Intersections of Law and Memory

This book elaborates a new framework for considering and understanding the relationship between law and memory.

How can law influence collective memory? What are the mechanisms law employs to influence social perceptions of the past? And how successful is law in its attempts to rewrite narratives about the past? As the field of memory studies has grown, this book takes a step back from established transitional justice narratives, returning to the core sociological, philosophical and legal theoretical issues that underpin this field. The book then goes on to propose a new approach to the relationship between law and collective memory based on a conception of "legal institutions of memory." It then elaborates the functioning of such institutions through a range of examples – taken from Japan, Iraq, Brazil, Portugal, Rwanda, and Poland – that move from the work of international tribunals and truth commissions to more explicit memory legislation. The book concludes with a general assessment of the contemporary intersections of law and memory, and their legal institutionalisation.

This book will be of interest to scholars with relevant interests in the sociology of law, legal theory and international law, as well as in sociology and politics.

Mirosław Michał Sadowski is Lecturer at the School of Law, University of Strathclyde in Glasgow, Scotland; Postdoctoral Researcher at the Centre for Global Studies, Aberta University in Lisbon, Portugal; Postdoctoral Fellow at CEBRAP – Brazilian Center of Analysis and Planning in São Paulo, Brazil; and Research Assistant at the Institute of Legal Sciences, Polish Academy of Sciences in Warsaw, Poland.

Intersections of Law and Memory

Influencing Perceptions of the Past

Mirosław Michał Sadowski

ROUTLEDGE
Routledge
Taylor & Francis Group
a GlassHouse Book

First published 2024
by Routledge
4 Park Square, Milton Park, Abingdon, Oxon OX14 4RN

and by Routledge
605 Third Avenue, New York, NY 10158

Routledge is an imprint of the Taylor & Francis Group, an informa business

a GlassHouse book

British Library Cataloguing-in-Publication Data
A catalogue record for this book is available from the British Library

Library of Congress Cataloging-in-Publication Data
Names: Sadowski, Mirosław Michał, 1995– author.
Title: Intersections of law and memory : influencing perceptions of the past / Mirosław Michał Sadowski.
Description: Abingdon, Oxon [UK]; New York, NY : Routledge, 2024. | Includes bibliographical references and index.
Identifiers: LCCN 2023047615 (print) | LCCN 2023047616 (ebook) | ISBN 9781032610160 (hardback) | ISBN 9781032610184 (paperback) | ISBN 9781003461548 (ebook)
Subjects: LCSH: Law—Social aspects. | Law—Philosophy. | Memory—Social aspects. | Sociological jurisprudence. | Transitional justice.
Classification: LCC K370 .S225 2024 (print) | LCC K370 (ebook) | DDC 340/.115—dc23/eng/20231012
LC record available at https://lccn.loc.gov/2023047615
LC ebook record available at https://lccn.loc.gov/2023047616

ISBN: 978-1-032-61016-0 (hbk)
ISBN: 978-1-032-61018-4 (pbk)
ISBN: 978-1-003-46154-8 (ebk)

DOI: 10.4324/9781003461548

Typeset in Sabon
by Apex CoVantage, LLC

To my parents, Irena and Mirosław, for their unwavering support in this ludicrous, exciting, frustrating, wonderful adventure.

Contents

Preface *xii*
Acknowledgements *xiv*
Prologue: France as a Law and Memory Hub *xvi*

Introduction: Intersections of Law and Memory Take the Stage 1
Why Law and Memory? 1
Why "Intersections"? 1
What State of Intersections of Law and Memory? 3
How Intersections of Law and Memory? 5
What Intersections of Law and Memory? 8

PART I
The Theory: Defining and Demarcating Law and Memory's Intersections 13

Introduction to Part I 13

1 Sociology, Memory, and Law: From Halbwachs to Agents of Memory 15
Introduction 15
Setting the Stage for Collective Memory: Maurice Halbwachs 16
What Came Later: From Collective to Global Memory 21
The Past/Present Dichotomy 22
The Society/Culture Dichotomy 23
The Formal/Global Dichotomy 25
The Innovative/Critical Dichotomy 28
Going the Opposite Way: Collective Forgetting 31
When the Past Weighs in on the Present: Trauma as a Collective Phenomenon of Memory 36

Bringing the Past into the Present: Agents and Carriers of Memory 44
Agents of Memory 44
Carriers of Memory 46
Conclusion: Return to Halbwachs or Law and Collective Memory 48

2 Philosophy, Memory, and Law: The French Four 50
Introduction 50
Institutions, Rituals, and Memory: Émile Durkheim 51
Memory's "Third Way": Henri Bergson 55
Memory, Morality, and Law: Emmanuel Levinas 59
The Power of Collective Memory: Michel Foucault 63
Conclusion: Law, Memory, Philosophy – Intersections 68

3 Collective Memory, Law, and Theory: From Human Rights and International Law to the Concept of Transitional Justice 69
Introduction 69
Memory and Human Rights Law: Direct and Indirect Intersections 69
Memory and International Law: From Everyday to Extraordinary Intersections 73
Transitional Justice and the Big Absent: Collective Memory 78
Transitional Justice – What's in a Name? 79
Transitional Justice and Collective Memory 83
Conclusion: Between Law and Memory 89

Conclusion to Part I: Law and Collective Memory, Collective Memory and Law 91

PART II
The Concept: Framing Law and Memory's Intersections 93

Introduction to Part II 93

4 Collective Memory and Law: Three Types of Institutions 95
Introduction 95
Soft Institution I. Law, Memory, and State to Victims Transfers: Reparations 96
Symbolic Reparations: The Case of Public Apologies 100
Soft Institution II: Law and Memory Intersecting High Above – International Tribunals 106

Medium Institution I. Law and Memory Walking Hand in Hand: Lustration 116
Medium Institution II. Past Atrocities, Divergent Memories, One (?) Narrative: Truth (and Reconciliation) Commissions 123
Hard Institution I. Law Repressing Memory: Legal Amnesia between Amnesty and Collective Forgetting 132
Hard Institution II. Law Forcing Memory: Memory Legislation 141
Conclusion: Legal Institutions of Memory as a Basis of the Understanding of Law and Memory Intersections 149

5 The Hidden Power of Law and Memory Intersections: From Memory Politics to a Right to Memory 152
Introduction 152
At the Crossroads of Memory and Power: The Politics of Memory 152
Politicisation of Memory in Practice: Institutionalising Remembrance 158
The Right to Memory: Between Conceptualisation and Unacknowledged Presence in Law and its Mechanisms 164
The Right to Remember 167
The Right to Be Remembered 170
The Right to Forget 172
The Right to Be Forgotten 173
What Right to Memory? 176
Conclusion: Law and Memory Intersections Between Memory Politics and the Right to Memory 178

Conclusion to Part II: A New Law and Memory Framework 179

PART III
The Practice: Reviewing Law and Memory's Intersections 183

Introduction to Part III 183

6 Placing Soft Legal Institutions of Memory Within the New Framework 189
Introduction 189
Soft Institution I in Practice: Between Material and Symbolic Reparations in the Case of Japan 189

Material Reparations in Japan 190
Symbolic Reparations in Japan 194
Japanese Reparations at the Intersections of Law and Memory 196
Soft Institution I in Practice Again: A Very Particular Public Apology, or the Letter of Polish to German Bishops 199
The Adoption and Contents of the 1965 Letter 200
The Letter's Immediate Aftermath 202
Polish Symbolic Reparations at the Intersections of Law and Memory 206
Soft Institution II in Practice: ECtHR – Conflicting Memories, Singular Narratives 209
The Court, the Memory, and the Law 209
ECtHR and the Perinçek *Case* 213
ECtHR and the Vasiliauskas *and* Drėlingas *Cases* 215
ECtHR at the Intersections of Law and Memory 217
Soft Institution II in Practice Again: Opportunity Missed, or the Katyń *Case before ECtHR* 220
The Case of Janowiec (and Others) *v.* Russia *Before the ECtHR* 222
The Katyń *Case at the Intersections of Law and Memory* 224
Conclusion: Soft Legal Institutions of Memory in Practice 226

7 **Placing Medium Legal Institutions of Memory within the New Framework** 227
Introduction 227
Medium Institution I in Practice: Leaving the Past Behind with the (A)Typical Lustration in Iraq 227
Lustration in Iraq 228
De-Ba'athification at the Intersections of Law and Memory 232
Medium Institution I in Practice Again: A Never-Ending Story, or the Case of Polish Lustration 236
A Bumpy Road Between Nowhere and Somewhere of Polish Lustration 237
The Polish Lustration at the Intersections of Law and Memory 242
Medium Institution II in Practice: (Never) Too Late for Truth in the Case of Brazilian Commission 245

The Long and Winding Road to a Truth Commission 246
Brazilian National Truth Commission 249
Brazil's National Truth Commission at the Intersections of Law and Memory 252
Conclusion: Medium Legal Institutions of Memory in Practice 255

8 **Placing Hard Legal Institutions of Memory within the New Framework** 256
Introduction 256
Hard Institution I in Practice: Forgetting and Evoking with Law, or the Case of Portugal's Legal Amnesia 256
Legal Amnesia in Portugal Between Revolution and Reaction 258
Portuguese Legal Amnesia at the Intersections of Law and Memory 263
Hard Institution II in Practice: Law Forcing Memory and What Comes Next in Rwanda's Memory Legislation 268
Memory Laws Proper in Rwanda 270
Rwandan Memory Legislation at the Intersections of Law and Memory 273
Hard Institution II in Practice Again: Memory Politics of Civil Law, or Polish Memory Legislation 276
The Wide Array of Polish Memory Legislation 277
Polish Memory Legislation at the Intersections of Law and Memory 283
Conclusion: Hard Legal Institutions of Memory in Practice 286

Conclusion to Part III: Applying the New Law and Memory Framework and What Happened 287

Conclusions: Intersections of Law and Memory – Remarks After the Inquiry 289
What About Law and Memory? 289
The State of Intersections of Law and Memory 291
What Future for Intersections of Law and Memory? 297

Index 299

Preface

This book, written on two continents, between Montréal, Wrocław, and Glasgow, and in many places in between, was not born in a vacuum; rather, it represents the culmination of over nine years of my research interest in the matters of memory: from the high school essay on Proust which got me to the final of the National Competition of the Polish Language and Literature, to the first steps taken at conferences during my Master of Law studies at the University of Wrocław, to my Doctor of Civil Law studies at McGill University at the very Faculty I first visited in 2017 as a bright-eyed student for a conference coming to a conclusion with the defence of the thesis on which this book is based.

Looking back now at the myriad motivations behind this book, I realise that my interest in memory stretches back much further, going beyond the high school infatuation with Proust. Eerily, my earliest "complete" recollection is that of sitting cross-legged in front of the TV on a certain September afternoon, fresh from preschool, while my mum is preparing dinner, and my dad is flipping channels during a Cartoon Network commercial which interrupted my programme. Finally, he settled on a newscast reporting live from New York on a plane that apparently hit a skyscraper by accident. Soon afterwards, however, I was to see, agape, a second plane, flying – almost cartoonish in doing that – into the second tower. The memory is completed by, shortly afterwards, pieces of paper flying all around Manhattan, as well as small dots appearing and disappearing at the World Trade Centre's windows. Watching this event alongside millions of other people all over the world, the six-year-old me involuntarily, and not aware of what exactly was taking place, participated in the establishment of one of his first global collective memories – as Szymborska put it, writing about the victims of 9/11, "the photograph halted them in life, and now keeps them above the face of the earth toward the earth"[1] – permanently suspended in our memories.

1 Wisława Szymborska, "Fotografia z 11 września" ["Photograph from 11 September"] in Clare Cavanagh and Stanisław Barańczak (trs), *Chwila/Moment* (Cracow: Znak, 2011) at 66–67.

In the years that followed, more global collective memories were to come – after all, as I was often told as a child, the worst fate there could be was "may you live in interesting times" – be that the Bible closed by the wind at John Paul II's funeral, or my mother waking me on a Saturday morning to inform me of the Smoleńsk plane catastrophe, these collective memories were later complemented by the significant ones that came during the writing of this book – the COVID-19 pandemic, the Russian invasion of Ukraine, and the death of Elizabeth II – each event symbolic in its own way, each a memory shared by billions around the globe, all the more so with the arrival of social media.

In their wake, throughout the years, I had to learn to become comfortable with the not easily relatable feeling for a small child about the surrounding world being familiar and unfamiliar at the same time, which I read about so many years ago in *Prince Caspian*: when the main characters are transported back to Narnia in what for them on Earth was only a short period of time, but for the parallel land they used to rule had been hundreds of years, they find themselves among the ruins of the very castle they inhabited, but do not realise it at first, as the fortress now lays in ruins; ultimately, the recognition comes that this world is one and the same, so familiar, yet so different, upon finding a chess piece from their own set, as well as their treasury, with "something sad and a little frightening about the place, because it all seemed so forsaken and long ago."[2] In a way, written under a similar *weltschmerz*, this book is the outcome of a number of years of feeling the almost tangible presence of memory in my very proximity, of the various collective memories concerning the events I remember myself, in futile attempts at holding on to the *World of Yesterday*, not unlike Stefan Zweig himself in his love letter to memories of a (for him not too) distant past of *belle époque*.[3]

The goal of my research has always been to bring matters of collective memory and law closer to the general public. While the hope that one's work will "end up under the roofs," to quote a Polish poet, Adam Mickiewicz, clearly represents only a vain aspiration, I have confidence that this book will be of help to any and all adepts in the study of the relationship between memory and law. Two things are certain: first, that it could not have happened if it was not for the support of a number of different people, whom I venture to give thanks in the acknowledgement section of this book; and second, that all errors and mistakes, of course, remain my own. In spite of them, I hope if anything, my work represents not only an enjoyable read but also an opportunity for a better understanding of the ways in which law works within society.

Glasgow, August 2023

2 C. S. Lewis, "Prince Caspian" in C. S. Lewis (ed.), *The Complete Chronicles of Narnia* (New York, NY: HarperCollins, 2000) 210 at 223.

3 Stefan Zweig, *The World of Yesterday* (London: Pushkin Press, 2011).

Acknowledgements

No work is brought to paper through the sheer power of one's will alone; rather, it comes together through the support, through conversations, through encouragement, through lending a helping hand, through simply "being there." I am lucky to say that I have received all this – and more – when writing this book. Although it is impossible to thank everyone who helped and supported me in the years of my research into the matters of law and memory, I will venture to do so in this brief acknowledgement section, at the same time being grateful to all those whom I met on my path, and, for the reason none other than a faulty memory, forgot to include in this limited list.

To my family: my parents, Irena and Mirosław, as well as my great-aunt Maria Pawlik, thank you for your unwavering support and willingness to read the piles of drafts throughout all these years.

To my closest friends: Sandrine Ampleman-Tremblay, Seyed Mohammad Amin Zavarei, Giusto Amadeo Boccheni, Luisa Castañeda-Quintana, Kamil Gaweł, Stefan-Michael Wedenig, thank you for being there for me during the many long-night discussions in the various places around the world.

To my DCL thesis supervisor and my committee members: Prof. Helge Dedek, Prof. Payam Akhavan, Prof. Evan Fox-Decent, thank you for your constructive criticism, suggestions, and support.

To my other close friends and colleagues in Montréal, Wrocław, Glasgow, and places in between: Lucas Clover Alcolea, Luter Atagher, Vincet Dalpé, Upasana Dasgupta, David DesBaillets, Michał Janusz Ekiert, Patricia Dudar, Katarzyna Dudys, Andreas Giorgallis, Aniel Guxholli, François Le Moine, Vito Di Mei, Ermanno Napolitano, Michael Poon, Oana-Maria Ştefănescu, Samuel White, Christopher Whitehead, Yuxiao Zhang, thank you for being there both to share your own stories and to listen to mine.

To the wonderful academics at McGill and the University of Wrocław: Dean Robert Leckey, Prof. Andrea Bjorklund, Prof. Darren Rosenblum, Prof. Shauna Van Praagh, Prof. Frédéric Mégret, Prof. René Provost, Prof. Zbigniew Pulka, Dr. Michał Paździora, thank you for finding the time to discuss my different ideas and hopes.

To the one-of-a-kind administrators and librarians at McGill and the University of Wrocław: Silvana Solitiero, Bianca Bourgeois, Katarina Daniels, Patrycja Cicha, for their help in organising my university life.

To unique people, many of whom I am now happy to call my friends, that I met at the different conferences and events in the past years: Prof. Thomas B. Gold, Prof. Andreas Philippopoulos-Mihalopoulos, Prof. Janet Ulph, Prof. Anne Wagner, Prof. Karol Żakowski, Prof. José M. Aroso Linhares, Prof. Alfons Bora, Prof. Aleksandra Matulewska, Prof. Dominik Markl, Prof. Marcin Grabowski, Prof. Pedro Caridade de Freitas, Prof. Hano Ernst, Prof. Martin K. Dimitrov, Prof. André Gustavo Corrêa de Andrade, Prof. Emilian Kavalski, Dr. Sophie Vigneron, Dr. Stephen Connelly, Dr. Samir Forić, Dr. Raza Saeed, Dr. Simon Lavis, Dr. Jānis Pleps, Dr. Markéta Štěpáníková, Dr. Yumei Chi, Dr. Jason Keith Fernandes, Dr. Sara Ross, Dr. Evgeny Tikhonravov, Dr. Paolo Caroli, Dr. Edvaldo Moita, Ferenc Németh, Adam Bohar, Pierre Druart, Fortunato Mangiola, Vinícius Alves Barreto da Silva, Pishko Shamsi, thank you for all the discussions, conversations, and comments which allowed me to take my research to a different level.

To the members of the research teams I am proud to be a part of at the Aberta University in Lisbon, the Polish Academy of Sciences, CEBRAP – Brazilian Center of Analysis and Planning, as well as other initiatives and collaborations: Prof. José Eduardo Franco, Prof. Maria Hermínia Tavares de Almeida, Prof. Renato Cymbalista, Prof. Cosmin Cercel, Dr. Susana Alves-Jesus, Dr. Aleksandra Gliszczyńska-Grabias, Dr. Uladzislau Belavusau, Dr. Gianluigi Mastandrea Bonaviri, Dr. Aleksandra Mercescu, Dr. Rafał Mańko, Dr. Paula Rhein-Fischer, Dr. Rui G. Maia Rego, Dr. André Carmo, Dr. Mariana Kuhn de Oliveira, Dr. Leonardo Esteves, Dr. Lívia Maria Tiéde, Hani El Debuch, thank you for your enlightening work.

To my new colleagues at the University of Strathclyde: thank you for making me feel welcome these past couple of months.

To the editorial team, which made the publication of this book possible: Dr. Colin Perrin and Naomi Cahalin, thank you for your guidance and insights.

And, ultimately, to Marcel Proust, thank you for being a lifelong inspiration in the pursuit of the essence of memory.

To each and every one, once again – thank you!

Prologue: France as a Law and Memory Hub

Any study of the intersections of law and memory would not be complete without investigating France, a country that not only has a large number of memory laws in place but also engages in a particularly vivid debate regarding their presence. As such, it makes a perfect case to open the debate on the relationship between law and memory in this book, used in a way as the "patient zero" of the issues I research in the next pages.

France's journey with memory laws began in 1990 with the adoption of the *Law aiming to suppress all racist, antisemitic and xenophobic acts*,[1] known after an MP who proposed it, Jean-Claude Gayssot, as *loi Gayssot*. Of particular interest for my investigations is article 9 of this law, which, by adding article 24 bis to the 1881 *Law on the freedom of press*, prohibited Holocaust denial under punishment, stipulating that:

> Those who contest, using one of the means listed in article 23, the existence of one or many crimes against humanity as defined by article 6 of the *Charter of the International Military Tribunal – Annex to the Agreement for the prosecution and punishment of the major war criminals of the European Axis* of the 8th of August 1945 and which were committed either by the members of an organisation declared as criminal by the application of article 9 of this Charter or by a person recognised as guilty of said crime by a French or international jurisdiction, will be punished with one of the punishments listed in the sixth paragraph of article 24.

The means from article 23 referred to there include, among others, written texts, drawings, prints, paintings, emblems, and images,[2] and the punishments from article 24 are five years of imprisonment and a €45,000 fine.[3]

1 JORF n° 0162 du 14 juillet 1990 page 8333, Loi n° 90–615 du 13 juillet 1990 tendant à réprimer tout acte raciste, antisémite ou xénophobe.
2 Article 23 of the *Loi du 29 juillet 1881 sur la liberté de la presse.*
3 Article 24 of the *Loi du 29 juillet 1881 sur la liberté de la presse.*

The second French memory law devoted to the protection of genocide from denial concerns the Armenian massacre of 1915. Comparable with the one regarding the Holocaust, it proved much more challenging to adopt, beginning with a 2001 simple, one-sentence commemorative act stating that "France publicly recognises the Armenian genocide of 1915."[4] While short, it already provides a single, clear narrative regarding the Turkish massacre of the Armenians, recognising it as a genocide (a designation which Turkey staunchly opposes to this day).

The 2001 law was followed by three attempts to grant the Armenian genocide a similar or the same level of protection from revisionism as the Holocaust has received. The first one, in 2006, failed to be passed by the Senate after having been blocked by the government,[5] while another, passed by the National Assembly in 2011 and by the Senate in 2012, was later found unconstitutional by the Constitutional Council. The Council argued that the law breached the constitution, as it punished the denial of a crime recognised as a genocide by the government itself, unlike the *loi Gayssot*, which made reference to the Nuremberg Tribunal as a source of recognition of the Holocaust as a crime against humanity.[6]

Ultimately, the penalisation of the Armenian – and any other mass atrocity recognised as genocide's denial – was introduced in such a way as to circumnavigate the Constitutional Council's objections, with a 2017 amendment to article 24 bis of the 1881 *Law on the freedom of* press, which added several paragraphs to the ones introduced by *loi Gayssot*. Nevertheless, the Council once again declared parts of the law unconstitutional.[7] Today, following the 2021 amendment, the now "unified" French mass atrocity memory law takes the following form:

> Those who contest, with the means listed in article 23, the existence of one or many crimes against humanity as defined by article 6 of the *Charter of the International Military Tribunal – Annex to the Agreement for the prosecution and punishment of the major war criminals of the European Axis* of the 8th of August 1945 and that were committed either by the members of an organisation declared as criminal by the application of

4 Loi n° 2001–70 du 29 janvier 2001 relative à la reconnaissance du génocide arménien de 1915. "La France reconnaît publiquement le génocide arménien de 1915."

5 L'Obs, "Génocide arménien", online: L'Obs <nouvelobs.com/societe/20110505.OBS2485/genocide-armenien-laisser-faire-les-negationnistes-est-une-insulte-a-la-diaspora.html>.

6 Décision n° 2012–647 DC du 28 février 2012. Loi visant à réprimer la contestation de l'existence des génocides reconnus par la loi, online: Conseil Constitutionnel <conseil-constitutionnel.fr/decision/2012/2012647DC.htm>.

7 Décision n° 2016–745 DC du 26 janvier 2017. Loi relative à l'égalité et à la citoyenneté, online: Conseil Constitutionnel <conseil-constitutionnel.fr/actualites/communique/decision-n-2016-745-dc-du-26-janvier-2017-communique-de-presse>.

> article 9 of this Charter or by a person recognised as guilty of said crime by a French or international jurisdiction will be punished with one year of imprisonment and a €45,000 fine.
>
> In the same way there will be punished those who deny, diminish or trivialise in an outrageous way, with the means listed in article 23, the existence of a crime of genocide other than mentioned in the first paragraph of this article, other crimes against humanity, the crime of enslavement or of the exploitation of an enslaved person, or a war crime as defined by articles 6, 7 and 8 of the Statute of the International Criminal Court signed in Rome on the 18th of July 1998 and by articles 211–1 to 212–3, 224–1 A to 224–1 C and 461–1 to 461–31 of the Criminal Code, if: (1°) the crime resulted in a condemnation by the French or international jurisdiction.

Thus, in its contemporary shape, French article 24 bis creates two memory laws: one protecting the Holocaust specifically from denial, and another protecting all other mass atrocities – genocides, crimes against humanity, war crimes and slavery – from revisionism. Moreover, in 2019, the French president passed a decree establishing April 24 as the Armenian Genocide Commemoration Day.[8]

In addition to memory laws concerning genocide, in the first years of the 21st century two laws concerning the French colonial past were also adopted. The first one,[9] known as one of the three *loi Taubira* after an MP, and later on a government minister, Christiane Taubira, who proposed them, recognised slavery as a crime against humanity. Composed of five articles, the law states in its first article that

> The French Republic recognises that the transatlantic as well as the Indian Ocean slave trade on the one hand, and putting into slavery on the other, perpetrated from the 15th century in the Americas and in the Caribbean, in the Indian Ocean and in Europe on the African, Amerindian, Malagasy and Indian populations, constitutes a crime against humanity.

The following two articles concern the granting of an adequate place to slavery in teaching and research and putting in an official request to several international organisations regarding the recognition of the slave trade as a crime against humanity.

8 Gouvernement.fr, "Génocide arménien: Chaque année, une journée de commémoration", online: Goivernemnet.fr gouvernement.fr/genocide-armenien-chaque-annee-une-journee-de-commemoration>.

9 Loi n° 2001–434 du 21 mai 2001 tendant à la reconnaissance de la traite et de l'esclavage en tant que crime contre l'humanité.

The second post-colonial memory law in France is the 2005 *Law granting the recognition of the Nation and the national contribution to the repatriated French.*[10] Its main function is to acknowledge the role of those who contributed to the creation and functioning of the old French colonies, most notably in Maghreb and Indochina. With the law seen as controversial in general, its article 4 provoked so much debate – both in France and abroad[11] – that it was in place for less than a year,[12] being ultimately repealed by President Jacques Chirac, who promised its rewriting to calm down the public.[13] While article 4's second paragraph is now simply absent,[14] it nevertheless remains a particularly good example of a way in which law attempts to directly influence collective memory, and thus, its now-repealed wording is worth invoking here:

> The school curricula will particularly acknowledge the positive role of the French overseas presence, especially in North Africa, and grant an eminent place to the history and sacrifice of the French army fighters in these territories, which they are due.

It is remarkable how in just one sentence, not leaving any room for negotiation or debate, the complete narrative about the French colonial past was set by this law, ready to be imposed on the unsuspecting students, potentially shaping their minds for years to come. While the dangers of such a use – or abuse – of legal regulations were soon recognised in France, that is often not the case in other countries, as, for example, the latter case study of Rwanda will show.

Before delving deeper into the French opposition to memory laws, one more question needs to be posed first: Why did France choose to adopt all the memory laws mentioned here?

In regard to *loi Gayssot*, the answer seems to be quite simple – this law not only helped mitigate the memories of Vichy but also "reflected the quasi-universal moral and political consensus with regards to the Holocaust."[15] The memory law recognising the 1915 Turkish massacre of the Armenians

10 Loi n° 2005–158 du 23 février 2005 portant reconnaissance de la Nation et contribution nationale en faveur des Français rapatriés.

11 Peter Dunwoodie, "Postface: History, Memory and Identity – Today's Crisis, Yesterday's Issue" (2006) 20 French History 318 at 319–320.

12 Vivian Grosswald Curran, "Evolving French Memory Laws in Light of Greece's 2014 Anti-Racism Law" (2014) 41 Legal Studies Research Paper Series 1 at 8.

13 Sévane Garibian, "Pour Une Lecture Juridique Des Quatre Lois 'Mémorielles'" (2006) 2 Esprit 158 at 160.

14 Article 4 of the *Loi portant reconnaissance de la Nation et contribution nationale en faveur des Français rapatriés.*

15 Stiina Löytömäki, *Law and the Politics of Memory* (Oxon: Routledge, 2014) at 12–13.

has been linked to the French rejection of the admission of Turkey to the EU,[16] but perhaps another, more pragmatic explanation also exists connected to the significant political influence of the Armenian diaspora in France.[17]

In turn, the two post-colonial laws served opposite purposes: one was supposed to right the historical wrongs of the French colonial expansion, and the other, along with honouring those who helped build the French colonies, whitewashed their much more sombre history. Furthermore, the former, *loi Taubira*, is said to have been motivated by the country's "evolution into a multicultural society" and the political pressure of various interest groups; it still, however, as Löytömäki notes, "involves a clash of memories: the French commemorate the abolition of slavery whereas the descendants of the enslaved people want to remember enslavement itself."[18]

On the other hand, the latter, *Law granting the recognition . . .*, was supposed to be both an answer to the "demand of memory" from the forgotten repatriates from Maghreb,[19] ill-treated by France after the Algerian War and today actively engaged in French "memory wars,"[20] and a rejection of the "anti-colonial memory," which supposedly stresses only the dark side of colonialism.[21] It was also supposed to officially introduce the question of colonialism to the school curriculum for the first time – until 2005, it was a topic "systematically" avoided by textbooks.[22]

Together, the French memory laws provide a detailed picture of how law can be employed to alter social perceptions of the past. They also show why memory laws in general are regarded as a slippery slope: once a government begins – even with best intentions – prohibiting genocide denial, it is difficult to stop – and the authorities can end up deciding to resolve various complex past issues with law, ultimately provoking even more controversies.

As mentioned earlier, France is an interesting case study not only due to its several adopted laws but also because of broad intellectual debates

16 *Ibid.* at 32.

17 See Michel Marian and Christian Makarian, "The French Armenian Diaspora and Turkey: The Possibility of Dialogue?" (2011) 5 Note Franco-Turque 1 at 10; Tigran Yegavian, "The Armenian Identity in France in the Grip of Memorialization" (2015), online: Repair <repairfuture.net/index.php/en/identity-standpoint-of-armenian-diaspora/the-armenian-identity-in-france-in-the-grip-of-memorialization>.

18 Löytömäki, *supra* note 15 at 96.

19 Claire Eldridge, "Blurring the Boundaries Between Perpetrators and Victims: *Pied-noir* Memories and the *harki* Community" (2010) 3 Memory Studies 123 at 134.

20 Eric Savarese, "The Post-Colonial Encounter in France" in Dietmar Rothermund (ed.), *Memories of Post-Imperial Nations: The Aftermath of Decolonization, 1945–2013* (Daryaganj, Delhi: Cambridge University Press, 2015) 76 at 80–91.

21 Löytömäki, *supra* note 15 at 103.

22 Ann L. Stoler, "Colonial Aphasia: Disabled Histories and Race in France" in Ann L. Stoler (ed.), *Duress: Imperial Durabilities in Our Times* (Durham: Duke University Press, 2016) 122 at 130.

surrounding their adoption. While certain researchers regard memory laws as a necessary means of protecting human dignity and a defence against the repetition of the past,[23] the resistance to memory laws in the country is notable, centred around the group of influential historians known as *Liberté pour l'Histoire* (Freedom for History) – or just *Liberté* – formed in 2005 in response to the first attempts at punishing the denial of Armenian genocide.[24] With their opposition grounded in four beliefs – (1) that historical debate should be free from political debate; (2) that memory laws violate the historians' role as guardians of French national identity; (3) that "a broad range of multicultural commemorations" is not desirable for French society; (4) and that penalisation of Holocaust denial is the only acceptable memory law (an issue that remains thorny and vague for the group)[25] – the collective not only has a significant online presence but manages to lobby, to an extent, the French government and to influence the country's society in general.[26]

Excluding any other broadly understood memory laws other than the aforementioned ones from their work,[27] the historians-members of the group have raised a number of particularly poignant questions regarding French – and, looking globally, all – memory laws, to which there seem to be no good answers: How broad should the term "crimes against humanity" be? To whom *loi Taubira* can actually apply? How to proceed now that a number of memory laws are in place?[28] Is France going too far in its repentance for the past?[29] And, perhaps most importantly, one asked by Timothy Garton Ash, who, speaking about the penalisation of the Armenian genocide denial, asked: "If France can ban this, what can't France ban?"[30]

At the same time, it needs to be stressed that the adoption of memory laws – at least those regarding denialism – is openly encouraged by the EU, with the 2008 *Framework Decision on combating certain forms and expressions of racism and xenophobia by means of criminal law*[31] in place. The decision,

23 Sévane Garibian, "Taking Denial Seriously: Genocide Denial and Freedom of Speech in the French Law" (2008) 9 Cardozo Journal of Conflict Resolution 479 at 488.

24 Robert A. Kahn, "Does It Matter How One Opposes Memory Bans? A Commentary on Liberté Pour L'histoire" (2016) 15 Washington University Global Studies Review 55 at 56.

25 *Ibid.* at 57, 75–76.

26 *Ibid.* at 64–65, 67.

27 Gilles Manceron, "Sur quelles bases aborder le débat sur la loi, la mémoire et l'histoire?" (2009) 9 Tracés. Revue de Sciences Humaines 29 at 31.

28 Kahn, *supra* note 24 at 83–84.

29 Manceron, *supra* note 27 at 39.

30 Kahn, *supra* note 24 at 70.

31 Council of the European Union, 28 November 2008, Council Framework Decision on combating certain forms and expressions of racism and xenophobia by means of criminal law, 2008/913/JHA in Official Journal of the European Union L 328/55.

adopted in response to the rise of xenophobia and racism,[32] and seen as a part of "commemorative obsession" and the post-9/11 tendency for "broader, preventive and protective" tendencies,[33] requires all Member States to adopt the necessary means to punish the public, intentional,

> condoning, denying or grossly trivialising crimes of genocide, crimes against humanity and war crimes as defined in Articles 6, 7 and 8 of the Statute of the International Criminal Court, directed against a group of persons or a member of such group defined by reference to race, colour, religion, descent or national or ethnic origin when the conduct is carried out in a manner likely to incite to violence or hatred against such a group or a member of such group.[34]

The decision, along with the increase in the number of new memory laws adopted – as the French legislation introduced here and the later case studies of Rwanda and Poland will show – as well as the deeming of the penalisation of Holocaust denial as an adequate means of combatting hate crimes by both the UN Human Rights Committee and the ECtHR,[35] demonstrate that the opponents of memory laws, at least in Europe, have already lost. Whether or not this should be regarded as a positive development, is it possible to answer the aforementioned *Liberté* historians' questions and, perhaps most importantly, are there limits to law's influence on collective memory? These are some of the main goals of this book, as we begin this journey of law and memory's intersections.

32 Emanuela Fronza, "The Crime of Historical Denialism and International Law" in Emanuela Fronza (ed.), *Memory and Punishment: Historical Denialism, Free Speech and the Limits of Criminal Law* (The Hague: TMC Asser Press, 2018) 51 at 58.

33 Emanuela Fronza, "Post-vérité, terrorisme et mémoire historique: la justice pénale et la liberté d'expression" (2018) 40 Archives de politique criminelle 23 at 33.

34 Article 1 let. c of the Council Framework Decision on combating certain forms and expressions of racism and xenophobia by means of criminal law.

35 Ioanna Tourkochoriti, "Challenging Historical Facts and National Truths: An Analysis of Cases from France and Greece" in Ladzislau Belavusau and Aleksandra Gliszczyńska-Grabias (eds), *Law and Memory: Towards Legal Governance of History* (Cambridge: Cambridge University Press, 2016) 151 at 169–171.

Introduction

Intersections of Law and Memory Take the Stage

Why Law and Memory?

The final words of Marcel Proust's *Time Regained* (and thus the end of the whole *In Search of Lost Time* cycle)[1] are one of the main reasons I became an academic. Far from being just a fleeting inspiration, Proust's *magnum opus*, read during one high school summer, motivated me to take a research interest in the relationship of memory, first with culture, then, once I started my studies, mostly with law. As I soon learned, the two are not as far apart from each other as it may seem at first glance – after all, culture and law address similar issues regarding "borders and boundaries,"[2] with memory playing a notable role in the existence of both. Thus, it could be said that my research into the broadly understood relationship between law and collective memory in one sense proposes to imagine replacing "men" in the initial quotation from Proust with "the laws" and examining how memory is influenced by law (in some cases itself influencing legal provisions), surpassing the spatial and temporal boundaries that constrain it on a usual basis.

Why "Intersections"?

In my initial, brief, sketch-like study of the question of law and collective memory, I proposed to call their interactions "an unobvious relationship."[3] While I stand by this characterisation, here, in this book, I choose to perceive

1 "I would therein describe men, if need be, as monsters occupying a place in Time infinitely more important than the restricted one reserved for them in space, a place, on the contrary, prolonged immeasurably since, simultaneously touching widely separated years and the distant periods they have lived through – between which so many days have ranged themselves – they stand like giants immersed in Time." Marcel Proust, "Time Regained", online: Project Gutenberg Australia <gutenberg.net.au/ebooks03/0300691.txt>.

2 Mirosław M. Sadowski, "Urban Cultural Heritage: Managing and Preserving a Local Global Common in the Twenty-First Century" (2018) 2 Journal of Heritage Management 125 at 126.

3 Mirosław M. Sadowski, "Law and Memory: The Unobvious Relationship" (2018) 16 Warsaw University Law Review 262.

DOI: 10.4324/9781003461548-1

the relations between the two as intersections: points where the lines of memory and law meet. The choice of this particular categorisation of the interplay between law and memory was inspired by an impactful for my research edited collection by Gisler et al., *Intersections of Law and Culture*, which in their introduction remark that:

> The notion of intersection proves to be quite an elastic concept. It can mean anything from the deliberate marshalling of a minor issue to attain a political end . . . to the urgent convergence of social and political needs with moments of historical readiness . . . The societal reactions to such intersections can range from the equivalent of a polite nod to a metaphorical collision that can derail entire political systems. Intersections are, therefore far from trivial phenomena.[4]

As this book demonstrates, the intersections of law and memory are as far removed from being a banal afterthought as possible – they become of major importance to all societies that need to grapple with a difficult past, whether the more recent one or laying further in time, always, importantly, with a certain hold on contemporary times. While memory's larger relationship with history, as will be noticed further, remains outside of the scope of this book, perhaps the most notable *leitmotif* of my study is the difficult past, which never leaves completely; and its memory rather becomes instrumentalised by law in different ways, with a potential – oftentimes unrealised – to transform the society in question and lead, if not to reconciliation, then at least to a certain level of the collectivity's acceptance of its trauma.

At the same time, the infamous adage proposing that "history is written by the victors"[5] is true only up to a certain point – while most certainly control over the official narrative is of major importance to the general shape of collective memories of the events in question, as the persistent impact of Greeks and Romans on our perception of antiquity shows,[6] ultimately, unlike history, collective memory is written not by specialists but by the people themselves, the different groups at the base of a society, which, when necessary, establish counter-narratives to the ones promoted by the authorities. In certain cases, described in this book, they succeed in turning them into parts of the official discourse with the help of various legal institutions, thus also showing the further investigated links between law, memory, and politics.

4 Priska Gisler, Sara Steinert Borella, and Caroline Wiedmer, "Setting the Stage: Reading Law and Culture" in Priska Gisler, Sara Steinert Borella, and Caroline Wiedmer (eds), *Intersections of Law and Culture* (Houndmills: Palgrave Macmillan, 2012) 1 at 2.

5 Matthew Phelan, "The History of 'History Is Written by the Victors'," online: Slate <slate.com/culture/2019/11/history-is-written-by-the-victors-quote-origin.html>.

6 Richard Heersmink, "Materialised Identities, Cultural Identity, Collective Memory, and Artifacts" (2021) Review of Philosophy and Psychology 1 at 14.

What State of Intersections of Law and Memory?

Importantly, this book does not appear in a vacuum: a certain proliferation of the study of memory across various disciplines, or a "hypertrophy of memory," has been remarked upon in recent years.[7] It must be noted, however, that law has not one but two relationships with memory – one with individual memory and another with collective memory. The former has been investigated in detail since a greater interest in the broadly understood courtroom psychology was sparked in the previous century – whether with regard to witness testimony,[8] punishment,[9] the courtroom as a socio-legal space,[10] trial in general,[11] or, more recently, in connection with cognitive psychology[12] and neuroscience.[13]

On the other hand, law's relationship with collective memory still lacks a profound, comprehensive examination, with the ones currently available focusing only on a limited number of aspects of law and memory's intersections, as has already been observed.[14] While a myriad of papers,[15] book chapters,[16] and books[17] have been written on various intersections between law and memory in recent years, none of them provides a comprehensive

7 Mirosław M. Sadowski, "Psychological, Social, Cultural, Literary, and Legal Dimensions of Memory" (2015) 5 Wrocław Review of Law, Economics and Administration 141.

8 John M. Maguire and Charles W. Quick, "Testimony: Memory and Memoranda" (1957) 3 Howard Law Journal 1; Mark W. Bennet, "Unspringing the Witness Memory and Demeanor Trap: What Every Judge and Juror Needs to Know About Cognitive Psychology and Witness Credibility" (2015) 64 American University Law Review 1331; Carla Stentzel, "Eyewitness Misidentification: A Mistake That Blinds Investigations, Sways Juries, and Locks Innocent People Behind Bars" (2017) 50 Creighton Law Review 515.

9 O. Carter Snead, "Memory and Punishment" (2011) 64 Vanderbilt Law Review 1196.

10 Amos Megged, "Between History, Memory, and Law: Courtroom Methods in Mexico" (2014) 45 Journal of Interdisciplinary History 163; Jennifer S. Bard, "'Ah Yes, I Remember It Well': Why the Inherent Unreliability of Human Memory Makes Brain Imaging Technology a Poor Measure of Truth-Telling in the Courtroom" (2016) 94 Oregon Law Review 295.

11 Christopher T. Lutz, "Memory" (2000) 26 Litigation 38; Lynn Nadel and Walter P. Sinnott-Armstrong (eds), *Memory and Law* (New York: Oxford University Press, 2012).

12 Michael Laris, "Debate on Brain Scans as Lie Detectors Highlighted in Maryland Murder Trial" (2012), online: Washington Post <washingtonpost.com/local/crime/debate-on-brain-scans-as-lie-detectors-highlighted-in-maryland-murder-trial/2012/08/26/aba3d7d8-ed84-11e1-9ddc-340d5efb1e9c_story.html?utm_term=.23313e73f300>.

13 Michael S. Gazzaniga, "Neuroscience in the Courtroom" (2011), online: Scientific American <scientificamerican.com/article/neuroscience-in-the-courtroom/>.

14 Adam Czarnota, "Law, History and Collective Memories: A Contribution to the Historical Sociology of Law" (2014) 1 Miscellanea Historico-Iuridica 203.

15 See, e.g., Jonathan Crowe and Constance Youngwon Lee, "Law as Memory" (2015) 26 Law Critique 251.

16 See, e.g., Moshe Hirsch, "Collective Memory and International Law" in Moshe Hirsch (ed.), *Invitation to the Sociology of International Law*, 1st ed. (Oxford: Oxford University Press, 2015) at 47.

17 See, e.g., Stewart Motha and Honni van Rijswijk, *Law, Memory, Violence: Uncovering the Counter-Archive* (London: Routledge, 2016); Uladzislau Belavusau and Aleksandra Gliszczyńska-Grabias (eds), *Law and Memory: Towards Legal Governance of History* (Cambridge: Cambridge University Press, 2016).

analysis of the relationship. The latter is a good example – despite its promising title, *Law and Memory*, it focuses solely on the question of memory laws, providing their broad review, but without venturing further into the field of the different legal institutions of memory.

In my previous research, which I regard as the basis for my book, I myself proposed several different approaches to the question of the relationship between law and collective memory. The ongoing analyses may be divided into four groups: focusing on the post-colonial socio-legal reality;[18] focusing on the place of heritage and identity within the city;[19] focusing on the theoretical aspects of the intersections of law and memory;[20] and focusing on Central Europe.[21]

18 Mirosław M. Sadowski, "Crossroads of the World, Crossroads of the Law: Hong Kong and Macau Legal Systems Approaching 20 Years Post-Transition" (2016) 7 Comparative Law Review 1; Mirosław M. Sadowski, "The Rule of Law, the Rule of Conflict? Hong Kong and Democracy – Past and Present Revisited" (2019) Hors-série (décembre 2019) Revue québécoise de droit international/Quebec Journal of International Law 19; Mirosław M. Sadowski, "Hong Kong, the Virus and Illiberalism: Between Flattening the Curve and an Authoritarian Slide?" (2022) 35:3 International Journal for the Semiotics of Law – Revue internationale de Sémiotique juridique 961.

19 Sadowski, *supra* note 2; Mirosław M. Sadowski, "Cultural Heritage and the City: Law, Sustainable Development, Urban Heritage, and the Cases of Hong Kong and Macau" (2018) 8 Romanian Journal of Comparative Law 208; Mirosław M. Sadowski, "Mapping the Art Trade in South East Asia: From Source Countries via Free Ports to (a Chance for) Restitution" (2020) International Journal for the Semiotics of Law – Revue internationale de Sémiotique juridique 669; Mirosław M. Sadowski, "City as a Locus of Collective Memory: Streets, Monuments and Human Rights" (2020) 40:1–2 Zeitschrift für Rechtssoziologie – The German Journal of Law and Society 209, 263; Mirosław M. Sadowski, "Heritage Strikes Back: The Al Mahdi Case, ICC's Policy on Cultural Heritage and the Pushing of Law's Boundaries" (2022) 2 Undecidabilities and Law – The Coimbra Journal for Legal Studies 99; Mirosław M. Sadowski and Seyed M. A. Zavarei, "Changing Presents, Shifting Past(s): The Diverse Interests of Transitional Justice and Cultural Heritage in the Case of the Iranian Revolution" (2023) Law and Humanities 1.

20 Sadowski, *supra* note 7; Mirosław M. Sadowski, "Fluttering the Past in the Present: The Role of Flags in the Contemporary Society: Law, Politics, Identity and Memory" in Anne Wagner and Sarah Marusek (eds), *Flags, Color, and the Legal Narrative: Public Memory, Identity, and Critique* (Cham: Springer, 2021) at 85.

21 Mirosław M. Sadowski, "Collective Memory and Historical Determinacy: The Shaping of the Polish Transition" in Balázs Fekete and Fruzsina Gárdos-Orosz (eds), *Central and Eastern European Socio-Political and Legal Transition Revisited: The CEE Yearbook*, vol. 7 (Frankfurt am Mein: Peter Lang, 2017) 175; Mirosław M. Sadowski, "Central Europe in Search of (Lost) Identity: Literary and Legal Findings" (2018) 50 Fascicle Administration: Theory Didactics Practice 130; Mirosław M. Sadowski, "Central Europe in the Search of (Lost) Identity: The Illiberal Swerve" in Alexandra Mercescu (ed.), *Constitutional Identities in Central and Eastern Europe: The CEE Yearbook*, vol. 8 (Berlin: Peter Lang, 2020) 173; Mirosław M. Sadowski, "Law and Collective Memory in the Service of Illiberalism. Through the Looking-Glass: Transformation or a Reactionary Revolution?" (2021) XVIII:1 Krakowskie Studia Międzynarodowe – Krakow International Studies 107.

My main findings have thus far confirmed that memory is a major political instrument, an important factor contributing both to the shape law takes and to the way it functions in a society. As the links between law and collective memory still lack a broad and comprehensive examination, particularly with regard to Central Europe and most notably Poland, the present-day theoretical research often focuses only on the transitional justice aspects of the law and memory intersections, neglecting the other ones and treating the legal institutions of memory as separate entities, dismissing how examining them together would help understand the more general law and memory processes, and overlooking the need for a new conceptualisation of the right to memory.

As such, I hope to fill this gap by bringing together the work done by many disciplines[22] – with a critical review of the investigations in the three most important disciplines from the perspective of my research conducted in the first part of this study – in order to uncover the many ways in which law influences collective memory, while also remarking on the various ways in which the collective memories of the past influence law – and, most importantly, to provide a new framework for the understanding of these intersections, as well as to answer my main research questions set out in the next section. My research would thus become, as proposed by Stef Craps, a part of the most recent and most critical, fourth wave of memory studies, looking into memory from the perspective of the Anthropocene and its "spatiotemporal magnitudes."[23]

How Intersections of Law and Memory?

My book attempts to prove the hypothesis that law and memory intersect in a variety of ways, resulting in one influencing the other and vice versa, supported by the secondary book that these intersections have a profound effect on the shape of law, society, and politics. With the main research questions being: (1) 'How can the intersections of law and memory be framed?' (2) 'Can a right to memory be conceived amongst the politics of memory?', and (3) 'What applying a new framework might tell us about particular instances of law and memory intersections?', this book takes the viewpoint that, as the intersections of law and memory affect society as a whole, or different groups within society, and as law imposes certain narratives upon them, the actual act of evoking does not take place in the vacuum. Ultimately, it is an individual who remembers – or is it? This both challenging and fascinating transition from the abstract and collective to the particular and individual from

22 Matthew Graves and Elizabeth Rechniewski, "From Collective Memory to Transcultural Remembrance" (2010) 7 PORTAL Journal of Interdisciplinary Studies 1.

23 Stef Craps et al. (eds), "Introduction, Memory Studies and the Anthropocene: A Roundtable (2018) 11:4 Memory Studies 498 at 500.

a research perspective is going to be most noticeable in the proposed concept of the right to memory, but its traces will be remarked upon throughout the book, as it is emblematic of law, collective memory, and their intersections.

Why are these research questions important? Answering them will allow me to show the scale of the intersections between law and memory, which, both in the past and in the present day, is extremely wide, transcending legal systems and political, legal, and social circumstances, as well as cultural contexts. As such, I agree with Huyssen that memory and law are "umbilically linked to state and nation, to citizenship issues and the invention of national traditions,"[24] as they impact each other in a number of ways, with the most notable ones analysed in this book.

I aim to answer my research questions using the law and humanities methodological approach as recently put forward by, *inter alia*, Andreas Philippopoulos-Mihalopoulos, which balances the theoretical and applied by undertaking legal analysis that is sensitive to both the conceptual and material situatedness of law. This approach argues that to respond to present-day problems, it is important to consider "material, emplaced and embodied, yet equally theorised" elements, acknowledging dynamic intersections with other disciplines,[25] in the case of my book in social sciences and humanities in particular. The intersections of law and memory are undoubtedly such a topical contemporary issue, with, as Part III of the book demonstrates, their repercussions impacting the everyday reality of contemporary countries even when the collective memories in question relate to a distant past.

Claims that "law *needs* extra-legal knowledge," and thus a new multidisciplinary (rather than interdisciplinary) method, appear regularly in the literature[26] – while the law and humanities methodological approach was not fully conceptualised back in the day, António Manuel Hespanha explained the advantages of such a broad, diverse method he compared to "a kaleidoscope," by arguing that in the present day, the "epoch of pluralism," we have to uncover and analyse the unofficial, "everyday" law, "look beyond the appearances" of the law from different (i.e., not only legal) perspectives to understand the official law.[27] Intersections of law and memory, the interplay between the official narrative and counter-memory, fit this description very well, and their study will benefit from a multidisciplinary perspective.

24 Andreas Huyssen, "International Human Rights and the Politics of Memory: Limits and Challenges" (2011) 53:4 Criticism 607 at 607.

25 Andreas Philippopoulos-Mihalopoulos, "Introduction" in Andreas Philippopoulos-Mihalopoulos (ed.), *Routledge Handbook of Law and Theory* (Oxon: Routledge, 2018) 1 at 1–6.

26 Victoria Guijarro, "The Missing Chapter – Some Thoughts About the Socio-Legal Lab", online: Rechtswirklichkeit <barblog.hypotheses.org/3485>.

27 António M. Hespanha, *O caleidoscópio do direito: O direito e a justiça nos dias e no mundo hoje* [*The Kaleidoscope of Law: The Law and Justice in the Present Day and World*] (Coimbra: Almedina, 2007) at 9–10, 16.

It is through this kaleidoscopic lens that I approach the research questions in this book, understanding the "humanities" in law and humanities approach more broadly than the typical definition proposes, providing a list of different disciplines (such as literature, history, philosophy, and fine arts). Rather, I perceive the humanities here as including all of cultural products, not only the intangible knowledge, related to various disciplines but also different material artefacts, which, as I note further in the book, can play a very important role as memory carriers.

As such, this approach will also allow me to acknowledge the basic principle of the law and spatial studies subfield in my research, that law takes place in space. This emphasis on the spatial situatedness of law should prove key in the later analysis, allowing me to approach my research questions from additional angles without losing sight of the role and operations of law as situated (and contested) in space. As my research thus far shows, and as I further remark upon in the conclusions, in spite of being immaterial, law and memory intersect in space, with a number of different spatial dimensions of the law and memory relationship uncovered thanks to my chosen methodology.

Additionally, the kaleidoscopic nature of the chosen methodology will allow me to profit from a more-diverse-than-usual perspective in my study, giving me the necessary tools to go well beyond legal texts, resulting in a more enriched analysis of the intersections between law and memory, ultimately uncovering their true nature for the "naked legal eye." As I have to reconcile a number of approaches in my research – socio-legal, dogmatic, law and theory, critical legal theory, law and culture, law and literature, and comparative law – applying the law and humanities methodological approach will also help me avoid the problems regarding their traditional use separately, crossing their boundaries instead.

Last, and perhaps most importantly, the law and humanities approach is not an interdisciplinary method in the traditional sense but multidisciplinary, as already remarked upon in this section. This means that while the different disciplines will continue to inform one another, providing the wide variety of perspectives on the law and memory relationship fundamental for its in-depth analysis, it will be conducted with a primacy of law among disciplines, never losing it out of sight, even when the main focus of the part of the study in question is on the non-legal, e.g., sociology or philosophy.

Thus, the multidisciplinary approach will permit me to reconcile the richness of the body of research on collective memory with the first and foremost legal perspective I take throughout this book, allowing me to make the necessary compromises and build bridges between the different disciplines. While noticeable throughout the book, it is perhaps most visible in the first, theoretical chapters, whereby the inherent differences between sociological, philosophical, and legal theoretical approaches to collective memory are analysed through a kaleidoscopic and multidisciplinary but nonetheless legal lens, which allows me to bring the different perspectives together, answering the question as to what collective memory is for law and ultimately opening the door to further analysis.

What Intersections of Law and Memory?

My book proposes to approach the research questions in three parts and eight chapters. Before moving on to an overview of what this book is about, however, it needs to be remarked that, as in any research work on such a broad question, there are certain notable absences from its pages that I need to comment on: history, memory studies, the Holocaust, Paul Ricoeur, Canada, and colonialism.

History is often put together with law and memory as a departure point of their investigations;[28] however, in my research, while the shadows of the past continue to be a major factor impacting the present, I choose to turn towards the contemporary, rather than that of the yesteryear, introducing the historical background only when absolutely necessary, perceiving, as Halbwachs did, history and memory as not synonymous but similar terms, with a number of differences I remark upon in Part I of this book. In a similar vein, I decided not to investigate the intersections of law and memory from the perspective of memory studies – while proposed as a separate, cross-disciplinary discipline in recent years bringing together any and all aspects of research connected to the questions of collective memory,[29] I do not agree that an interdisciplinary approach to the understanding of collective memory is beneficial for the study of its relationship with law. It is from a legal perspective that I conduct the research in my book, and it is with regard to law that I propose what collective memory is at the end of Part I, using this single-discipline perspective throughout the rest of my study. At the same time, I also choose not to investigate the Holocaust as a separate case study: while of major importance to the development of international law[30] and a focal point of global collective memory,[31] its dedicated research would take my

28 See, e.g., Austin Sarat and Thomas R. Kearns (eds), *History, Memory and the Law* (Ann Arbor, MI: University of Michigan Press, 2002).

29 See, e.g., Wulf Kansteiner, "Finding Meaning in Memory: A Methodological Critique of Collective Memory Studies" (2002) 41 History and Theory 179; Henry L. Roediger III and James V. Wertsch, "Creating a New Discipline of Memory Studies" (2008) 1:1 Memory Studies 9; Anamaria Dutceac Segesten and Jenny Wüstenber, "Memory Studies: The State of an Emergent Field" (2017) 10:4 Memory Studies 474.

30 Mary J. Gallant and Harry M. Rhea, "Collective Memory, International Law, and Restorative Social Processes After Conflagration: The Holocaust" (2010) 20:3 International Criminal Justice Review 265.

31 Aleida Assmann, "The Holocaust – a Global Memory? Extensions and Limits of a New Memory Community" in Aleida Assmann and Sebastian Conrad (eds), *Memory in a Global Age: Discourses, Practices and Trajectories* (Houndsmills/New York, NY: Palgrave Macmillan, 2010) at 97.

book too deeply into the past; as such, the tragedy of Shoah will be analysed only incidentally when linked to other elements of my book.

In turn, the other two omissions are more personal in nature: while focusing on contemporary French philosophy regarding memory issues, I choose not to ponder the thought of Paul Ricoeur, who, while writing widely on matters on collective memory, has not only already been particularly often interpreted in this context[32] but also whose approach does not fit into the proposed framework. Similarly, while Canada, with its symbolic reparations and truth and reconciliation commission, could provide for an interesting case study, the fact that its reconciliation process is still ongoing, as well as, as I also note further, its certain popularity as an object of research,[33] means that the country's legal institutions of memory would require a much more profound study than one that may be provided in this book.

Last, while a number of case studies that I choose to investigate in this book were either colonies (Brazil, Iraq, Rwanda) or metropoles (Japan, Portugal), I do not engage in an analysis from a post-colonial perspective. As I agree with Saeed that "colonialism not just influenced legal and normative orderings in the colonies, but laid the very terrain in which law and normative systems function" and thus "the examination of law in these contexts . . . cannot escape the re-articulation of the shared history of law and colonialism,"[34] adding this viewpoint to the law and memory would require a much more detailed historical study than proposed for the purposes of the book. Nevertheless, echoes of colonialism may be found throughout the last chapters of this work, particularly in the cases of Iraqi and Rwandan memory policies.

Beginning with the Prologue – "France as a Law and Memory Hub," which, by introducing the main themes on the example of France, a country particularly rich in the intersections of law and memory, sets the stage for later investigations – this book is divided into three parts – theoretical, conceptual, and practical – with Parts I and III each composed of three chapters

32 See, e.g., Abdelmajid Hannoum, "Paul Ricoeur On Memory" (2005) 22:6 Theory, Culture and Society 123; Jeffrey A. Barash, "The Place of Remembrance: Reflections on Paul Ricoeur's Theory of Collective Memory" in Brian Treanor and Henry Isaac Venema (eds), *A Passion for the Possible: Thinking with Paul Ricoeur* (New York, NY: Fordham University Press, 2010) at 147.

33 See, e.g. Gail Guthrie Valaskakis, Madeleine Dion Stout, and Eric Guimond (eds), *Restoring the Balance First Nations Women, Community, and Culture* (Winnipeg, MB: University of Manitoba Press, 2009); Rosemary L. Nagy, "The Scope and Bounds of Transitional Justice and the Canadian Truth and Reconciliation Commission" (2013) 7 The International Journal of Transitional Justice 52; Ronald Niezen, *Truth and Indignation: Canada's Truth and Reconciliation Commission on Indian Residential Schools* (North York, ON: University of Toronto Press, 2017).

34 Raza Saeed, "Law and Coloniality of Empire: Colonial Encounter and Normative Orderings in the Indian Sub-Continent" (2018) 19:1 Yearbook of Islamic and Middle Eastern Law 103 at 104.

and Part II of two. Part I, entitled "The Theory: Defining and Demarcating Law and Memory's Intersections," provides the bases for my later investigations. Focusing on the theoretical approaches to the relationship between law and collective memory, it traces the links between them in three disciplines – sociology, philosophy, and theory of law – each in a dedicated chapter.

In the first chapter, "Sociology, Memory, and Law: From Halbwachs to Agents of Memory," I introduce the main sociological ideas that I will use throughout the book, most notably the concept of collective memory, presenting not only its classical Halbwachsian understanding but also proposing a division of various contemporary approaches to the question of social memory, categorising them into four groups based on their dichotomies (past/present; society/culture; formal/global; and innovative/critical). Further in the chapter, I also analyse other key elements of the theory of collective memory, i.e., collective forgetting, cultural trauma (which I propose to reread as collective trauma-memory), and the notion of agents and carriers of memory.

The second chapter, "Philosophy, Memory and Law: The French Four," is devoted to a review of approaches to the questions of memory and law by four French thinkers, chosen, as I elaborate later in the book, based on the suitability of their thought for my proposed new framework of law and memory intersections. As such, I turn to Émile Durkheim and his theory that law and its rituals replaced religion in modern societies, Henri Bergson's particular understanding of memory, one escaping the typical individual/collective division, Emmanuel Levinas and his diachronic, memory-entrenched theory of ethics, and Michel Foucault's observations on the questions of authority and power over social memory, as well as his concepts of countermemory heterotopias.

In the third, final chapter of Part I, "Collective Memory, Law and Theory: From Human Rights and International Law to the Concept of Transitional Justice," I shift my attention to the question of legal theory. I focus on the deep relationship between and influence on human rights law and international law of collective memory, later deconstructing the concept of transitional justice most typically used to describe law and memory's intersections in the present day, remarking upon the failings of its supposed universality. Ultimately, the first part of the book closes with a concluding section, "Law and Collective Memory, Collective Memory and Law," in which I propose to define what collective memory is for law.

In turn, Part II of the book, entitled "The Concept: Framing Law and Memory's Intersections," focuses on the development of the new framework for the understanding of law and memory's intersections. To establish such a different approach, I propose to base the new framework on three key points. The first, introduced in Chapter 4, "Collective Memory and Law: Three Types of Institutions," is the concept of legal institutions of memory, i.e., those institutions of law that attempt to impact the social perceptions of the past the most, dividing them into soft, medium, and hard, depending on the degree of their direct impact on memory. I recognise six such institutions: two soft (reparations, both material and symbolic, and international tribunals), two medium (lustration and truth and reconciliation commissions), and two hard (legal amnesia and memory legislation).

The fifth chapter, "The Hidden Power of Law and Memory Intersections: From Memory Politics to a Right to Memory," represents a continuation of the development of the new framework, as such introducing its two other fundaments. The first of these is memory politics, i.e., the question of the instrumental use of the issues of the past by politicians in order to achieve particular political goals, in certain cases using the existing, in others creating new state and semi-independent entities to the disseminate the official narrative. The final element laying at the basis of the new framework is the question of the right to memory. While its existence has been mused by a number of researchers in recent years, with some arguing it already appears in various international law provisions, I propose to perceive it as a double-sided right, composed of the right to evoking (based on the right to remember and be remembered) and the right to disremembering (formed from the right to forgot and to be forgotten), whose different aspects need to be balanced, particularly in contemporary times. Ultimately, Part II of the book concludes with the elaboration of the proposed new law and memory framework.

Part III, the final part of the book, entitled "The Practice: Reviewing Law and Memory's Intersections," proposes to apply the new law and memory framework in particular circumstances, chosen on the basis of their singularity, as they all challenge the model of their respective institution, while nonetheless remaining within its limits, with selected case studies coming from around the world and a particular focus on Poland.

In Chapter 6, "Placing Soft Legal Institutions of Memory Within the New Framework," I analyse each of the soft legal institutions of memory. As such, I investigate reparations on the case of Japan and Poland and international tribunals on the example of the European Court of Human Rights (ECtHR) in regard to three cases. Chapter 7, "Placing Medium Legal Institutions of Memory Within the New Framework," is devoted to the medium legal institutions of memory; it analyses lustration in the cases of Iraq and Poland, and truth commissions in the example of Brazil. Then, the eighth chapter, "Placing Hard Legal Institutions of Memory Within the New Framework," turns to the question of hard legal institutions of memory, with studies of legal amnesia in the case of Portugal and memory legislation in the example of Rwanda and Poland.

The outcomes of these focused studies are then compared in Part III's conclusion, "Applying the New Law and Memory Framework and What Happened." Ultimately, the results of my investigations throughout the whole book are brought together in the work's conclusion, "Intersections of Law and Memory: Remarks After the Inquiry."

Part I

The Theory

Defining and Demarcating Law and Memory's Intersections

Introduction to Part I

The investigations of law and memory's intersections, like many others, need to be grounded in theory. As I already explained in the Introduction to this book, I will not look in the field of memory studies for the basis of my analysis, perceiving it as too fragmented and too far removed from law to provide a structured argument. Instead, I intend to focus on three disciplines, chosen and ordered not arbitrarily, but in such a way as to provide a clear demarcation of the intersections of law and memory, supplementing clear definitions and concepts that are going to be used throughout the book, as well as providing an understanding of the major theoretical questions surrounding the eponymous intersections.

Thus, I propose to start this journey with a sociological analysis, one which will introduce and attempt to explain a wide variety of collective memory phenomena, providing the book with an extensive vocabulary used later not only in this theoretical part but also throughout the conceptual and practical parts. Moving forward towards the field of philosophy, I will focus on four thinkers whose concepts grant a certain depth towards the sociological ideas presented in the earlier chapter, allowing us to understand their inner workings on a different level. While questions of law are a recurring *leitmotiv* in the first two chapters, they will be a sole focus of the third chapter, opening the grounds for the analysis to come in the following parts of the book. Ultimately, this theoretical opening of my investigations will close with an answer to one of the key questions of my research: What is collective memory for law? First, however, let me introduce the concept in general.

DOI: 10.4324/9781003461548-2

Chapter 1

Sociology, Memory, and Law

From Halbwachs to Agents of Memory

Introduction

Sociology is the discipline that has coined the term "collective memory," and it is for this reason that I choose to open the first, theoretical part, whose goal is to conceptualise collective memory in relation to law, with the analyses of the intersections between memory and society. Permanently provisional, constantly "vibrating," as it aims to "encapsulate events that have occurred in the ever quickly receding past of social time and cultural space,"[1] collective memory appears to be a rather elusive concept.

The difficulties in its conception notwithstanding, understanding collective memory is crucial for the study of various socio-cultural and socio-political processes – as Golka notes, society's existence is dependent on collective memory because it links the current generations to those of the past. As memory fluctuates, always being the effect of a consensus, society develops as well.[2] Adding that "individual memory is the trait of our 'me' in the singular, and social memory is a trait of our different 'us',"[3] he proceeds to distinguish over 40 various types of social memory.

I, in turn, propose a different focus: beginning with the first full conceptualisation of the collective memory concept, I move to the analysis of the ways in which it has been developed over the years, later introducing collective memory–related theories with a life of their own (collective forgetting and cultural trauma), closing the analysis with the introduction of the various agents and carriers of collective memory.

1 Robin Wagner-Pacifici, "Memories in the Making: The Shapes of Things That Went" (1996) 19:3 Qualitative Sociology 301 at 301–302.

2 Marian Golka, *Pamięć społeczna i jej implant* [*Social Memory and Its Implants*] (Warsaw: SCHOLAR, 2009) at 8.

3 *Ibid.* at 11.

DOI: 10.4324/9781003461548-3

Setting the Stage for Collective Memory: Maurice Halbwachs

Maurice Halbwachs is considered the "father" of collective memory.[4] While the idea appeared earlier in academia,[5] it was Halbwachs who fully conceptualised it in his 1925 *Social Frames of Memory* (translated into English as *On Collective Memory*)[6] and two later publications, *The Legendary Topography of the Gospels in the Holy Land: A Study of Collective Memory*[7] and the posthumous, unfinished *The Collective Memory*.[8] After falling into oblivion following his death in a concentration camp, Halbwachs's input on sociology has been recognised in recent years,[9] with his work considered to be fundamental for the discipline of memory studies.[10]

The collective, the group, is at the centre of Halbwachs's theory of remembering; however, for him, collective memories realise themselves only within the individual ones – as he argues, our memories are created in a sort of interplay between the individual and their social unit: "one may say that the individual remembers by placing himself in the perspective of the group, but one may also affirm that the memory of the group realises and manifests itself in individual memories."[11] For Halbwachs, collective memory is dynamic, ever-changing, and "constantly transformed," as the groups that are behind it are also constantly changing, with old members leaving and new members coming all the time.[12]

The individuals may stay behind the scenes in Halbwachs's work, and they may often be overlooked in the analysis of his theory; however, Halbwachs never loses the singular person out of sight, stressing that "while the collective memory endures and draws strength from its base in a coherent body of people, it is individuals as group members who remember."[13] It is also the individual who is "the site through which society exists and therefore

4 Sarah Gensburger, "Halbwachs' Studies in Collective Memory: A Founding Text for Contemporary 'Memory Studies'?" (2016) 16:4 Journal of Classical Sociology 396 at 397.
5 Jeffrey K. Olick, "Products, Processes, and Practices: A Non-Reificatory Approach to Collective Memory" (2006) 36:1 Biblical Theology Bulletin: Journal of Bible and Culture 5 at 10.
6 Maurice Halbwachs, *On Collective Memory* (Chicago, IL/London: University of Chicago Press, 1992).
7 Maurice Halbwachs, *La topographie légendaire des Évangiles en Terre Sainte: Étude de Mémoire Collective* (Paris: Presses Universitaires de France, 1941).
8 Maurice Halbwachs, *The Collective Memory* (New York, NY: Harper Colophon Books, 1980).
9 Csaba Pléh, "Remembering the Collective Memory of Maurice Halbwachs" (2000) 128:3–4 Semiotica 435 at 435–436.
10 Gensburger, *supra* note 4 at 398.
11 Halbwachs, *supra* note 6 at 40.
12 Anne Whitehead, *Memory* (Oxon: Routledge, 2009) at 128.
13 Halbwachs, *supra* note 8 at 48.

the place where the social dynamic of memory takes place."[14] I would argue that this acknowledgement of the individual even when speaking about the collective is one of the reasons why his theory remains relevant today and will prove useful in the creation of collective memory's definition from a legal viewpoint.

Individual memories exist for Halbwachs; however, for him, they are "effectively displaced" and ultimately "absorbed into the collective memory":[15] he argues that it is "on the basis of memory patterns" within our social groups that "the originally episodic memories become semantic ones, and get decontextualised,"[16] as "it is in society that people normally acquire their memories. It is also in society that they recall, recognise, and localise their memories," because "most of the time, when I remember, it is others who spur me on; their memory comes to the aid of mine and mine relies on theirs."[17] To put it succinctly, when one remembers, he or she "moves in a frame of reference common to all the members of his – wider or narrower – social group."[18]

Every one of us is a member of a large number of different groups at the same time – family, church, class, nation – and while some of the members of one of our groups also belong to another one of ours, or may be together with us in a larger group, they never overlap completely: for example, pupils in two different classes of second-graders at the same school are all members of the same educational community at the same time, but they share only similar memories, not the same collective memory. Each group "has its own original collective memory, keeping alive for a time important remembrances,"[19] and this collective memory "serves as a reference to define what is important and meaningful for this particular group," providing "the frame within which (or against which) individuals try to make sense of their own personal experiences."[20]

Social groups "frame" our memory by constructing "thought patterns, cognitive schemata, that guide our perception and memory in particular directions," thus forming "the all-encompassing horizon in which our perception and memory is embedded."[21] These social frameworks or "conceptual

14 Gensburger, *supra* note 4 at 403.
15 Whitehead, *supra* note 12 at 129.
16 Pléh, *supra* note 9 at 440.
17 Halbwachs, *supra* note 6 at 38.
18 J. C. Nyíri, *Tradition and Individuality: Essays* (Dodrecht: Springer Science+Business Media, 1992) at 28–29.
19 Halbwachs, *supra* note 8 at 78.
20 Erika Apfelbaum, "Halbwachs and the Social Properties of Memory" in Susannah Radstone and Bill Schwarz (eds), *Memory: Histories, Theories, Debates* (New York: Fordham University Press, 2010) 77 at 85.
21 Astrid Erll, *Memory in Culture* (Houndmills: Palgrave Macmillan, 2011) at 15.

schemes" of memory provide a space where "individual memories come to be located," thus establishing limits of individual memory.[22]

It is also "groups themselves" who "share publicly articulated images of collective pasts,"[23] with two types of collective memory distinguished by Halbwachs: "autobiographical memory," encompassing collective memories of one's own life; and "historical memory," encompassing those memories that no one in the group may personally recollect but through which "groups claim a continuous identity through time."[24]

The two overlap, as one's autobiographical memory is shaped by the historical memory,[25] allowing the former "to be heard in a context of broad social meaning."[26] It is precisely this mechanism that is used by the various agents of memory aiming to influence our memories and "refashion" a society's past[27] through the "politics of memory,"[28] employing those "long-lasting traces" of the past that remain "deeply and permanently engraved, often without our realising it, in traditions, institutions, and cultural heritage, as well as in the physical environment itself,"[29] buildings, streets, monuments, and other carriers of collective memory, as well as the legal institutions of memory, which I analyse in Part II of the book. As a result, one's autobiographical memory is linked not only to the "collective memories of the various groups to which he or she is affiliated but also to the broader historical memory of the society in which he or she lives,"[30] allowing a larger sense of identity (regional, national) to be born.

Nota bene, Halbwachs turns his focus to other, smaller groups than that of the nation, arguing that apart from some major events, the nation is a group "too remote from the individual"[31] to be of significance to his or her collective memory. Today, however, this remark should be regarded rather as showing that his thinking about the nation still belonged more to the 19th century than to the 20th. I would argue that since the arrival of mass media and the resulting collective national identity formation on an everyday basis (upon which I will remark upon further), Halbwachs's concept of collective memory may also be applied to the nation and, in the 21st century, to the whole world in certain instances (e.g., 9/11, COVID-19 pandemic).

22 Barbara A. Misztal, *Theories of Social Remembering* (Maidenhead: Open University Press, 2003) at 57.
23 Olick, *supra* note 5 at 11.
24 Olick, *supra* note 5 at 11.
25 Halbwachs, *supra* note 8 at 52.
26 Apfelbaum, *supra* note 20 at 89.
27 Misztal, *supra* note 22 at 52.
28 Apfelbaum, *supra* note 20 at 89.
29 Apfelbaum, *supra* note 20 at 91.
30 Apfelbaum, *supra* note 20 at 91.
31 Halbwachs, *supra* note 8 at 77.

Returning to the dichotomy of collective memory, to give an example, an autobiographical memory would be a memory of the first day at university, shared only by the members of the individual's entering class, while a historical memory would be the memory of the founding of this university, shared by all members of the community, bringing them together as a group. As the autobiographical collective memories of the establishment of the institution are unavailable, all members of the university group (current students, alumni, professors, etc.) have to rely on historical memory. As Douglas notes, "in so far as there is pressure toward coherent principles of organisation, so will the justificatory stories of the past be amalgamated and rationalised as part of the social process" – ultimately leading to the creation of a collective out of individuals, as "coherence and complexity in public memory will tend to correspond to coherence and complexity at the social level."[32]

It must be emphasised that for Halbwachs, historical memory does not equal history: in his theory, collective memory and history are opposed, with the latter oriented towards the past and the former leaning towards the present.[33] Moreover, the two are fundamentally different for him, as what becomes a part of the official narrative (history) is selected not by the groups that might have had a collective memory of the event, but by the historian, who "is guided in his selection and evaluation by reasons having little to do with the opinion of that time, which no longer exists."[34]

Since for Halbwachs, "history is what is no longer included within the sphere of thought of existing groups," its conception "must wait until old groups have disappeared, until their thoughts and memory have vanished,"[35] beginning only "when tradition ends and the social memory is fading or breaking up."[36] As a result, the ever-changing collective memory of a social group connects it with the past, being constantly adapted to fit the group's current needs, thus bringing it into the present, whereas history shows us what is different about the past in the present, reminding us that society is constantly changing.[37] To cite Fowler's evocative observation, for Halbwachs, "history fixes dates and places precisely on the banks, collective memory offers a social current within which we 'bathe midstream.' "[38]

For example, collective memories of the origins of various religions seem "to be fixed once and for all,"[39] which means they do not necessarily

32 Mary Douglas, *How Institutions Think* (New York: Syracuse University Press, 1986) at 80.
33 Erll, *supra* note 21 at 17.
34 Halbwachs, *supra* note 8 at 106.
35 Halbwachs, *supra* note 8 at 106.
36 Halbwachs, *supra* note 8 at 78.
37 Whitehead, *supra* note 12 at 131.
38 Bridget Fowler, "Collective Memory and Forgetting Components for a Study of Obituaries" (2005) 22:6 Theory, Culture & Society 53 at 55.
39 Halbwachs, *supra* note 6 at 92.

correspond with the historical account of these events – they are based on "culturally constructed knowledge about a distant past and its transmission through the creation of traditions," rather than on a historical narrative.[40] Ultimately, a religious group is a social group similar to others, and its collective memory "obeys the same laws as every collective memory."[41] The only factor that is different is that the vast majority of the original social groups that were present at the time most of the religions were born have long disappeared, whereas the social group of a particular religion withstood the test of time, bringing its often-antiquated collective memories to the present. This proves what Misztal calls "the persistence of memory"[42] – as long as a group exists, its collective memories persist, in some cases even standing the test of time through the ages.

Importantly, in Halbwachs's theory, the past and present continuously influence one another, with our current experiences impacting the perceptions of our past and vice versa, together forming "a coherent whole" as "discoveries of fact are but traditions of most recent date."[43] An individual memory is thus a reconstruction of the past on the basis of what is present in a society at a given moment.[44] As a result, the things we remember, our recollections, "are not just simple imprints; they are truly active selections and reconstructions of this past," as they are "continuously evaluated and shaped by confrontations with collective memory, which confer legitimacy on our memory."[45]

However, as Bastide poignantly remarks, for Halbwachs, the present does not immediately create memories, which instead rest in the "treasury" of collective memories, acting like a "lock" or a "filter" for what exactly is brought back in the process of evoking,[46] preventing other, unnecessary memories from coming back (here we may see echoes of Bergson's theory of memory, analysed in Chapter 2). Ultimately, remembering involves more than simply "reconstituting the image of a past event a piece at a time" – it needs to begin "from shared data or conceptions" which "are present in our mind as well as" the minds of other members of the group.[47]

40 Erll, *supra* note 21 at 18.
41 Halbwachs, *supra* note 6 at 119.
42 Misztal, *supra* note 22 at 55.
43 Nyíri, *supra* note 18 at 29.
44 Paul Sabourin, "Perspective sur la mémoire sociale de Maurice Halbwachs" ["Perspective on the Social Memory of Maurice Halbwachs"] (1997) 29:2 La mémoire sociale 139 at 148.
45 Apfelbaum, *supra* note 20 at 85.
46 Roger Bastide, "Mémoire collective et sociologie du bricolage" ["Collective Memory and the Sociology of Bricolage"] (1970) 21 L'Année sociologique, online: UQAC <classiques.uqac.ca/contemporains/bastide_roger/memoire_collective_socio_bricolage/memoire_coll_texte.html> 5 at 18.
47 Halbwachs, *supra* note 8 at 31.

Before moving on to the analysis of the various concepts of collective memory proposed following Halbwachs in the next section, it is important to remark after Pleh that Halbwachs presented his idea at a particular moment in history: "in a society with a broken sense of temporal continuity, in France after the Great War."[48] It could be argued that the 21st-century globalised society also lost its "temporal continuity" due to the COVID-19 pandemic, thus rendering Halbwachs's theory even more useful for my analysis.

What Came Later: From Collective to Global Memory

Collective memory, as any other concept, has not stood still in academia over the years. Halbwachs may have provided the foundations; however, the idea has been developed, redeveloped, and criticised ever since its conception. Thus, to fully answer the question of what collective memory is in relation to law, a further examination of the evolution of the concept is warranted.

Brian Conway attempted to organise the increasingly nebulous memory-related phenomena by dividing them into three categories on the basis of the "goal" of a particular concept of memory: those concerning "agency and actorhood in relation to commemoration and remembrance" (e.g., memory works); those concerning "the contexts in which memory is (re)produced" (e.g., postmemory); and those concerning "the constitutive forces for memory" (e.g., cultural trauma).[49] While looking into the goal of the different aspects of collective memory makes for an interesting intellectual exercise, by putting together the various concepts of collective memory alongside such phenomena as carriers and subdivisions of collective memory, his distinction is rendered unhelpful in the long run, only leading to greater confusion.

Instead of looking at what different theories view as the goal of collective memory, I propose to focus on their roots, asking what the different concepts regard as key in the creation of collective memory. Earlier in my work,[50] I proposed a basic threefold distinction of the various theories of collective memory into past-oriented, social-oriented, and mixed. Here, I would like to introduce a broader categorisation, which, while by no means all-encompassing or exclusionary, helps navigate the extremely crowded sea of ideas attempting to provide an understanding of collective memory. Proposing to investigate them in a comparative way, one that attempts to bring order while also showing the fluid boundaries between various theories, I distinguish the following concepts of collective memory: past-oriented and

48 Pléh, *supra* note 9 at 441.

49 Brian Conway, "New Directions in the Sociology of Collective Memory and Commemoration" (2010) 4:7 Sociology Compass 442 at 445–446.

50 Mirosław M. Sadowski, "Law and Memory: The Unobvious Relationship" (2017) 16:2 Warsaw University Law Review 262 at 266–268.

present-oriented; social and cultural; formal and global; and innovative and critical.

The Past/Present Dichotomy

In some instances, collective memory theorists choose to focus on the interplay between memories and time, regarding either the *past* or the *present* as the key element in the construction of collective memories. With regard to the former, the link between the present day and what has happened before is particularly stressed, seen as influencing one's behaviour today, with collective memory conceptualised as a social memory, shared by a group or a community, and understood "as the set of symbols and practices referring to the past."[51] As Gudehus explains further, being "narrative constructions of the past of an ideal nature," our collective memories' purpose is to "frame histories about the represented entity (person, group, institution)" in order to give significance and orientation, thus providing coherence[52] to a set of otherwise individual people with their own stories and experiences. As a result, collective memory is not free from power relations, legitimising the group's elites, which in particularly complex societies (such as contemporary nations) means "the past becomes the subject of strategies seeking to impose the representations that conform most to the dominant interests,"[53] such as legal institutions of memory analysed in Chapter 2 of the book.

When the focus is turned towards the *present*, the concepts of collective memory do not disregard the past, stressing, however, the personal histories and behaviour of contemporary group members as of major significance. In this view, collective memory is both "what people really remember through their own experience" and "the constructed past which is constitutive of the collectivity."[54] As "collectively created and collectively held," collective memory plays the role of "a crucial element in the translation of experience into future action."[55] It also results in a shared identity providing "an interpretative code" through which one perceives his or her experiences, synbooking "the private and public spheres together by conferring momentous

51 Lorenzo Zamponi, "Collective Memory and Social Movements" in David A. Snow, Donatella della Porta, Bert Klandermans, and Doug McAdam (eds), *The Wiley-Blackwell Encyclopedia of Social and Political Movements* (Malden, MA: Wiley-Blackwell, 2013, Wiley Online Library) at 1.

52 Christian Gudehus, "Sobre a Significância do Passado para a Ação Presente e Futura" ["About the Significance of the Past for the Present and Future Action"] (2014) 2:3 História, Histórias 109 at 118.

53 Paolo Jedlowski, "Memory and Sociology: Themes and Issues" (2001) 10:1 Time and Society 29 at 34.

54 Misztal, *supra* note 22 at 13.

55 Howard Schuman and Jacqueline Scott, "Generations and Collective Memories" (1989) 54:3 American Sociological Review 359 at 378–379.

historical events with significance for the individual, and by constructing a chronological history."[56] This presentist perspective on collective memory would thus be particularly helpful when analysing the processes of transitional justice (the concept of which is introduced in Chapter 3), when the public memory needs to account for various conflicting personal narratives.

The Society/Culture Dichotomy

Another dichotomy of the collective memory theories I propose to distinguish focuses on the interactions between memories and the key medium in their conception: *society* and *culture*. In the case of the former, social interactions taking place on the various stages of one's life lay at the root of collective memory, linked first to shared experiences among children, then later encompassing the memories of "family and cultural experiences steeped in rich experiences" among adolescents, ultimately also including the "collective knowledge of familial and cultural history that informs the richer narratives"[57] in adulthood. Importantly, all collective memories need to be shared by the members of a group, be that deliberately or accidentally, even if they took place in the past for some or all of the group's members, as they continue to have an impact in the present.[58] In this view, collective memory is composed of individual memories, but, akin to public opinion, it differs "from the sum total of the personal recollections of"[59] the group's members. What lies at its core is the "distribution throughout society of what individuals know, believe, and feel about the past, how they judge the past morally, how closely they identify with it, and how much they are inspired by it as a model for their conduct and identity"[60] in the present day. The *social* theories of memory are thus perhaps closest to the "classical" definition proposed by Halbwachs and most useful when analysing the various social processes and products influenced by narratives and perceptions of the past, including, for example, memory legislation analysed in Part II of the book.

While some theorists of collective memory focus on society, others choose to turn their attention to one of its products – *culture*. The main theory of

56 Lorraine Ryan, "Memory, Power and Resistance: The Anatomy of a Tripartite Relationship" (2010) 4:2 Memory Studies 154 at 156.

57 Elaine Reese and Robyn Fivush, "The Development of Collective Remembering" (2008) 16:3 Memory 201 at 209.

58 John Sutton, "Between Individual and Collective Memory: Coordination, Interaction, Distribution" (2008) 75:1 Social Research 23 at 31.

59 Eviatar Zerubavel, "Social Memories: Steps to a Sociology of the Past" (1996) 19:3 Qualitative Sociology 283 at 293–294.

60 Barry Schwartz, "Rethinking the Concept of Collective Memory" in Anna Lisa Tota and Trever Hagen (eds), *Routledge International Handbook of Memory Studies* (London/New York, NY: Routledge, 2016) 9 at 10.

the interactions between culture and collective memory has been proposed by Jan and Aleida Assmann, who created the concept of cultural memory, describing it as different from communicative/everyday memory as well as from science.[61] Communicative memory is, for them, a type of collective memory that encompasses everyday communications turned oral history, stretching up to only 80 or 100 years to the past.[62] Once no first-hand collective memories are available (as those of World War I in the present day, for example), a transition takes place from communicative memory to objectivised culture,[63] and ultimately cultural memory, distant from the present and unchanging through time, is born.[64] Between the two, there exists "a shifting 'floating gap' that moves along with the passage of time."[65]

Defining cultural memory as a particular type of collective memory conveying collective cultural identity, the Assmanns argue it is a form of an institution, "exteriorized, objectified, and stored away in symbolic forms," which is always "stable and situation-transcendent" and "may be transferred from one situation to another and transmitted from one generation to another" with the help of cultural objects.[66] As it is "purposefully established and ceremonialized,"[67] cultural memory "has its specialists, both in oral and in literate societies": troubadours, priests, artists, scholars, etc.[68]

Importantly, as Erll remarks, cultural memory does not need to be chronologically distant. What matters is the meaning that the collective memories of a particular event carry with them. For example, in the present day, 9/11 was an event of such magnitude and repercussions that it was transformed *ad hoc* from a recent past to "foundational history," sharing "basic characteristics with the memory of 'distant,' 'mythical' times and fulfil[ling] the same functions."[69]

The Assmanns propose their concept of cultural memory as bridging the gap in Halbwachs's theory,[70] arguing that he focused only on communicative memory,[71] seemingly mistaking his distinction between collective memory and history for a limitation on his part of collective memories to those that

61 Jan Assmann, "Collective Memory and Cultural Identity" (1995) 65 New German Critique 125 at 126.
62 *Ibid.* at 126–127.
63 *Ibid.* at 128.
64 *Ibid.* at 129.
65 Erll, *supra* note 21 at 28.
66 Jan Assmann, "Communicative and Cultural Memory" in Astrid Erll and Ansgar Nünning (eds), *Cultural Memory Studies: An International and Interdisciplinary Handbook* (Berlin/New York, NY: Walter de Gruyter, 2008) 109 at 110–111.
67 Erll, *supra* note 21 at 28.
68 Assmann, *supra* note 66 at 114.
69 Erll, *supra* note 21 at 32.
70 Assmann, *supra* note 66 at 111–113.
71 Assmann, *supra* note 61 at 126.

are only "in the living memory." As I have shown in the previous section, Halbwachs's concept also includes very distant events as elements of collective memory (for example, the origins of religions), as long as they continue to influence the present. While the Assmanns' distinction sheds light on the differences between what I would call a group's major collective memories and a collectivity's regular collective memories, I am not sure what exactly it brings to the metaphorical "collective memory table" and whether it is actually needed – on the one hand, it is also the everyday collective memories that determine a group's survival, and on the other, some of them will become recognised as of such importance that they will be carried for generations, perhaps taking the place of some of the collective memories belonging to the "fixed past" along the way.

While most often analysed, the Assmanns' concept is by no means the only attempt at conceptualising collective memory through *culture* – more recently, for example, Qi Wang stressed the influence of cultural differences and evolution of culture on collective memory, proposing to understand it as "a dynamic cultural practice that sustains the cultural continuity of a community and in the meantime adapts to the cultural transformation of the community in a historical era."[72] This viewpoint is particularly insightful when linked to the question of globalisation and global collective memories analysed next, as in the present day cultural practices become more uniform, with the number of collective memories shared around the world increasing exponentially in recent years.

In a similar vein, also looking into the inner workings of cultural practices, Aaron Beim argues that collective memory should be understood as the cultural "schemata produced through individual interaction with other individuals and among institutional representations of history,"[73] which are used "to make sense of the past."[74] Bringing forward a sketch of such a schema, Beim stresses the role of cultural objects in the production of collective memory, calling them collective memory objects.[75] Looking into them as carriers of collective memory, I will analyse them further in this chapter.

The Formal/Global Dichotomy

Another dichotomy of the collective memory theories is based on two opposing vectors, with *formal* theories focusing on the hermetic world of institutions and *global* theories venturing to describe processes taking place in the

72 Qi Wang, "On the Cultural Constitution of Collective Memory" (2008) 16:3 Memory 305 at 315.

73 Aaron Beim, "The Cognitive Aspects of Collective Memory" (2007) 30:1 Symbolic Interaction 7 at 15.

74 *Ibid.* at 21.

75 *Ibid.* at 19–20.

whole of the present-day world. With regard to the former, I use the term *formal* collective memory to encompass two major concepts of memory that rely on formalisation as a way of preservation: organisational memory and institutional memory.

Organisational memory refers to the "consciously designed, controlled and managed" collective memory of an entity, constructed on the basis of its "ability to collect, transfer and employ knowledge" it has gained throughout its years in operation[76] – for example, a company's trade secrets and inner modes of working. Thus, regarded as an intangible asset, organisational memory may be of substantive value to an entity.[77] As a type of collective memory, organisational memory shares its general traits. It is based on past experiences; however, it can also "entail time embedded information or the anticipation of experiences not yet experienced," for example, projections, forecasts, and strategic plans,[78] which, akin to collective memories in the 'classical' definition, reach out from the past to influence the present and aim to shape the future. Importantly, as Aksu notes, organisational memory is strictly limited to those groups (collectives) that are organised, while collective memory in general does not require organisation within a group for its conception; however, the appearance of collective memory may accelerate the process of a group's formalisation, ultimately leading to the appearance of organisational memory.[79]

The second *formal* concept of collective memory is institutional memory, which, similar to organisational memory, has a purpose and "a considerable organisational dimension";[80] however, it also involves managing the past by elites to create a narrative for the rest of society suited to their political needs, with various "versions" of the past propagated by different interest groups at the same time.[81] As such, institutional memory is a major factor in the process of nation building, and, wherever it is lacking, disorder ensues.[82] With law playing a vital role in the inner workings of institutional memory, a number of legal institutions of memory analysed in Part II of the book

76 Mark N. Wexler, "Organizational Memory and Intellectual Capital" (2002) 3:4 Journal of Intellectual Capital 393 at 395.
77 *Ibid.* at 395.
78 *Ibid.* at 396–397.
79 Eşref Aksu, "Global Collective Memory: Conceptual Difficulties of an Appealing Idea" (2009) 23:2 Global Society 317 at 322.
80 *Ibid.* at 323.
81 Richard N. Lebow, "The Memory of Politics in Postwar Europe" in Richard N. Lebow, Wulf Kansteiner, and Claudio Fogu (eds), *The Politics of Memory in Postwar Europe* (Durham: Duke University Press, 2006) 1 at 13.
82 Francis Fukuyama, "Nation-Building and the Failure of Institutional Memory" in Francis Fukuyama (ed.), *Nation-Building: Beyond Afghanistan and Iraq* (Baltimore, MD: Johns Hopkins University Press, 2006) 1 at 11.

(most notably memory legislation) could be classified more specifically as legal institutions of formal memory.

The closed-off, hermetic concept of formal memory may be contrasted with the idea of *global* memory, one "shared by all or most human beings," with its substance and its carriers derived "from across the world, regardless of the well-known power asymmetries in world politics," incorporating or accommodating the various "experiences, viewpoints, value systems, and particular sensitivities" present around the world.[83] While I would argue that the arrival of great religions in all corners of the world in the 16th–18th centuries (through various, often not peaceful means) also resulted in the establishment of first *global* collective memories, we are living in a truly globalised society only since the second half of the 19th century.

With increasingly rapid access to information, events of particular magnitude are remembered by millions of people, influencing their behaviour for decades, for example, the bombing of Hiroshima and Nagasaki, which installed the fear of an atomic war and thus impacted the world's geopolitics in the 1960s; the Holocaust, which, after decades of international commemoration and presence in mass media,[84] turned into a "de-contextualised symbol," becoming a point of reference for other acts of genocide;[85] and 9/11 and other terrorist attacks, which permanently changed the way flights are organised all over the world.[86] One could argue that every time we go through airport security, putting our liquids in a clear bag before travelling, we participate in a ritual, collectively remembering that fateful day and the later failed plots.

Importantly, *global* memory, as a type of collective memory, shares its traits with the presence of different, even contradictory perceptions of the same event; this is particularly notable in multicultural societies.[87] As memories cross national borders, the lines between past and present begin to fade, and people not only become increasingly aware of the presence of different narratives within society but also realise the need to rectify the mistakes of the past,[88] which in turn leads to calls for transitional justice, a concept analysed in Chapter 3.

83 Aksu, *supra* note 79 at 324.

84 Daniel Levy and Natan Sznaider, "Memory Unbound: The Holocaust and the Formation of Cosmopolitan Memory" (2002) 5:1 European Journal of Social Theory 87 at 100.

85 *Ibid.* at 102.

86 Aksu, *supra* note 79 at 325.

87 Matthew Graves and Elizabeth Rechniewski, "From Collective Memory to Transcultural Remembrance" (2010) 7:1 PORTAL Journal of Interdisciplinary Studies 1 at 2.

88 Henry Rousso, "Vers une Mondialisation de la Mémoire" (2007) 94 Vingtième Siècle: Revue d'histoire 3 at 6.

The Innovative/Critical Dichotomy

The final pair of collective memory theories is particularly elusive, with viewpoints that cannot be easily classified and are thus grouped together as either *innovative* or *critical* concepts. With regard to the former, I focus on four that are, in my opinion, most helpful in broadening the understanding of collective memory: Wertsch and Roedinger's concept of collective remembering; Olick's proposal of distinguishing collected memories from collective memories; Levabre's theory of collective memory, laying at the intersections of various theoretical concepts related to past and remembering; and Russell's idea of the evolution of collective memory, which I have analysed elsewhere,[89] showing how it ventures to establish the difference between the understanding of collective memory before modern times (pre-Halbwachsian memories) and after the contemporary concept of identity was born,[90] following the birth of nation-states (Halbwachsian memories), demonstrating the differences that need to be taken into account when analysing the processes of remembering and forgetting in modern societies and those of the past.

In turn, acknowledging the existing "elusiveness" of the concept of collective memory, Wertsch and Roedinger propose delineating their approach on the basis of three antimonies: collective memory and collective remembering; history and collective remembering; and individual remembering and collective remembering.[91] The first of these distinctions proposes to understand collective memory "as a static base of knowledge," while collective remembrance is a dynamic process of evoking, involving "social and political contestation."[92] The second distinction proposes to regard history as an attempt "to provide an accurate account of the past," while collective remembering is deeply connected to identify and, providing a permanent link between past and present, may ignore or distort events it perceives as dangerous to the identity in question.[93] Ultimately, the third opposition aims to distinguish between the individual and collective remembering, conceding that culture is key in understanding the difference between the two, as "what makes collective memory collective" is sharing "a similar set of cultural tools, especially narrative forms, when understanding the past."[94] Wertsch and Roedinger's approach thus interestingly shifts the focus of collective memory from the established narratives about the past to the dynamic

89 Sadowski, *supra* note 50 at 268–269.

90 Nicholas Russell, "Collective Memory Before and After Halbwachs" (2006) 79:4 The French Review 792 at 800.

91 James V. Wertsch and Henry L. Roediger III, "Collective Memory: Conceptual Foundations and Theoretical Approaches" (2008) 16:3 Memory 318 at 319.

92 *Ibid.* at 319.

93 *Ibid.* at 320.

94 *Ibid.* at 324.

identity processes taking place in the present, rendering it particularly useful when analysing post-transitional societies, once "the dust settles" and the links with the past have already been reforged but are still competing for dominance, potentially leading to conflict.

Olick also bases his *innovative* theory of collective memory on a distinction between two types of collective memory: collected memories and "actual" collective memory. The former, he argues, includes "the aggregated individual memories of members of a group," with the singular person at the centre of collected memory. In this concept, "only people have lives" of their own – and not memories. While "social frameworks shape what individuals remember, . . . it is only individuals who do the remembering," with the various "shared symbols and deep structures . . . only real insofar as individuals (albeit sometimes organised as members of groups) treat them as such or instantiate them in practice."[95] Such an approach allows free collective memory of its ideological aspects and opens it, as well as its outcomes, to psychological and other social discipline analyses.[96]

In turn, what Olick calls collective memory is linked to the "classical" concept of collective memory, one asserting "that collectivities have memories, just like they have identities, and that ideas, styles, genres, and discourses, among other things, are more than the aggregation of individual subjectivities," thus encompassing more than the collected approach proposed earlier, and also providing an explanation for heritage, traditions, and myths passed on through participation collective rituals (acts of collective "re-member-ing").[97]

Olick leaves open his argument on the understanding of collective memory, proposing three ways of moving forward with this question: abandoning the concept altogether; restricting it only "to public discourses about the past as wholes or to narratives and images of the past that speak in the name of collectivities";[98] or broadening the term exponentially to describe the "wide variety of mnemonic processes, practices, and outcomes, neurological, cognitive, personal, aggregated, and collective" under the new name of "social memory studies."[99]

While Olick leans towards the third suggested option, I have to disagree with each of his proposals. Dropping the concept of collective memory is not helpful, as it leaves the field of research with an enormous gap in the possible ways of analysing social practices of remembrance, just as expanding it *ad infinitum* would prove unhelpful when putting together the different

95 Jeffrey K. Olick, "Collective Memory: The Two Cultures" (1999) 17:3 Sociological Theory 332 at 338.
96 *Ibid.* at 339–342.
97 *Ibid.* at 342.
98 *Ibid.* at 345.
99 *Ibid.* at 346.

by nature social, psychological, and physiological workings of memory. In turn, limiting it only to public or collective discourses regarding the past seems to lose sight of collective memory's effect on individuals' actions in the present. Instead, both of his ideas regarding the collected and "actual" collective memory should be taken into account only as enriching the study of the collective memory processes, the former bringing the individual perspective to the front of analysis, and the latter stressing the importance of collective forms of remembering deeply entrenched with societies (a viewpoint akin to that of Durkheim, analysed in Chapter 2).

The final *innovative* theory of collective memory, which I find particularly useful in understanding its concept, has been proposed by Lavabre, who, heavily influenced by Halbwachs, introduces collective memory as being at the centre of the various theoretical crossroads between history and memory on the one hand and between the different forms of memory – historic, shared, and ultimately collective – on the other. Noting that the distinction between history and memory is fundamental for the understanding of collective memory,[100] Lavabre defines the former as a systematic "intellectual operation," one whose goal is "knowledge and intelligibility of the past," while memory has a number of faces: historic (one employing history for political needs, including identity and legitimisation purposes), shared (one concerning what the society may actually remember at a given moment through various generations alive at a given moment in time),[101] and collective, laying at the intersections of the three aforementioned concepts.[102]

Importantly, in Lavabre's concept, history, historic memory, and shared memory are not static (and thus collective memory is not static either), influencing one another in the following movements: shared memory moves towards history (as what one has lived as a member of different groups at the same time may turn them into an objective "historian" of a particular experience or period) and historic memory (as one's experiences may turn them into subjective representatives of the past); history moves towards historic memory (becoming politicised), and historic memories move towards shared memories (influencing people's perceptions of lived experiences).[103]

While ambiguous, Lavabre's dynamic concept of collective memory manages to capture the essence of the idea in question, linking the past with the present, the objective with the subjective, and the individual with the collective, and will prove particularly helpful when answering this chapter's eponymous question: what does collective memory mean for law?

100 Marie-Claire Lavabre, "La 'mémoire collective' entre sociologie de la mémoire et sociologie des souvenirs?" (2016) HAL Archive ouverte en Sciences de l'Homme et de la Société, online: HALSH <halshs.archives-ouvertes.fr/halshs-01337854> 1 at 9.

101 *Ibid.* at 10.

102 *Ibid.* at 11.

103 *Ibid.* at 12.

The innovative concepts, going beyond the traditional realms of collective memory, in some cases end up negating its existence (as in one of the cases proposed by Olick). Thus, I propose to put them together with *critical* views on collective memory, those putting its various particularities into question. Kansteiner, for example, remarks on collective memory's Eurocentrism,[104] one which may be motivated by its blindness towards the major differences between oral and writing-based societies.[105] Gedi and Elam dismiss collective memory as a fad that has replaced history, which will lead to its "disintegration" as a discipline,[106] arguing that it may be understood only as a metaphor,[107] nothing more than a myth, a social stereotype, "a fabricated version of that same personal memory adjusted to what the individual mind considers . . . as suitable in a social environment."[108] In a similar vein, Susan Sontag dismisses collective memory as "not a remembering but a stipulating: that this is important, and this is the story about how it happened, with the pictures that lock the story in our minds," arguing that it is the ideologies that "create substantiating archives of images, representative images, which encapsulate common ideas of significance and trigger predictable thoughts, feelings."[109]

This brief analysis of the various concepts of memory shows us, on the one hand, that despite its being an elusive phenomenon, researchers do not shy away from aiming to describe it and that, on the other hand, the inflation of its concepts does not necessarily help clear the proverbial waters of what it actually is, with even negating theorists taking a stance and proposing a suitable (in their mind) replacement. One thing that comes out of this collective memory fog, however, is that it is clearly malleable as a concept, and as such, various disciplines try to adapt the basis laid out by Halbwachs to best fit their particular frames. Before venturing out to do so for law, however, several other terms related to the concept of collective memory need to be introduced first.

Going the Opposite Way: Collective Forgetting

The analysis of collective memory has resulted in the birth of related concepts, also ones that do not necessarily fit any of its numerous definitions

104 Wulf Kansteiner, "Finding Meaning in Memory: A Methodological Critique of Collective Memory Studies" (2002) 41 History and Theory 179 at 183.

105 Pléh, *supra* note 9 at 442.

106 Noa Gedi and Yigal Elam, "Collective Memory – What Is It?" (1996) 8:1 History and Memory 30 at 40.

107 *Ibid.* at 43.

108 *Ibid.* at 47.

109 Susan Sontag, *Regarding the Pain of the Others* (New York: Farrar, Strauss and Giroux, 2003) at 85–86.

or categories given that the phenomena they are describing take place in particular circumstances. One of them, also vital in the study of memory's intersections with law, as it lays at the basis of one of the legal institutions of memory, legal amnesia, and is a vital element of other law and memory's intersections, is created in opposition to collective memory: collective forgetting.

Even though our collective memories are as fallible as the individual ones,[110] and while it has been noted that "what is not remembered is as critical to forming . . . identity as what is remembered,"[111] collective forgetting has been researched less substantively than its reciprocal, most often analysed from the viewpoint of "how" and "why," with studies hoping to uncover its nature, rather than to provide a definition. (I will attempt to rectify this by proposing my own understanding of this phenomenon at the end of this section.)

Asking "how memory accessibility may be manipulated"[112] and what mechanisms are employed in the process of collective forgetting, Connerton distinguishes seven of them (perhaps following Schachter's *The Seven Sins of Memory*, focused on the individual processes of remembrance and forgetting),[113] grouped into five categories on the basis of their agents: the authorities and official institutions (Types 1 and 2); individuals and families, as well as other groups based on kinship (Types 3 and 4); individuals and various groups of different sizes (Type 5); all those who are a part of the "entire system of economic production" (Type 6); and civil society (Type 7).[114] While I will follow Connerton's classification, as it has been noted, instead of focusing on their agents, the mechanisms of collective forgetting may also be divided on the basis of their purpose: oriented on the shaping of the past to fit the current narrative and goals (Types 1–3); oriented on the future and the shaping of a new identity (Type 7); oriented on the present and the unification of various narratives available at the same time (Type 4); and focused on dealing with "information overload" (Types 5–6).[115]

The first category, as proposed by Connerton, includes *repressive erasure* (Type 1) and *prescriptive forgetting* (Type 2) and, as such, will be most

110 Laura Spinney, "Our Collective Memory, Like Individual Memory, Is Shockingly Fallible" (2016), online: Research Digest: The British Psychological Society <digest.bps.org.uk/2016/01/22/our-collective-memory-like-individual-memory-is-shockingly-fallible/>.

111 Charles B. Stone and William Hirst, "(Induced) Forgetting to Form a Collective Memory" (2014) 7:3 Memory Studies 314 at 315.

112 Jefferson A. Singer and Martin A. Conway, "Should We Forget Forgetting?" (2008) 1:3 Memory Studies 279 at 280.

113 Matthew H. Erdelyi, "Forgetting and Remembering in Psychology: Commentary on Paul Connerton's 'Seven Types of Forgetting' (2008)" (2008) 1:3 Memory Studies 273 at 273.

114 Paul Connerton, "Seven Types of Forgetting" (2008) 1:1 Memory Studies 59 at 69–70.

115 Inke Wessel and Michelle L. Moulds, "How Many Types of Forgetting? Comments on Connerton (2008)" (2008) 1:3 Memory Studies 287 at 291.

important in my further research. Repressive erasure includes these cases of collective forgetting when the authorities are set on removing certain memories from the public sphere and is used as a method "to deny the fact of a historical rupture as well as to bring about a historical break" by both totalitarian regimes (directly) and all governments set on promoting certain narratives or ideologies (indirectly).[116] Within democratic societies, for example, memory legislation may be used as a legal mechanism of repressive erasure. In turn, prescriptive forgetting is used by authorities to reconcile a society that has been subject to cultural trauma: for example, following a transition to democracy, when for it to be able to function, members of the former regime need to be reintegrated.[117] Legal mechanisms of prescriptive forgetting would thus be the various institutions of legal amnesia that, as noted later in the book, not only are implemented directly but also often hide in the background of various other institutions.

The second category includes *forgetting as a constitutive part of a new identity* (Type 3) and *structural amnesia* (Type 4). The former type of collective forgetting includes sliding into oblivion of these memories, which are not in line with the current shape of identity, so as not to "provoke too much cognitive dissonance."[118] Connerton provides examples based on family relations; however, I would argue that this type of collective forgetting may also apply to societies as a whole: for example, Protestant states choosing to forget about their Catholic past often destroyed cultural-religious objects directly referring to the "dissonant" past back in the days of transition (in England or the Netherlands, for example). Structural amnesia, in turn, refers to those cases of collective forgetting involving remembering only what is "socially important" in one's pedigree.[119] Connerton once again includes only familial examples; however, in the present day, societies choose to link their identity to distant origins or overlook major historical events that do not fit the national collective memories, for example, in contemporary Turkey (stressing links with the Hittites), Greece (aiming to establish continuity with ancient times), Mongolia (building upon the legacy of Genghis Khan),[120] and France (choosing to leave out any past related to immigration from the national collective memory).[121] In some cases, as in Hungary and Latvia, even

116 Connerton, *supra* note 114 at 60–61.
117 Connerton, *supra* note 114 at 61–62.
118 Connerton, *supra* note 114 at 63–64.
119 Connerton, *supra* note 114 at 64.
120 Michael Wood, "The Use of the Pharaonic Past in Modern Egyptian Nationalism" (1998) 35 Journal of the American Research Center in Egypt 179 at 179.
121 Gerald Noiriel, "Immigration: Amnesia and Memory" (1995) 19:2 French Historical Studies 367 at 368–370.

preambles to the countries' constitutions[122] are used as a tool of forgetting as a constitutive part of a new identity. Importantly, as noted later in the book, truth commissions can be used directly to introduce this type of collective forgetting.

Forgetting as annulment (Type 5) refers to those instances when there is too much information, too many memories to remember at hand, and thus some of them become relegated to the archive (whether in a traditional sense of the word or digital), and once stored, the society may be able to "afford to forget them."[123] From the perspective of legal institutions of memory, lustration may be regarded as leading to this type of collective forgetting, being based on the principle that the opulent and divisive collective memory inherited from the previous regime needs to be stored in an archive, where its details will sooner or later be forgotten in general, made public only in particular situations, when law itself will allow to do so.

The sixth type of collective forgetting, *forgetting as planned obsolesce*, is, Connerton argues, "built into the capitalist system of consumption" and refers to the fleeting nature of the created products, which, as the services industry continues to grow, renders the present obsolete at an increasing speed; thus, forgetting becomes an intrinsic part of the market.[124] Using music as an example, he makes one think of social media, Snapchat and TikTok in particular, as an even better illustration of forgetting as planned obsolesce: while we collectively participate in the creation of various memories by watching the many short videos, they may quickly disappear, and we will soon forget them as new ones take their place on the global e-stage.

Ultimately, the final type of forgetting distinguished by Connerton, *forgetting as humiliated silence* (Type 7), describes a "covert, unmarked and unacknowledged," as well as "widespread" patterns "of behaviour in civil society," including state apparatus, set on making the group in question forget about certain shameful acts committed in the past.[125] Such was the case of the collective memories of the involvement of ordinary German citizens in Nazi crimes in the 1950s and 1960s,[126] as well as of the Austrian role in them until the mid-1980s (with the country portraying itself as a victim),[127] which

122 Filip Cyuńczyk, "Prawo, historia a pamięć zbiorowa: Odwołania do przeszłości w preambułach do konstytucji Łotwy i Węgier na tle innych państw postkomunistycznych" ["Law, History and Collective Memory: References to the Past in the Preambles to the Constitution of Latvia and Hungary in Comparison with Other Post-Communist Countries"] (2016) XV:1 Miscellanea Historico – Iuridica 221 at 229–232.

123 Connerton, *supra* note 114 at 64–66.

124 Connerton, *supra* note 114 at 66–67.

125 Connerton, *supra* note 114 at 67–69.

126 Alf Lüdtke, "'Coming to Terms with the Past': Illusions of Remembering, Ways of Forgetting Nazism in West Germany" (1993) 65:3 The Journal of Modern History 542 at 554.

127 Jenny Wüstenberg and David Art, "Using the Past in the Nazi Successor States from 1945 to the Present" (2008) 617 Annals AAPSS 72 at 73.

were collectively forgotten. To this day, examples of forgetting as humiliated silence are often noticeable in the school curricula, particularly history textbooks, which, through particular wording and omissions, hide the shameful past from the new generations, as in the case of the Japanese narrative on World War II[128] and the American narrative on the US World War II internment camps for the Japanese.[129] It may also be noted in public speeches, which, in addition to reinforcing memories, commemorating events, and providing information, can also lead to the "impairing" of "some memories over others" through poignant silences on certain details, resulting in "a gradient of forgetting."[130]

Silence is at the centre of another major analysis of the nature of collective forgetting proposed by Vinitzky-Seroussi and Teeger, who argue that *overt silences* (characterised as the "complete absence of any narrative" on a particular topic) and *covert silences* (characterised as "veiled by much mnemonic talk") are key to the understanding of collective memory and forgetting.[131] In the case of the latter, overt silence refers to cases of collective forgetting that are induced by a complete lack of reference to the event in question in the public sphere[132] and could be classified as Connerton's repressive erasure. In turn, covert silence includes those instances of collective forgetting when commemoration of a difficult past takes place (as, for example, its absence would cause criticism) but in such a way as to lessen its impact, for example, by linking the celebrated person or event with other ones of mnemonic importance.[133] This type clearly escapes Connerton's classification and could be regarded as the eighth way of collective forgetting, one where the authorities and institutions are the agents of memory and which is oriented on shaping the present to help reconcile different narratives, *forgetting through distorted connotation.*

As the various analyses of its nature introduced here show, collective forgetting may at times act as an "explicit or tacit ally of oppression and silence," and at others as "a necessary and adaptive reaction to the alternative of painful or destructive memory,"[134] in these cases related to the question

128 See, e.g., Roger B. Jeans, "Victims or Victimizers? Museums, Textbooks, and the War Debate in Contemporary Japan" (2005) 69:1 The Journal of Military History 149; Matiko Oi, "What Japanese History Lessons Leave Out" (2013), online: BBC News <bbc.com/news/magazine-21226068>.

129 See, e.g., Jeffrey M. Hawkins and Michael Buckendorf, "A Current Analysis of the Treatment of Japanese Americans and Internment in United States History Textbooks" (2010) 1:1 Journal of International Social Studies 34.

130 Stone and Hirst, *supra* note 111 at 322.

131 Vered Vinitzky-Seroussi and Chana Teeger, "Unpacking the Unspoken: Silence in Collective Memory and Forgetting" (2010) 88:3 Social Forces 1103 at 1108.

132 *Ibid.* at 1110–1111.

133 *Ibid.* at 1114–1116.

134 Singer and Conway, *supra* note 112 at 279.

of collective forgiveness,[135] being a "*sine qua non* of a peaceful society,"[136] which lays on the basis of the legal institution of symbolic reparations introduced later in the book, most notably of public apology.

Thus, I would propose to understand collective forgetting as a socio-cultural phenomenon of pushing certain collective memories outside of the official narrative of a particular group with the goals of maintaining its unity, sheltering it from facing the difficult past, helping it manage the presence of too many, often contradictory memories and preserving its elite's power. Importantly, the forgotten collective memories do not disappear, living on as counter-memories (a concept that I analyse in the next chapter) and in some instances coming to the surface in the process of collective evoking,[137] thus entering the official narrative, as, for example, in the case of the acknowledgement of the dark colonial past by the former metropoles.

When the Past Weighs in on the Present: Trauma as a Collective Phenomenon of Memory

The second concept related to the study of intersections between memory and law is referred to as collective trauma, cultural trauma, historical trauma, social trauma, or political trauma. The traumatic processes of memory lay at the basis of the identity of numerous groups and may shape perceptions, influence policy, and lead to the creation of new institutions. After all, as Markl poignantly notes, the official "narratives regularly invoke heroism and victory in war, but the notion of cultural trauma indicates that collective suffering from violence can serve narratives that strengthen collective identity as well."[138]

Beginning with a review of the more established concept of cultural trauma, in the later analysis, I propose not to divide the various approaches towards trauma proposed by researchers into separate groups, but rather to examine its similar but different theories as complementary. Keeping the terminology of each concept's author, I venture to look into them from a more general perspective of trauma as a collective phenomenon of memory, or collective trauma-memory, which will be of major importance in my later research, laying at the basis of many a legal institution of memory.

Studying trauma from a collective perspective, one focuses on those events in a group's history that are of tremendous magnitude (including, for example, "genocide, war, terrorism, civil and ethnic strife and radical

135 Whitehead, *supra* note 12 at 154.

136 David Rieff, *In Praise of Forgetting: Historical Memory and Its Ironies* (New Haven, CT: Yale University Press, 2016) at 57.

137 Sadowski, *supra* note 50 at 270.

138 Dominik Markl, "Triumph and Trauma: Justifications of Mass Violence in Deuteronomistic Historiography" (2022) 8 Open Theology 412 at 414.

regime transitions") and that "generate serious and often catastrophic challenges to communal self-understandings," with "the 'memory' of such 'traumas' play[ing] a significant and sometimes elemental role in shaping subsequent political perceptions, affiliations and action."[139] In the analysis of this process, one needs to depart from individual theories of trauma given that the "conceptual framing" of collective trauma is completely different – "conceptualised from the start, when groups turn against other groups, and when enacted, it is enacted as a specimen of a concept" – ultimately developed and fostered as an idea "in social discourse."[140]

Among many others, the major and most widely used in the social discourse is the concept of *cultural* trauma, based on the idea that traumatic experiences "demand a response from culture" and that every culture "develops specific forms and mechanisms of social healing."[141] Notably, while each of the cultural trauma researchers proposes a slightly different understanding of cultural trauma, as I said, their viewpoints are in general complementary, and I venture to present them as such here.

The result of "an invasive and overwhelming event that is believed to undermine or overwhelm one or several essential ingredients of a culture or the culture as a whole,"[142] cultural trauma is defined as "a memory accepted and publicly given credence by a relevant membership group and evoking" the traumatic event on which it is based. For a trauma to be cultural, three conditions need to be fulfilled: it must be not only "laden with negative affect," but also "represented as indelible" and "regarded as threatening a society's existence or violating one or more of its fundamental cultural presuppositions."[143]

Additionally, collective trauma will become a cultural trauma only when a social crisis turns into a cultural crisis.[144] This process may be traced to

139 Duncan Bell, "Introduction: Memory, Trauma and World Politics" in Duncan Bell (ed.), *Memory, Trauma and World Politics: Reflections on the Relationship Between Past and Present* (Houndmills/New York, NY: Palgrave Macmillan, 2006) 1 at 5.

140 Andreas Hamburger, "Introduction to Part I" in Andreas Hamburger (ed.), *Trauma, Trust, and Memory: Social Trauma and Reconciliation in Psychoanalysis, Psychotherapy, and Cultural Memory* (Oxon/New York, NY: Routledge, 2018) 3 at 3.

141 John P. Wilson, "Culture, Trauma, and the Treatment of Post-Traumatic Syndromes: A Global Perspective" in Anthony J. Marsella, Jeannette L. Johnson, Patricia Watson, and Jan Gryczynski (eds), *Ethnocultural Perspectives on Disaster and Trauma Foundations, Issues, and Applications* (New York, NY: Springer Science+Business Media, 2008) 351 at 351, 359.

142 Neil J. Smelser, "Psychological Trauma and Cultural Trauma" in Jeffrey C. Alexander, Ron Eyerman, Bernhard Giesen, Neil J. Smelser, and Piotr Sztompka (eds), *Cultural Trauma and Collective Identity* (Berkeley, CA/London: University of California Press, 2004) 31 at 38.

143 *Ibid.* at 44.

144 Jeffrey C. Alexander, "Toward a Theory of Cultural Trauma" in Jeffrey C. Alexander, Ron Eyerman, Bernhard Giesen, Neil J. Smelser, and Piotr Sztompka (eds), *Cultural Trauma and Collective Identity* (Berkeley, CA/London: University of California Press, 2004) 1 at 10.

one – or several at the same time – of the following four sources: (1) a contact or a confrontation with a different culture, potentially leading to conflict;[145] (2) increased mobility, when people, either as refugees and emigrants or as travellers, are exposed to a different culture;[146] (3) a major "change of fundamental institutions or regimes," be that political or economic;[147] and (4) "the change of ideas," an exposure to radically different viewpoints.[148] With this backdrop in place, along with the "triggering, precipitating factors" – a "set of conditions or situations, perceived as pernicious, dangerous, or threatening" – trauma emerges.[149]

Looking into the process of cultural trauma's creation more closely, one may distinguish four such conditions that need to be fulfilled. The first is the appearance of "carrier groups," "the collective agents of the trauma process," who I would call agents of traumatic memory, tasked with formulating " 'claims' about the shape of social reality, its causes, and the responsibilities for action such causes imply."[150]

The second requirement includes the forming of a "spiral of signification," i.e., "a compelling framework of cultural classification,"[151] which in turn rests on four elements: (1) the nature of the pain, what happened to the traumatised group, and what effect it has on a larger collectivity;[152] (2) the nature of the victim, whether a particular group was traumatised, or generally "the people";[153] (3) the relation of the trauma victim to the larger audience, the number of people who feel the relation between themselves and the traumatised group;[154] and (4) the attribution of responsibility, properly identifying the perpetrator, or the "antagonist."[155]

The third condition is the creation of institutional arenas whereby the "new master narrative of social suffering" plays out, which may be religious, linking trauma to theodicy;[156] aesthetic, aiming to "produce imaginative identification and emotional catharsis";[157] scientific, turning trauma into a sub-

145 Piotr Sztompka, "The Trauma of Social Change: A Case of Postcommunist Societies" in Jeffrey C. Alexander, Ron Eyerman, Bernhard Giesen, Neil J. Smelser, and Piotr Sztompka (eds), *Cultural Trauma and Collective Identity* (Berkeley, CA/London: University of California Press, 2004) 155 at 162.
146 *Ibid.* at 162–163.
147 *Ibid.* at 163.
148 *Ibid.* at 163–164.
149 *Ibid.* at 164.
150 Alexander, *supra* note 144 at 11.
151 Alexander, *supra* note 144 at 12.
152 Alexander, *supra* note 144 at 13.
153 Alexander, *supra* note 144 at 13–14.
154 Alexander, *supra* note 144 at 14–15.
155 Alexander, *supra* note 144 at 15.
156 Alexander, *supra* note 144 at 15.
157 Alexander, *supra* note 144 at 15–16.

ject of research;[158] mass media, which allow "traumas to be expressively dramatised and permit some of the competing interpretations to gain enormous persuasive power over others";[159] state bureaucracy, the decisions of branches of government venturing to "channel the representational process";[160] and legal, focused on issuing "a definitive judgement of a legally binding responsibilities and to distribute punishments and material repartitions,"[161] as in the case of the intersections between collective memory and human rights and international law analysed in Chapter 3.

Ultimately, the fourth requirement for the creation of cultural trauma is the appearance of stratificational hierarchies, which mediate the "constraints imposed by institutional arenas" through the "uneven distribution of material resources and the social networks that provide differential access" to them.[162]

Once all conditions are fulfilled, cultural trauma is set in motion – and, as Stamm et al. show, while in each case influenced by a number of different variables,[163] it is cyclical by nature. Beginning its path from the initial cultural stability to disruption by either a cultural challenge or contact with a particularly different culture, cultural trauma may lead to either cultural loss, traumatic stress (and ultimately to cultural extinction – in this case, the cycle is broken), or reorganisation and revitalisation (collective healing), and ultimately back to cultural stability.[164] To resolve cultural trauma and "return to normal," Eyerman notes, collective memory and collective identity need to come into play, with the new narratives, however, forever marred by the traumatic experience, as they are "modified with the passage of time, filtered through cultural artifacts and other materialisations, which represent the past in the present."[165]

Focusing also on memory, but using the concept of cultural trauma only as a backdrop, Hałas proposes approaching collective trauma in a slightly different way, as a *cultural memory of trauma*, trying to rectify some of the deficiencies of cultural trauma theory. She stresses the future orientation and the role of collective memories of trauma that at the same time "divide and

158 Alexander, *supra* note 144 at 18.
159 Alexander, *supra* note 144 at 18–19.
160 Alexander, *supra* note 144 at 19–21.
161 Alexander, *supra* note 144 at 16–17.
162 Alexander, *supra* note 144 at 22.
163 B. Hudnall Stamm, Henry E. Stamm IV, Amy C. Hudnall, and Craig Higson-Smith, "Considering a Theory of Cultural Trauma and Loss" (2004) 9 Journal of Loss and Trauma 89 at 103.
164 *Ibid.* at 102.
165 Ron Eyerman, *Cultural Trauma: Slavery and the Formation of African American Identity* (Cambridge: Cambridge University Press, 2003) at 14.

connect" as memories "both shared and divided"[166] – shared by the society on which trauma had been inflicted, but divided both between victims and perpetrators and on the local and global scales.[167] While I agree with her that in understanding the phenomenon of collective trauma, the collective memories of those affected by trauma, as well as those who come after them, need to be stressed, I propose departing further from the cultural perspective on trauma, which, while providing an explanation as to how collective trauma is established, loses not only the memorial viewpoint but also people from the horizon, focusing on the questions of culture instead.

To fully conceptualise collective trauma and understand the healing processes that need to take place to reconcile the divergent, difficult collective memories in its aftermath (which are related to the concept of transitional justice and the various legal institutions of memory linked to it), as mentioned at the beginning of this chapter, I propose looking at the traumatic collective processes as collective trauma-memories, a viewpoint synthesised from several different perspectives on collective trauma.

Duran et al. speak about *historical* trauma, proposing to understand it as a phenomenon that spans long periods of time, encompassing numerous generations as a result. Based on "multigenerational, collective, historical, and cumulative psychic wounding," historical trauma is "an ongoing process via pressures brought by acculturative stress" and as such may lead to numerous psychological issues passed on from parents (agents of memory) to children, ultimately including "the aftereffects of racism, oppression, and genocide."[168] These "haunted traces of past" do not cease to influence the present and "rise up, trouble and call out in loud and visceral ways"[169] instead – as Hamburger, speaking about *social* trauma, also stresses, unresolved trauma may be "transmitted not only to survivors' families, but also to the society as a whole."[170]

Importantly, various studies of, *inter alia*, the children of Holocaust survivors seem to confirm this concept, showing that through "the conjunction of

166 Elżbieta Hałas, "Time and Memory: A Cultural Perspective" (2010) 14:4 Trames 307 at 316–317.

167 *Ibid.* at 319.

168 Eduardo Duran, Bonnie Duran, Maria Yellow Horse Brave Heart, and Susan Yellow Horse-Davis, "Healing the American Indian Soul Wound" in Yael Danieli (ed.), *International Handbook of Multigenerational Legacies of Trauma* (New York, NY: Springer Science+Business Media, 1998) 341 at 342–343.

169 Kim Wale, Pumla Gobodo-Madikizela, and Jeffrey Prager, "Introduction: Post-Conflict Hauntings" in Kim Wale, Pumla Gobodo-Madikizela, and Jeffrey Prager (eds), *Post-Conflict Hauntings: Transforming Memories of Historical Trauma* (Cham: Palgrave Macmillan, 2020) 1 at 14.

170 Andreas Hamburger, "New Thoughts on Genocidal Trauma" in Andreas Hamburger (ed.), *Trauma, Trust, and Memory: Social Trauma and Reconciliation in Psychoanalysis, Psychotherapy, and Cultural Memory* (Oxon/New York, NY: Routledge, 2018) 13 at 14–15.

discourse and the narrative practice of emplotment,"[171] collective trauma-memory may result in transgenerational transmission of traumatic experiences,[172] leading to the progeny of trauma survivors undertaking "the requisite memory work" and thus reconstituting themselves "as wounded descendants of trauma,"[173] in some cases even culminating in secondary post-traumatic stress disorder.[174]

I concur with Volkan et al., who argue that the passing on of collective trauma-memories is only one of the possible outcomes of a traumatic event for a society. Others may include an obligation not only to mourn but also to look for solutions to "reverse helplessness" (through, for example, transitional justice processes), as well as "biosocial regeneration," i.e., increased birth – rate in the aftermath of a trauma, or "biosocial degradation," i.e., hesitancy to establish families among trauma survivors, depending on the circumstances.[175] Irrespective of the coping strategy employed by a society with regard to collective trauma-memories, the new generations are permanently "haunted" by them, perpetually enclosed in a trauma "time warp," forced to "live in the past" and adopt different roles (for example, of the victimiser or of the victim), recreating "mental representations of the past history in seemingly endless and various 'replays' in interpersonal relations."[176] Examples of several societies enclosed in such trauma "time warps" due to unresolved past issues are analysed in Part III of this book.

Explaining how past traumas may cease to shape the contemporary politics of a society,[177] Prager links the *social* concept of trauma with law, noting its vital role in the process of reworking through trauma via trials or truth (and reconciliation) commissions[178] and stressing the need for collective healing in post-traumatic societies, which in some cases involves the creation of new institutions,[179] several of which I analyse both theoretically and in practice as legal institutions of memory further in the book. Such "social

171 Carol A. Kidron, "Surviving a Distant Past: A Case Study of the Cultural Construction of Trauma Descendant Identity" (2004) 31:4 Ethos 513 at 533.

172 Natan P. F. Kellermann (executive director), "Transmission of Holocaust Trauma – an Integrative View" (2001) 64:3 Psychiatry 256 at 265.

173 Kidron, *supra* note 171 at 533.

174 Kellermann, *supra* note 172 at 258.

175 Vamik D. Volkan, Gabriele Ast, and William F. Greer Jr., *The Third Reich in the Unconscious: Transgenerational Transmission and Its Consequences* (New York, NY: Brunner-Routledge, 2002) at 2–3.

176 *Ibid.* at 4.

177 Jeffrey Prager, "Danger and Deformation: A Social Theory of Trauma Part I: Contemporary Psychoanalysis, Contemporary Social Theory, and Healthy Selves" (2011) 68:3 American Imago 425 at 436.

178 *Ibid.* at 432.

179 *Ibid.* at 433.

redress,"[180] he argues, is necessary to prevent trauma from remaining permanently anchored in the present and allow society a reorientation "toward the future."[181]

While it is not an easy process – given the aforementioned transgenerational transmission which creates "communities of distrust, alienation, and hatred," enduring "even when legal and institutional measures are implemented to dismantle" them[182] – it may succeed, as in the case of present-day Israel, which, Prager argues, is now "less haunted by the ghosts from the past" thanks to its policy of acknowledging and talking about the traumatic past, with "rituals, rites and sites" (carriers – places of memory analysed further in this chapter) allowing the society to establish a clear line of separation between the past and the present, thus becoming "less encumbered by earlier traumas," while continuing to remember.[183] In spite of being seemingly successful, as case studies in Part III of this book will show, such an approach is not widely implemented when approaching collective trauma-memories, as various legal institutions of memory are rather established.

Despite the fact that every society deals with them differently, either making peace with the past, locked permanently in a time warp, or somewhere in between, similar processes may be distinguished following every collectively traumatic event. As Iguarta and Paez note, there are three phases in the life of *collective* trauma: denial; appearance of "a conventional view of the situation"; and ultimately, the "positive reconstruction of the past," leading to reconciliation and social reconstruction.[184]

Importantly, as the case of Israel shows, collective trauma-memories have implications along the lines not only of past–present but also of present–future, leading to the emergence of political communities and thus organising "a social habitat."[185] Speaking in a similar context about *political* trauma, Fierke remarks it is based on the "assimilation of a past context of trauma" in such a way that it shapes "identity within a linguistic world of action and interaction vis-à-vis others" and on the repetition of past experiences in the present due to either a prevalence of one narrative of the traumatic events, or their complete denial, resulting in whole societies being "bound to one

180 Jeffrey Prager, "Danger and Deformation: A Social Theory of Trauma Part II: Disrupting the Intergenerational Transmission of Trauma, Recovering Humanity, and Repairing Generations" (2015) 72:2 American Imago 133 at 136.

181 Prager, *supra* note 177 at 433–432.

182 Prager, *supra* note 180 at 146–147.

183 Prager, *supra* note 180 at 152.

184 Juanjo Igartua and Dario Paez, "Art and Remembering Traumatic Collective Events: The Case of the Spanish Civil War" in James W. Pennebaker, Dario Paez, and Bernard Rimé (eds), *Collective Memory of Political Events: Social Psychological Perspectives* (Mahwah, NJ: Lawrence Erlbaum Associates, 1997) 79 at 83.

185 Adrian Parr, *Deleuze and Memorial Culture: Desire, Singular Memory and the Politics of Trauma* (Edinburgh: Edinburgh University Press, 2008) at 5–6.

way of looking at the present," making its members "unaware of the role of his or her actions in reproducing that past."[186] Furthermore, she regards collective memories as providing "a script for re-enacting of a cultural package inherited from the past," with both collective memory and political trauma "binding together" the group's identity, ultimately proposing to understand trauma as a socio-political concept.[187]

The question of the relationship between collective memory and collective trauma is a particular one – Fierke sees both as vital for the survival of a group's identity, while Sarat et al. propose a fourfold perspective on their intersections. They argue that traumatic events have a particular "mnemonic structure," one with its own time and as such prone to repression; that traumatic events result in "an injunction to remember" imposed on the different commemoration practices – carriers of memory; that as such, remembrance of traumatic events works in a particular way, not only through the usual "repetition and recollection," but also other means (for example "material compensation"), and has the potential to lead to collective healing; and that, ultimately, traumatic events have a unique function preserving the "collective identity over time," in some cases "healing trauma" through either recognition of what happened or collective forgetting.[188]

I, however, would propose a different perspective on the relationship, one returning to the idea that I had expressed earlier: of trauma as a collective phenomenon of memory. Perceiving collective trauma as a type of collective memory, a collective trauma-memory, I define it as a collective memory that is traumatic in its nature, and because of that, particularly powerful, having a major impact on the society, ultimately influencing various short- and long-term processes, such as the legal institutions of memory of reparations, lustration, and truth (and reconciliation) commissions, ultimately leading to a reconstruction of society through incorporation of collective trauma-memories into collective identity on par with, and in some cases of bigger importance than, other collective memories. In certain instances, as the case of Poland will show, collective identity may include layers upon layers of collective trauma-memories, while Brazil and Portugal will have only a couple, nevertheless of major significance. Always, however, collective trauma-memories – similar to the "regular" collective memories – may take their

186 K. M. Fierke, "Bewitched by the Past: Social Memory, Trauma and International Relations" in Duncan Bell (ed.), *Memory, Trauma and World Politics: Reflections on the Relationship Between Past and Present* (Houndmills/New York, NY: Palgrave Macmillan, 2006) 116 at 132–133.

187 *Ibid.* at 133.

188 Austin Sarat, Nadav Davidovitch, and Michal Alberstein, "Trauma and Memory Between Individual and Collective Experiences" in Austin Sarat, Nadav Davidovitch, and Michal Alberstein (eds), *Trauma and Memory: Reading, Healing, and Making Law* (Stanford, CA: Stanford University Press, 2007) 4 at 9–10.

rightful place on the pedestal of collective identity only through the work of various agents and carriers, which are the focus of the next section.

Bringing the Past into the Present: Agents and Carriers of Memory

Having studied what collective memory might be and the ways in which it is created, the final question I would like to ruminate on in this chapter is how it may be passed upon and influenced. While in the literature, the two terms are often used interchangeably,[189] here I would like to propose a clear distinction, which will prove useful in the later research of the legal institutions of memory – between agents (actors, entrepreneurs) of memory, i.e., active creators, bearers, and influencers of collective memory; and carriers of memory (the aforementioned collective memory or cultural objects), i.e., passive vessels created by agents of memory that have the collective memories attached to them.

Agents of Memory

Agents of memory – family members, politicians, religious leaders, journalists, teachers, researchers, artists[190] – instrumentally influence and manipulate collective memories, creating a "useable past"[191] through the establishment and maintenance of both local and global "meta-narratives" of collective memories. Taking on various positions within a society, they engage in "battles" with those agents propagating a different narrative than that of their group, ultimately trying to construct a bridge between the past and the future of the collectivity.[192] Agents of memory often take the narrative beyond its

189 I have used them interchangeably myself in "Fluttering the Past in the Present: The Role of Flags in the Contemporary Society: Law, Politics, Identity and Memory" in Anne Wagner and Sarah Marusek (eds), *Flags, Color, and the Legal Narrative: Public Memory, Identity, and Critique* (Cham: Springer, 2021) 85; see also: Carol A. Kidron, "In Pursuit of Jewish Paradigms of Memory: Constituting Carriers of Jewish Memory in a Support Group for Children of Holocaust Survivors" (2009) 23:1 Dapim: Studies on the Holocaust 7 at 10; Motti Neiger, Oren Meyers, and Eyal Zandberg, "On Media Memory: Editors' Introduction" in Motti Neiger, Oren Meyers, and Eyal Zandberg (eds), *On Media Memory Collective Memory in a New Media Age* (Houndmills/New York, NY: Palgrave Macmillan, 2011) 1 at 7.

190 Michael Bernhard and Jan Kubik, "A Theory of the Politics of Memory" in Michael Bernhard and Jan Kubik (eds), *Twenty Years After Communism: The Politics of Memory and Commemoration* (New York, NY: Oxford University Press, 2014) 8 at 10.

191 Rafi Nets-Zehngut, "Origins of the Palestinian Refugee Problem: Changes in the Historical Memory of Israelis/Jews 1949–2004" (2011) 48:2 Journal of Peace Research 235 at 236.

192 Dovilė Budrytė, "Experiences of Collective Trauma and Political Activism: A Study of Women 'Agents of Memory' in Post-Soviet Lithuania" (2010) 41:3 Journal of Baltic Studies 331 at 331.

original social frames, aligning themselves with political groups, either those in power or those countering it, creating "functioning social networks" if successful, but at a cost of "emotional" or "irrational" politics.[193] In the case study of Poland in Part III of the book, several examples of such emotional politics influenced by agents of memory are analysed.

Agents of memory may be divided, following Benhard and Kubik, as well as Gutman, into five categories: (1) mnemonic warriors (those with one, clear version of the past which they use as a socio-political basis to further their socio-political goals);[194] (2) mnemonic pluralists (those who accept the existence of other viewpoints on the past, hoping to engage in dialogue and find common points with other groups);[195] (3) mnemonic abnegators (those who have no interest in engaging with the past, either because it has already been broadly agreed on or because of their present-day focus);[196] (4) mnemonic prospectives (those who are revolutionaries, believing to have uncovered the truth about the past and present's wrongs, which they will use to establish a "post-historical" society);[197] and (5) mnemonic activists (those hoping to make the silenced past – counter-history, as it is analysed in the following chapter – known, despite it's bringing controversy and rejection).[198]

This division will later provide a particularly useful perspective when analysing the various legal institutions of memory, both conceptualising them in the second chapter and in practice in the third, as different institutions are employed by different types of agents (for example, in the case of Japan, where successive governments, acting as agents of memory–memory warriors, continued a particular policy with regard to reparations in hopes of sustaining a unified narrative about the past).

Looking into agents of memory at work, the case of passing on collective trauma-memories to future generations analysed in the previous section is a good, albeit extreme example of the ways in which they work: those who suffered the trauma act as the original agents of collective memory, while their children take on the role of new agents of the same memories, passing them on to their descendants and creating new carriers of memory.[199] Moreover, agents of traumatic memory often align themselves with political groups,

193 *Ibid.* at 334–335.
194 Bernhard and Kubik, *supra* note 190 at 13–14.
195 Bernhard and Kubik, *supra* note 190 at 14.
196 Bernhard and Kubik, *supra* note 190 at 15.
197 Bernhard and Kubik, *supra* note 190 at 15.
198 Yifat Gutman, *Memory Activism: Reimagining the Past for the Future in Israel-Palestine* (Nashville, TN: Vanderbilt University Press, 2017) at 19.
199 Rebecca Kook, "Agents of Memory in the Post-Witness Era: Memory in the Living Room and Changing Forms of Holocaust Remembrance in Israel" (2020) October Memory Studies 971 at 971–972.

and as a result, the narrative of trauma may ultimately lay at the basis of the national meta-narrative.[200]

Nota bene, in a contemporary society, whether one is dealing with collective trauma-memories or "regular" ones, the role of media as particular agents of memory needs to be stressed. Thanks to their ability to create "instant" collective memories,[201] the media often become unintentional agents of memory, using the past to gain credibility, to explain an event or to frame the present within its boundaries,[202] also reaching out to influence the future.[203] The media may also play a conscious, political role as memory agents, advancing the goals of a particular group[204] and delineating who belongs and who does not belong within its limits.[205] Importantly, in the present day, social media give individuals the power to become instantaneous agents of memory and influence collective memories of large numbers of people with one viral post.[206] Additionally, the media in general strongly influence various carriers of memory,[207] but in turn, through their creations – broadcasts reaching different people at the same time[208] – become carriers of memory themselves.

Carriers of Memory

Carriers of memory are objects and rituals that "narrate a past event as part of a shared group identity,"[209] thus allowing agents to mobilise a particular

200 See for example how Palestinian children reframe their own experiences within collective memories of the past providing a new narrative: Janette Habashi, "Palestinian Children: Authors of Collective Memory" (2013) 27 Children and Society 421 at 431.

201 Yoram Peri, "The Media and Collective Memory of Yitzhak Rabin's Remembrance" (1999) 49:3 Journal of Communication 106 at 107.

202 Michael Schudson, "Journalism as a Vehicle of Non-Commemorative Cultural Memory" in Barbie Zelizer and Keren Tenenboim-Weinblatt (eds), *Journalism and Memory* (Houndmills/New York, NY: Palgrave Macmillan, 2014) 85 at 95.

203 Keren Tenenboim-Weinblatt, "Bridging Collective Memories and Public Agendas: Toward a Theory of Mediated Prospective Memory" (2013) 23 Communication Theory 91 at 96.

204 Neiger, Meyers, and Zandberg, *supra* note 189 at 4–5.

205 Motti Neiger, "Theorizing Media Memory: Six Elements Defining the Role of the Media in Shaping Collective Memory in the Digital Age" (2020) 14:5 Sociology Compass 1 at 4.

206 *Ibid.* at 4.

207 Michael Meyen, "Mass Media as Memory Agents: A Theoretical and Empirical Contribution to Collective Memory Research" in Nicole Maurantonio and David W. Park (eds), *Communicating Memory and History* (New York/Bern/Berlin/Brussels/Oxford/Vienna: Peter Lang, 2019) 77 at 80.

208 Peri, *supra* note 201 at 122.

209 Hiro Saito, "From Collective Memory to Commemoration" in John R. Hall, Laura Grindstaff, and Ming-Cheng Miriam Lo (eds), *Handbook of Cultural Sociology* (London/New York, NY: Routledge, 2010) 629 at 630.

group.[210] Ranging from monuments, textbooks, and museums, to public speeches and movies,[211] to lawsuits and trials, their success relies on the ability to link private and public collective memories.[212] In certain instances, law itself may be regarded as a carrier of memory, a way of "encoding into binding norms of the lessons of past experience,"[213] for example, in numerous provisions of human rights law, which were introduced as a way of preventing various atrocities that took place in the past (the perspective which I analyse further in Chapter 3).

Carriers of memory may be divided in two ways: either to intentional (created by agents of memory, e.g., a monument) and unintentional ("residues" of the past which continue to influence the present, e.g., the legacy of Watergate and its impact on the American political and legal sphere);[214] or to conventional (which fit the usual expectations of what a carrier might be, e.g., a typical monument) and anomalous (which somehow break the convention for carriers of memory, e.g., a monument the form of which has been somehow reformulated). These in turn may be either permanent (created to withstand the test of time, e.g., a museum) or temporary (which, at least initially, are supposed to mobilise a group only in a particular moment, e.g., a travelling exhibition).[215]

Importantly, there exists an interplay, "an irreducible tension"[216] between agents and carriers of memory. While the latter are created by the former, given that ultimately it is always individual people who remember, they may choose to approach particular collective memories in a different way from the official way.[217] Additionally, demographic and economic changes may lead to the replacement of one type of agent of memory with another, thus resulting in a reconceptualisation and recontextualisation of certain carriers of memory.[218]

A particular case among the many different carriers of memory (and of particular interest from the legal perspective) are places of memory, both material – monuments, street names, plaques, flags, archives, museums, or

210 Noiriel, *supra* note 121 at 380.

211 Michael Schudson, "Lives, Laws, and Language: Commemorative Versus Non-Commemorative Forms of Effective Public Memory" (1997) 2:1 The Communication Review 3 at 3.

212 Wagner-Pacifici, *supra* note 1 at 312.

213 Schudson, *supra* note 211 at 8.

214 Schudson, *supra* note 211 at 5–6.

215 Wagner-Pacifici, *supra* note 1 at 309–311.

216 James V. Wertsch, "The Narrative Organization of Collective Memory" (2008) 36:1 Ethos 120 at 122.

217 Jay Winter, "Historians and Sites of Memory" in Pascal Boyer and James V. Wertsch (eds), *Memory in Mind and Culture* (Cambridge/New York, NY: Cambridge University Press, 2009) 252 at 258.

218 Saito, *supra* note 209 at 635.

even cities as a whole[219] – and immaterial – events, public commemorations, generations, or songs.[220] They may be political, with some belonging to the main narrative and others to the counter-narrative,[221] always framing our collective memory; they may exist in reality, but they may also only have a place in our memories, having been destroyed, altered, or passed away,[222] which was noted already by Halbwachs, who remarked on the role "spatial images" play in the formation and sustaining of collective memories.[223]

It was Pierre Nora, however, who, based on his research on Halbwachs's distinction between history and memory,[224] proposed a major theory of places of memory as *lieux de mémoire*, explaining why they have such significance. Places of memory in a material (e.g., an archive), symbolic (e.g., a minute of silence), and functional (e.g., a veterans' meeting) sense,[225] *lieux de mémoire* carry more than a simple historical meaning.[226] Having "survived" in the post-memorial present, they "mark the rituals of a society without ritual," produced by the interplay between memory and history,[227] where there is an intention to remember.[228] Importantly, they are "forever open to the full range of . . . possible significations,"[229] with the ability to transform and adapt along with the changing collective memories of a society.

Conclusion: Return to Halbwachs or Law and Collective Memory

Together, as Golka notes, the various forms and types of collective memory one may distinguish form a "continuum," within the infinite frames of which exists "the opulent world of social memories."[230] It is true that while the

219 For the analysis of particular carriers of memory, see my study of the intersections between urban places of memory and the law "City as a Locus of Collective Memory: Streets, Monuments and Human Rights" (2020) 40:1–2 Zeitschrift für Rechtssoziologie – The German Journal of Law and Society 209; and my study of the relationship between flags as carriers of memory and the law, *supra* note 189.

220 Bill Schwarz, "Memory, Temporality, Modernity: Les lieux de mémoire" in Susannah Radstone and Bill Schwarz (eds), *Memory: Histories, Theories, Debates* (New York: Fordham University Press, 2010) 41 at 50.

221 Menachem Klein, "Jerusalem's Alternative Collective Memory Agents" (2020) 35:1 Israel Studies Review 1 at 12.

222 Sadowski, *supra* note 50 at 213.

223 Halbwachs, *supra* note 8 at 130.

224 Whitehead, *supra* note 12 at 141.

225 Pierre Nora, "Between Memory and History: Les Lieux de Mémoire" (1989) 26 Representations 7 at 18–19.

226 *Ibid.* at 9.

227 *Ibid.* at 12.

228 *Ibid.* at 19.

229 *Ibid.* at 23.

230 Golka, *supra* note 2 at 34.

different theories, concepts, and approaches provide us with a better understanding of the collective memory phenomenon, at the same time, it becomes quite clear that memory studies researchers are in a way still enclosed within the frames provided by Halbwachs almost a century ago, in particular his division between memory and history, adapting his and later work to the particular circumstances they are investigating. Halbwachs's insights also remain crucial for my study today.

While this chapter dealt with sociology, it has provided not only the conceptual basis but also a number of insights into my further research on law and memory, showing, among other things, how the two are entangled on a number of levels and how law, itself a product, is shaped by agents of memory and may often be regarded as a carrier of memory in its own right, with memory and law changing positions as a subject and an object in their relationship at different times. However, sociology on its own is not enough to provide a clear theoretical definition of what collective memory is with regards to law. In order to fully approach this question, I propose to reach into two other disciplines, first philosophy, followed by theory of law itself.

Chapter 2

Philosophy, Memory, and Law

The French Four

Introduction

Sociology, the focus of Chapter 1, has conceptualised the idea of collective memory; philosophy, however, has taken an interest in the study of memory from its very beginning and continues it to this day.[1] While the actual term "collective memory" rarely appears in philosophical works, the concept may be found lingering in the shadows of many a treaty and convention. Thus, as the intersections between law, memory, and philosophy remain largely unexplored, a philosophical analysis will prove helpful in understanding the various institutions of collective memory.

In the context of law and memory, Ubuntu philosophy – a traditional African concept centred around the notion of humanness, which underlines the need for reconciliation[2] – and, as remarked upon in the Introduction, the late writings of Paul Ricoeur – who linked up "the question of memory with that of justice and the problem of constructing new polities"[3] – are often considered. For consistency purposes, realising the limitations that will necessarily follow, I propose to narrow my investigations to only four Western thinkers, those providing particular insight into my investigations of the meaning of collective memory with regard to law: (1) Émile Durkheim, who shows the hidden power of contemporary rituals; (2) Henri Bergson, who

1 See, e.g., Sven Bernecker and Kourken Michaelian (eds), *The Routledge Handbook of Philosophy of Memory* (Oxon/New York: Routledge, 2017); Kourken Michaelian, Dorothea Debus, and Denis Perrin (eds), *New Directions in the Philosophy of Memory* (New York/Oxon: Routledge, 2018).

2 See, e.g., Michael Battle, *Reconciliation: The Ubuntu Theology of Desmond Tutu* (Cleveland, OH: Pilgrim Press, 2009); Dani W. Nabudere, "Ubuntu Philosophy: Memory and Reconciliation" (2005), online: Texas ScholarWorks <repositories.lib.utexas.edu/handle/2152/4521>.

3 Steve H. Clark, "Introduction: Paul Ricoeur: Memory, Identity, Ethics" (2010) 27:5 Theory, Culture & Society 3 at 4. See also: Justyna Jezierska, "Między obowiązkiem pamięci a jej zdradą. Analiza rozważań Avishaia Margalita i Paula Ricoeura" ["Between the Duty of Memory and Its Betrayal: Analysis of the Thought of Avishai Margalit and Paul Ricoeur"] (2020) 24:1 Prace Kulturoznawcze 33.

DOI: 10.4324/9781003461548-4

helps us perceive the power of law laying in memory; (3) Emmanuel Levinas, for whom memory lays at the basis of ethics; and (4) Michel Foucault, who provides a particular insight into memory's power relations.

Remaining in the realm of 20th-century French philosophy was a narrowing but much-needed choice for a thorough analysis of the relationship between law, philosophy, and memory, one made consciously with the knowledge of how influential the various thinkers were for one another – for example, Henri Bergson, had an impact on both Emmanuel Levinas[4] and Maurice Halbwachs, the father of collective memory analysed in Chapter 1, who, in turn, was also influenced by Durkheim.[5] Thus, I propose to examine their work chronologically, beginning with the latter.

Institutions, Rituals, and Memory: Émile Durkheim

Émile Durkheim is regarded first and foremost as a sociologist whose work helped elevate the discipline to its contemporary stance in academia.[6] However, his study of the intertwining of religion, law, rituals, and memories often crosses the border with philosophy; hence, I propose reading it along with the three other philosophers key to my research into the intersections of law and collective memory.

Before I move to its analysis, it has to be noted that Durkheim's theory has been criticised as being too generalising, attributing "one collective memory or set of memories to entire, well-bounded societies."[7] While this is certainly true, collective memory research can only be generalised, and collective memory practices by their nature attempt to unify social perceptions of the past. Durkheim's concept can thus be particularly helpful in my study.

Importantly, Durkheim never used the term collective memory *per se*; however, the role collective memories have in a society is visible throughout his oeuvre, helping us understand the purpose of official commemorations in the past and in the present day – and why they may lead to conflict – as well as providing us with a sense of law's collective rituals, such as lustration and truth (and reconciliation commissions).

4 Keith Ansell-Pearson, *Philosophy and the Adventure of the Virtual: Bergson and the Time of Life* (London/New York: Routledge, 2002) at 10.

5 Marcin Rebes, "Miejsce pamięci z perspektywy filozoficznej" ["The Place of Memory from a Philosophical Perspective"] in Kinga A. Gajda and Aneta Pazik (eds), *Pozytywne Miejsca Pamięci Europejskiej* [*Positive Places of European Memory*] (Cracow: Instytut Europeistyki Uniwersytetu Jagiellońskiego, 2015) 42 at 42.

6 Tara Milbrandt and Frank Pearce, "Émile Durkheim" in George Ritzer and Jeffrey Stepnisky (eds), *The Wiley-Blackwell Companion to Major Social Theorists* (Chichester: Blackwell Publishing, 2011) 236 at 236.

7 Jeffrey K. Olick, "Products, Processes, and Practices: A Non-Reificatory Approach to Collective Memory" (2006) 36:1 Biblical Theology Bulletin: Journal of Bible and Culture 5 at 11–12.

His view of society remarkably rests on, among other elements, what we today understand as collective memory, with Durkheim's observation seemingly echoed by Halbwachs in his definition of collective memory, as cited in the previous chapter:

> when we start life we find established and all around us a complex of ideas, beliefs and behaviours, which others have acknowledged and practiced before us . . . we have the feeling that there is an impersonal force beyond us, one which took shape before we were born, which will outlast us, and which dominates us; and that force is society.[8]

The key to understanding Durkheim's view of what determines a society is *conscience collectif* (most often translated as collective consciousness),[9] a term defined by him as

> the totality of beliefs and sentiments common to average citizens of the same society . . . independent of the particular conditions in which individuals are placed; they pass on and it remains . . . it does not change with each generation, but, on the contrary, it connects successive generations with one another.[10]

The collective consciousness is, thus, a shared set of beliefs that holds society together over the years. I would argue that, while not entirely synonymous,[11] collective memory should be understood as one of the elements of the collective consciousness,[12] passed on by "socialising agencies, such as schools, religious communities and 'ethnically-grounded' communities,"[13] and ultimately present in the main societal institutions, such as religion and law.

Both of them are of interest to Durkheim, who notes poignantly that "law is meaningless if it is detached from religion, which has given it its main

8 Émile Durkheim, *Moral Education: A Study in the Theory and Application of the Sociology of Education* (New York: Free Press of Glencoe, 1961) at 246.

9 Kenneth Thompson, "Preface to the First Edition" in Kenneth Thompson (ed.), *Readings from Émile Durkheim* (London/New York: Routledge, 2005) xv at xv.

10 Émile Durkheim, *The Division of Labor in Society* (Glencoe, IL: The Free Press of Glencoe, Illinois, 1960) at 79–80.

11 Werner Gephart, "Memory and the Sacred: The Cult of Anniversaries and Commemorative Rituals in the Light of *The Elementary Forms*" in N. J. Allen, W. S. F. Pickering, and W. Watts Miller (eds), *On Durkheim's Elementary Forms of Religious Life* (Oxon: Routledge, 1998) 127 at 129.

12 Similarly, Aaron Beim, "The Cognitive Aspects of Collective Memory" (2007) 20:1 Symbolic Interaction 7 at 9.

13 Gephart, *supra* note 11 at 130.

distinguishing marks, and of which it is partially only a derivation."[14] Like religion, "law is a site and an instrument of power and conflict . . . it may also be a focus of commitment, attachment and solidarity."[15] Moreover, as Misztal notes, in Durkheim's eyes, the institutions of law "are seen as mechanisms of systematising remembering and forgetting, while the role of the state and its institutions is to sustain the authority of law, and, by the same token, ensure moral integration, as the precondition of social cohesion."[16] In turn, Blom argues, for Durkheim, religion is "a celebration of a mythical past that confers identity on individuals and groups. Religion then allows us to understand shared memory as a key element of social life. Society is memory, and memory is recognition, identity."[17]

Thus, in his analysis of religion – and law, which takes on religion's function in modern societies as the place where "shared beliefs and understandings are imbued in"[18] – we may yet again find collective memory hidden behind the scenes as one of the main forces bringing society together through ceremonies and rituals – mnemonic devices,[19] which not only result in closer interpersonal bonds[20] but also allow people to forget about their everyday activities[21] and focus on "their common beliefs, their common traditions, the memory of their great ancestors, the collective ideal of which they are the incarnation."[22]

As Gephart notes, in Durkheim's theory, "commemorative symbols, norms, a commemorative social organisation and rituals as specialised or non-specialised social interactions are at the basis of collective memory."[23] We may thus propose an application of Durkheim's observations on religious ceremonies to contemporary events (he noticed the similarities himself),[24] such as independence day celebrations, city feasts, and memorials that take the form of public commemorations, with speeches, unveilings of monuments,

14 Émile Durkheim, *The Rules of Sociological Method and Selected Texts on Sociology and Its Method* (London/Basingstoke: The Macmillan Press, 1982) at 205.
15 Roger Cotterrell, *Émile Durkehim: Law in a Moral Domain* (Stanford, CA: Stanford University Press, 1999) at 50.
16 Barbara A. Misztal, "Durkheim on Collective Memory" (2003) 3:2 Journal of Classical Sociology 123 at 134.
17 Ina Blom, "Introduction: Rethinking Social Memory: Archives, Technology, and the Social" in Ina Blom, Trond Lundemo, and Eivind Røssaak (eds), *Memory in Motion: Archives, Technology, and the Social* (Amsterdam: Amsterdam University Press, 2017) 11 at 14.
18 Misztal, *supra* note 16 at 130.
19 Misztal, *supra* note 16 at 126.
20 Émile Durkheim, *The Elementary Forms of the Religious Life* (London: George Allen & Unwin, 1964) at 348.
21 *Ibid.* at 348.
22 *Ibid.* at 348–349.
23 Gephart, *supra* note 11 at 131.
24 Durkheim, *supra* note 20 at 427.

laying of the flowers, etc. In fact, they have the same goal as religious rituals of yesteryear: bringing a social group together through reinforcing their common collective memories. Participation, as Hoskins remarks,[25] is key for the survival of a collectivity.

Similarly, trial, also seen by Durkheim as a form of a ritual,[26] may become a carrier of collective memories,[27] especially if its role is supposed to be extraordinary, for example, in the case of truth (and reconciliation) proceedings, lustration processes, or international tribunal judgements on national crimes. As whole nations "participate" in a trial, this collective experience strengthens their bonds as a society.

Durkheim's theory may also be applied to certain carriers of collective memory, the aforementioned symbolic objects around which rituals take place, explaining their unique significance. Swingewood gives an example of the flag, noting that "the soldier who dies for his country dies for the flag and this is the symbol which has priority in his consciousness,"[28] while Misztal turns her attention to law, arguing that "memory is codified in law."[29]

In Durkheim's concept, the relationship between rituals, collective memory, and a society's existence becomes a vicious circle: "the unity of a society is closely connected with its collective memory which guarantees social identity. However, this memory is dependent on organisation and on collective symbols which need to be ritualized."[30] Should rituals stop, society would dissolve.[31] Thus, with the role of religion diminishing in modern societies, he underlined (already noting the politicisation of collective memory in contemporary times) the need for patriotism to take religion's role as the organising force of a group, with schools responsible for instilling it onto future generations.[32]

With that, as Misztal remarks, Durkheim "implies that the state and its institutions should ensure the representation of a national past that glorifies abstract values, not values of particular groups," which may also "offer us something emotional and capable of arousing in us sentiments and

25 Andrew Hoskins, "Memory of the Multitude: The End of Collective Memory" in Andrew Hoskins (ed.), *Digital Memory Studies: Media Pasts in Transition* (New York/Oxon: Routledge, 2018) 85 at 94.
26 Joachim J. Savelsberg and Ryan D. King, "Law and Collective Memory" (2017) 3 Annual Review of Law and Social Science 189 at 192–193.
27 Misztal, *supra* note 16 at 133.
28 Alan Swingewood, *Cultural Theory and the Problem of Modernity* (New York: St. Martin's Press, 1998) at 55.
29 Misztal, *supra* note 16 at 132.
30 W. S. F. Pickering, "Introduction" in N. J. Allen, W. S. F. Pickering, and W. Watts Miller (eds), *On Durkheim's Elementary Forms of Religious Life* (Oxon: Routledge, 1998) 1 at 9.
31 Durkheim, *supra* note 20 at 375.
32 Émile Durkheim cited in Ruth A. Wallace, "Émile Durkheim and the Civil Religion Concept" (1977) 18:3 Review of Religious Research 287 at 289.

attachments to traditions and beliefs."[33] This is clearly visible today in the various actions undertaken by the authorities to promote a single, official narrative of the past through the various legal institutions of memory analysed in Part II of this book.

Memory's "Third Way": Henri Bergson

Henri Bergson is a particular philosopher among this group of four – while none of them used the actual term of collective memory, elements of the concept may be found within the work of three of them. Bergson, however, proposes a "third way" of looking at memory, perceiving it as a "synthesis of the past and the present with a view to the future."[34] His understanding of memory is suspended between what is usually regarded as collective and individual memory: since "no individual is wholly asocial, and no society exists without individuals, individual and collective memory are always implied in one another," with the possibility of looking at the two "in terms of combinatory and overlapping body-images."[35]

While memory is the object of a number of Bergson's investigations (as Lawlor notes, "Bergsonism is a 'primacy of memory' "[36]), its concept is presented most comprehensively in *Matter and Memory*, where he argues that memory is at the basis of our daily existence, as every single one of our perceptions is marred with one's past experiences, and it is "memory, and not the senses, which creates our perception of the world."[37] Given that memory is in a "constant and fertile interaction with matter,"[38] we always "mingle a thousand details out of our past experience. In most cases, these memories supplant our actual perceptions, of which we then retain only a few hints, thus using them merely as 'signs' that recall to us former images."[39]

He distinguishes two – or in fact, as I will show later on, three – different forms of remembering. Using an example of learning a poem by heart, he demonstrates the difference between actually remembering what was learnt, i.e., when something is "imprinted on" one's memory, and evoking the memories of the process of learning, i.e., remembering a particular moment in one's life story.[40]

33 Misztal, *supra* note 16 at 134.
34 Henri Bergson, *Matter and Memory* (London: George Allen & Unwin; New York: Humanities Press, 1970) at 294.
35 James Burton, "Bergson's Non-Archival Theory of Memory" (2008) 1:3 Memory Studies 321 at 336.
36 Leonard Lawlor, *The Challenge of Bergsonism* (London: Continuum, 2003) at 28.
37 Piotr Herbich, "Koncepcja pamięci w *Materii i pamięci* Henri Bergsona" ["The Concept of Memory in Henri Bergson's *Matter and Memory*"] (2004) 13:1 Przegląd Filozoficzny 61 at 66.
38 Pete A. Y. Gunter, "Bergson and Jung" (1982) 43:4 Journal of the History of Ideas 635 at 636.
39 Bergson, *supra* note 34 at 24.
40 Bergson, *supra* note 34 at 89.

Lawlor illustrates this difference between the two types of memory by giving another example, of a person learning how to drive: at first, they are conscious of every single light and sign, but ultimately they begin to take them in without actually thinking about them.[41] This way, the habit memory is created, or, as Bergson calls it, "prolongation," the memory of repetition, born out of and "bent upon action, seated in the present and looking only to the future. . . . it no longer represents our past to us, it acts it." It is still memory, but unlike the other type of memory, it does not conserve "bygone images, but . . . prolongs their useful effect into the present moment."[42]

However, if one was to think back to the memories of their driving lessons, they would find precisely these "memory-images," the "representational memory," or the memory which imagines, recording "all the events of our daily life as they occur in time[.] By this memory is made possible the intelligent, or rather intellectual, recognition of a perception already experienced."[43] This type of memory is regressive, taking one back into the past, but, despite different vectors, both types are connected.[44]

Habit memory and representational memory are two ways of recollecting, suited to the "requirements of the present."[45] However, Bergson's understating of memory is actually "tripartite" – he also distinguishes "pure memory," i.e., "the true means by which the past is prolonged into the present."[46] It constitutes one's "personal recollections, exactly localised, the series of which represents the course of our past existence," making up, "all together, the last and largest enclosure of our memory."[47] This "record" of one's every single memory is available for "the perceiving, recalling consciousness,"[48] stretching out "towards the situation to be interpreted."[49] Pure memory is thus responsible for ensuring that "only those past images come into operation that can be co-ordinated with a present perception and so enabling a useful combination to emerge between past and present images,"[50] allowing us to lead our daily lives not only habitually but also intellectually.

Ultimately, the tripartite understanding of memory is at the same time encompassing the future (habit memory), the present (representational

41 Lawlor, *supra* note 36 at 32.
42 Bergson, *supra* note 34 at 93.
43 Bergson, *supra* note 34 at 92.
44 Lawlor, *supra* note 36 at 35.
45 Keith Ansell-Pearson, "Bergson on Memory" in Susannah Radstone and Bill Schwarz (eds), *Memory: Histories, Theories, Debates* (New York: Fordham University Press, 2010) 61 at 66.
46 Burton, *supra* note 35 at 326.
47 Bergson, *supra* note 34 at 129.
48 Burton, *supra* note 35 at 329.
49 Jean Hyppolite, "Various Aspects of Memory in Bergson" in Leonard Lawlor (ed.), *The Challenge of Bergsonism* (London: Continuum, 2003) 112 at 118.
50 Ansell-Pearson, *supra* note 4 at 173.

memory), and the past (pure memory).[51] To visualise this concept, Bergson proposed an image of a cone[52] or an inverted pyramid, which I analyse in greater detail elsewhere.[53] What needs to be repeated here is that with this figure, Bergson shows exactly how his theory of memory works: pure memories lay at the base of the cone/inverted pyramid, "prior to their instantiation,"[54] with our past experiences registered as various memory-images doubling up on one another (the main body of the cone/inverted pyramid), weighing in on our perception of the present (the tip of the cone/inverted pyramid).

The cone/inverted pyramid exemplifies how our "past always both conditions the present as what makes the passing of the present possible and affects the present as our character which supports every decision we make."[55] Because, in Bergson's concept, "past and present coexist, the past existing as virtuality and the present as actuality."[56] As such, whenever one wants to recall a past event, they do not need to return from their "position in the present, through all the events that separate" the current moment and the past event,[57] but simply adjust themselves, doing "something like the focussing of a camera."[58] We may "trail behind us, unawares, the whole of our past; but our memory pours into the present only the odd recollection or two that in some way complete our present situation."[59]

Nota bene, while, as I remarked earlier, Bergson's theory escapes the traditional realms of the division between the individual and collective memory, Bergson was aware of the ways social perceptions of the past can influence the present, observing that:

> an event belongs to the past, and enters into history, when it is no longer of any direct interest to the politics of the day . . . As long as its action makes itself felt, it adheres to the life of a nation and remains present to it.[60]

51 Anna Kuchta, "Meandry pamięci: Między koncepcją pamięci Henri Bergsona a wizją postpamięci Marianne Hirsch – próba zestawienia" ["Meanders of Memory: Between Henri Bergson's Concept of Memory and Marainne Hirsch's Vision of Post-Memory – an Attempt at Comparison"] (2017) 34 Maska 145 at 148.

52 Bergson, *supra* note 34 at 211.

53 Mirosław M. Sadowski, "Law and Memory: The Unobvious Relationship" (2017) 16:2 Warsaw University Law Review 262 at 273–275.

54 Mark Sinclair, *Bergson* (Oxon: Routledge, 2020) at 101.

55 Lawlor, *supra* note 36 at 58.

56 Grant D. Bollmer, "Virtuality in Systems of Memory: Toward an Ontology of Collective Memory, Ritual, and the Technological" (2011) 4:4 Memory Studies 450 at 455.

57 Sinclair, *supra* note 54 at 102.

58 Bergson, *supra* note 34 at 171.

59 Henri Bergson, *Creative Evolution* (New York: Camelot Press, 1911) at 167.

60 Henri Bergson, "The Perception of Change" in Keith A. Pearson and John Mullarkey (eds), *Henri Bergson: Key Writings* (London/New York, NY: Presses Universitaires de France/Continuum, 2002) 248 at 262.

This remark helps us understand how a group's identity is forged – with "the production of the collective itself," at the same time "the actualisation of history as (a) movement (in several senses of the word)" takes place, and ultimately "a collective is formed out of the actualisation of history as memory."[61]

Importantly, Bergson's concept of memory may be applied to law, deepening our understanding of the various law and memory processes. Thus far, it has most often been used to explain the relationship between memory and common law, with, for example, Mawani regarding law "as ever changing, as becoming," a "temporal force,"[62] inherently similar to Bergson's theory of memory, since both share the "commitment to the past, present, and future";[63] Lefebvre arguing that "judgments are composites of perception and memory";[64] and Crow and Youngwon Lee seeing law as "searching for the common ground between the past and the present,"[65] with the meaning of various laws changing as time goes by and – just like human perception does according to Bergson – with the judge perpetually "in search of a meaning that shifts dynamically with the context."[66]

I would argue, however, that Bergson's theory of memory escapes the singular common law applications – in civil law systems, the judge is also often responsible for applying a rule to the changing context, which is particularly noticeable in the work of the constitutional tribunals, tasked with reconciling the unchanging rules of the constitution and the evolving times. Additionally, Bergson's concept is helpful in the context of the intersections between law and collective memory, allowing us to better understand the seemingly irresponsible political decisions made by certain countries, which are in reality rooted in the collective memories harboured by whole nations, a point that I develop further in the next chapter, engaging with the intersections between collective memory and international law.

A similar "ignorance" of the nature of memory may be observed in certain processes of transitional justice, rendering them ineffective. They perceive collective memory "as a sequence of presents," which "makes it difficult to understand and resolve the deeply contrasting memories of the same events that may surface following a civil conflict."[67] Only by realising that collective memories, similar to Bergosonian memories, should be regarded as

61 Bollmer, *supra* note 56 at 458.
62 Renisa Mawani, "The Times of Law" (2015) 40:1 Law and Social Inquiry 253 at 260.
63 *Ibid.* at 257.
64 Alexandre Lefebvre, *The Image of Law: Deleuze, Bergson, Spinoza* (Stanford, CA: Stanford University Press, 2009) at 127.
65 Jonathan Crowe and Constance Youngwon Lee, "Law as Memory" (2015) 26 Law Critique 251 at 252.
66 *Ibid.* at 257.
67 *Ibid.* at 258.

constructed of layers upon layers of memories coming from different periods of time may reconciliatory processes reach a different conclusion, the thought which I will explore further in the next chapter.

Memory, Morality, and Law: Emmanuel Levinas

Emmanuel Levinas, like other philosophers analysed in this chapter, does not use the term "collective memory" directly; however, the concept may be noticed throughout his work, which, when analysed, allows us to better understand the difference between individual and collective memory and provides a yet another perspective on the links between law and collective memory. Importantly, Levinas's oeuvre as a whole is an example of the reworking of cultural trauma-memory – as he noted himself, his work "is dominated by the presentiment and the memory of the Nazi horror"[68] – with Shoah constantly influencing him "as a memory, as a trace of what has receded irrecuperably into the past,"[69] his thought in certain cases is "inseparable from the memory of the crimes of the twentieth century,"[70] functioning "as an act of memory."[71]

With the difference between individual and collective memory a key to understanding the various processes of law and memory, and given the analysis of the different sociological viewpoints on that matter in the previous chapter, it is perhaps surprising to see Levinas poignantly showing the difference between the two in the dedications to his magnum opus *Otherwise than Being*.[72] There are two dedications there, one in French (translated into other languages in the various editions of the book) and another in Hebrew (not translated to French even in the original). The first dedication reads:

> To the memory of those who were closest among the six million assassinated by the National Socialists, and of the millions on millions of all confessions and all nations, victims of the same hatred of the other man, the same anti-semitism.

68 Emmanuel Levinas, *Difficult Freedom: Essays on Judaism* (Baltimore, MD: Johns Hopkins University Press, 1997) at 291.

69 Michael Bernard-Donals, "In Memoriam: Levinas, the Holocaust, and the Immemorial" (2007) 40:3 Mosaic: An Interdisciplinary Critical Journal 1 at 1.

70 Marc Crépon, *The Thought of Death and the Memory of War* (Minneapolis, MN: University of Minnesota Press, 2003) at 53.

71 James Hatley, "Nameless Memory: Levinas, Witness, and Politics" (2017) 33 Religion and Public Life 33 at 40.

72 Emmanuel Levinas, *Otherwise Than Being or Beyond Essence* (Dordrecht: Springer Science+Business Media, 1997) at v.

The second, in its main part, is devoted " 'To the memory of the spirit of my father, Yehiel, son of Avraham Halevi, my mother Devorah, daughter of Moshe,' [Levinas's] two brothers and his wife's mother."[73]

The interplay between these two functions takes place on several different levels, but above all, it clearly demonstrates the difference between collective and individual memory. The first, "collective" dedication, is easily accessible to the reader and, while directed to all the victims of Nazism, clearly speaks to every human being, evoking our shared perceptions of the past. The second dedication is much more intimate, accessible in general only to fellow Jews, and speaks of the individual memories of the author, those that cannot be shared by the majority of his readers. Levinas is clearly aware of these differences between the individual and the collective memory; hence, he limits the audience of his second dedication.

The two dedications are also Levinas's way of reworking his collective trauma-memories. As Bernard-Donals remarks, between them there exists "a trace of memory, a notion that is integral to the task of living – and of bearing witness – after the Holocaust." More than mere dedications, "they mark, in palimpsest, the relation between naming, post-Holocaust memory, and ethics that is foundational to Levinas."[74] The second dedication, composed of the names of Levinas's family members who perished in the Holocaust, "proceeds" towards "the memory of the six million" at the same time making us reach the conclusion that "those closest among the six million renders 'the six million' impossible to recall."[75]

These traces of collective memory may be found throughout *Otherwise than Being*, and, importantly, Levinas returns to the two dedications at the end of his work, remarking that one would not be able to "recall the *beyond essence*," if Western history did not convey, "in its margins, the trace of events carrying another signification, and if the victims of the triumphs which entitle the eras of history could be separate from its meaning."[76] As Herzog notes, these are the same victims Levinas speaks about in the dedication, with the reading of the book going "backward, to a beginning anterior to the beginning itself," thus re-establishing memory.[77] With his work, Levinas wants to "give a place in the very history of thought to history's defeated,"[78] giving them back their voice.

73 Bernard-Donals, *supra* note 69 at 3.
74 Bernard-Donals, *supra* note 69 at 2.
75 Bernard-Donals, *supra* note 69 at 5.
76 Levinas, *supra* note 72 at 178.
77 Annabel Herzog, "Levinas, Memory and the Art of Writing" (2005) XXXVI:3 The Philosophical Forum 333 at 338.
78 Orietta Ombrosi, *The Twilight of Reason: Benjamin, Adorno, Horkheimer and Levinas Tested by the Catastrophe* (Boston: Academic Studies Press, 2012) at 169.

In a way, the two dedications also set the stage for Levinas's diachronic theory of ethics, giving "a palpable presence both to the names that are substituted for the events of history and the effect of the events themselves; to what has been written"[79] and to "the proximity of one to the other, the commitment of an approach, the one for the other, the very signifyingness of signification."[80]

In Levinas's view, ethics are "the first philosophy,"[81] superseding ontology[82] (which in turn means that justice "precedes discourse"[83]). Asking the question as to whether one's relations to others are justified,[84] his ethical system is based on "the face-to-face encounter between self and other," and in its creation is both akin to and linked with collective memory, as one's ethics are being put together from the experiences with other people, meeting after meeting,[85] over the years showing in one's "passive sythesis of these repeated encounters,"[86] which leads to "a general attitude towards social life."[87]

Levinas' ethics begin "in the face of the other – that face which enlists my responsibility by its human expression," with the meaning of ethical responsibility contained in the fact that "no one can substitute himself for me when it is I who am responsible."[88] It is this focus on the others that makes us human, laying at the basis of our "capacity to fear injustice more than death, to prefer to suffer than to commit injustice, and to prefer that which justifies being over that which assures it."[89]

As our ethics are based on the memories of our various encounters, the past "is on the hither side of every present and every re-presentable . . . included in the extraordinary and everyday event of my responsibility for

79 Bernard-Donals, *supra* note 69 at 3.
80 Levinas, *supra* note 72 at 5.
81 Herzog, *supra* note 77 at 337.
82 Nahanni Freeman, "American Cultural Symbolism of Rage and Resistance in Collective Trauma: Racially-Influenced Political Myths, Counter-Myths, Projective Identification, and the Evocation of Transcendent Humanity" in David M. Goodman, Eric R. Severson, and Heather Macdonald (eds), *Race, Rage, and Resistance: Philosophy, Psychology, and the Perils of Individualism* (Oxon: Routledge, 2020) 46 at 49.
83 Jonathan Crowe, "Lévinas on Shared Ethical Judgments" (2011) 42:3 Journal of the British Society for Phenomenology 233 at 240.
84 Lisbeth Lipari, "Rhetoric's Other: Levinas, Listening, and the Ethical Response" (2012) 45:3 Philosophy and Rhetoric 227 at 229.
85 Crowe and Youngwon Lee, *supra* note 65 at 262.
86 Crowe, *supra* note 83 at 239.
87 Jonathan Crowe, "Levinasian Ethics and Legal Obligation" (2006) 19:4 Ratio Juris 421 at 425.
88 Emmanuel Levinas, "Martin Buber, Gabriel Marcel, and Philosophy" in Haim Gordon and Jochanan Bloch (eds), *Martin Buber: A Centenary Volume* (Negev: KTAV Publishing, 1984) 305 at 317.
89 Emmanuel Levinas, "Ethics as First Philosophy" in Seán Hand (ed.), *The Levinas Reader* (Oxford: Basil Blackwell, 1989) at 85.

the faults or the misfortune of others."[90] Through "retention, memory and history, nothing is lost, everything is presented or represented, everything is consigned and lends itself to inscription, or is synthetized or . . . assembled," leading to "a transcending diachrony"[91] and "an 'unrepresentable, immemorial, pre-historical' sense of our shared ethical responsibilities."[92]

Ultimately, this "ethical memory" (collective, social memory) comes "before everything", becoming – or rather, being – the "memory of the immemorial,"[93] memory "of the trace of the infinity that is present in the face of the victims,"[94] when "the otherness is everything except the present of consciousness."[95] And it is this memory, the memory expressed in the first dedication, that "paradoxically . . . proves to be more graspable than particular memory"[96] expressed in the second. We all share collective memories, and through them we may participate, among other things, in the many individual traumas of singular people – and these "social encounters" humanise us.

As Crowe and Youngwon Lee remark, the diachronic concept of ethics leads Levinas straight to law, as it "contains the secret of sociality,"[97] and thus brings to the surface the ethical foundations of law, whose "continual search for the past produces a dynamic amalgam of the past and present, continually oscillating and shaping one another."[98] In Levinas's concept, law needs to be grounded in ethics,[99] and it may do that only "if it allows itself to be influenced by the weight of the past"[100] made present with collective memories.

Keynan argues that Levinas's view on ethics and law may be used "in the safe space of mutual empathetic recognition and witnessing by the former enemies"[101] to reach reconciliation. It certainly helps us understand the rationale behind the various mechanisms of transitional justice, particularly

90 Levinas, *supra* note 72 at 10.
91 Levinas, *supra* note 72 at 9.
92 Crowe and Youngwon Lee, *supra* note 65 at 263.
93 Herzog, *supra* note 77 at 338.
94 Manuel Losada-Sierra, "Memory and History: The Overcoming of Traditional Theodicy in Levinas and Metz" (2019) 10 Religions 1 at 7.
95 Sophie Galabru, "Paul Ricoeur et Emmanuel Levinas: Vulnérabilité, mémoire et narration. Peut-on raconter la vulnérabilité?" (2019) 10:1 Études ricoeuriennes/Ricoeur Studies 125 at 131.
96 Herzog, *supra* note 77 at 342.
97 Emmanuel Levinas, *On Thinking of the Other: Entre nous* (New York, NY/Chichester: Columbia University Press, 1998) at 169.
98 Crowe and Youngwon Lee, *supra* note 65 at 265.
99 Crowe, *supra* note 87 at 433.
100 Crowe and Youngwon Lee, *supra* note 65 at 264.
101 Irit Keynan, "Ethics of Memory, Trauma and Reconciliation" in Kim Wale, Pumla Gobodo-Madikizela, and Jeffrey Prager (eds), *Post-Conflict Hauntings Transforming Memories of Historical Trauma* (Cham: Palgrave Macmillan, 2020) 47 at 62.

truth (and reconciliation) commissions, which aim to give voice to the victims and accommodate the various collective memories with respect to one another. This legal institution of memory will be analysed alongside others in the subsequent parts of the book; however, it needs to be remarked here that in their present form, truth (and reconciliation) commissions seem not to be enough to fulfil the criteria of Levinas's ethics: as Hatley observes, "if there is to be peace, the political memory of violence must move beyond merely expressing an outrage for wrongs suffered."[102] It, Levinas tells us, needs to also be felt by others.

The Power of Collective Memory: Michel Foucault

The final thinker whose concepts I would like to analyse in the context of my research is Michel Foucault. While in his vast oeuvre he does not use the term "collective memory" *per se*, speaking about memory only together with and in the context of history, it has to be noted that his understanding of history[103] is much closer to one of the contemporary perceptions of collective memory as encompassing more than just small social groups – and this is why his thoughts prove useful in the later chapters.

As it has been observed earlier, by the end of the second half of the twentieth century, our understanding of memory had in general become much more social and more collective, linking "hip new linguistic practices with some of the oldest senses of memory as a union of divine presence and material object,"[104] in a way taking history's place in the academic debate.[105] I agree with Klein that in Foucault's works, memory, even if it is referred to as history, "becomes a subject in its own right, free to range back and forth across time," with one using the term able to examine a "memory of events that happened hundreds of years distant or to speak of the memory of an ethnic, religious, or racial group."[106]

Foucault was particularly interested in history and memory with regard to his investigations of the question of power. He was well aware of the force official narratives have over people, noting that thanks to the omnipresence of the Gaullist version of the events of World War II in French popular culture, the whole country was "exonerated by de Gaulle, while the right . . .

102 Hatley, *supra* note 71 at 49.
103 Allan Megill, "Foucault, Structuralism, and the Ends of History" (1979) 51:3 The Journal of Modern History 451 at 499–500.
104 Kerwin L. Klein, "On the Emergence of Memory in Historical Discourse" (2000) 69 Representations 127 at 129.
105 *Ibid.* at 128.
106 *Ibid.* at 136.

was purified and sanctified by him."[107] This has in turn resulted in a certain "reprogramming [of] popular memory, which existed but had no way of expressing itself." In such cases, he argued, "people are shown not what they were, but what they must remember having been."[108] Additionally, as he further observed, the question of collective memory is clearly linked to that of power: "if one controls people's memory, one controls their dynamism. In addition, one also controls their experience, their knowledge of previous struggles."[109]

Foucault's work will be particularly important for my research in the analysis of those instances when collective memory intersects with law, resulting in conflict. Thus, I would like to introduce here two of his concepts more closely: heterotopia and counter-memory/history, which will make clearer, among other things, why the aforementioned places of memory, notably street names and monuments, are regarded as not only powerful carriers of collective memories but also objects of power, in some instances provoking protests.

I propose to look at places of memory as heterotopias in the Foucauldian sense, which he defines as places whereby:

> all the other real sites that can be found within the culture, are simultaneously represented, contested, and inverted. Places of this kind are outside of all places, even though it may be possible to indicate their location in reality. . . . these places are absolutely different from all the sites that they reflect and speak about.[110]

Monuments, street names, and some other carriers of memory clearly fit this definition, carrying with them various collective memories and constant reflections of the past in the everchanging present.

Foucault further explains his concept of heterotopia, proposing six principles by which such a place is characterised. First, heterotopias are omnipresent in every culture around the world, taking different forms. Foucault distinguishes "crisis heterotopias," e.g., boarding schools and military service, and "heterotopias of deviation," e.g., prisons and retirement homes – in general places that provide societies with a space for certain abnormal behaviour.[111] While at first glance places of memory do not seem to pass this principle, I would argue that in fact they play such a role, being often an outlet for local, ethnic, and national groups to rework their collective

107 Michel Foucault, "Film and Popular Memory: An Interview with Michel Foucault" (1974) 251:2 Cahiers du Cinéma 24 at 25.
108 *Ibid.* at 25.
109 *Ibid.* at 25.
110 Michel Foucault and Jay Miskowiec, "Of Other Spaces" (1986) 16:1 Diacritics 22 at 24.
111 *Ibid.* at 24–25.

trauma-memories, celebrate their heroes, and perform memorial rituals, but in a way that allows the past to exist separately from the present.

The second principle characterises heterotopias as each having a particular function in a society, one that may change with time,[112] while the third argues that although every heterotopia is a "single real place," it may carry with it several other places, often incompatible.[113] This is again true about places of memory, which, while in general holding a commemorative function, may change their meaning (e.g., a headquarters of secret police being changed into a memorial after a transition to democracy) and at the same time have various conflicting collective memories attached to them (e.g., a monument to the hero of a former regime).

According to the fourth principle, heterotopias are umbilically connected to "slices in time," whether accumulating time in perpetuity (e.g., libraries and museums), places where "time never stops building up and topping its own summit," or spaces where time is "transitory," unreal (e.g., holiday villages and fairgrounds).[114] Places of memory clearly fit into the first category, accumulating various, often conflicting collective memories over generations, perhaps changing their meaning along the way.

Ultimately, the fifth principle characterises heterotopias as places that, even when they seem easily accessible, in reality have a certain exclusion to them,[115] with the sixth principle noting that heterotopias influence all spaces around them, either exposing "every real space . . . as . . . illusory," or creating a place that is as ideal as the remaining space is not.[116] Places of memory again could clearly be characterised as such, monuments in particular – they may seem to be an integral part of the cityscape but are in fact separate from the rest of the city, most often meticulously kept and renovated, even with the buildings behind them dilapidated. They always carry one into the past due to the collective memories connected to them, even involuntarily and unknowingly to the person in question. *Nota bene*, as a good illustration of this point, the artistic project of an Israeli artist who changed the background of "fun" pictures taken at the Berlin Holocaust Memorial to that of concentration camps[117] comes to mind – while people who had their pictures taken there may not have felt as if they were in a sacred space themselves, the general public's understanding of the monument's role was immediate, regarding it as a separate entity from the rest of the city.

112 *Ibid.* at 25.
113 *Ibid.* at 25–26.
114 *Ibid.* at 26.
115 *Ibid.* at 26.
116 *Ibid.* at 26.
117 Joel Gunter, "'Yolocaust': How Should You Behave at a Holocaust Memorial?," online: BBC News <bbc.com/news/world-europe-38675835>.

As Topinka notes in his analysis of heterotopias, they "combine and juxtapose many spaces in one site, creating an intensification of knowledge that can help us re-see the foundations of our own knowledge; but they cannot take us outside of this knowledge or free us from power relations."[118] Replacing the word "knowledge" with "collective memory" in this citation allows us to further see how the concept of heterotopia deepens our perception of places of memory while making us aware of their power – and their limits. A different concept of Michel Foucault helps us also understand why certain places of memory – certain heterotopias – become "sites of reordering,"[119] turn controversial, and lead to conflict: that of counter-memory/history.

The term "counter-memory" can be understood in a variety of different ways, used to describe, for example, both memory legislation and a personal memento; however, in Foucault's perception, it means "the residual or resistant strains [of memory] that withstand official versions of historical continuity."[120] He approached the question of counter-memories/histories in several of his works, regarding counter-memory as a result of such a "use of history that severs its connection to memory, its metaphysical and anthropological model," and transforms it "into a totally different form of time."[121]

Remarking upon "the intimate connection between the construction of knowledge about ourselves through the human sciences and the increasingly more refined way power is exerted by and upon persons,"[122] Foucault argued that people "experience the world in ways which necessarily depend upon the influence upon them of social forces such as power/knowledge,"[123] distinguishing "subjugated knowledges," i.e., those memories that were hidden, repressed or banished from official narratives.[124]

His focus was on the counter-memories, memories of struggles, engaging in what Foucault called "genealogy," the process of "coupling together of scholarly erudition and local memories,"[125] hoping to "reactivate" them.[126] As Colwell notes, "if history is the collective memory of a particular social group then genealogy is a counter-memory composed of the same elements

118 Robert J. Topinka, "Foucault, Borges, Heterotopia: Producing Knowledge in Other Spaces" (2010) 9 Foucault Studies 54 at 70.

119 *Ibid.* at 56.

120 Natalie Z. Davis and Randolph Starn, "Introduction" (1989) 26 Representations 1 at 2.

121 Michel Foucault, *Language, Counter-Memory, Practice* (Ithaca, NY: Cornell University Press, 1996) at 160.

122 Frank Pignatelli, "Critical Ethnography/Poststructuralist Concerns: Foucault and the Play of Memory" (1998) 29 Interchange 403 at 416.

123 Mark Bevir, "Foucault, Power, and Institutions" (1999) XLVII:2 Political Studies 345 at 358.

124 Michel Foucault, *"Society Must Be Defended" Lectures at the Collège de France 1975–76* (New York, NY: Picador, 2003; London: Penguin Books, 2004) at 7.

125 *Ibid.* at 8.

126 *Ibid.* at 10.

repeated and arranged in a different manner."[127] Through such a genealogical analysis, he hoped to uncover the basis of power in a society,[128] arguing that one of history's roles was (is) to reaffirm the current hierarchies.[129] Analysing the place of history in modernity, Foucault notes that throughout the creation of a contemporary society, the discourse was filled with not one, unified story, but two: (the official, one reaffirming power) history and (the divergent, unofficial, that of struggle) counter-history.[130]

Importantly, while speaking at this point about the official history's place in the Roman civilisation and the Middle Ages, he also remarked on a function it holds to this day, memorialisation – noting that history "makes things memorable and, by making them memorable, inscribes deeds in a discourse that constraints and immobilises minor actions in monuments that will turn them into stone and render them . . . present forever."[131]

Foucault's analysis of the power relations resulting from the existence of official memory/history and the unofficial counter-memories/histories can be applied to transitional situations (as I will attempt to do later in this book), when a "critical reconstruction and re – evaluation of our beliefs can (and should) be reopened and resumed[,] whenever new standpoints appear on the scene but also whenever we discover that certain voices or perspectives were never considered or were not given equal weight."[132] It helps us understand why people are so eager to change and remove the supposedly unimportant elements of their everyday lives, such as street names and monuments, after a regime transformation.

While Medina argues that Foucault's concept does not allow for the turning of counter-memories into "a heterogenous collective memory" but rather makes them one of the many divergent collective memories present in a society at the same time,[133] I disagree: through such changes to the cityscape or through lustration and truth (and reconciliation) commissions, people want to reassert the power shift by turning their counter-memories/histories into the official discourse. After a certain time in power, these will become official history. At the same time, the collective memories of former regime members will become counter-histories, as observed later on in this part of the book when proposing the concept of collective memory inversion.

127 C. Colwell, "Deleuze and Foucault: Series, Event, Genealogy" (1997) 1:2 Theory & Event, online: Project Muse <>https://muse.jhu.edu/article/32453>.
128 Foucault, *supra* note 124 at 17.
129 Foucault, *supra* note 124 at 66.
130 Foucault, *supra* note 124 at 70.
131 Foucault, *supra* note 124 at 67.
132 José Medina, "Toward a Foucaultian Epistemology of Resistance: Counter-Memory, Epistemic Friction, and Guerrilla Pluralism" (2011) 12 Foucault Studies 9 at 21.
133 *Ibid.* at 24.

It must be noted that Foucault's concept has also been used in various studies of racial relations in the United States, with Medina giving the example of Charles W. Mills's analysis of "white ignorance," resulting from the "socially orchestrated, exclusionary processes of both remembering and forgetting,"[134] which Mills calls "the management of memory."[135] Richard Delgado, in turn, shows how official, "white" memories and unofficial counter-memories of minorities function side by side, noting how only through the incessant attempts at bringing the counter-memories into the official discourse can an all-encompassing change be implemented[136] – once society's collective memories become "mutated"[137] (to use Colwell's term). These observations will prove particularly helpful in the later analysis of such legal institutions of memory as reparations and truth (and reconciliation) commissions.

Conclusion: Law, Memory, Philosophy – Intersections

The thought of four philosophers analysed in this chapter lends a helping hand to the previous sociological study in the search for the definition of collective memory, bringing us another step closer to uncovering its understanding with regard to law in Part II of this book devoted to the workings of the legal institutions of memory.

Importantly, the conducted philosophical analysis reminds us of a point oftentimes lost in the sociological deliberations on the subject: that law and collective memory are not perpetually focused only on the past but rather encompass society's present and future as well, with their power interplay always in the background. As Colebrook poignantly notes, both in the context of law and collective memory, "to remember is never simply to retain and recall a past, but always to do so from the point of view of a present that anticipates a future."[138]

134 *Ibid.* at 31.

135 Charles W. Mills, "White Ignorance" in Shannon Sullivan and Nancy Tuana (eds), *Race and Epistemologies of Ignorance* (Albany: State University of New York Press, 2007) 13 at 28.

136 Richard Delgado, "Storytelling for Oppositionists and Others: A Plea for Narrative" (1989) 87:8 Michigan Law Review 2411 at 2441.

137 Colwell, *supra* note 127.

138 Claire Colebrook, "The Intensity of the Archive" in Stef Craps et al., "Memory Studies and the Anthropocene: A Roundtable" (2018) 11:4 Memory Studies 498 at 507.

Chapter 3

Collective Memory, Law, and Theory

From Human Rights and International Law to the Concept of Transitional Justice

Introduction

Following the analysis of the intersections of collective memory, law and two other disciplines belonging to the social sciences and humanities families, respectively, I would like to close this first part of my theoretical research with the investigation of the relationship between collective memory and theory of law. Once again, limiting the field to those aspects most relevant to my book, I choose to centre my research on three instances of their intersections: regarding human rights law, international law, and the concept whereby elements of the two come together – transitional justice – in particular focusing on the intersections of one of the aforementioned extraordinary rituals of Durkheim, i.e., those trials when whole nations come together. While analysing these three particular fields of law, I hope to uncover certain general rules regarding the intersections of law and memory, which later on in the book will prove particularly useful in the research of the legal institutions of memory, one of the elements of the proposed law and collective memory framework.

Memory and Human Rights Law: Direct and Indirect Intersections

Huyssen remarks that human rights and collective memory are "two stars that shed light on each other in the same galaxy but remain different in their trajectories toward historical justice."[1] As this chapter will show, he is right in making the evocative assertion, but only to a point: he fails to take into account the fact that the light of these stars intersects in certain instances, be that directly, in the cases of collective memory's influence on the shape

1 Andreas Huyssen, "Historical Justice and Human Rights: A New Constellation" in Klaus Neumann and Janna Thompson (eds), *Historical Justice and Memory* (Madison, WI: University of Wisconsin Press, 2015) 27 at 44.

DOI: 10.4324/9781003461548-5

of human rights law, or indirectly, "mirrored" through various institutions applying human rights law.

The direct intersections between human rights law and collective memory have a particularly long history, predating the birth of the contemporary human rights movement. It has been argued that it is through the collective memory of the various judicial means available for redress that civil and human rights came to be – as such, both in the past and today, when broader parts of society are aware of what to expect and demand from law, the "mutual claim making among powerholders and ordinary people takes place within the frames of shared memory."[2] Moreover, as Misztal remarks, the collective memory of certain rights granted in the past through legal documents allows us to comprehend the "beginnings and values" of societies such as those of the United Kingdom or the United States, which lay at the basis of their founding myths, with the influence of the Magna Carta and the Declaration of Independence continuing to this day.[3]

Since the second half of the 20th century, the direct intersections of human rights law and collective memory have been particularly notable with regard to the questions of cultural rights and human rights violations. In regard to the former, the understanding of collective memory as a part of culture[4] creates a number of obligations on the part of the state parties to the various cultural rights treaties, including the need for consultations and/or consent for the transformation of cultural spaces belonging to local communities and the allowing of various collective memories and narratives to exist in the public sphere, as well as in education and history.[5] Importantly, these issues are directly linked to the question of the right to memory, as introduced in Part II of the book.

It is the cases of the abuses of human rights violations, however, that carry particular weight in contemporary times: it was the collective trauma-memories of the first half of the 20th century, along with "the legacies of the natural law tradition," which led to the adoption of the Universal Declaration of Human Rights (UDHR) and the United Nations' Convention on the

2 Charles Tilly, "Afterword: Political Memories in Space and Time" in Jonathan Boyarin and Charles Tilly (eds), *Remapping Memory: The Politics of Time Space* (Minneapolis, MN: University of Minnesota Press, 1994) 241 at 249.

3 Barbara A. Misztal, "Legal Attempts to Construct Collective Memory: The Necessity and Difficulties of Aiming for Both Truth and Solidarity" (2001) 133 Polish Sociological Review 61 at 61.

4 William E. Conklin, "Which Takes Precedence: Collective Rights or Culture?" in Almed Momeni-Rad, Arian Petoft, and Alireza Sayadmansom (eds), *Cultural Rights: An Anthology* (Tehran: Iranian Cultural Services Society, 2015) 115 at 146.

5 Pok Yin S. Chow, "Culture as Collective Memories: An Emerging Concept in International Law and Discourse on Cultural Rights" (2014) 14:4 Human Rights Law Review 611 at 644–645.

Prevention and Punishment of the Crime of Genocide;[6] I would argue that they were in a way one of the means of the reworking of trauma of World Wars I and II and their aftermaths by the international society, which ultimately cemented the human rights role as "a locational discourse for reviewing past injustice."[7]

Also today, in the 21st century, "effective rights depend on shared memories":[8] without the memory of past grievances, human rights law would be "in danger of losing historical grounding and risks legalistic abstraction and political abuse."[9] It is the existence of certain global collective trauma-memories, the concepts of which I analysed in Chapter 1, including in particular those of the Holocaust and the destruction of Hiroshima and Nagasaki, and their aforementioned decontextualisation through globalisation, that nurtures "the future of human rights in the world,"[10] creating a "global cultural 'memory imperative'" of which human rights are an expression,[11] as they "matter only to the extent that their universality is recognised."[12] Only when the "historical specificity and context" of a particular infraction are pushed "beyond national confinement"[13] can the collective memories born out of them serve as a legitimisation for human rights law.[14]

In turn, with regard to the indirect intersections of human rights law and collective memory, the function of trials is key to their understanding. Their role in general as "sites of memory production,"[15] which may provide long-lasting effects on collective memory,[16] has already been remarked upon by Durkheim, as I noted in the previous chapter. Today, this function is particularly visible on the national level in trials regarding human rights abuses, with the "global spread of the language of human rights," resulting in a

6 Andreas Huyssen, "International Human Rights and the Politics of Memory: Limits and Challenges" (2011) 53:4 Criticism 607 at 608.

7 Kalliopi Chainoglou, Barry Collins, Michael Phillips, and John Strawson, "Introduction: Injustice, Memory and Faith in Human Rights" in Kalliopi Chainoglou, Barry Collins, Michael Phillips, and John Strawson (eds), *Injustice, Memory and Faith in Human Rights* (Oxon/New York, NY: Routledge, 2018) 1 at 1.

8 Tilly, *supra* note 2 at 244.

9 Huyssen, *supra* note 1 at 28.

10 Huyssen, *supra* note 1 at 28.

11 Daniel Levy and Natan Sznaider, *Human Rights and Memory* (University Park, PA: Pennsylvania State University Press, 2010) at 4.

12 *Ibid.* at 14.

13 Huyssen, *supra* note 1 at 38.

14 Huyssen, *supra* note 6 at 614.

15 Joachim J. Savelsberg, "Tribunals, Collective Memory, and Prospects of Human Rights" in Werner Gephart, Jürgen Brokoff, Andrea Schütte, and Jan Christoph Suntrup (eds), *Tribunale* (Frankfurt am Main: Klostermann, 2013) 117 at 118.

16 Dario R. Paez and James Hou-Fu Liu, "Collective Memory of Conflicts" in Daniel Bar-Tal (ed.), *Intergroup Conflicts and Their Resolution: A Social Psychological Perspective* (New York, NY/Hove: Psychology Press, 2011) 105 at 110.

"growing number of nations addressing their respective past wrongdoings,"[17] not only through trials but also through various legal institutions of memory introduced in the following chapter. Overall, a legal engagement with human rights infractions has become "a central factor for [the] legitimate standing in the international community and increasingly also a domestic source of legitimacy,"[18] thus allowing human rights law to "cut against its own grain and construct legal spaces for the expression of collective memory."[19]

Trials concerning human rights infractions are particularly challenging because, to paraphrase Osiel, in their instances, human rights law has other than traditional objectives,[20] with the potential for changing collective memory taking centre stage. Through these trials, the legal system has the possibility to construct "collective memories of injustice as a basis for redress," as well as to "shake or salve" "the psyche of a people," being able to use collective memory both regressively and progressively[21] to achieve its goals, potentially leading to reconciliation, in turn one of the goals of transitional justice, analysed further in this chapter.

Importantly, during such trials, global trauma-memories come into play once again: since making decisions regarding human rights abuses "involves a certain level of abstraction," it is only with such memories that the transitory processes may "attain their transnational power of affect and mobilisation beyond the communities of the victims themselves"[22] and avoid "slipping too quickly into ahistorical abstraction."[23] Despite their different trajectories, this represents a major similarity between the direct and indirect intersections of human rights law and collective memory: both rely on and refer to global collective memories throughout their processes.

Importantly, whether a trial will have an impact on collective memory depends on the trial's actors' willingness to go beyond the "narrow, lawyerly approach" of simply determining facts and using them to prove which rights were violated – in order to be collective memory-changing, human rights abuse trials need to also take into account the present and past collective memories of each group in question.[24]

17 Misztal, *supra* note 3 at 62.
18 Levy and Sznaider, *supra* note 11 at 19.
19 Patrick Macklem, "Rybná 9, Praha 1: Restitution and Memory in International Human Rights Law" (2005) 16:1 The European Journal of International Law 1 at 13.
20 Mark Osiel, *Mass Atrocity, Collective Memory, and the Law* (Oxon/New York, NY: Routledge, 2017) at 2.
21 Sharon K. Hom and Eric K. Yamamoto, "Collective Memory, History, and Social Justice" (2000) 47 UCLA Law Review 1747 at 1764.
22 Huyssen, *supra* note 1 at 36.
23 Huyssen, *supra* note 4 at 617.
24 Hom and Yamamoto, *supra* note 21 at 1764.

This, in turn, may only be achieved thanks to the role played by other, non-judicial parties – agents of memory. As it has been noted, "the active prosecution of human rights violations in the courts also depends on the strength of memory discourses in the public sphere: in journalism, films, media, literature, the arts, education, and even urban graffiti."[25] However, the role of human rights activists and organisations goes far beyond that of motivating trials: as "credible local or in-group leaders," they may have greater success in ensuring a society's coming to terms with its own past than external actors.[26] It is through their "memory work" that they can shape "the ways in which ordinary people make sense of human rights violations,"[27] often "forcefully" introducing certain issues that otherwise would have been collectively forgotten into the social debate.[28] Ultimately, not only "the law under which the trials are held" but also their "social context" has a major impact on what becomes a part of collective memory following a prosecution.[29]

The results of human rights law and collective memory's intersections (such as the aftermath of trials) have been noted to positively affect the level of respect for human rights in a society's future, as well as the stability of democratic regimes. Nevertheless, they are governed by the singular "institutional logic of the judicial world," which means that certain groups have easier access to legal protection, that certain violations of human rights are more "compatible" with the legal language than others, and that certain categories of victims and perpetrators fit the already existing categories in law more than others[30] – thus, their potential for influencing collective memories of the whole society is greater. To fully understand the peculiarity of these processes and what has been done to counteract law's "logic" on a global level, another, interconnected perspective on the intersections between law and collective memory needs to be investigated: within the realm of international law.

Memory and International Law: From Everyday to Extraordinary Intersections

Collective memory and international law have a particular relationship: on the one hand, just as in the case of human rights law, to which it is also

25 Huyssen, *supra* note 1 at 32.
26 Paez and Liu, *supra* note 16 at 119.
27 Barbara Sutton, "Collective Memory and the Language of Human Rights: Attitudes toward Torture in Contemporary Argentina" (2015) 42:3 Latin American Perspectives 73 at 88.
28 See, e.g., Zvika Orra and Daphna Golan, "Human Rights NGOs in Israel: Collective Memory and Denial" (2014) 18:1 The International Journal of Human Rights 68.
29 Savelsberg, *supra* note 15 at 122.
30 Joachim J. Savelsberg, "Violações de direitos humanos, lei e memória coletiva" ["Human Rights Violations, Law, and Collective Memory"] (2007) 19:2 Tempo Social, revista de sociologia da USP 14 at 32.

linked,[31] they intersect in cases of extreme violations of law, with international law aiming to do what domestic jurisdictions cannot or will not do. These instances of intersections, while particularly memorable and thus having an unusually strong impact on collective memories, both in the affected societies and globally, take place only from time to time – which is why I propose distinguishing them as extraordinary intersections. On the other hand, the day-to-day workings of international law do not include major conflicts and crimes but still involve interactions with collective memory – hence their designation as everyday intersections.

With regard to the latter, the everyday relations between international law and collective memory take place on a number of levels, with both implicit and explicit references. While not occurring as often as their implicit counterparts, some of the everyday intersections of international law and collective memory are explicit; for example, the international cultural heritage protection legal framework, based on, among other elements, heritage's inherent relationship with collective memory, or internationally designated days of remembrance, such as Holocaust Remembrance Day.[32]

The more common implicit intersections involve, among others, collective memories influencing "the interpretation of international treaties,"[33] with various mechanisms of international law acting as carriers of memory among expert groups with regard to some of the "principles of international customary law."[34] Additionally, as in the case of memory and human rights law intersections, a number of international law institutions, including the United Nations and the International Criminal Court, were created in response to the collective memories of past atrocities.[35]

Importantly, major "treaties or international institutions' resolutions" may themselves become a part of collective memories, particularly when relating to a group's recognition or "concerning some major international conflicts."[36] For example, the November 11, 1918, armistice is remembered in collective memory as the end of a four-year conflict in some countries and as the beginning of independence in others.

31 Peter D. Rush, "Dirty War Crimes: Jurisdictions of Memory and International Criminal Law" in Kevin Jon Heller and Gerry Simpson (eds), *The Hidden Histories of War Crimes Trials* (Oxford: Oxford University Press, 2013) 367 at 383.

32 Moshe Hirsch, *Invitation to the Sociology of International Law* (Oxford: Oxford University Press, 2015) at 55–56.

33 *Ibid.* at 58.

34 *Ibid.* at 48.

35 Eric Langenbacher, "Collective Memory as a Factor in Political Culture and International Relations" in Eric Langenbacher and Yossi Shain (eds), *Power and the Past: Collective Memory and International Relations* (Washington, DC: Georgetown University Press, 2010) 13 at 19.

36 Hirsch, *supra* note 32 at 53–54.

International law and collective memory also intersect implicitly in those instances that I introduced in the previous chapter, remarking on Bergson's theory of memory: when "images frozen within collective memory formulate strong messages" connecting past events to present ones, at the same time linking past images with present-day "knowledge and perception" of an interpreter,[37] whole countries' "positions and conduct regarding implementation of international legal rules"[38] may be affected, potentially leading to "the formation of intermediate doctrines that affected international law."[39]

Examples of such cases include: Germany, in terms of both its fiscal policy, which is heavily influenced by the memory of 1920s hyperinflation, with a notable impact on the EU response to the 2010s eurozone crisis,[40] and its foreign policy, which, whether during the Bonn or Berlin periods continues to be under the influence of collective memories of World War II, used to provide an often contradictory basis for the country's stance on military interventions;[41] Argentina, where collective memories of foreign interventions and the Calvo Doctrine born in their wake motivated the country's unwelcoming stance towards the ICSID tribunals in the 2007–2013 period;[42] the United States, whose trade policy continues to be influenced by collective memories of past trade wars, most notably with Japan in the 1980s;[43] or Europe, the regional identity of which has its basis in the collective memory of the Holocaust[44] becoming, to a certain degree, frozen and during the Cold War.[45] While these examples may be considered "limit cases for the impact of collective memory," as it has been noticed, collective memory to some degree influences the foreign policy of each country and region[46] – and thus also international law.

In turn, extraordinary intersections of collective memory involve trials, which, as in the case of human rights law and indirect intersections with collective memory, stem from their Durkheimian role as rituals. There are a number of significant disparities, however, between domestic human rights

37 Sungjoon Cho, "The Undead Past: How Collective Memory Configures Trade Wars" (2021) 95:3 Tulane Law Review 487 at 491–492.

38 Hirsch, *supra* note 32 at 58.

39 Hirsch, *supra* note 32 at 48–49.

40 Hirsch, *supra* note 32 at 64–73; see also: Patrick O'Callaghan, "Collective Memory in Law and Policy: The Problem of the Sovereign Debt Crisis" (2012) 32:4 Legal Studies 642 at 657.

41 Ruth Wittlinger and Martin Larose, "No Future for Germany's Past? Collective Memory and German Foreign Policy" (2007) 16:4 German Politics 481 at 492–493.

42 Hirsch, *supra* note 32 at 73–89.

43 Cho, *supra* note 37 at 498–513.

44 Henning Grunwald, "Genocide Memorialization and the Europeanization of Europe" in Christian Karner and Bram Mertens (eds), *The Use and Abuse of Memory: Interpreting World War II in Contemporary European Politics* (Milton: Taylor and Francis, 2017) 23 at 25–26.

45 *Ibid.* at 36.

46 Langenbacher, *supra* note 35 at 15.

trials and trials involving international institutions that aim to rectify the aforementioned shortcomings of domestic legal systems, given that the former "[operate] in existing domestic constellations" and the latter "typically [actualise] in a broader context of condemning the past and reorienting for the future."[47] While the particularities of the international tribunals' inner workings with regard to collective memory will be analysed in Part II of the book, those differences need to be highlighted here.

The first major difference relates to the question of the classification of the crime: trials involving international institutions are reserved for major atrocities, those affecting the whole of humanity, which then has an obligation to act "against the unpresentability"[48] of war crimes, crimes against humanity, ethnic cleansing, and the crime of genocide.[49] These trials' aim is the pursuit of "chief violators," discouraging "potential offenders"[50] and acknowledging the victims of these crimes,[51] as well as creating "a space for the airing of personal and collective memories of . . . terror and trauma."[52]

It also needs to be noted that these crimes themselves have a particular relationship with collective memory: for them to be committed, various narratives about the past need to be consolidated[53] and mobilised. Since they are also particularly powerful creators of collective trauma-memories, similar mechanisms govern both their commemoration[54] and persecution[55] of their perpetrators. They never "belong to the past but are, on the contrary, extremely current," continuously influencing global society.[56] Importantly, the judicial recognition of any crime of international law "constructs an object,"[57] a carrier of memory," a particularly strong one in regard to

47 Immi Tallgren, "The Finnish War-Responsibility Trial in 1945–6: The Limits of Ad Hoc Criminal Justice?" in Kevin Jon Heller and Gerry Simpson (eds), *The Hidden Histories of War Crimes Trials* (Oxford: Oxford University Press, 2013) 430 at 448.

48 Rush, *supra* note 31 at 380.

49 David Hirsch, *Law Against Genocide: Cosmopolitan Trials* (London: GlassHouse Press, 2003) at xiii.

50 Thijs B. Bouwknegt, "Unravelling Atrocity Between Transitional Justice and History in Rwanda and Sierra Leone" in Uğur Ümit Üngör (ed.), *Genocide: New Perspectives on Its Causes, Courses, and Consequences* (Amsterdam: Amsterdam University Press, 2016) 219 at 222.

51 Caroline Fournet, *The Crime of Destruction and the Law of Genocide: Their Impact on Collective Memory* (Aldershot/Burlington, VT: Ashgate, 2007) at 125.

52 Nicola Henry, *War and Rape: Law, Memory and Justice* (Oxon/New York, NY: Routledge, 2011) at 2.

53 Hirsch, *supra* note 49 at 141.

54 Dan Stone, *The Holocaust, Fascism and Memory: Essays in the History of Ideas* (Houndmills: Macmillan, 2013) at 143.

55 *Ibid.* at 154.

56 Fournet, *supra* note 51 at xxx.

57 Kirsten Campbell, "The Laws of Memory: The ICTY, the Archive, and Transitional Justice" (2012) 22:2 Social and Legal Studies 247 at 254.

genocide, which, contrary to other classifications including crimes against humanity, grants its collective memories a unique level of notoriety, making them particularly resistant to diminishment or fading into oblivion.[58]

The second difference is related to the question of jurisdiction, as the institutions of international law are strictly limited both externally and internally. Most often they can take action only if so agreed upon by the state parties and/or the international community and ensuring due process[59] – as a result, "significant historical events are often not addressed by" them,[60] with, for example, Rwanda becoming "a synonym for a tropical version of the Holocaust"[61] thanks to the work of the International Criminal Tribunal for Rwanda (ICTR), while a number of other large-scale atrocities slide into oblivion due to the lack of persecution, granting a "*de facto* forgiveness for the crimes perpetrated."[62] At the same time, as they are increasingly aware of their role in creating collective memories, international bodies' selection of cases may be "affected by the goal of ensuring that the historical narrative emerging from the tribunal's case law will present the various aspects of the event."[63]

This is directly connected to the third difference: compared to domestic courts, international institutions "are less influenced by the distorting narratives of national identity,"[64] as global-scale "atrocities no longer have nationalities."[65] The evidence presented during such trials is obviously "strongly coloured" by a group's collective memories; however, their "output aims to be free from national particularity," with the goal of creating global collective memories.[66] Importantly, these collective memories "may be pitted against" some of the collective memories of local communities,[67] who may regard themselves as victims and not perpetrators, for example. In order to "realign" them, some of the international law's institutions have even begun establishing special "legacy officers" in the aftermath of trials,

58 Fournet, *supra* note 51 at 134–136.

59 Mark J. Osiel, "Why Prosecute? Critics of Punishment for Mass Atrocity" (2000) 22:1 Human Rights Quarterly 118 at 132.

60 Hirsch, *supra* note 32 at 57.

61 René Lemarchand, *Forgotten Genocides: Oblivion, Denial, and Memory* (Philadelphia, PA: University of Pennsylvania Press, 2016) at vii.

62 Fournet, *supra* note 51 at xxxii.

63 Hirsch, *supra* note 32 at 54–55.

64 Nena Tromp, "Understanding the Milošević Case: Legacy of an Unfinished Trial" in H. G. van der Wilt, J. Vervliet, G. K. Sluiter, and J. Th. M. Houwink ten Cate (eds), *The Genocide Convention The Legacy of 60 Years* (Leiden/Boston, MA: Martinus Nijhoff, 2012) 27 at 31.

65 Bouwknegt, *supra* note 50 at 221.

66 Hirsch, *supra* note 49 xix.

67 Mary J. Gallant and Harry M. Rhea, "Collective Memory, International Law, and Restorative Social Processes After Conflagration: The Holocaust" (2010) 20:3 International Criminal Justice Review 265 at 272.

aiming to extend their "didactic and historical reach,"[68] or ordering particular reparations,[69] thus acknowledging their bond with collective memory.

Last, without trials conducted by institutions of international law, "the emergence of the collective memory of the crime [is] greatly impeded,"[70] particularly in regard to global collective memories and creating a narrative close to the historical truth. While they are not "the only vector for memory," they play a key role in its construction,[71] at times becoming a major part of collective memories of the events in question[72] – for example, the International Criminal Tribunal for the former Yugoslavia (ICTY) being part of the narratives of the war in the Balkans – which in turn may also lead to the appearance of a universal recognition of the magnitude of certain crimes, such as rape.[73]

The extraordinary intersections of international law and collective memory not only produce powerful narratives of the past but also may begin the process of reconciliation,[74] preventing "a cycle of condemnation, blame and renewed violence"[75] from taking place in their absence and providing "resources for working through unsettled history."[76] This role closely relates to the question of transitional justice, which is the focus of the next section.

Transitional Justice and the Big Absent: Collective Memory

Transitional justice is a set of socio-legal processes that follow and are intrinsically linked to the processes surrounding transitions from one political regime to the next. These processes, among other things, involve a need for some kind of a response towards the recent difficult past, whereby transitional justice mechanisms come into play. Thus, transitional justice, influenced by both human rights and international law, is organically linked to collective memory. However, their relationship is fraught and often remains unacknowledged or not taken properly into account by those in charge of putting the transitional justice processes into motion, which in turn diminishes their effectiveness – as this section will demonstrate, also proposing responses towards their betterment.

68 Henry, *supra* note 52 at 10.

69 See, e.g., Mirosław M. Sadowski, "Heritage Strikes Back: The Al Mahdi Case, ICC's Policy on Cultural Heritage and the Pushing of Law's Boundaries" (2022) 2 Undecidabilities and Law – The Coimbra Journal for Legal Studies 99.

70 Fournet, *supra* note 51 at xxxii.

71 Fournet, *supra* note 51 at 127.

72 Henry, *supra* note 52 at 19.

73 Sara De Vido, "Collective Memory of Rape: An Analysis from an International Law Perspective" (2016) 3 Sociologia del diritto 101 at 126.

74 Henry, *supra* note 52 at 26.

75 Gallant and Rhea, *supra* note 67 at 273.

76 Rush, *supra* note 31 at 384.

Transitional Justice – What's in a Name?

First, however, to better understand its inner workings, I propose to focus more closely on the question of transitional justice itself. Laying on four foundations – truth, justice, reparation, and guarantees of non-recurrence[77] – it has been defined as "a set of measures and processes,"[78] whether formal or informal, which are "implemented by a group or institution of accepted legitimacy around the time of a transition"[79] following "regime changes, violent conflicts, wars, and other historical injustices"[80] to identify and realise "the necessary ideal and practical interventions required in post-conflict situations, while operating in the most challenging circumstances,"[81] with the main aim of rendering "justice to perpetrators and their collaborators, as well as to their victims."[82]

In addition, four main goals of transitional justice may be distinguished: two intermediate ones – recognition, i.e., the establishment of truth regarding the crimes and victims of the previous regime,[83] and civic trust, i.e., attaining a certain level of support for the new authorities;[84] and two ultimate ones – reconciliation, i.e., the integration of various parts of society as one community,[85] and democracy, i.e., a system with the rule of law,[86] which allows us to "institutionalise revenge and deter future wrongdoing."[87]

To achieve these goals, different mechanisms have been employed throughout the years, "used and adapted around the world in varying contexts,"[88]

77 Ariel Dulitzky, "Memory, an Essential Element of Transitional Justice" (2014) 20 Peace in Progress 45 at 45.
78 Roman David, "What We Know About Transitional Justice: Survey and Experimental Evidence" (2017) 38:1 Advances in Political Psychology 151 at 151.
79 Marek M. Kaminski, Monika Nalepa, and Barry O'Neill, "Normative and Strategic Aspects of Transitional Justice" (2006) 50:3 Journal of Conflict Resolution 295 at 295.
80 David, *supra* note 78 at 151.
81 Giada Girelli, *Understanding Transitional Justice: A Struggle for Peace, Reconciliation, and Rebuilding* (Cham: Palgrave Macmillan, 2017) at 3.
82 Kaminski, Nalepa and O'Neill, *supra* note 79 at 295.
83 Pablo de Greiff, "Theorizing Transitional Justice" in Melissa S. Williams, Rosemary Nagy, and Jon Elster (eds), *Transitional Justice NOMOS LI* (New York, NY: New York University Press, 2012) 31 at 42–44.
84 *Ibid.* at 44–48.
85 de Greiff, *supra* note 83 at 48–52.
86 de Greiff, *supra* note 83 at 52–58.
87 Samar El-Masri, Tammy Lambert, and Joanna R. Quinn, "Changing the Context: Can Conditions Be Created That Are More Conducive to Transitional Justice Success?" in Samar El-Masri, Tammy Lambert, and Joanna R. Quinn (eds), *Transitional Justice in Comparative Perspective* (Cham: Palgrave Macmillan, 2020) 1 at 3.
88 Yifat Gutman, Amy Sodaro, and Adam D. Brown, "Introduction: Memory and the Future: Why a Change of Focus Is Necessary" in Yifat Gutman, Adam D. Brown, and Amy Sodaro (eds), *Memory and the Future Transnational Politics, Ethics and Society* (Houndmills/New York, NY: Palgrave Macmillan, 2010) 1 at 3.

from the aforementioned trials, be they domestic or international, to amnesty and collective forgetting, to reparations, lustration, and truth (and reconciliation) commissions, to various memorialisation practices[89] – all in hopes of allowing the society to work through its collective trauma-memories, which is linked to Prager's concept of social redress introduced in the first chapter. Since they may also be used in non-transitional contexts, I will provide their detailed analysis in Part II of the book, investigating them as legal institutions of memory.

Leaving the peculiarities of their inner workings aside, it needs to be noted here that the processes of transitional justice can be divided either historically or according to their character. Looking into the former distinction, putting the early endeavours at transitional justice – its "prehistory" dating back to ancient Athens,[90] a case that I analyse in Part II of the book in the context of legal amnesia – aside, it could be said that, similar to human rights law, transitional justice is the product of the horrors of the first half of the 20th century, with the first attempts at its realisation on a major scale taking place with the convening of the Nuremberg trials.[91] Its three contemporary – and more "conscious" with regard to their extrajudicial role – phases, however, encompass (1) the period of "the waning dictatorships" between the 1970s and early 1990s, focusing on reconciliation after an oppressive regime; (2) the period of "the ethnic identity conflicts," focusing on reconciliation after attempts at ethnic cleansing in the 1990s; and (3) the period of a certain dichotomy: a growing lack of faith towards reconciliatory processes after 9/11[92] and the ambiguous transitions (e.g., the Arab Spring) that followed,[93] coinciding with the institutionalisation of the mechanisms of transitional justice[94] and the beginning of work by the International Criminal Court (ICC).[95] I would argue, however, that the 21st century also brought a fourth phase of the transitional justice processes, one that sees a certain return to the questions of justice in post-transitional societies (the "post-transition reckoning"[96]), as well as a turn towards it in societies that did not undergo a major transition. The peculiarities of this fourth phase will be analysed in the case studies in the following parts of the book.

89 El-Masri, Lambert, and Quinn, *supra* note 87 at 4.

90 Michał Krotoszyński, *Modele sprawiedliwości tranzycyjnej* [*Models of Transitional Justice*] (Poznań: Wydawnictwo Naukowe UAM, 2017) at 36–39.

91 Girelli, *supra* note 81 at 293.

92 Pierre Hazan, *Judging War, Judging History: Behind Truth and Reconciliation* (Stanford, CA: Stanford University Press, 2010) at 29–30.

93 Krotoszyński, *supra* note 90 at 40.

94 Hazan, *supra* note 92 at 29–30.

95 Hazan, *supra* note 92 at 42.

96 Stephanie R. Golob, "Volver: The Return of/to Transitional Justice Politics in Spain" (2008) 9:2 Journal of Spanish Cultural Studies 127 at 128.

With regard to the question of their characteristic, several different classifications have been distinguished, dividing the processes of transitional justice into endogenous (coming from the society itself) and exogenous (motivated by outside forces);[97] formal (legal) and informal processes (linked to symbolic measures of coming to terms with the past); tangible (with visible effects, e.g., prosecutions) and intangible (with shifts in the collective memory);[98] retributive (e.g., trials), reconciliatory (e.g., reparations), revelatory (e.g., truth [and reconciliation] commissions and lustration) and reparatory processes (e.g., the different attempts at redressing the oppressive past).[99] In most cases, however, transitional justice processes cannot be easily classified: during the same transition, some of them may take place informally on the national level, with formal ones happening internationally; while different mechanisms can take on several functions, for example, truth (and reconciliation) commissions, which play reconciliatory, reparatory, and revelatory roles at the same time. Importantly, intersections with collective memory always follow transitional justice processes, as analysed next.

Before moving to this question, however, I need to stress that the concept of transitional justice is not without its issues. When employed in unstable political regimes, for example, not fully democratic ones or without an established rule of law and respect for human rights, its processes are "less likely to work efficiently," first requiring changes in the level of civic trust,[100] which, along with democracy, is in turn one of the goals of transitional justice, as noted earlier. Thus, the application of transitional justice in practice may lead to a certain conundrum: while "only a democratic state can guarantee truth and justice, only truth and justice can sustain a democratic state."[101]

Even if used in contexts of more established democracies, where such vicious circles are absent, transitional justice processes tend to create "commitments that will likely remain unfulfilled in the immediate period of transition,"[102] particularly with regard to the question of reconciliation. As I remarked upon in the previous chapter, Levinas may provide us with certain insights into this matter, having noted that reconciliation will fail unless its processes will move beyond simple acknowledgements of the oppression. Given that large-scale reckoning with the past within a society is not possible immediately following a transition, as states are trying to focus on stability – and the "successor elites may be put off by the many delicate and explosive

97 Kaminski, Nalepa and O'Neill, *supra* note 79 at 295–296.
98 David, *supra* note 78 at 153.
99 David, *supra* note 78 at 154.
100 El-Masri, Lambert and Quinn, *supra* note 87 at 8–9.
101 Mark Arenhövel, "Democratization and Transitional Justice" (2008) 15:3 Democratisation 570 at 581.
102 de Greiff, *supra* note 83 at 65.

aspects of such [an] assignment"[103] – ultimately, reconciliation may become a self-fulfilling promise in its own right, not truly based on the prosecution of former oppressors and the admission of truth about past events, but rather a basis for the new democratic order, which cannot become unravelled by the quest for justice. This use of the aforementioned policy of prescriptive forgetting, while useful for the new authorities, may result in a disjunction of priorities between "those who have to live with their neighbours" and the transitional justice mechanisms,[104] limited by due process.[105]

This impossibility of "striking a delicate balance between essential but seemingly irreconcilable goals,"[106] as well as between the "actors and needs, operating in contexts where everything is urgently needed, and nothing is easy to achieve"[107] and law's own internal limitations,[108] pushing the authorities towards choosing what is pragmatic,[109] and the resulting politicisation of the whole process, often lead to frustration among large parts of the post-transitory society. This sentiment is expressed particularly well by a former GDR oppositionist, Bärbel Bohley, who, following the lack of large-scale prosecutions of the various actors of the former regime in the unified Germany, underlined "the gap between the politico-juridical and the moral dimension"[110] of transitions, proclaiming that "we wanted justice and got the rule of law."[111] As will be noted in greater detail, while bringing short-term stability, these unresolved questions will continue to haunt societies for long periods of time, showing that in most cases, transitional justice processes "do not appear any more successful . . . than retributive justice."[112]

103 Luc Huyse, "Justice After Transition: On the Choices Successor Elites Make in Dealing with the Past" (1995) 20:1 Law and Social Inquiry 51 at 64.

104 Rosalind Shaw and Lars Waldorf, "Introduction: Localizing Transitional Justice" in Rosalind Shaw, Lars Waldorf, and Pierre Hazan (eds), *Localizing Transitional Justice: Interventions and Priorities After Mass Violence* (Stanford, CA: Stanford University Press, 2010) 3 at 11.

105 Alexandra Barahona de Brito, Carmen González-Enríquez, and Paloma Aguilar, "Introduction" in Alexandra Barahona de Brito, Carmen González-Enríquez, and Paloma Aguilar (eds), *The Politics of Memory and Democratization* (Oxford: Oxford University Press, 2001) 1 at 27.

106 Girelli, *supra* note 81 at 4.

107 Girelli, *supra* note 81 at 293.

108 Adam Czarnota, "Między polityką a prawem, czyli o sprawiedliwości okresu przejściowego" ["Between Politics and Law, or About Transitional Justice"] (2015) 27 Acta UnIversitatis Lodziensis. Folia Philosophica. Ethica Aesthetica Practica 13 at 21.

109 Osiel, *supra* note 59 at 147.

110 Arenhövel, *supra* note 101 at 580.

111 Roderick Guemm Galam, " 'We Wanted Justice and Got the Rule of Law': Literary Representations of the State, the Rule of Law and Urban Squatting" (2003) 77:4 Philippine Law Journal 476 at 477.

112 Lars Waldorf, "Mass Justice for Mass Atrocity: Rethinking Local Justice as Transitional Justice" (2006) 79:1 Temple Law Review 1 at 16–17.

Disillusionment aside, it also needs to be noted that transitional justice is an inherently Western concept,[113] which may be imposed on societies following a transition "by other states or international organisations."[114] As a result, it is often "marked by disconnections between international legal norms and local priorities and practices,"[115] and thus less effective, particularly in those communities whereby collective forgetting may take precedence over remembering,[116] when the transition in question was not to a liberal system,[117] or in societies that have negative experiences with democracy.[118] Additionally, in cases where international law steps in, moving a trial to a foreign court may undermine its legitimacy, as it becomes removed from the contexts within which its "target public" operates.[119]

Finally, another major issue concerning transitional justice processes – one of particular interest for my investigations – is the absence of consciousness regarding collective memory, the taking of the zeitgeist,[120] and the social reality whereby they are taking place for granted,[121] which is one of the main reasons behind the problems transitional justice faces noted above. In the next subsection, I will take a closer look into the intersections between the two.

Transitional Justice and Collective Memory

In regard to the relationship between transitional justice and collective memory, the two are extremely close, as "the fundament of any justice with regards to the past . . . is the memory about it," which means that collective memory "plays a major role . . . in the building of the basis of new normativity"[122] following a transition. From this perspective, transitional justice has been

113 Hazan, *supra* note 92 at 48.
114 Arenhövel, *supra* note 101 at 578.
115 Shaw and Waldorf, *supra* note 104 at 3.
116 Galina Nelaeva and Natalia Sidorova, "Transitional Justice in South Africa and Brazil: Introducing a Gendered Approach to Reconciliation" (2019) VI:2 BRICS Law Journal 82 at 99.
117 Thomas O. Hansen, "Transitional Justice: Toward a Differentiated Theory" (2011) 13 Oregon Review of International Law 1 at 41.
118 Barahona de Brito, González-Enríquez and Aguilar, *supra* note 105 at 17.
119 Ivor Sokolić, *International Courts and Mass Atrocity Narratives of War and Justice in Croatia* (Cham: Palgrave Macmillan, 2018) at 30.
120 Nanci Adler, "Conclusion" in Alexandra Barahona de Brito, Carmen González-Enríquez, and Paloma Aguilar (eds), *The Politics of Memory and Democratization* (Oxford: Oxford University Press, 2001) 303 at 307.
121 Nanci Adler, "Introduction: On History, Historians, and Transitional Justice" in Nanci Adler (ed.), *Understanding the Age of Transitional Justice: Crimes, Courts, Commissions and Chronicling* (New Brunswick, NJ: Rutgers University Press, 2018) 1 at 7.
122 Czarnota, *supra* note 108 at 28.

described as a "disjuncture" in the "cycles of social memory-making,"[123] a "contest over history and memory, in which past events are reconstructed and reinterpreted according to current events and needs."[124] These processes are directly linked to the power shift taking place within a society during a transition,[125] with their changes also impacting its memory narratives.[126] To build on the earlier analysis of Foucault's thought, along with transitional processes, a certain inversion of counter-memories takes place: as transitional justice brings the former counter-memories to the forefront of a society's collective memory, the previous one becomes counter-memory itself[127] (in certain instances still potent should the members of a previous regime retain some level of influence[128]), with former victims turned into the agents of transitional justice[129] – and thus agents of memory. Moreover, following the earlier established patterns of passing on collective-trauma memories to future generations, it needs to be noted that transitional justice may amplify these processes through its mechanisms, providing "a space where" even the people "who did not live through trauma come to identify strongly with it," thus allowing them "to continue the struggle to mete out justice, speak the truth, memorialise victims and build a better society."[130] These actions may motivate the aforementioned fourth phase of transitional justice processes.

At the same time, collective memories are "employed to grant legitimacy"[131] to transitional justice processes and used in the establishment of the truth through the remembering and rectifying of "historical injustice," which is in turn recognised as one of the goals of transitional justice.[132] It is also through collective memories that certain "crimes in the collective past" come to light

123 Alexandra Barahona de Brito, "Transitional Justice and Memory: Exploring Perspectives" (2010) 15:3 South European Society and Politics 359 at 364.
124 Astrid Bothman, *Transitional Justice in Nicaragua 1990–2012: Drawing a Line Under the Past* (Wiesbaden: Springer Fachmedien Wiesbaden, 2015) at 47–48.
125 Francesca Lessa, *Memory and Transitional Justice in Argentina and Uruguay: Against Impunity* (New York, NY: Palgrave Macmillan, 2013) at 21.
126 Peter Manning, *Transitional Justice and Memory in Cambodia: Beyond the Extraordinary Chambers* (Oxon/New York, NY: Routledge, 2017) at 32.
127 For the analysis of this process in practice on the example of Iranian cultural heritage see: Mirosław M. Sadowski and Seyed M. A. Zavarei, "Changing Presents, Shifting Past(s): The Diverse Interests of Transitional Justice and Cultural Heritage in the Case of the Iranian Revolution" (2023) Law and Humanities 1–22.
128 Nora Taha, "Practices of Memory in Transitional Justice: The Construction of a Collective Memory in Tunisia" (2016), online: Global Campus Open Knowledge Repository <repository.gchumanrights.org/handle/20.500.11825/782> at 9.
129 Hazan, *supra* note 92 at 40.
130 Camilla Orjuela, "Passing on the Torch of Memory: Transitional Justice and the Transfer of Diaspora Identity Across Generations" (2020) 14 International Journal of Transitional Justice 360 at 364.
131 Lessa, *supra* note 125 at 22.
132 El-Masri, Lambert and Quinn, *supra* note 87 at 3.

during the transition.[133] However, as Dulitzky notes, collective memory is not recognised as one of the foundations of transitional justice, which means that its questions "are rarely integrated into wider strategies of democracy building and are diluted or made invisible in the transitional justice processes."[134] Invisible, but nonetheless potent – ultimately, it is the collective memories of the pre-transition atrocities that, along with law, lay at the basis of the key belief of transitional justice that the two "can expel – if not mitigate – the violence in divided societies"[135] through the building of "a new 'anamnestic solidarity' . . . based upon the ethical framework circumscribed by both the knowledge of the truth and the official acknowledgement of its history."[136] In contrast, in certain cases, societies may engage in collective forgetting[137] before the transition or create selective collective memories – which are deconstructed and remade throughout the transitional justice processes. This particular *circulus vitiosus* of the relationship between collective memory and transitional justice is demonstrated in Figure 3.1.

Importantly, this lack of a proper acknowledgement of the role collective memory plays during a transition often leads to conflict and negatively influences the newly implemented mechanisms of transitional justice. As collective memories "can work to re-establish solidarities but also to unsettle existing ones" during the time of transition,[138] without their proper and diverse "expression" in the "public domain,"[139] and the reckoning that the society in question was not created by the transition but existed as a community under the previous regime, reconciliation,[140] one of the main goals of transitional justice, cannot take place.

In such situations, to fill in the official vacuum, various collective memories come into play, becoming "a privileged object of 'memory struggles' where diverse actors compete to establish their interpretation of the events of

133 Arenhövel, *supra* note 101 at 571.
134 Dulitzky, *supra* note 77 at 46.
135 Hazan, *supra* note 91 at 30.
136 Vladimir Tismaneanu, "Democracy, Memory, and Moral Justice" in Vladimir Tismaneanu and Bogdan C. Iacob (eds), *Remembrance, History, and Justice: Coming to Terms with Traumatic Pasts in Democratic Societies* (Budapest/New York, NY: Central European University Press, 2015) 145 at 149–150.
137 Janine N. Clark, "Re-Thinking Memory and Transitional Justice: A Novel Application of Ecological Memory" (2021) 14:4 Memory Studies 695 at 699–700.
138 Donatella della Porta, Massimiliano Andretta, Tiago Fernandes, Eduardo Romanos, and Markos Vogiatzoglou, "Memory in Movements: A Preface" in Donatella della Porta, Massimiliano Andretta, Tiago Fernandes, Eduardo Romanos, and Markos Vogiatzoglou (eds), *Legacies and Memories in Movements: Justice and Democracy in Southern Europe* (New York, NY: Oxford University Press, 2018) vii at xi.
139 Hazan, *supra* note 92 at 36.
140 Czarnota, *supra* note 108 at 32–33.

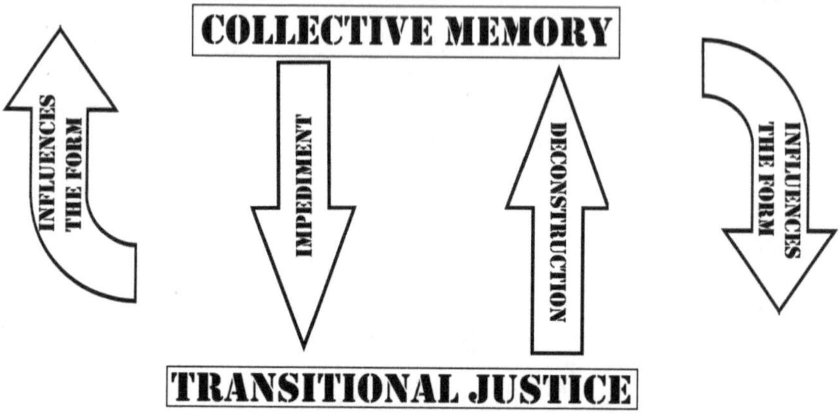

Figure 3.1 The interactions between collective memory and transitional justice
Source: Author.

the past as the prevailing representation,"[141] which in some instances means putting the narratives of the former victims "into competition" with one another.[142] Ultimately, following a transition, only certain collective memories are going to become a part of the official narratives, elevated to this status by the very transitional justice mechanisms that they motivated[143] (see Figure 3.1). Even these narratives, however, will change over time,[144] becoming "eroded and defeated by other constructions of meanings,"[145] because of those collective counter-memories present at the time of transition that remained unacknowledged, as they often prove to be particularly enduring.

If societies, whether as a whole or from the viewpoint of their certain parts, for example minorities, feel that justice did not actually take place following a transition, even in those cases where the mechanisms of transitional justice have been employed, the demands for a proper reckoning with the past will continue – often returning with force years or decades after the original transition took place, as "the passage of time" does "not fully exonerate the ghosts of [the] past."[146] Here, Levinas's theory comes into play once again – as collective memory provides a basis for ethics, the unresolved

141 Eugenia Allier-Montaño and Emilio Crenzel, "Introduction" in Eugenia Allier-Montaño and Emilio Crenzel (eds), *The Struggle for Memory in Latin America Recent History and Political Violence* (New York, NY: Palgrave Macmillan, 2010) 1 at 1.
142 Hazan, *supra* note 92 at 155.
143 Lessa, *supra* note 125 at 22.
144 Lessa, *supra* note 125 at 28.
145 Allier-Montaño and Crenzel, *supra* note 141 at 10.
146 Huyse, *supra* note 103 at 77.

memories of a difficult past may slowly implode the system; hence, calls for retribution will continue until larger-scale remedies are implemented. Several such cases – including, most notably, Brazil and Poland – will be analysed in Part III of this book, examples of the fourth phase of transitional justice.

Yet another dimension of the "invisible" intersections of collective memory and transitional justice needs to be acknowledged, one linked to the presentist concepts of collective memory. In the absence of legal responses to atrocities during the times of an oppressive regime, narratives regarding the crimes of that time become unified, leading to the reshaping of individual memories with collective ones. The collective memory of oppression thus constructed "provides a more complete understanding of the system of violence than individual testimony,"[147] but it also means that "local communities are endeavouring to turn the page of violence and conflict in ways that may contrast distinctly from the official approaches of the state."[148] As such, when transitional justice ultimately arrives in its various forms, the legal proceedings' emphasis on singular witness statements requires a deconstruction of the already established narratives on the side of the former victims (as observed in Figure 3.1), "potentially undoing the healing that has been accomplished through dialogue and community identification," even leading to re-traumatisation,[149] as the former victims become once again alienated from the rest of society.[150] Ultimately, this process of "collective memory's exclusion from the law is akin to forced forgetting and undermines the broader goals of reconciliation and nation-building"[151] following a transition.

To alleviate these negative effects of the striving for justice, several concepts worthy of implementing to ensure more successful processes of transitional justice need to be mentioned: state-sponsored public spaces for the sharing of collective memories;[152] the possibility of presenting community statements on its collective memories by, for example, common interveners during legal proceedings;[153] and the prescription of not only individual but also collective remedies.[154] Such initiatives could further the coming to terms

147 Rachel López, "The (Re)Collection of Memory after Mass Atrocity and the Dilemma for Transitional Justice" (2015) 47 International Law and Politics 799 at 842.

148 Camilo Tamayo Gomez, "Victims' Collective Memory and Transitional Justice in Post-Conflict Colombia: The Case of the March of Light" (2019) 15:2 Memory Studies 376 at 379.

149 Rachel López, "Legalising Collective Remembrance After Mass Atrocities" in S. Elizabeth Bird and Fraser M. Ottanelli (eds), *The Performance of Memory as Transitional Justice* (Cambridge/Antwerp/Portland, OR: Intersentia, 2015) 23 at 23–24.

150 López, *supra* note 147 at 838.

151 López, *supra* note 149 at 37.

152 López, *supra* note 147 at 837–838.

153 López, *supra* note 149 at 38–40.

154 López, *supra* note 147 at 805.

with the past following a transition, allowing not only the former "forefront" victims (political prisoners, for example) to preserve their memories of the oppression as part of a larger narrative, but also giving the same opportunity to other members of the society, who suffered from "everyday" injustice at the hands of the previous regime (through, for example, food, goods, and utilities shortages, prevailing fear of the secret police, etc.).

Last, while in general collective memory remains invisible for transitional justice processes, with regard to their ultimate goal – reconciliation – its role is often noticed, but at the same time abused and consciously politicised, with transitional justice regarded as a potential "mediator between different collective memories."[155] At the same time, given the so-called "memory's economy," which makes plurality of different narratives a burden for a society's transition,[156] in order to achieve the goal of reconciliation processes, 'accommodation' of the diverse collective memories takes place, simplifying and unifying them around "a common horizon."[157] To achieve this, transitional justice mechanisms may "privilege particular types of knowledge and memory," at the same time silencing others,[158] thus turning reconciliation endeavours into symbolic but empty gestures,[159] which do not reflect any major shift among the collective memories of the majority of the group in question. In certain instances, to placate the more vocal counter-memories still present within the post-transition society and to stop the erosion of social stability, attempts at reconciliation through the inclusion of plurality of narratives may appear, taking the form of reparations – also monetary, but in particular symbolic – a legal institution of memory analysed in the following chapter.

In reality, there are no easy solutions for reconciliation, just as "there is no definitive 'closure'"[160] following a transition: memory shifts within a society are years in the making.[161] This is in a way a reflection of how, "as societies move further from their authoritarian past," what becomes the key element of collective memory is not the previous regime's "structure or its harsh everyday reality but rather its persistent collective psychological

155 Chrisje Brants and Katrien Klep, "Transitional Justice: History-Telling, Collective Memory, and the Victim-Witness" (2013) 7:1 International Journal of Conflict and Violence 36 at 38.

156 Emilios Christodoulidis and Scott Veitch, "Reconciliation as Surrender: Configurations of Responsibility and Memory" in François Du Bois and Antje Du Bois-Pedain (eds), *Justice and Reconciliation in Post-Apartheid South Africa* (Cambridge/New York, NY: Cambridge University Press, 2008) 9 at 29–30.

157 *Ibid.* at 10.

158 Clark, *supra* note 137 at 701.

159 Ann Rigney, "Reconciliation and Remembering: (How) Does It Work?" (2012) 5:3 Memory Studies 251 at 253–254.

160 Barahona de Brito, González-Enríquez and Aguilar, *supra* note 105 at 35.

161 Nico Wouters, "Transitional Justice and Memory Development in Europe" in Nico Wouters (ed.), *Transitional Justice and Memory in Europe (1945–2013)* (Cambridge: Intersentia, 2014) 369 at 400–408.

dimension,"[162] in a way another reincarnation of Figure 3.1's vicious circle, with what happened in the years following the transition taking transitional justice's place on the diagram. It is only through the acknowledgement of transitional justice's limitations, the reckoning with the various narratives present at the same time, and the conceptualisation of the right to memory, also analysed later in the book, that the cycle may be broken and a true inclusion of diverse collective memories can take place, potentially leading to reconciliation.

Conclusion: Between Law and Memory

Human rights law, international law, and transitional justice all intersect, with collective memory seemingly at humanity's worst, responding to the violations of law, be that singular, periodical, or enduring. Always acting as their *spiritus movens*, however, collective memory represents a certain promise: on the one hand, it allows societies to remember and grieve when the time is right, giving them the possibility of working through their collective trauma-memories; on the other hand, once again following the Bergsonian cone of memory, it allows societies to put the current difficult experiences into perspective, showing that change is possible in the future, just as better times came to be in the past.

One of the major elements of that promise is the law, which, while never arriving quite on time,[163] gives hope for retribution in the future. It is through the concept of transitional justice, which also includes the various mechanisms of human rights and international law, that this promise comes to truly realise itself in law.

The analysis of transitional justice presented in this chapter, however, points me towards the conclusion that it does not exist *per se*, as a separate entity, being rather used to describe a set of law and collective memory's intersections – intersections *par excellence* (as demonstrated in Figure 3.1) – but still only a set of already pre-existing intersections, one more visible in extreme conditions of a transition. As I will demonstrate in the following chapter, the so-called mechanisms of transitional justice exist in both transitionary and post-transitory situations, which is why I propose to investigate them as general legal institutions of memory instead, allowing their analysis to apply also in situations concerning what I call the fourth phase of transitional justice, taking place in societies that have not seen a formal transition or that have seen it only decades ago and cannot be regarded as

162 Jane L. Curry, "When an Authoritarian State Victimizes the Nation: Transitional Justice, Collective Memory, and Political Divides" (2007) 37:1 International Journal of Sociology 58 at 71.

163 Rush, *supra* note 31 at 380.

being governed by the same rules as those that have just emerged from an oppressive regime.

I would argue that adopting this perspective, focusing less on the contexts of transition and more on the question of collective memory, may liberate us from the "illusion" of the possibility of "locking away the past,"[164] instead providing us with answers as to why the effectiveness of the transitional justice mechanisms on the processes of reconciliation, society's integration or democratisation is debatable – we expect too much of them by granting them a special status and perceiving them differently, separating them from other examples of legal institutions of memory. However, while law and memory's intersections are potent in general, they all function within the already existing social frames, which, on the one hand, may give them only so much influence, and on the other hand, have similar effects whether in transitionary or non-transitional contexts – only taken *ad extremum* in the case of the former.

As such, major trials, for example, project on social perceptions of the past similarly under any social circumstances; truth (and reconciliation) commissions may be convened in societies that have not seen any major shift in perception of its past; public apologies may not reflect the opinions of the society on behalf of which they are made; and international institutions may decide on matters of collective memory that do not pertain to any ongoing transitory processes. The analysis of the specifics of these legal institutions of memory, one attempting to be free from the looming spectre of transitional justice, will thus be continued in the following chapters. Before that, however, I would like to return to the question at the core of this first part of my book: the understanding of collective memory with regard to law.

164 Hazan, *supra* note 92 at 157.

Conclusion to Part I: Law and Collective Memory, Collective Memory and Law

Throughout this first part of the thesis, the term "collective memory" has been used in a number of contexts. I have analysed sociology's proliferation of various approaches towards it, meant to describe every potential phenomenon of memory, philosophy's attempts to fit in collective memory within its various theories without directly engaging with it, and law at the crossroads as to how approach it, both politicising and ignoring it, most often without acknowledging its presence not only when its forces come into play, but even when it would be beneficial for law itself.

Thus, the question remains: what is collective memory with regard to law? Both are social products, both rely on each other in certain instances, and, ultimately, both influence each other on a number of levels, intersecting during local commemorations, in the process of a national reckoning with the past, and in an international courtroom, to name but a few of the many instances analysed in this part.

Elsewhere, I defined collective memory as "a social memory, one which is not created individually, but within a group, with one person having a wide array of collective memories functioning on different levels" and, importantly, potentially "influenced by a number of factors, in particular by governments, both on the local and the national level."[1]

I now propose to fit law into this general definition, taking collective memory from its dark matter-like relation with law[2] to the forefront of their intersections, which in turn allows for a proper inclusion of the individuals and their role in the reception of collective memory, and, following Lavabre,

1 Mirosław M. Sadowski, "City as a Locus of Collective Memory: Streets, Monuments and Human Rights" (2020) 40:1–2 Zeitschrift für Rechtssoziologie – The German Journal of Law and Society 209 at 211.

2 Here I paraphrase Poole's remark on the prerogative power in Hobbesian theory, which, akin to dark matter, while "rarely visible, its residual presence holds together the more prominent and, in the normal course of events, more important stuff of political life." Thomas Poole, "Hobbes on Law and Prerogative" in David Dyzenhaus and Thomas Poole (eds), *Hobbes and the Law* (Cambridge/New York, NY: Cambridge University Press, 2012) 68 at 90.

DOI: 10.4324/9781003461548-6

also to acknowledge the interplay between the objective and the subjective, crucial both for law and collective memory.

Thus, I propose to understand collective memory throughout this book as a social memory. This social memory is not created or established solely individually but within various groups to which one belongs, in particular the local community and the nation, but today also the global society. As such, it is being influenced by those in power in order to further different goals, from social unison to the inclusion of diverse voices into the official narratives, using various means, among which law stands out as a particularly potent one. At the same time, collective memory influences various social products, including law, in a perpetual case of *circulus vitiosus*. To fully understand these mutual influences – or intersections – their new conceptualisation needs to be proposed, which is the focus of the next part of the book.

Part II

The Concept

Framing Law and Memory's Intersections

Introduction to Part II

Part I of the book established a firm theoretical basis for the analysis of law and memory intersections, one stretching from the various sociological ideas that help comprehend the different law and memory processes, through the thoughts of four selected philosophers that provide the much-needed conceptual fundament for the new law and memory framework, to the law and theory analysis of specific concepts established in attempts to approach the question of the relationship between law and memory by other researchers. This culminated in a definition of collective memory from a legal perspective, proposing to perceive it as:

> A social memory. This social memory is not created or established solely individually but within various groups to which one belongs, in particular the local community and the nation, but today also the global society. As such, it is being influenced by those in power in order to further different goals, from social unison to the inclusion of diverse voices into the official narratives, using various means, among which law stands out as a particularly potent one. At the same time, collective memory influences various social products, including law, in a perpetual case of *circulus vitiosus*.

In turn, on the basis of these theoretical deliberations, this part of the book attempts to create a new framework, a new approach to the understanding of the intersections between law and memory. I propose the new framework as based on three elements: (1) the concept of legal institutions of memory, of which I distinguish six, divided into three types, soft – reparations and international institutions, medium – lustration and truth (and reconciliation) commissions, and hard – legal amnesia and memory laws; (2) the understanding of memory politics as having a major impact on the functioning and employment legal institutions of memory; and (3) the introduction of the right to memory as a potential new human right, in an attempt to solve various legal conundrums caused by law and memory's intersections.

DOI: 10.4324/9781003461548-7

Various approaches towards the questions of law and memory intersections have been proposed over the years, with, for example, Adam also putting forward a six-way categorisation of what he called social "strategies" to a collective "grappling" with the political crimes of the past: amnesia, trials and justice, lustration, negotiated restitution, political re-education and truth commissions.[1] While interesting, his proposal not only visibly blurs the lines between the legal, the social, and the political mechanisms and ignores the question of highly influential memory laws, but also remains deeply rooted in 20th-century ways of thinking by including re-education as a viable strategy to solve the issues of the past.

As such, my framework for the understanding of law and memory intersections proposed in this chapter in a way stands alone, not only focusing on purely legal institutions and including all the major instances of law and memory intersections but also departing from the traditional transitional justice approaches, proposing a new path for the studies of the law–memory relationship, one fit for the challenges law faces when dealing with issues concerning collective memory. The new framework, as proposed in this part of the book, will then be put to work in the following practical part of my investigations.

1 Heribert Adam, "Divided Memories: Confronting the Crimes of Previous Regimes" (2000) 118 Telos 87 at 88–89.

Chapter 4

Collective Memory and Law

Three Types of Institutions

Introduction

(Re-)framing law and memory's intersections may seem like a daunting task. On the one hand, the more established concepts venturing to provide their understanding, most notably the transitional justice mechanisms perspective introduced in the previous chapter, are those most often encountered. On the other, the relationship between law and collective memory is much broader than the classical attempts at its comprehension may suggest, not only going beyond the transitional situations but also including processes independent from those that may be implemented during a regime change.

Thus, I propose framing the intersections between law and collective memory through their rereading as legal institutions of memory, i.e., those instances when law's mechanisms, institutions, and/or prestige[1] become carriers of memory, actively influencing society's collective memory, be that on a local, national, or global scale. They are particularly prolific carriers of memory – despite being the means employed by those in power, their operations blur the line between the agents and carriers of memory, akin to the media. As such, I distinguish three types of such institutions, depending on the direct level of law's attempted influence on collective memory: *soft* (including reparations and international tribunals), *medium* (including lustration and truth [and reconciliation] commissions), and *hard* (including legal amnesia and memory legislation). In this chapter, I will provide an analysis of these institutions, showing their particularities and differences, beginning with the least direct ones. For the most part I follow the schema of introducing an institution, analysing its design and goals, reviewing its issues,

1 I understand the concept of law's prestige, or respect for law following Adam Podgórecki, who perceived it as a measurable level of law's authority within the society. See: Adam Podgórecki, *Prestiż prawa* [*Law's Prestige*] (Warsaw: Książka i Wiedza, 1966); Agata Przylepa-Lewak, "Wkład Adama Podgóreckiego w powstanie i rozwój socjologii prawa" ["Adam Podgórecki's Contribution to the Establishment and Development of Sociology of Law"], online: UMCS Digital Library <dlibra.umcs.lublin.pl/Content/31982> at 208–210.

DOI: 10.4324/9781003461548-8

and ultimately shifting the focus to its intersections with collective memory, focusing on its concept, and, in the process, trying to use as few examples as possible to focus only on their idea at this point of the book – with the exception of the case of France introduced in the Prologue employed here to deepen the understanding of memory laws (reread as memory legislation).

Nota bene, there are two major intersections of law and collective memory that I choose to exclude from the concept of legal institutions of memory. One such intersection is trials, with their general links to collective memory already analysed in the previous part of the book, given that, as Durkheim already noted, a trial's influence on collective memory is organic, pertaining to every trial, and as such I would argue it lacks the special connection required for it to be recognised as a legal institution of memory in its own right.[2] The other intersection involves the memory interactions taking place in the cityscape, which, while pertaining to the relationship between administrative law and collective memory, are particularly complex, taking place on a number of levels, related to Nora's idea of *lieux de mémoire* and Foucault's concept of heterotopias, in certain cases involving some of the legal institutions of memory, such as memory legislation, thus requiring a more holistic and detailed approach, which puts them outside of the scope of this book.[3]

Soft Institution I. Law, Memory, and State to Victims Transfers: Reparations

Reparations are the first legal institution of memory that I choose to investigate and historically the oldest, functioning in international law for centuries as an element of peace treaties.[4] In the 20th century, however, the meaning of reparations has evolved, and it is not the classical, international law one, focused on state-to-state transfer of goods,[5] that is of interest to my deliberations. Rather, it is the second meaning, which stems from "a novel international standard that privileges ethical with traditional realpolitik

2 I propose, however, to regard international tribunals as one of the legal institutions of memory, given that their relationship with collective memory goes far beyond the fact of conducting a trial itself, as introduced in the previous part of the book, and analysed further in one of the following sections of this chapter.

3 For my preliminary analysis of said memory interactions within the cityscape, see the aforementioned Mirosław M. Sadowski, "City as a Locus of Collective Memory: Streets, Monuments and Human Rights" (2020) 40:1–2 Zeitschrift für Rechtssoziologie – The German Journal of Law and Society 209.

4 See, e.g., Eugene N. White, "Making the French Pay: The Costs and Consequences of the Napoleonic Reparations" (2001) 5:3 European Review of Economic History 337.

5 Stephen Peté and Max du Plessis, "Reparations for Gross Violations of Human Rights in Context" in Max du Plessis and Stephen Peté (eds), *Repairing the Past? International Perspectives on Reparations for Gross Human Rights Abuses* (Antwerpia/Oxford: Intersentia, 2007) 3 at 11.

considerations"[6] and is influenced by human rights law.[7] This innovative understanding of reparations focuses on the state to victims of mass atrocities transfer of goods, with the state in question not necessarily being a foreign power but in certain instances the nation-state of the victims.[8]

Reparations of this type are directly connected to the question of law and collective memory, as they are attempts at reconciliation and the reworking of collective trauma-memories. As such, they are employed in some cases as one of the mechanisms used during transitionary processes, often perceived by the victims as "the most tangible manifestation of the efforts of the state to remedy the harms they have suffered."[9] It needs to be noted, however, that not all abuses will be met with reparations: while some may be recognised as not "gross" enough,[10] others may have happened too long ago for the reparations to be determined.[11] Such debates are always, however, "intrinsically rooted" in the collective memories of the mass atrocity in question.[12]

In the context of reparations in the sense of a legal institution of memory, researchers often distinguish between material and symbolic reparations, with the former including different forms of compensation, i.e., "payments in either cash or negotiable instruments," as well as various "service packages, which may in turn include provisions for education, health, and housing," and the latter concerning, *inter alia*, "official apologies, rehabilitation, the change of names of public spaces, the establishment of days of commemoration, the creation of museums and parks dedicated to the memory of victims, etc."[13] It has also been noticed that the way both types of reparations act is different: while material reparations address "specific harms," symbolic reparations pertain "to the wrongness of the act itself."[14]

As Moon acutely remarks, however, the distinction between two forms of reparation is not particularly useful in the long run: given their goals analysed in this section, it needs to be stressed that once they are received,

6 Elazar Barkan, *The Guilt of Nations: Restitution and Negotiating Historical Injustices* (New York, NY/London: W. W. Norton & Company, 2000) at 317.
7 Peté and du Plessis, *supra* note 5 at 12.
8 Pablo de Greiff, "Justice and Reparations" in Pablo de Greiff (ed.), *The Handbook of Reparations* (Oxford/New York, NY: Oxford University Press, 2006) 452 at 454.
9 Pablo de Greiff, "Introduction. Repairing the Past: Compensation for Victims of Human Rights Violations" in Pablo de Greiff (ed.), *The Handbook of Reparations* (Oxford/New York, NY: Oxford University Press, 2006) 2 at 3.
10 Peté and du Plessis, *supra* note 5 at 17–20.
11 Peté and du Plessis, *supra* note 5 at 20–27.
12 Kevin Hearty, "Problematising Symbolic Reparation: 'Complex Political Victims', 'Dead Body Politics' and the Right to Remember" (2020) 29:3 Social and Legal Studies 334 at 335.
13 de Greiff, *supra* note 8 at 454.
14 Susan Sharpe, "The Idea of Reparation" in Gerry Johnstone and Daniel W. Van Ness (eds), *Handbook of Restorative Justice* (Oxon/New York, NY: Routledge, 2011) 24 at 27.

"the symbolic freight of [also] the material gesture is rendered immediately visible,"[15] and it conveys "both tangible and intangible meanings."[16] While sharing the traits of material reparations, however, symbolic reparations have an even stronger relationship with collective memory, and as such, their most popular form, public apology, merits a closer investigation following this general analysis of the institution of reparations.

Whether material or symbolic, reparations have three functions – repairing psychological, economic, and/or physical abuse; vindicating victims; and determining responsibility[17] – and four main goals: recognition, i.e., the re-recognising of victims both as human beings[18] and as equal citizens, which they were due by the rest of society;[19] civic trust, i.e., its reconstitution both between the victims and the rest of society, and between the society and the state;[20] solidarity, i.e., the (re)taking of interest of the society as a whole with all of its parts, including the victims;[21] and a shift in collective memory, i.e., the bringing of the victims' counter-memories to the forefront of official narratives.[22] As such, they privilege "multiple group identities as simultaneously influencing and contributing to the . . . narrative"[23] through the regulation of "the range of political and historical meanings with which the crimes of the past are endowed and through which they are interpreted and acted upon."[24] This fourth goal is particularly interesting for my investigations.

Importantly, reparations in the law and memory sense are a unique legal institution, not only because of their particular goals, but also due to their very nature: they are tasked not with righting an "infrequent and exceptional" wrong, as in the case of typical criminal law restitutions, but rather with responding to "massive and systematic" violations,[25] which were often incurred by the state itself. Thus, in lieu of the usual "case-by-case" response to crime undertaken before the courts, in regard to collective abuse, a collective response is also needed.[26]

15 Claire Moon, "'Who'll Pay Reparations on My Soul?' Compensation, Social Control and Social Suffering" (2012) 21:2 Social and Legal Studies 187 at 190.
16 Roman David, "What We Know About Transitional Justice: Survey and Experimental Evidence" (2017) 38:1 Advances in Political Psychology 151 at 167.
17 Moon, *supra* note 15 at 190.
18 Christopher Kutz, "Justice in Reparations: The Cost of Memory and the Value of Talk" (2004) 32:3 Philosophy and Public Affairs 277 at 281.
19 de Greiff, *supra* note 8 at 461–462.
20 de Greiff, *supra* note 8 at 462–465.
21 de Greiff, *supra* note 8 at 465–467.
22 Kutz, *supra* note 18 at 283.
23 Barkan, *supra* note 6 at 322.
24 Moon, *supra* note 15 at 188.
25 de Greiff, *supra* note 8 at 455.
26 de Greiff, *supra* note 8 at 458.

While collectively awarded reparations in many cases mean smaller awards than those that might have been awarded by the courts, they not only satisfy the "conditions of justice" but, most importantly, allow for swift and large-scale administrative proceedings with a large number of successful recipients in the end.[27] Moreover, only such all-encompassing attempts at redress have the ability to affect collective memories of not only individual groups but also society as a whole, thus achieving the institution of reparations' "fourth goal." If employed instead, the case-by-case approach often results in the victims' stories fading into the background and monetary issues taking centre stage,[28] thus losing the possibility of the reparations serving as a focal point "in the grieving process"[29] and being a part of the new narrative, one with the collective trauma-memories ultimately reworked within the society and the aforementioned trauma "time warps," which also encompass the generations following those of the victims, broken. Importantly, reparations may also have an effect on the collective memories of the perpetrators, assuaging their guilt,[30] and, if combined with "group affirmation," can lead to a meaningful change in relations between victims and perpetrators,[31] potentially preventing reconciliation.

Should reparations be successful in achieving their goals, they need to be not only externally (created in conjunction with other legal institutions of memory) and internally (encompassing different forms of reparations) coherent,[32] but also specifically tailored to the atrocity they are meant to rectify, decided upon with the participation of both the perpetrators and the victims, offered or agreed upon rather than mandated,[33] and taking into account the collective memories of the atrocity in question, thus allowing for the most suitable forms of reparations to be adopted.[34] The relationship between reparations and collective memory is thus twofold: on the one hand, their shift is one of the goals of the institution; on the other, no meaningful

27 de Greiff, *supra* note 8 at 460.

28 de Greiff, *supra* note 8 at 460.

29 Brandon Hamber and Richard A. Wilson, "Symbolic Closure Through Memory, Reparation and Revenge in Post-Conflict Societies" (2002) 1:1 Journal of Human Rights 35 at 38.

30 Aarti Iyer, Colin Wayne Leach, and Anne Pedersen, "Racial Wrongs and Restitutions: The Role of Guilt and Other Group-Based Emotions" in Nyla R. Branscombe and Bertjan Doosje (eds), *Collective Guilt International Perspectives* (Cambridge/New York, NY: Cambridge University Press, 2004) 262 at 269.

31 Gregory R. Gunn and Anne E. Wilson, "Acknowledging the Skeletons in Our Closet: The Effect of Group Affirmation on Collective Guilt, Collective Shame, and Reparatory Attitudes" (2011) 37:11 Personality and Social Psychology Bulletin 1474 at 1485.

32 de Greiff, *supra* note 8 at 468.

33 Sharpe, *supra* note 14 at 29–32.

34 Rachel López, "The (Re)Collection of Memory After Mass Atrocity and the Dilemma for Transitional Justice" (2015) 47 International Law and Politics 799 at 853.

change will take place unless those pre-existing ones are taken into account when designing it.

It needs to be stressed, however, that there are certain limitations to what reparations may achieve, both in general and in the sphere of collective memory. Complete "restitution is rarely, if ever, satisfied" by reparations[35] – as it is not possible in the majority of cases to quantify harm[36] and reparations are only a way of making "the best of a situation."[37] But they also may not be enough to break the established narratives that are behind the systemic patterns of abuse or discrimination within society,[38] in some cases only reinforcing "selective interpretations of the past."[39] Moreover, reparations work best not only when their different forms (material and symbolic) are employed at the same time,[40] but also, as I mentioned earlier, when adopted in conjunction with other legal institutions of memory, such as truth (and reconciliation) commissions or lustration. Reparations help "to keep those other measures from fading into irrelevance for most victims,"[41] but more importantly, they themselves rely on other legal institutions of memory in order not to be branded as attempts at buying the victims "acquiescence"[42] or "silence,"[43] and to prevent the intensification of social suffering (as they tend to do in certain instances).[44] This is the reason why I propose categorising them as a soft legal institution of memory.

Symbolic Reparations: The Case of Public Apologies

With material reparations taking a number of different forms, it is rather peculiar that symbolic reparations most often take only one shape: that of a public apology. Such a "public display of remorse" can often resonate particularly strongly both locally and internationally and – somewhat counter-intuitively for an act of little juridical power – may herald a true end of a

35 de Greiff, supra note 9 at 14.
36 Kutz, *supra* note 18 at 279.
37 Michael Freeman, "Back to the Future: The Historical Dimension of Liberal Justice" in Max du Plessis and Stephen Peté (eds), *Repairing the Past? International Perspectives on Reparations for Gross Human Rights Abuses* (Antwerp/Oxford: Intersentia, 2007) 29 at 41.
38 Sharpe, *supra* note 14 at 36.
39 Hearty, *supra* note 12 at 336.
40 David, *supra* note 16 at 170.
41 de Greiff, *supra* note 8 at 462.
42 Pablo de Greiff, "Theorizing Transitional Justice" in Melissa S. Williams, Rosemary Nagy, and Jon Elster (eds), *Transitional Justice NOMOS LI* (New York, NY: New York University Press, 2012) 31 at 37.
43 Wiseman Chirwa, "Collective Memory and the Process of Reconciliation and Reconstruction" (1997) 7:4 Development in Practice 479 at 480.
44 Moon, *supra* note 15 at 188.

conflict,[45] providing "moral restitution" and "offering recipients something of nonmaterial value" as a way of reparation.[46]

A public apology is an act of "the recognition of a past violation or harm in conjunction with the admission of responsibility and the plea for forgiveness,"[47] with "collective responsibility . . . assumed and guilt . . . accepted without excuse and justification for the past,"[48] thus putting the apologising group "into a position of vulnerability since [it] risks admitting [its] guilt without being forgiven."[49] Apologies are "transactional" in character,[50] directed as much towards the victim group as they are towards the apologising one, with the latter engaging in introspection and its members speaking "to themselves and try[ing] to create a new moral identity by focusing their collective guilt and transforming their collective memory.[51] Public apologies are also intergenerational, with responsibility and obligations, as well as victimhood, passed on from ancestors to descendants.[52]

As such, apologies consist of three elements: the verdictive, i.e., what happened, a clear and official acknowledgement of the harm caused by the apologising group; the attributive, i.e., who committed the harm, the acknowledgement of the blame laying on the part of the apologising group, potentially connected with the question of forgiveness; and the participatory, i.e., who apologises and to whom the apology is given.[53] Should one of these elements be missing or deficient, an apology will not achieve its intended effect.[54]

An important aspect of the participatory element of public apologies is the person or people delivering it,[55] as for its "collective remorse" to be

45 Christopher Daase, "Addressing Painful Memories: Apologies as a New Practice in International Relations" in Aleida Assmann and Sebastian Conrad (eds), *Memory in a Global Age: Discourses, Practices and Trajectories* (Houndmills/New York, NY: Palgrave Macmillan, 2010) 19 at 20.

46 Robert R. Weyeneth, "The Power of Apology and the Process of Historical Reconciliation" (2001) 23:3 The Public Historian 9 at 31.

47 Daase, *supra* note 45 at 20.

48 Daase, *supra* note 45 at 27.

49 Daase, *supra* note 45 at 24.

50 Stephen Winter, "Theorising the Political Apology" (2015) 23:3 The Journal of Political Philosophy 261 at 263.

51 Daase, *supra* note 45 at 28.

52 Janna Thompson, "Apology, Historical Obligations and the Ethics of Memory" (2009) 2:2 Memory Studies 195 at 205–207. See also: Pramod K. Nayar, "Contrition Chic and the Politics of Public Apology" (2016), online: The Wire <thewire.in/history/contrition-chic-or-the-politics-of-public-apology>.

53 Winter, *supra* note 50 at 264.

54 Borja Martinovic, Karen Freihorst, and Magdalena Bobowik, "To Apologize or to Compensate for Colonial Injustices? The Role of Representations of the Colonial Past, Group-Based Guilt, and In-Group Identification" (2021) 34:20 International Review of Social Psychology 1 at 2.

55 A public apology may be delivered by social representatives instead of public figures, but in such a case it would be recognised as a societal apology, and not an official apology. See: Rafi Nets-Zehngut, "Societal Apology (vs. Official Apology) in the Context of Collective Political Violence" (2021) 4:10 International Journal of Latest Research in Humanities and Social Science 24.

considered true, and for an apology to have greater resonance, it needs to "be transmitted through the whole group, that is, through an official representative," who, importantly, needs to give not a "personal avowal," but an "official statement for the entire" collectivity.[56] Importantly, the "higher the representative is ranked in the state hierarchy and the more official and public the statement is," the more effective an apology is considered to be.[57] However, public apologies may also be delivered by organs or institutions that are not "best positioned" to apologise, in those instances when a public apology is needed at a particular moment in time.[58] The actual act of an apology can take forms other than a statement, both emblematic – such as a pardon[59] or a day of remembrance[60] – and physical, for example, a plaque or a memorial.[61]

Apart from their form, public apologies may be divided in two different ways: either to interstate, i.e., from one state to another; national, i.e., from one group to another within the same state; and transnational, i.e., from one state to a particular group outside of (and potentially also inside) the same state;[62] or to contemporaneous, i.e., concerning events that have taken place relatively recently, with the event "still within living memory," and retrospective, i.e., regarding events that are part of a more distant past.[63] Although it may seem that apologising for atrocities committed in the past is not feasible in the present day, public apologies have a direct link with the question of the universal, "retroactive and perpetual" human rights, which are their background and inspiration; this allows them to realise the aforementioned transgenerational dimension of public apology and for them to be retrospective, granting a "formal recognition to the suffering and unwanted memories stemming from state-crafted atrocities in the past."[64] This mechanism takes place through the symbolic connection of the "personal hurt in the present with a collective that was responsible for the wrongdoings done

56 Daase, *supra* note 45 at 26.
57 Daase, *supra* note 45 at 26.
58 Nick Smith, "An Overview of Challenges Facing Collective Apologies" in Daniël Cuypers, Daniel Janssen, Jacques Haers, and Barbara Segaert (eds), *Public Apology Between Ritual and Regret: Symbolic Excuses on False Pretenses or True Reconciliation Out of Sincere Regret?* (Amsterdam/New York, NY: Rodopi, 2013) 29 at 38.
59 Weyeneth, *supra* note 46 at 16.
60 Weyeneth, *supra* note 46 at 20.
61 Weyeneth, *supra* note 46 at 15.
62 Ąžuolas Bagdonas, "Historical State Apologies" in Berber Bevernage and Nico Wouters (eds), *The Palgrave Handbook of State-Sponsored History After 1945* (London: Palgrave Macmillan, 2018) 775 at 779.
63 Weyeneth, *supra* note 46 at 21.
64 Ridwan Laher Nytagodien and Arthur G. Neal, "Collective Trauma, Apologies, and the Politics of Memory" (2004) 3:4 Journal of Human Rights 465 at 466.

in the past,"[65] thus reaffirming "the value of the protection of the rights of individuals and certain groups . . . against states,"[66] as well as the vital role of collective memory in the whole process.

This connection, in turn, is based on the understanding of the state as "a corporate actor that transcends time and government change,"[67] as well as on the everlasting effect of the harm done towards the victimised group, which in their collective memory remains "an injustice that resonates beyond its temporal context, a crime that is aimed at all members of the group as a unit and cannot be forgiven" simply with the passage of time.[68] Thus, while both types of apologies, contemporary and retrospective, are directly related to the matters of collective memory – as I argued in Part I of this book, an event does not need to be a part of a distant past in order to be considered a major element of collective memory –retrospective apologies in particular may lead to profound shifts in collective memory, challenging, recasting,[69] and ultimately changing long-established official narratives,[70] putting the counter-memories forward.

Public apologies also have several different goals, corresponding with, but at the same time broader than, those of reparations in general: restoration of the lost reputation; closure, i.e., "a meaningful conclusion to a difficult" past; the establishment of "accountability," providing the basis for "a future relationship"; the placation of difficult situations; the initiation of the reconciliation process; and, perhaps most importantly, forgiveness.[71] It needs to be stressed, however, that while being one of the goals of an apology from the apologiser's perspective, forgiveness is by no means a "precondition for an apology": only by taking "the risk that forgiveness will not be granted"[72] does the apology have a real possibility of transforming "the relationship between victim and offender and their respective identities,"[73] addressing "the causes and consequences" of harm.[74] It is this future-orientation that is one of the main, and in my view most important, characteristics of a public apology.

65 Michael J. A. Wohl, Matthew J. Hornsey, and Catherine R. Philpot, "A Critical Review of Official Public Apologies: Aims, Pitfalls, and a Staircase Model of Effectiveness" (2011) 5:1 Social Issues and Policy Review 70 at 84.
66 Bagdonas, *supra* note 62 at 780.
67 Nava Löwenheim, "A Haunted Past: Requesting Forgiveness for Wrongdoing in International Relations" (2009) 35:3 Review of International Studies 531 at 534.
68 *Ibid.* at 540.
69 Barkan, *supra* note 6 at 323.
70 Bagdonas, *supra* note 62 at 788.
71 Weyeneth, *supra* note 46 at 21–25.
72 Daase, *supra* note 45 at 25.
73 Daase, *supra* note 45 at 28.
74 Hearty, *supra* note 12 at 337.

It is in its orientation on the future that the main long-term goal of public apology lies, the breaking "with a repressive past"[75] and the opening of the door to reconciliation, an aim clearly connected to the question of forgiveness: as it has been noticed, apologies may cause "a strong cathartic effect" on both the apologising and the apologised to group, thus "fostering the (re-) approachment between" the two, allowing for the latter's "acknowledgement and demonstrating a real commitment to change" on behalf of the former.[76] Should apologies lead to reconciliation, however, several conditions, or steps,[77] need to be fulfilled first: in addition to the aforementioned need for an official representative of the state delivering the apology, public apologies also have to be credible, need to express a certain level of remorse, stem from an actual need to apologise within the culpable group,[78] and may be received only within a receptive intergroup context[79] and by a group whose culture is responsive towards such an act[80] – one which believes that the apologising group has freed itself from the behaviour that led to the harm in the past,[81] and whose members perceive change as possible in general within social groups.[82] Moreover, the aftermath of an apology (the "post-apology" commitment) is also important to its long-term effects, involving the ongoing engagement of the apologising group with its promises of reconciliation and a change in behaviour, ultimately leading to the reestablishment of the relationship between the two groups.[83]

75 Freeman, *supra* note 37 at 50.

76 Giada Girelli, *Understanding Transitional Justice: A Struggle for Peace, Reconciliation, and Rebuilding* (Cham: Palgrave Macmillan, 2017) at 3.

77 See Wohl, Hornsey, and Philpot's staircase model of an apology: Wohl, Hornsey, and Philpot, *supra* note 65 at 88.

78 Daase, *supra* note 45 at 26.

79 Catherine R. Philpot and Matthew J. Hornsey, "What Happens When Groups Say Sorry: The Effect of Intergroup Apologies on Their Recipients" (2008) 34:4 Personality and Social Psychology Bulletin 474 at 485.

80 As studies show, while the perception that a public apology may lead to reconciliation can be found throughout different regions, there are certain discrepancies between the number of people who hold such a view: from 30% in the South and SE Asia, to 20% in Africa, Middle East, East Asia, and Latin America, to 13% in Russia and the Balkans, to 9% in Western Europe, to 6% in the Anglo-Saxon region. See: Kimberly A. Rapoza and Marineh Laliki, "Integrative Summary on Apology and Forgiveness" in Kathleen Malley-Morrison, Andrea Mercurio, and Gabriel Twose (eds), *International Handbook of Peace and Reconciliation* (New York, NY/Heidelberg/Dordrecht/London: Springer, 2013) 431 at 435.

81 Michael J. A. Wohl, Smadar Cohen-Chen, Eran Halperin, Julie Caouette, Nicole Hayes, and Matthew J. Hornsey, "Belief in the Malleability of Groups Strengthens the Tenuous Link Between a Collective Apology and Intergroup Forgiveness" (2015) 41:5 Personality and Social Psychology Bulletin 714 at 715.

82 *Ibid.* at 722.

83 Wohl, Hornsey, and Philpot, *supra* note 65 at 94.

Importantly, the possibility for reconciliation and a "new beginning" between groups notwithstanding, public apologies are not free from controversy. On the one hand, they have been criticised as "a slippery slope of ill-conceived revisionism," as it is not feasible to apologise for each and every wrong committed in the past; on the other hand, apologies can be perceived as cynical, only "empty rhetoric that salves guilty modern consciences," poorly replacing any real action.[84] Moreover, giving public apologies may lead to unintended, exclusionary consequences: while the act of apology should lead to "open conversation" about the past,[85] in reality, as any legal institution of memory, it is a part of the creation of a new official narrative, which, although inclusionary, means that some counter-memories will not be able to fit in, be that anymore or still.[86]

At the same time, it needs to be stressed that not only making a public apology may cause tension among the victim and the oppressor groups, but so may the lack of it,[87] negatively impacting not only the victims trapped with their collective trauma-memories but also the perpetrator group, whose reputation will remain damaged should it continue to refuse to apologise.[88] Importantly, the question of whether a public apology will be given depends largely on the collective memory of the perpetrator group: the more important a particular official narrative is to the group's identity, the less likely it is to offer an apology.[89]

Directly linked to the matters of collective memory is also the final aspect of public apologies on which I will focus in their analysis, the question of the source of their power – after all, public apologies are always "a form of state-sponsored" official narrative,[90] an attempt at changing collective memory. Moreover, symbolic reparations in general, and public apologies in particular, complement material reparations in different ways, on the one hand tentatively addressing issues which cannot be resituated or repaired, such as physical injuries and death, and on the other "redressing the injury of injustice itself," going "to a layer underneath specific harms."[91] Their power to do so lies in their performative dimension:[92] a public apology in a way allows

84 Weyeneth, *supra* note 46 at 30.

85 Kora Andrieu, "'Sorry for the Genocide': How Public Apologies Can Help Promote National Reconciliation" (2009) 38:1 Millennium: Journal of International Studies 3 at 13.

86 Jan Löfström, "Historical Apologies as Acts of Symbolic Inclusion and Exclusion? Reflections on Institutional Apologies as Politics of Cultural Citizenship" (2011) 15:1 Citizenship Studies 93 at 104–105.

87 Weyeneth, *supra* note 46 at 31.

88 Löwenheim, *supra* note 67 at 546–547.

89 Bagdonas, *supra* note 62 at 791.

90 Bagdonas, *supra* note 62 at 775.

91 Sharpe, *supra* note 14 at 32.

92 Erin K. Wilson and Roland Bleiker, "Performing Political Apologies" in Erica Resende and Dovile Budryte (eds), *Memory and Trauma in International Relations: Theories, Cases, and Debates* (London: Routledge, 2014) 42 at 43.

for the Levinasian "face to face encounter with the Other," a meeting which may lead to reconciliation, although in such a case between groups and not individuals.[93] As such, like material reparations, but all the more so, public apologies are collective rituals in the Durkheimian sense, as introduced in Chapter 2 – it is through them that groups are established and sustained,[94] "the values at the basis of the legal system"[95] are reaffirmed, and ultimately collective memory is reshaped,[96] in a way establishing this particular form of reparations as an almost legal institution of memory in its own right, albeit still a soft one, given its limited, resting on multiple factors capacity at influencing collective memory.

Soft Institution II: Law and Memory Intersecting High Above – International Tribunals

International tribunals play a major role in the creation of collective memory on a global scale – as noted in Part I of the book in the section on international law, trials before international institutions can be regarded as extraordinary intersections of collective memory and law, with a particular category of cases heard before them, restrictive jurisdiction, a certain level of imperviousness to official narratives of singular countries (but, as I will note, not necessarily an ability to change them), and, in some instances, a major role in the reconciliation process, all leading to the creation or shifting of collective memories, which are "fashioned out" of tribunals' judgements,[97] with a large number of them becoming instant global collective memories.

As such, I propose distinguishing international tribunals as the second soft type of legal institution of memory, departing, however, from the traditional focus in this context only on the intersections between international criminal tribunals and collective memory, as proposed in Mark Osiel's

93 *Nota bene*, Levinas himself was cautious about transferring his concept of ethics from the individual to the collective, ultimately leaving, however, this possibility open. See: Danielle Celermajer, "Apology and the Possibility of Ethical Politics" (2008) 9:1 Journal for Cultural and Religious Theory 14 at 29–31.

94 Andrieu, *supra* note 85 at 18.

95 Daniël Cuypers, "When Sorry Seems to Be the Hardest Word: An Apology with a Legal Disclaimer" in Daniël Cuypers, Daniel Janssen, Jacques Haers, and Barbara Segaert (eds), *Public Apology Between Ritual and Regret: Symbolic Excuses on False Pretenses or True Reconciliation Out of Sincere Regret?* (Amsterdam/New York, NY: Rodopi, 2013) 9 at 20.

96 Wilson and Bleiker, *supra* note 92 at 53.

97 Victoria Vanneau, "Le tribunal pénal international doit-il faire l'événement? Ou les paradoxes d'une Justice pour l'Histoire" ["Should International Criminal Tribunals Make Headlines? Or the Paradoxes of Justice for History"] (2011) 32 Sociétés & Représentations 135 at 150.

seminal work,[98] instead following Moshe Hirsch.[99] I would argue that in terms of their relationship with collective memory, all international tribunals, both criminal and non-criminal, can be regarded as legal institutions of memory, given that the former always, and the latter in many instances, are "tribunals of history," and the two are in all instances "tribunals of human rights." Thus, both types of tribunals intersect – as I show in this chapter in general and in Chapter 6 on the case study of ECtHR, in particular – with collective memory in various ways. Importantly, these interactions take place not only in criminal trial contexts directly in the aftermath of abuse, but also in a detemporalised context many years following the events in question.

The power of international tribunals over collective memory comes from – to follow Durkheim once again – their role as extraordinary rituals, "historiographical dramas,"[100] carried, on the one hand, "under the auspices of the 'international community,' " and, on the other, "under exceptional circumstances,"[101] rendering them a "last judgement" quality, which means they "operate simultaneously at the level of legal mechanism and performance."[102] With "the *niveau* within which the meaning of the past is determined – from the national to the transnational" shifted,[103] international tribunals offer more symbolic power than any national court and may be perceived, to follow Vanneau, as "entirely juridical practices which take morality for witness, history for the horizon and the event for instrument."[104] As such, they truly become places of collective rituals in the Durkheimian sense – rituals "of collective mourning and the exercise of tolerance and reflectivity about the past, which is then translated into" collective memory.[105]

In their role as legal institutions of memory, international tribunals intersect with collective memory on a number of different levels, depending on their mandate (meaning that not all tribunals will interact with collective

98 See: Mark Osiel, *Mass Atrocity, Collective Memory, and the Law* (Oxon/New York, NY: Routledge, 2017).

99 See: Moshe Hirsch, "The Role of International Tribunals in the Development of Historical Narratives" (2018) 20 Journal of the History of International Law 391 at 402–403.

100 Nicola Henry, "Memory of an Injustice: The 'Comfort Women' and the Legacy of the Tokyo Trial" (2013) 37:3 Asian Studies Review 362 at 362.

101 Paul Muldoon, "Beginning a New Exceptional Institutions and the Politics of Ritual" in Kalliopi Chainoglou, Barry Collins, Michael Phillips, and John Strawson (eds), *Injustice, Memory and Faith in Human Rights* (Oxon/New York, NY: Routledge, 2018) 93 at 95.

102 *Ibid.* at 99.

103 Katarina Ristić, "The Legacy of the ICTY in Croatia, Bosnia and Serbia" in Annalisa Ciampi (ed.), *History and International Law: An Intertwined Relationship* (Northampton: Edward Elgar Publishing, 2019) 168 at 172.

104 Vanneau, *supra* note 97 at 153.

105 Katarina Ristić, *Imaginary Trials: War Crime Trials and Memory in Former Yugoslavia* (Leipzig: Leipziger Universitätsverlag, 2014) at 80.

memory in the same way – the war criminal ones will intersect in all four, and others in one, two, or three ways). The four such points of intersection are, first, the individualisation of guilt in order to expunge the blame of the society in question (only war criminal tribunals); second, perhaps most importantly, the establishment of truth (legal truth), and thus of an official narrative and ultimately collective memories (both war criminal and non-criminal tribunals); third, the provision of a forum to re-work collective trauma-memories for the victims (war crime tribunals and potentially non-criminal tribunals); fourth, reconciliation, built up upon the basis of the previous three effects of an international tribunal's judgement on collective memory (war crime tribunals and potentially non-criminal tribunals). However, in practice, this ideal model of an international tribunal as a legal institution of memory faces numerous challenges.

With regard to the question of individualising guilt, the symbolic dimension of international tribunals' decisions needs to be stressed once again: as "a few war criminals stand for a much larger group of guilty individuals," this "individual justice actually becomes a *de facto* way of exonerating many of the guilty,"[106] with the exceptional ritual taking place before the international tribunal able "to generalise rather than to personalise injustice," which may be both beneficial and detrimental[107] for the perpetrators' society, as I will show. In addition to the question of symbolism, however, practical concerns leading to the individualisation of guilt need to be observed: on the one hand, a broad process of social cleanse could "spark a nationalist backlash";[108] on the other, law's – and the tribunals' – own limitations need to be acknowledged, given that "even the broadest application of legalistic principles will only allow the conviction of actual perpetrators – those who really committed crimes" and not the "wider circle of bystanders and collaborators."[109] Prosecuting an ideology or a larger part of the society *in abstracto*, "with no 'live' defendants," might prove to be virtually impossible.[110]

The decisions to prosecute but a select few have a major impact on the perpetrators' society collective memory, potentially belittling the "everyday," "mundane" atrocities by focusing only on major ones,[111] thus "by implication exonerating the remainder of the population and closing the

106 Gary J. Bass, *Stay the Hand of Vengeance: The Politics of War Crimes Tribunals* (Princeton, NJ: Princeton University Press, 2014) at 300.

107 Muldoon, *supra* note 101 at 102–104.

108 Bass, *supra* note 106 at 301.

109 Bass, *supra* note 106 at 298.

110 Sergey Toymentsev, "Legal but Criminal: The Failure of the 'Russian Nuremberg' and the Paradoxes of Post-Soviet Memory" (2011) 48:3 Comparative Literature Studies 296 at 302–303.

111 Lawrence Douglas, "The Didactic Trial: Filtering History and Memory into the Courtroom" (2006) 14:4 European Review 513 at 517.

book on retribution."[112] This allows the particular groups to leave the contentious issues in the realm of the past without any introspection, and thus foster collective memories which have little to no relation to the truth – most importantly those of also being the victims (albeit "dissociated"[113]), in their case "suffering in consequence of the machinations of omnipotent criminal leaders,"[114] on which the perpetrators' society is able "to vicariously take revenge" through the work of a tribunal.[115] Nevertheless, "the hope" of the international community in establishing the tribunals is that "these rituals" will have a strong enough effect on the perpetrator society, substituting "for more enduring acts of collective accountability and public acknowledgement."[116]

The tribunals' decisions individualising guilt have an effect of rehabilitating the society which committed the atrocities not only "inside," allowing it to move forward, but also "outside," reconstituting the narratives and collective memories of a particular society on a global stage, taking on a role of "international labelling agencies."[117] This effect of tribunals' decisions shows their function as creators of global memory, which is in place whether or not the society in question perceives the tribunal as successful, e.g., the International Military Tribunal in Nuremberg (IMT Nuremberg), seen outside of Germany as "the most spectacular element in a broader Allied program of denazification," gaining "prestige" from the successful "process of turning a fascist enemy into a democratic ally," but regarded sceptically for several decades inside the very country it concerned, which demonstrates that a tribunal's decisions are never "a quick fix, but part of a much more ambitious and time-consuming project of social engineering."[118] Another example includes Japan, a country which to this day holds an ambiguous

112 Madoka Futamura, "Memory of War and War Crimes: Japanese Historical Consciousness and the Tokyo Trial" in Jenny Macleod (ed.), *Defeat and Memory Cultural Histories of Military Defeat in the Modern Era* (Basingstoke/New York, NY: Palgrave Macmillan, 2008) 137 at 142.

113 *Ibid.* at 141–142.

114 Patrick Finney, "The Stories of Defeated Aggressors: International History, National Identity and Collective Memory After 1945" in Jenny Macleod (ed.), *Defeat and Memory Cultural Histories of Military Defeat in the Modern Era* (Basingstoke/New York, NY: Palgrave Macmillan, 2008) 97 at 98.

115 Graham T. Blewitt AM, "The Importance of a Retributive Approach to Justice" in David A. Blumenthal and Timothy L. H. McCormack (eds), *The Legacy of Nuremberg: Civilising Influence or Institutionalised Vengeance?* (Leiden/Boston, MA: Brill/Martinus Nijhoff Publishers, 2008) 32 at 33.

116 Michael Humphrey, "International Intervention, Justice and National Reconciliation: The Role of the ICTY and ICTR in Bosnia and Rwanda" (2003) 2:4 Journal of Human Rights 495 at 502.

117 Moshe Hirsch, "Introduction: Sociological Perspectives on International Tribunals" (2020) 34 Temple International and Comparative Law Journal 193 at 199.

118 Bass, *supra* note 106 at 295–296.

view of the International Military Tribunal for the Far East in Tokyo (IMTFE Tokyo). However, Japan continues to use it to build an identity of "a peaceful and law-abiding member of the international community,"[119] which fits their broader memory politics, analysed in greater detail in Part III of this book.

As such, the establishment of truth, or rather the establishment of legal truth, could be regarded as the main point of intersection between the international tribunals' work and collective memory, given that it allows us to uncover certain atrocities for the official narrative,[120] with the linking of a particular "ideology or geopolitical goal . . . to the commission of atrocity" considered "the *pièce de résistance* of the contribution that international" tribunals"[121] make to collective memory. At the same time, "the absence of a well-established historical record facilitates denial that atrocities ever happened,"[122] with events that did not become a part of the official record – often for political reasons[123] – susceptible to collective forgetting.[124]

It needs to be stressed once again, however, that the truth established by a tribunal will only be legal truth in that the court's work is always limited by the temporal boundaries of its mandate[125] (certain major events may become collectively forgotten after not being included in the prosecution), as well as the selection of the reviewed historical events within them (in some cases a tribunal refuses "to address issues that are of undoubted historical importance but essentially irrelevant for the purposes" of a particular case), the "legal definition"[126] of the events in question, the possibility of guilty pleas,[127] the provision of space for the accused's distorted narrative on par

119 Kerstin Lukner, "From Tokyo to The Hague: War Crime Tribunals and (shifting?) Memory Politics in Japan" (2015) 27:3 Japan Forum 321 at 333.

120 Futamura, *supra* note 112 at 141.

121 Shea E. Esterling and Michael John-Hopkins, "The Creation and Protection of History Through the Prism of International Criminal Justice in Al Mahdi" (2018) 9 Journal of Humanitarian Legal Studies 1 at 36–37.

122 Bass, *supra* note 106 at 304.

123 Kerstin von Lingen, "Nuremberg, Rome, Tokyo: The Impact of Allied War Crimes Trials on Post-War Memory and Identity in Germany, Italy and Japan After 1945" (2009) 8 Working Papers in Military and International History, online: University of Salford <usir.salford.ac.uk/32968/1/MIH_1_no_8_-_LINGEN_K_-_Nuremberg%2C_Rome%2C_Tokyo.pdf> 1 at 22.

124 Henry, *supra* note 100 at 369–370.

125 Futamura, *supra* note 112 at 140.

126 Pieter Lagrou, "'Historical Trials': Getting the Past Right – or the Future?" in Christian Delage and Peter Goodrich (eds), *The Scene of the Mass Crime: History, Film, and International Tribunals* (Oxon/New York, NY: Routledge, 2013) 9 at 13.

127 William A. Schabas, "Building the Narrative: The UN Tribunals for the Former Yugoslavia, Rwanda and Sierra Leone" in Christian Delage and Peter Goodrich (eds), *The Scene of the Mass Crime: History, Film, and International Tribunals* (Oxon/New York, NY: Routledge, 2013) 23 at 31.

with that of the prosecution,[128] and, as will be described in greater detail, the choice of witnesses. Importantly, as it has been correctly noted, trials before international tribunals are not so much about past and history; they are future-oriented, "judging the past" but also expressing the official narrative "to remodel the present and the future."[129] Ultimately, their effect is "not so much making history in the courtroom," but rather "trying to contribute to the history of the courtroom, affirming their jurisdiction, making legal history"[130] – and thus influencing collective memory on a global scale, with the potential to prepare also the perpetrators' society, and its, if not current, than at least "future elites for shouldering the[ir] moral burden" one day.[131]

This role of tribunals in establishing official narratives is not free from controversy, with the court representatives themselves both shying away from and embracing it under different circumstances[132] (as the case study of the ECtHR will show), well aware that during such a trial, law will ultimately summarise and distort history.[133] Nevertheless, the tribunals' decisions have a major impact on collective memories whether they acknowledge it or not, particularly when taking over the role of national "judicial or semi-judicial bodies" that choose to "deliberately conceal a significant historical event generating extensive harm to a disadvantaged group."[134] Of major importance in building the official narrative are decisions regarding the classification of a crime, particularly as genocide, and a failure to do so may potentially contribute to the denial of atrocities in question.[135] At the same time, also raising questions are the decisions to refuse to take into account the crimes on both sides of the conflict for fear of legitimising the "other side's" actions and thus "distort[ing] history rather than enhanc[ing] it."[136] In this regard, the long-term role of a tribunal's archives is also vital for the sustaining of collective memory established on the basis of its work.[137] In certain regions,

128 Donald Bloxham, "Defeat, Due Process, and Denial: War Crimes Trials and Nationalist Revisionism in Comparative Perspective" in Jenny Macleod (ed.), *Defeat and Memory Cultural Histories of Military Defeat in the Modern Era* (Basingstoke/New York, NY: Palgrave Macmillan, 2008) 117 at 130.
129 Vanneau, *supra* note 97 at 150–151.
130 Lagrou, *supra* note 126 at 20.
131 Blewitt AM, *supra* note 115 at 32.
132 Schabas, *supra* note 127 at 28.
133 Gerry J. Simpson, *Law, War and Crime: War Crimes Trials and the Reinvention of International Law* (Cambridge: Polity, 2007) at102.
134 Hirsch, *supra* note 99 at 394.
135 Caroline Fournet, *The Crime of Destruction and the Law of Genocide: Their Impact on Collective Memory* (Aldershot/Burlington, VT: Ashgate, 2007) at 134; see also Schabas, *supra* note 127 at 32.
136 Schabas, *supra* note 127 at 35.
137 Kirsten Campbell, "The Laws of Memory: The ICTY, the Archive, and Transitional Justice" (2012) 22:2 Social and Legal Studies 247 at 249.

an international court may engage in the fostering of a regional collective memory, e.g., the Inter-American Court of Human Rights (IACtHR).[138]

The establishment of an official narrative is directly connected to the place of victims in international tribunal trials, which provide them "with a space where their witnessed experiences can be ventilated,"[139] and, through the application of human rights law, give them an opportunity to recover their individual rights, an "attempt to reverse victimisation by state violence."[140] When appearing before tribunals, victims of an atrocity allow for their thus far individual memory[141] to enter into the collective realm of law[142] and thus have the power of changing the established narrative, creating a new narrative,[143] and ultimately providing "great educational value"[144] for the current and future generations, further cementing particular events in collective memory,[145] in certain cases even influencing international law. Examples of the latter include that of the International Criminal Tribunal for the former Yugoslavia's (ICTY) recognition of the war crime of sexual assault,[146] and the International Criminal Tribunal for Rwanda's (ICTR) recognition of rape as an element of genocide,[147] which constituted "an act of collective recognition, a collective memory of a wrong."[148] Conversely, exclusion of certain victims from becoming witnesses may further inequality and, as noted earlier, induce the process of collective forgetting of a particular crime, however widespread it may have been, which may span generations.[149]

Allowing victims to speak up is particularly important in the considerably "asymmetric settings" of power in regard to the construction of the official narrative,[150] as it opens up the space for the bringing of counter-memories to

138 Hirsch, *supra* note 99 at 409.
139 Ristić, *supra* note 103 at 172.
140 Humphrey, *supra* note 116 at 496.
141 Benjamin Thorne, "Liberal International Criminal Law and Legal Memory: Deconstructing the Production of Witness Memories at the International Criminal Tribunal for Rwanda" (2016) 9:s2 Journal of the British Academy 127 at 148.
142 Douglas, *supra* note 111 at 515.
143 Chrisje Brants and Katrien Klep, "Transitional Justice: History-Telling, Collective Memory, and the Victim-Witness" (2013) 7:1 International Journal of Conflict and Violence 36 at 41.
144 Fournet, *supra* note 135 at 130.
145 Brants and Klep, *supra* note 143 at 41.
146 Kirsten Campbell, "Sexual Assault, Memory, and International Humanitarian Law" (2002) 28:1 Signs 149 at 153.
147 Maja G. Burheim, *Authority to Tell: ICTR Contributions to Collective Memory of Sexual Violence in the Rwandan Genocide* (Oslo: University of Oslo, 2016) at 32.
148 Campbell, *supra* note 146 at 155.
149 Nicola Henry, *War and Rape: Law, Memory and Justice* (Oxon/New York, NY: Routledge, 2011) at 52–55.
150 Hirsch, *supra* note 99 at 394.

its forefront and for a public recognition of the victims' victimhood.[151] This acknowledgement is of major importance for the possibility of reworking collective trauma-memories by the victims – even if a tribunal's narrative will not be "accepted by the wider society" in question[152] – as it will enable their reintegration into collective memory and, at the same time, the wider group,[153] as well as open the door to reconciliation.[154]

Reconciliation as an effect of the work of international tribunals has become their increasingly important function in recent years, leading to their perception also as a tool of democratisation,[155] one necessary for the reconstitution of national law and the recreation of "moral social relationships and community and therefore national justice."[156] However, reconciliation can be achieved not simply through simply issuing judgements, but also through the process of explaining them[157] with media representation[158] and wide-ranging community outreach initiatives,[159] which have the power of "acting upon and reframing otherwise ambivalent or conflicting memory."[160]

The ICTY, for example, recognised its failure to proactively engage "with the peoples of former Yugoslavia proactively" and created the Outreach Program tasked with disseminating "information about its proceedings," as well as countering "misinformation" about its work,[161] which included meetings with the affected communities,[162] actively acknowledging its role in the creation of collective memory.[163] In turn, the Extraordinary Chambers in the Courts of Cambodia (ECCC) have chosen to rely on non-governmental organisations that complement their outreach, organising, *inter alia*, public

151 Fournet, *supra* note 135 at 132–133.
152 Hirsch, *supra* note 99 at 418.
153 Fournet, *supra* note 135 at 133.
154 Dejana Radisavljević and Martin Petrov, "Srebrenica and Genocide Denial in the Former Yugoslavia: What Has the ICTY Done to Address It?" in Paul Behrens, Nicholas Terry, and Olaf Jensen (eds), *Holocaust and Genocide Denial: A Contextual Perspective* (Oxon/New York, NY: Routledge/Taylor and Francis, 2017) 145 at 147–148.
155 Brigitte Weiffen, "From Domestic to International Instruments for Dealing with a Violent Past: Causes, Concomitants and Consequences for Democratic Transitions" in Aleida Assmann and Linda Shortt (eds), *Memory and Political Change* (New York, NY: Palgrave Macmillan, 2012) 89 at 97.
156 Humphrey, *supra* note 116 at 498.
157 Radisavljević and Petrov, *supra* note 154 at 156.
158 Vanneau, *supra* note 97 at 138.
159 Bloxham, *supra* note 128 at 132.
160 Peter Manning, "Governing Memory: Justice, Reconciliation and Outreach at the Extraordinary Chambers in the Courts of Cambodia" (2011) 5:2 Memory Studies 165 at 173.
161 Radisavljević and Petrov, *supra* note 154 at 151–152.
162 Hiroto Fujiwara, *The International Criminal Investigation and the Formation of Collective Memory in Post-Conflict Societies: An Analysis of Investigation Processes and an Epistemology of War Crimes* (Leuven: KU Leuven, 2019) at 287–289.
163 Henry, *supra* note 149 at 65.

hearings and court visits.[164] Building on the *ad hoc* tribunals' experience, the International Criminal Court (ICC) has the possibility – one that it uses – of choosing to include various forms of reparation aimed at community rebuilding as part of its decision.[165] Moreover, in certain cases, a tribunal may also choose to order a specific way of commemorating victims of an atrocity, as it has already done by the IACtHR.[166] The road to reconciliation, however, is always long, and a tribunal's decision – which always needs to find a balance "between forging peace and redressing the justified claims"[167] – is by itself, even when strengthened by outreach initiatives, not enough to bring a meaningful and permanent change,[168] further confirming the categorisation of international tribunals as soft legal institutions of memory.

In addition, international tribunals may face other problems in matters of memory that are not directly connected to the four points of law–memory intersection I outlined earlier. These include the weakening of a court's actual power in establishing the official narrative due to its physical distance from the place where the atrocity happened[169] and a lack of understanding of local, particularly non-Western cultural contexts,[170] which in turn may result in the failure to achieve a meaningful shift from "the discourses of self-victimisation" in the affected groups.[171] At the same time, the question of a certain familiarisation with mass atrocity that took place between 1945 and the 1990s, one resulting in the term "genocide" losing some of its "capacity to inspire outrage or response,"[172] also poses a major challenge for the narrative of international tribunals to become truly embedded in collective memory. It is further at a disadvantage due to its usually limited presence in the

164 Manning, *supra* note 160 at 167–169.

165 See: Mirosław M. Sadowski, "Heritage Strikes Back: The Al Mahdi Case, ICC's Policy on Cultural Heritage and the Pushing of Law's Boundaries" (2022) 2 Undecidabilities and Law – The Coimbra Journal for Legal Studies 99 at 110–111.

166 Hirsch, *supra* note 99 at 400.

167 Adam Czarnota, "Law as Mnemosyne and as Lethe: Quasi-Judicial Institutions and Collective Memories" in Emilios A. Christodoulidis and Scott Veitch (eds), *Lethe's Law: Justice, Law and Ethics in Reconciliation* (Oxford/Portland, OR: Hart Publishing, 2001) 115 at 122.

168 Kirsten Ainley, Rebekka Friedman, and Chris Mahony, "Transitional Justice: Interactions Between the Global and the Local in Evaluations of Success" in Kirsten Ainley, Rebekka Friedman, and Chris Mahony (eds), *Evaluating Transitional Justice Accountability and Peacebuilding in Post-Conflict Sierra Leone* (Houndmills: Palgrave Macmillan, 2015) 265 at 271–272.

169 Dmytro Koval, "Collective Memory and International Criminal Courts' Activity" (2015) 4 Юридичний Вісник 194 at 197.

170 Alexander Betts, "Should Approaches to Post-Conflict Justice and Reconciliation Be Determined Globally, Nationally or Locally?" (2005) 17:4 The European Journal of Development Research 736 at 748.

171 Faruk Hadžić, "Post-Genocidal Balkans Peace: Human Justice, Morality, Memory and Oblivion" (2021) 4:7 Journal of Balkan and Black Sea Studies 89 at 103.

172 Simpson, *supra* note 133 at 84–85.

perpetrator society's official discourse,[173] as well as its distortion in the local news outlets,[174] and the banalisation of its particularities in the international media[175] – hence the aforementioned importance of community outreach initiatives. Moreover, there often also exists a dissonance between the "illusion of unity" upon which these legal institutions of memory are established and their actual lack of ideological or cultural neutrality,[176] which – in conjunction with the influence of various agents of memory, such as governments, historians, and the media[177] – results in a sort of constant interplay between global and local collective memories.

Importantly, these issues of power over memory – exemplifications of Foucault's observations on the official narrative and authority introduced earlier – may decrease, alongside the individualisation of guilt mentioned previously, the possibility of acceptance of blame on the part of the perpetrators, which will regard the international proceedings as "partial, victor's justice."[178] This, in turn, may lead to either a passive acceptance of the judgement, resulting in a failure to engage with the reasons behind the committed atrocities,[179] never-ending debates on its merits, or even revisionism[180] – with the perpetrator society locked in the past,[181] ultimately constructing their own counter-memories around the international tribunal's decision. A particular example of these problems may be the legacy of ICTY, which on the one hand established a particular viewpoint on the events in the Balkans internationally but was used locally, as Ristić notes, to foster extremely divergent narratives: in Serbia, the "memory of the defeated," in Bosnia, the memory of victimhood, and in Croatia, "victor's memory."[182]

This example blatantly shows why, in spite of their global power, due to their limited local impact, especially in the short term, I choose to look at international tribunals as soft legal institutions of memory: while they develop the official narrative and thus collective memory, they also "provide

173 Madoka Futamura, "Japanese Societal Attitude Towards the Tokyo Trial: From a Contemporary Perspective" in Yuki Tanaka, Tim McCormack, and Gerry Simpson (eds), *Beyond Victor's Justice? The Tokyo War Crimes Trial Revisited* (Leiden/Boston: Martinus Nijhoff/Brill, 2011) 35 at 37–38.
174 Vanneau, *supra* note 97 at 139.
175 Mirza Velagic and Zlatka Velagic, "Do Court Rulings Matter? International courts and Journalists' Framing of the Srebrenica Genocide" (2014) 8:4 Journalism Practice 421 at 431.
176 Hirsch, *supra* note 99 at 413.
177 Hirsch, *supra* note 99 at 415.
178 Bloxham, *supra* note 128 at 125.
179 Futamura, *supra* note 112 at 147.
180 Futamura, *supra* note 173 at 46–47.
181 Madoka Futamura, "Individual and Collective Guilt: Post-War Japan and the Tokyo War Crimes Tribunal" (2006) 14:4 European Review 471 at 475.
182 Ristić, *supra* note 103 at 189.

a version that is flat and lacking in nuance,"[183] particularly for the different actors who bear witness to the actual atrocity. Moreover, an international tribunal wields little "power both over its own process and its impact, being dependent on other actors both to function and to bear influence,"[184] thus limiting the impact of these institutions. While working well on the international level, establishing a "legally true" narrative of the events in question for global memory, the collective memories created on the basis of the international tribunals' role as legal institutions of memory either fail or take a significant amount of time to engrain and meaningfully transform the communities most affected by their narrative, often crumbling in the face of the already established local one. In addition, through their inherently limited focus, international tribunals can often lead – unintentionally or intentionally – to collective forgetting. These are some of the reasons why certain societies choose to use medium legal institutions of memory, either in conjunction with or in lieu of some of the soft ones.

Medium Institution I. Law and Memory Walking Hand in Hand: Lustration

Lustration is an administrative legal institution of memory, employed in particular in the years following the post-1989 transitions in Central and Eastern Europe but also more broadly,[185] for example, in Ukraine after the 2014 government change (where lustration encompassed not only the ex-members of the communist regime but also the former Yanukovych administration and corrupt officials),[186] as well as in other transitional contexts, such as in Iraq after the 2003 invasion (where lustration concerned members of Saddam Hussein's Ba'ath Party, which is analysed in Chapter 7).[187]

With its name coming from the Latin word *lustratio*, or a purification rite with a sacrifice,[188] lustration is an institution of memory closely linked at its conceptual basis to the Durkheimian concept of ritual introduced earlier in the book, consisting of an administrative legal process[189] of creat-

183 Schabas, *supra* note 127 at 36.

184 Burheim, *supra* note 147 at 84.

185 Łukasz Krotoszyński, *Lustracja w Polsce w świetle modeli sprawiedliwości okresu tranzycji* [*Lustration in Poland in the Light of Transitional Justice Models*] (Warsaw: Helsińska Fundacja Praw Człowieka, 2014) at 35.

186 Nataliya Minyenkova, "Znaczenie lustracji w procesie demokratyzacji Ukrainy" ["The Meaning of Lustration in the Process of Ukraine's Democratisation"] (2017) 25 Kultura Bezpieczeństwa. Nauka-Praktyka-Refleksje 169 at 178.

187 Jens Meierhenrich, "The Ethics of Lustration" (2006) 20:1 Ethics and International Affairs 99 at 111.

188 Roman Boed, "An Evaluation of the Legality and Efficacy of Lustration as a Tool of Transitional Justice" (1999) 37:2 Columbia Journal of Transnational Law 357 at 358.

189 *Ibid.* at 364.

ing a ceremonial break with the former authorities[190] through the putting into practice of "transitional public employment laws"[191] in the process of screening,[192] or moral "purifying."[193] This practice is supposed to shield the society from the possibility of members and collaborators of a former regime holding actual power over the country's politics through the organising of a general vetting – lustration – of candidates for certain positions, thus gaining – and in certain instances making public – knowledge of their previous collusion, potentially, depending on the severity of lustration model adopted, inhibiting them from taking particular positions.[194]

As a medium legal institution of memory, lustration is introduced directly through either governmental decisions[195] or, more typically, legal acts of parliament that then fall under the constitutional court's review; however, this is where the parallels between different lustration laws end: in spite of the similar circumstances in which they are introduced, lustration regulations vary in terms of their scope (from secret police collaborators to all former regime members), the potential punishment (from internal self-explanation, to publicisation of names, to prohibition of holding certain posts), the person responsible for initiating the process (the individual or the institution), the availability of public access to the secret police files (from individual access, to availability to journalists and researchers, to the public in case of the individual holding a particular post), and their length in time (from limited to the years following a transition, to being extended, to introduced only for a longer time following a regime change).[196]

Lustration is often linked to the question of decommunisation; however, while the former may be a part of the latter in its broader sense (i.e., the expunging of the public sphere of any communist legacies),[197] the two are not

190 Brian K. Grodsky, *The Costs of Justice: How New Leaders Respond to Previous Rights Abuses* (Notre Dame, IN: University of Notre Dame Press, 2010) at 62.
191 Roman David, "Transitional Justice and Changing Memories of the Past in Central Europe" (2015) 50:1 Government and Opposition 24 at 30.
192 Hilary Appel, "Anti-Communist Justice and Founding the Post-Communist Order: Lustration and Restitution in Central Europe" (2005) 19:3 East European Politics and Societies 379 at 383.
193 *Ibid.* at 401–402.
194 Cynthia M. Horne and Margaret Levi, "Does Lustration Promote Trustworthy Governance? An Exploration of the Experience of Central and Eastern Europe" in János Kornai and Susan Rose-Ackerman (eds), *Building a Trustworthy State in Post-Socialist Transition* (New York, NY/Houndmills: Palgrave Macmillan, 2004) 52 at 52.
195 Pavlína Janebová, "Lustration in Slovakia" in Marcin Moskalewicz and Wojciech Przybylski (eds), *Understanding Central Europe* (Oxon/New York, NY: Routledge, 2018) 394 at 398.
196 Horne and Levi, *supra* note 194 at 53–54.
197 Adam Czarnota, "Decommunisation and Democracy: Transitional Justice in Post-communist Central-Eastern Europe" in Sven Eliaeson, Lyudmila Harutyunyan, and Larissa Titarenko (eds), *After the Soviet Empire: Legacies and Pathways* (Leiden: Brill, 2016) 165 at 167.

synonymous,[198] all the more so given that, as noted earlier, lustration may also be implemented with regard to former non-communist regimes. Similarly, parallels should not be drawn between decommunisation and denazification: while both are in a way measures implemented to counter a particular ideology,[199] lustration, despite being a punitive measure, "is not premised on the criminal responsibility of its targets";[200] its scope, however, reflects the "perpetrator-centred" approach taken by the society in question.[201]

An important factor in determining whether lustration is an adequate legal institution of memory to deal with collective trauma-memories of the society in question (and how far-reaching it should be once implemented) is the very nature of the pre-transition regime, which might have seen as broad collaboration across different parts of society through acts that, while morally dubious,[202] were then legal.[203] As such, "the line between victims, by-standers, and perpetrators might be thin and to distinguish precisely between the categories is complicated, if not impossible."[204] This means that lustration needs to incorporate "a different version of accountability for past action within the frame work of the past itself,"[205] bringing openness and transparency to the public sphere in its wake,[206] with one of its main goals being a certain "reset" of social "value systems" and a redefinition of "patterns of acceptable behaviour,"[207] which connects it indirectly with the matters of collective memory, as I will note further in this section.

An additional factor is the nature of the transition itself, which in the case of a negotiated transfer of power and the previous regime's members retaining some level of influence[208] may lead to the rule of law remaining for the large part a mere "façade form of justice and mask actual injustice,"[209] as

198 Grodsky, *supra* note 190 at 63. Cf. Krotoszyński, *supra* note 185 at 35.
199 Andrzej Kaniowski, "Lustration and Decommunisation: Ethical and Theoretical Debates" in Marcin Krygier and Adam Czarnota (eds), *The Rule of Law After Communism Problems and Prospects in East-Central Europe* (Oxon/New York, NY: Routledge, 2016) 212 at 234.
200 Boed, *supra* note 188 at 364–365.
201 David, *supra* note 191 at 31.
202 Czarnota, *supra* note 197 at 174.
203 Horne and Levi, *supra* note 194 at 55.
204 Martin Faix and Ondrej Onrej Svacek, "Dealing with the Past: Prosecution and Punishment of Communist Crimes in Central and Eastern European Countries" (2015) 16:3 Espaço Jurídico 31 at 36.
205 Michéle Harrison, "Choosing a Past: Choosing a Future. Lustration and Transition in the Czech Republic" (2003) 2 Slovak Foreign Policy Affairs 54 at 58.
206 Matt Killingsworth, "Lustration After Totalitarianism: Poland's Attempt to Reconcile with Its Communist Past" (2010) 43 Communist and Post-Communist Studies 275 at 279.
207 Roman David, *Lustration and Transitional Justice: Personnel Systems in the Czech Republic, Hungary, and Poland* (Philadelphia, PA: University of Pennsylvania Press, 2011) at 195.
208 Appel, *supra* note 192 at 403.
209 Czarnota, *supra* note 197 at 170.

the new authorities' focus on future issues may push the questions of dealing with the past to the background.[210] At the same time, the severity of the previous regime also plays a vital role in the process of choosing the model of lustration: for example, as Stan notes in the case of Hungary, the "liberalised communist past, negotiated transition and post-communist present" led to a "toothless lustration," as the so-called "goulash communism" (feeble Kádár regime in Hungary in the years following the 1956 revolution) resulted in "goulash justice" following 1989.[211] Another important factor is the availability of competent replacements for various bureaucratic positions,[212] which may be difficult to find among those not associated with the previous regime.

Proponents of lustration, who often include not only politicians but also NGOs (which can become influential actors in the process),[213] stress that "democratisation, the rule of law and the practice of lustration are inseparable,"[214] arguing that following a regime change, the process needs to be employed to "safeguard" the post-transitory developments.[215] Lustration's goals, in addition to the aforementioned "value reset," include ensuring that the former authorities and their supporters not only are not free of any punishment,[216] simply able to "enjoy their spoils in the new democratic system," but also that they cease to pose a significant danger to the new democratic government, as even with the best intentions towards the new authorities, they may always be blackmailed should the information regarding the extent or the very fact of their collaboration remain hidden.[217] Without early lustration, some of the nefarious members or supporters of the former regime may remain in power, later blocking attempts at lustration,[218] which could see the "personalisation and localisation" of their previous overreaches,

210 Dragoş Petrescu, "Rok 1989 jako powrót do Europy: O rewolucji, reformie i pojednaniu z traumatyczną przeszłością" ["Year 1989 as a Return to Europe: About Revolution, Reform and Reconciliation with a Traumatic Past"] in Krzysztof Brzechczyn (ed.), *Interpretacje upadku komunizmu w Polsce i w Europie Środkowo-Wschodniej. Studia i materiały poznańskiego IPN, t. XIV* [*Interpretations of the Fall of Communism in Poland and Central and Eastern Europe: Studies and Materials of Poznań IPN*] (Poznań: Instytut Pamięci Narodowej, 2011) 15 at 35.

211 Lavinia Stan, "Goulash Justice for Goulash Communism? Explaining Transitional Justice in Hungary" (2007) VII:2 Studia Politica. Romanian Political Science Review 269 at 279.

212 Andrei C. Macsut, "Lustration and Reform in Romania" (2011) I Annals of "Ştefan cel Mare" University of Suceava: Philosophy, Social and Human Disciplines 113 at 117.

213 Despina Angelovska, "The Failure of Macedonian Post-Communist Transitional Justice: Lustration, Between Cleansing and Parody" in Olivera Simić and Zala Volčič (eds), *Transitional Justice and Civil Society in the Balkans* (New York, NY/Heidelberg/Dordrecht/London: Springer, 2013) 51 at 58–60.

214 Czarnota, *supra* note 197 at 180.

215 Boed, *supra* note 188 at 359.

216 Boed, *supra* note 188 at 399.

217 Horne and Levi, *supra* note 194 at 68.

218 Mascut, *supra* note 212 at 123.

making them visible and tangible for the general public.[219] As such, lustration becomes one of the ways of "providing the new polity with political legitimacy,"[220] impacting, through the re-arranging "of the constitutional setting of society and state"[221] following a transition, "not only a democratic polity, but also a moral one,"[222] bringing the "value reset" mentioned earlier and ultimately breaking the ties established during the previous regime,[223] at the same time acting as a political "weapon" used to protect the new one.[224]

Opponents of lustration as a legal institution often focus on its highly political dimension, comparing it to a forced performance in a grotesque play,[225] participation in "the game of dossiers"[226] (belonging to the former regime's secret services, to which I turn in greater detail later in this section), or even "moral not legal" witch hunts.[227] While the broader issues of legal politicisation of collective memory, including the question of national memory institutes (directly linked to the matters of lustration), will be analysed further in this part of the book, the potential for using secret police files publicly (or behind closed doors, for the aforementioned blackmail purposes) against political opponents,[228] possibly creating "a cycle of escalation" as successive governments come into power[229] and thus turning the whole lustration process into "a function of political expediency,"[230] needs to be stressed here. As such, despite being employed to protect it, the process of engaging in lustration raises questions about the legal institution's compliance with the rule of law[231] – all the more so given that while it needs to achieve a broader consensus in the legislative body to be implemented,[232] in practice, it can take

219 Harrison, *supra* note 205 at 57.
220 Killingsworth, *supra* note 206 at 279.
221 Czarnota, *supra* note 197 at 175.
222 Liviu Damsa, "Lustration (Administrative Justice) and Closure in Post-Communist East Central Europe" (2011) 1:4 International Journal of Public Law and Policy 335 at 338.
223 Csilla Kiss, "We Must Remember Thus: Transitional Justice in Service of Memory in Hungary" (2014) XI Studia Universitatis Cibiniensis. Series Historica 71 at 72.
224 Appel, *supra* note 192 at 400.
225 Jiřína Šiklová, "Lustration or the Czech Way of Screening" in Marcin Krygier and Adam Czarnota (eds), *The Rule of Law After Communism Problems and Prospects in East-Central Europe* (Oxon/New York, NY: Routledge, 2016) 248 at 248.
226 Jan Stradowski, "Gry lustracyjne" ["Lustration Games"] (2005), online: Wprost <wprost.pl/72862/gry-lustracyjne.html>.
227 Šiklová, *supra* note 225 at 265.
228 Appel, *supra* note 192 at 399.
229 Horne and Levi, *supra* note 194 at 60.
230 Csilla Kiss, "The Misuses of Manipulation: The Failure of Transitional Justice in Post-Communist Hungary" (2006) 58:6 Europe-Asia Studies 925 at 927.
231 Kaniowski, *supra* note 199 at 238.
232 Lavinia Stan, "If I Could Turn Back Time: Justice and Memory in Post-Communism" (2009), online: Academia.edu <academia.edu/1657580/If_I_Could_Turn_Back_Time_Justice_and_Memory_in_Post_Communism> 1 at 5–6.

place even without structured lustration mechanisms in place.[233] Moreover, a correlation between stronger economic growth and growing support for lustration has been observed,[234] in a way stressing its political angle, which results in the process often not being applied consequently.[235] Conversely, it has been argued that lustration should be introduced immediately following a transition,[236] and not once the society in question has achieved stability, given that – as noted earlier in this section – one of its main goals is the protection of a post-transitory regime, with Calhoun stipulating that "a dose of controlled instability in the [then] present will inoculate the country against unpredictable outbursts in the future."[237] This suggests that, when implemented at a later stage, lustration has been noted to be of more political than legal nature and "far more expensive, time consuming and delicate to undertake,"[238] potentially creating more problems than remedies. However, not introducing it at all will not lead to collective forgetting and the disappearance of the underlying issues, as the question of lustration "has a remarkable ability to endure."[239]

In turn, its opponents argue that lustration may be perceived as leading "to new injustices,"[240] a means of "assigning collective guilt without a determination of an individual's responsibility for any harm caused."[241] This potentially violates "fair employment laws" and ultimately undermines the "right to due process and individual liberties inherent in a rule-of-law state," depending on the secret police files created by the authorities of the previous regime,[242] which oftentimes are of dubious quality[243] and large quantity, making their complete cataloguing an issue in itself.[244] It possibly also leads to the mislabelling of some innocent people as collaborators.[245]

The archives of the former regime's secret services on which the lustration process is based have a particular link with collective memory. They should be regarded as the aforementioned Foucauldian heterotopias – not mere

233 Lavinia Stan, *Transitional Justice in Post-Communist Romania: The Politics of Memory* (Cambridge: Cambridge University Press, 2012) at 253.
234 Grodsky, *supra* note 190 at 73.
235 Faix and Svacek, *supra* note 204 at 36.
236 David Kosař, "Lustration and Lapse of Time: 'Dealing with the Past' in the Czech Republic" (2008) 3 Eric Stein Working Paper 460 at 485.
237 Noel Calhoun, "The Ideological Dilemma of Lustration in Poland" (2002) 16:2 East European Politics and Societies 494 at 517.
238 Mascut, *supra* note 212 at 121.
239 Calhoun, *supra* note 237 at 496.
240 Grodsky, *supra* note 190 at 66.
241 Boed, *supra* note 188 at 359.
242 Appel, *supra* note 192 at 397.
243 Grodsky, *supra* note 190 at 64.
244 Czarnota, *supra* note 197 at 168–169.
245 Faix and Svacek, *supra* note 204 at 37.

archives, but rather not easily accessible[246] heterotopias of deviation, housing dossiers of former collaborators connected to the regime of yesteryear, now transformed into carriers of collective memory, influencing the society in question until lustration processes may be completed (which often remains an unattainable ideal),[247] as the differences in the adopted model of lustration will have a notable, if not easily predictable, impact on that society's perception of the former regime's collaborators.[248]

Importantly, lustration's links with collective memory go far beyond the archival question. As has been noted, the legal institution of memory has been used following the post-1989 transitions to reconceptualise[249] and assign "new meanings"[250] to the past in a way presupposing other, non-institutionalised memory processes taking place within the affected societies.[251] An element of the broader mechanisms of "recovering and bringing back memory"[252] and a basis for reconciliation[253] – which in turn is heavily influenced by various factors brought by the results of lustration, such as the individual reasons for previous collaboration becoming public[254] – lustration is not only past- but also future-oriented.[255] Although the later lustration is introduced, the less influence it has on a society's collective memory,[256] it always plays an important role in the interpretation of the past,[257] ultimately becoming a permanent part of the "political process and political struggle"[258] of the post-transitional days. As such, lustration is a legal institution of memory of major importance, vital in the delegitimisation of the previous regime,[259] re-establishing

246 Mascut, *supra* note 212 at 120.
247 Stan, *supra* note 233 at 233.
248 David, *supra* note 191 at 36–37.
249 Harrison, *supra* note 205 at 57.
250 David, *supra* note 207 at 196.
251 Cristian Tileagă, "Troubled Pasts, Collective Memory, and Collective Futures" in Constance de Saint-Laurent, Sandra Obradović, and Kevin R. Carriere (eds), *Imagining Collective Futures Perspectives from Social, Cultural and Political Psychology* (Cham: Palgrave Macmillan, 2018) 153 at 158.
252 Patrycja Bałdys and Katarzyna Piątek, "Collective Memory as a Tool for the Reconstruction of the Past in Central and Eastern Europe" in Patrycja Bałdys and Katarzyna Piątek (eds), *Alternative Memory-Alternative History: Reconstruction of the Past in the Central and Eastern Europe* (Gdynia/Bielsko Biała: Polish Naval Academy in Gdynia/University of Bielsko-Biala, 2015) 23 at 31.
253 Boed, *supra* note 188 at 400.
254 David, *supra* note 207 at 214–216.
255 Harrison, *supra* note 205 at 54.
256 Calhoun, *supra* note 237 at 519.
257 Piotr Pomostowski, "'Czeski błąd' i polski 'Kret': O różnych filmowych obliczach lustracji" ["'Czech Mistake' and Polish 'Mole': About Various Cinematic Faces of Lustration"] (2012) XI:20 Images 83 at 84–85.
258 Czarnota, *supra* note 197 at 172.
259 Harrison, *supra* note 205 at 55.

the ways in which it is going to be remembered, in particular among those who have not experienced it first-hand,[260] with the lustration-influenced collective memories contributing to the rebuilding of the legal culture[261] of the society in question. At the same time, however, the direct impact of lustration on collective memory is limited,[262] which is why, alongside the fact that questions of memory are of a secondary importance to lustration laws, I choose to classify it as a medium legal institution of memory.

Medium Institution II. Past Atrocities, Divergent Memories, One (?) Narrative: Truth (and Reconciliation) Commissions

In the face of a need to deal with troubling issues of the past, lustration is often put alongside and compared with another medium legal institution of memory, i.e., a commission of inquiry,[263] better known today by its "Orwellian name"[264] as truth – and in some cases truth and reconciliation – commission, presenting the two institutions as alternatives. I have argued myself elsewhere that implementing a truth and reconciliation commission in the countries of Central Europe might have given them a much-needed "revolutionary catharsis," which lustration was never able to achieve, thus potentially allowing them to conclusively deal with their collective trauma-memories.[265] However, it needs to be stressed here that lustration and truth commissions should not be considered interchangeable. While they share some of the same goals, namely, the reinforcing of the new regime through the support of particular values (main purpose of lustration, secondary for truth commissions) and the allowing for dealing with a difficult past (main task of truth commissions, secondary for lustration), their ideological construction is different. Where lustration is a method of administrative justice, truth commissions are, as this section will show, planned as a moral response to past atrocities, acting not so much in "the legal arena," but rather in

260 Tileagă, *supra* note 251 at 166.

261 Czarnota, *supra* note 197 at 177.

262 Michal Vit, "Lustration in Czech Politics" in Marcin Moskalewicz and Wojciech Przybylski (eds), *Understanding Central Europe* (Oxon/New York, NY: Routledge, 2018) 401 at 405.

263 Jemima Garcia-Goods, "Victim Reparations in the Peruvian Truth Commission and the Challenge of Historical Interpretation" (2008) 2:1 The International Journal of Transitional Justice 63 at 63.

264 Mark Freeman, *Truth Commissions and Procedural Fairness* (Cambridge/New York, NY: Cambridge University Press, 2006) at 11.

265 Mirosław M. Sadowski, "Law and Collective Memory in the Service of Illiberalism. Through the Looking-Glass: Transformation or a Reactionary Revolution?" (2021) XVIII:1 Krakowskie Studia Międzynarodowe – Krakow International Studies 107 at 118–119.

"the realms of ethics and emotions,"[266] constantly in between the questions of "legal-forensic and narrative historical," or truth and memory,[267] often concerned more with the past[268] than looking towards the future. (This is primarily why, in spite of its large impact on the social perceptions of the past, I consider the truth commission to be a medium legal institution of memory.) The two, lustration and truth commissions, should thus not be regarded as substitutes but as complementary methods, and they have been used as such in unified Germany following the fall of the German Democratic Republic (GDR) and reunification.[269]

A truth commission may be defined as a legal institution of memory created as a temporary non-judicial *ad hoc* measure implemented in response to a particular period of past atrocities in the society in question where large-scale prosecutions are not possible. Despite being established in the state by an organ of this state or, less often, an international organisation, they are semi-independent, and their main task is to determine (and bring to public knowledge, official narrative, and ultimately collective memory) the truth about the investigated events and their causes and consequences, by focusing mainly on victims and ultimately providing an official report and recommendations to the authorities and society at large.[270] Truth commissions have been employed notably in South America, Africa, and South Asia, and in transitional contexts,[271] but they have also been incidentally established in Central Europe and North America,[272] and many years following a transition,[273] as well as in non-transitional contexts.[274]

266 Greg Grandin, "The Instruction of Great Catastrophe: Truth Commissions, National History, and State Formation in Argentina, Chile, and Guatemala" (2005) 110:1 The American Historical Review 46 at 47.

267 Onur Bakiner, "One Truth Among Others? Truth Commissions' Struggle for Truth and Memory" (2015) 8:3 Memory Studies 345 at 346.

268 Nenad Dimitrijević, "Justice Beyond Blame Moral Justification of (the Idea of) a Truth Commission" (2006) 50:3 Journal of Conflict Resolution 368 at 373.

269 Molly Andrews, "Grand National Narratives and the Project of Truth Commissions: A Comparative Analysis" (2003) 25:1 Media, Culture & Society 45 at 50.

270 Freeman, *supra* note 264 at 3, 12–18.

271 David, *supra* note 16 at 155.

272 David Webster, "Introduction: Memory, Truth, and Reconciliation in Timor-Leste, Indonesia, and Melanesia" in David Webster (ed.), *Flowers in the Wall: Truth and Reconciliation in Timor-Leste, Indonesia, and Melanesia* (Calgary: University of Calgary Press, 2018) 1 at 4–5.

273 André Dias, "Memories About Truth: Journalistic Narratives, 'True Stories,' and the Clash of Memories in Brazil's National Truth Commission" in Véronique Tadjo (ed.), *The Culture of Dissenting Memory: Truth Commissions in the Global South* (Oxon/New York, NY: Routledge, 2019) 41 at 44.

274 Matt James, "A Carnival of Truth? Knowledge, Ignorance and the Canadian Truth and Reconciliation Commission" (2012) 6 The International Journal of Transitional Justice 182 at 185.

With large-scale prosecutions, as noted immediately previously but also in the section on international tribunals, impossible in the context of widespread atrocities or in the case of atrocities that took place in a distant past,[275] truth commissions are created as a response to the "many needs of victims and communities"[276] affected by these events. This is due most importantly to their "potential capacity for producing" an accurate official narrative,[277] clarifying the past and breaking social silences on the events in question,[278] and also turning the whole society's attention to the reasons for "the widespread culture of tolerance of injustice" being allowed to appear in the first place[279] back in the day.

The question of truth, i.e., the facts about the nature and extent of the investigated atrocities,[280] and the place of victims in this respect are of major importance for truth commissions: while the victims themselves are aware of the truth and do not necessarily learn "new truth" by participating in a commission's proceedings, they are offered a "powerful" and potentially "cathartic" experience of giving testimony[281] and thus, in a process noted earlier in the book, returning to society.[282] Their "reintegration"[283] takes place as the former victims' truth becomes "formally recognised"[284] for all of the group's members to see[285] for the very first time – provided that they are able to see it. Public reception is key should a truth commission be able to influence a society, which is why open and accessible ways of conducting the truth commission's proceedings are vital[286] and need to be followed by an active process of social dissemination of its findings – the final report – whereby a major role

275 Onur Bakiner, *Truth Commissions: Memory, Power, and Legitimacy* (Philadelphia, PA: University of Pennsylvania Press, 2006) at 43.
276 David, *supra* note 16 at 155.
277 Garcia-Godos, *supra* note 263 at 63.
278 Priscilla B. Hayner, *Unspeakable Truths: Confronting State Terror and Atrocity* (New York, NY: Routledge, 2001) at 24–25.
279 Dimitrijević, *supra* note 268 at 381.
280 Dimitrijević, *supra* note 268 at 375.
281 Hayner, *supra* note 278 at 139–140.
282 David A. Crocker, "Truth Commissions, Transitional Justice, and Civil Society" in Robert I. Rotberg and Dennis F. Thompson (eds), *Truth v. Justice: The Morality of Truth Commissions* (Princeton, NJ: Princeton University Press, 2000) 99 at 102.
283 Yasmin Sooka, "Dealing with the Past and Transitional Justice: Building Peace Through Accountability" (2006) 88:862 International Review of the Red Cross 311 at 319.
284 Hayner, *supra* note 278 at 26.
285 Judith L. Coullie, "Remembering to Forget: Testimony, Collective Memory and the Genesis of the 'New' South African Nation in 'Country of My Skull' " (2007) 19:2 Current Writing: Text and Reception in Southern Africa 123 at 124.
286 Crocker, *supra* note 282 at 101.

is played by civil society,[287] as well as the instigation of processes of not only collective remembering but also collective evoking.[288]

However, despite conducting – in most cases – a large number of interviews, truth commissions are usually able to fully investigate only a handful of cases while using others for analysis and statistical research.[289] It also means that the individual voices of the victims (the "micro truth") will ultimately be lost, reconstructed to create one official narrative (the "macro truth"),[290] and thus one collective memory from many individual memories – in certain cases also including various collective memories of local communities if investigated by a commission.[291] One memory, however, is now beneficial for society in a way liberated from the *circulus vitiosus* of collective trauma-memories.[292]

This is the second main goal of truth commissions: following the uncovering of the truth, they are tasked with the creation of an official narrative based on this newly established truth, and given that "their verdict on history carries the promise of official endorsement,"[293] a new "social consensus" may be forged[294] around it. To achieve this goal, a truth commission needs to "be rooted in the realities and possibilities of its particular environment," aiming to "understand the origins of past conflict and the factors that allowed abuses to take place," at the same time being "supportive of victims and inclusive of a wide range of perspectives."[295] This "social embeddedness," however, may limit a commission's ability to stay completely neutral[296] and may prove problematic should its work uncover some truths that will be uncomfortable for the victims of the atrocity in question.[297]

In addition to truth-finding and the establishment of a new official narrative, truth commissions may also have, depending on their mandate – which in case of additional tasks should be particularly clearly defined normatively to avoid undue politicisation[298] – secondary goals, which include the fostering

287 Webster, *supra* note 272 at 10.
288 Lisa J. Laplante, "The Peruvian Truth Commission's Historical Memory Project: Empowering Truth-Tellers to Confront Truth Deniers" (2007) 6:4 Journal of Human Rights 433 at 445.
289 Hayner, *supra* note 278 at 140.
290 Bakiner, *supra* note 275 at 78.
291 Elizabeth Nannelli, "Memory, Records, History: The Records of the Commission for Reception, Truth, and Reconciliation in Timor-Leste" (2009) 9:1–2 Archival Science 29 at 35.
292 Laplante, *supra* note 288 at 434.
293 Bakiner, *supra* note 267 at 346.
294 Bakiner, *supra* note 275 at 63.
295 Priscilla B. Hayner, "Truth Commissions: A Schematic Overview" (2006) 88:862 International Review of the Red Cross 295 at 296.
296 Bakiner, *supra* note 275 at 68.
297 Bakiner, *supra* note 275 at 69.
298 Dimitrijević, *supra* note 268 at 377.

of a new legal culture, based on democracy[299] and human rights,[300] enshrining new, moral values in society[301] and thus rehabilitating the state,[302] and reconciliation, which, to stress once again, is not always the aim of truth commissions (then known as truth and reconciliation commissions).[303] However, even if it remains beyond a commission's mandate, establishing a truthful, official narrative of past events is a prerequisite,[304] a "starting point"[305] for reconciliation; it may take place only once the new "metanarrative" becomes firmly entrenched in a society,[306] as the "sense that there are shared tragedies in" a society's history[307] allows it to put their collective trauma-memories behind.

In spite of their many potential benefits, truth commissions are not free from issues. Perceived as "high-risk endeavours," given the "diverse motives" behind their creation,[308] they are highly politicised by different actors.[309] This is in a way natural, given that, on a practical level, truth commissions need to relay on "state bureaucracy" in order to function,[310] and, on a conceptual level, "both produce and are produced by grand national narratives,"[311] as they are infused with a "set of values" adopted as key by the new regime.[312] However, their politicisation carries certain dangers within: it might lead to "depoliticising and generalising" past atrocities, using the commission's work as a starting point for a new socio-political future of the society in question,[313] or even recontextualising and rewriting it many years following

299 Donald W. Shriver Jr., "Truth Commissions and Judicial Trials: Complementary or Antagonistic Servants of Public Justice?" (2001) 16:1 Journal of Law and Religion 1 at 12–14.
300 Martha Minow, "Making History or Making Peace: When Prosecutions Should Give Way to Truth Commissions and Peace Negotiations" (2008) 7:2 Journal of Human Rights 174 at 181.
301 Shriver, *supra* note 299 at 15–26.
302 Michael Humphrey, "From Victim to Victimhood: Truth Commissions and Trials as Rituals of Political Transition and Individual Healing" (2003) 14:2 The Australian Journal of Anthropology 171 at 172.
303 Kevin Avruch, "Truth and Reconciliation Commissions: Problems in Transitional Justice and the Reconstruction of Identity" (2010) 47:1 Transcultural Psychiatry 33 at 35, 39–40.
304 Crocker, *supra* note 282 at 101.
305 Mona C. Schwartz, "Truth Commissions and Collective Memory in Latin America", online: ScholarWorks University of Montana <scholarworks.umt.edu/utpp/56/> at 21.
306 Avruch, *supra* note 303 at 38.
307 Coullie, *supra* note 285 at 139.
308 Freeman, *supra* note 264 at 37–38.
309 Kimberly R. Lanegran, "Truth Commissions, Human Rights Trials, and the Politics of Memory" (2005) 25:1 Comparative Studies of South Asia, Africa and the Middle East 111 at 112.
310 Chirwa, *supra* note 43 at 480.
311 Andrews, *supra* note 269 at 46.
312 Dimitrijević, *supra* note 268 at 376.
313 Heidi Grunebaum, *Memorializing the Past: Everyday Life in South Africa After the Truth and Reconciliation Commission* (Oxon/New York, NY: Routledge, 2017) at 25.

the completion of a commission's proceedings to fit the current socio-political reality.[314] Moreover, a truth commission's work may be impeded by certain elements of the current or former authorities,[315] or even mistrusted by those parts of society not directly affected by the previous regime[316] who remain sceptical towards the new, in their own way also "political" revelations.[317]

While truth commissions are considered to be a fertile ground for breeding new agents of memory "to confront status-quo keepers,"[318] once established, their additional goals of improving democracy and human rights within the society in question have been observed not to be actually impacted by the whole process[319] in the short term, rather, like international tribunals analysed earlier, first creating global memories, only having a truly meaningful impact on the society in question in the long term.[320] Immediately in their wake, truth commissions seem to provide an opportunity, "an advance," and not "a guarantee of either justice or democracy."[321]

Moreover, following the uncovering of truth categorisation of certain parts of society as victims and others as perpetrators, the potentially "easy" process of bridging social divisions may prove problematic, given the much more "complex social reality."[322] As such, once a commission finishes its work, social debates about the past will still persist,[323] inhibiting the possibility of reconciliation, which requires at least a minimum level of agreement on the past – and the future.[324] Additionally, the "metanarrative" established by a commission, while presented as a step towards social unity, may potentially be used as a veil for the commission's role "as an agent of nationalism."[325]

314 Francesca Lessa, *Memory and Transitional Justice in Argentina and Uruguay: Against Impunity* (New York, NY: Palgrave Macmillan, 2013) at 126–127.
315 Sooka, *supra* note 283 at 316.
316 Bakiner, *supra* note 267 at 349.
317 Monica Ciobanu, "Criminalising the Past and Reconstructing Collective Memory: The Romanian Truth Commission" (2009) 61:2 Europe-Asia Studies 313 at 334.
318 Laplante, *supra* note 288 at 441.
319 Eric Wiebelhaus-Brahm, *Truth Commissions and Transitional Societies: The Impact on Human Rights and Democracy* (London/New York, NY: Routledge, 2011) at 140–141.
320 James L. Gibson, *Overcoming Apartheid: Can Truth Reconcile a Divided Nation?* (New York: Russell Sage Foundation, 2004) at 77.
321 Charles S. Maier, "Doing History, Doing Justice: The Narrative of the Historian and of the Truth Commission" in Robert I. Rotberg and Dennis F. Thompson (eds), *Truth v. Justice: The Morality of Truth Commissions* (Princeton, NJ: Princeton University Press, 2000) 261 at 273.
322 Garcia-Godos, *supra* note 263 at 67.
323 Hayner, *supra* note 278 at 27.
324 Avruch, *supra* note 303 at 40.
325 Grandin, *supra* note 266 at 64.

It should also be stressed that, often as a direct result of political compromise,[326] truth commissions tend to have a limited mandate,[327] which may interact with several other potentially further restrictive factors in the social, political and legal sphere (some of them already outlined),[328] most importantly the premise of amnesty to perpetrators, which, if granted, may prove particularly problematic to the victims. Its negative effects, however, can be mitigated by linking truth commissions with other legal institutions of memory, such as reparations, both material and symbolic.[329] At the same time, another potential problem for victims is the lack of any long-term psychological support, which may often prove necessary following the recounting of their difficult experiences before the commission.[330]

What may also prove difficult for some of the victims is the understanding that, given their design as non-judicial bodies, truth commissions cannot provide complete justice on a legal level as courts do, such as imposing sanctions (apart from publicising the perpetrators' names in some cases), and, due to their focus on the victims, their investigations cannot be considered trials,[331] given that they often disrespect due process and other procedural matters as a result.[332] Moreover, they can only propose recommendations that require political will to put into work,[333] thus breaking Levinas's approach towards true reconciliation, which, as noted above, needs to move away from public outrage as a first step. However, they most definitely have the potential, in the case of prosecutions on the basis of their work,[334] to be "either a vital ingredient of justice" or, even in the (oftentimes) case of an amnesty, justice's "best available approximation."[335] As I mentioned before, due to this limited legal impact, I regard truth commissions as only a medium legal institution of memory, their meaningful influence on collective memory notwithstanding.

As Durkheimian performative[336] rituals,[337] truth commissions allow for "collective mourning"[338] and "narrativise" a society's past, intersecting

326 Maier, *supra* note 321 at 262.
327 Brants and Klep, *supra* note 143 at 47.
328 Bakiner, *supra* note 275 at 112.
329 David, *supra* note 16 at 156–158.
330 Hayner, *supra* note 278 at 135.
331 Freeman, *supra* note 264 at 71–72.
332 Hayner, *supra* note 295 at 296.
333 Rebekka Friedman, *Competing Memories: Truth and Reconciliation in Sierra Leone and Peru* (Cambridge: Cambridge University Press, 2017) at 158.
334 Hayner, *supra* note 278 at 29.
335 Freeman, *supra* note 264 at 83.
336 Grandin, *supra* note 266 at 46.
337 Dario R. Paez and James Hou-Fu Liu, "Collective Memory of Conflicts" in Daniel Bar-Tal (ed.), *Intergroup Conflicts and Their Resolution: A Social Psychological Perspective* (New York, NY/Hove: Psychology Press, 2011) 105 at 117–118.
338 Coullie, *supra* note 285 at 133.

with collective memory on several different levels, first by bringing former counter-memories to the forefront of debate[339] and then turning them, as previously noted, into one collective memory (or rather, given the diversity of collective memories, one "authorised" public version of it)[340] in the course of "flattening-out" the "complex memories and understandings of the past into an inclusive nation-building narrative."[341] Importantly, this process – to follow Foucault's observation outlined in Chapter 2 – "evens out"[342] the questions of power surrounding memory issues, as "the spectacle of the victim's pain and suffering" taking place before a commission "inverts the ritual of power," granting those suffering under the previous regime their humanity back.[343]

The key element in the establishment of new official narratives is the publication of a truth commission's final report, which is not a mere text[344] but a major carrier of memory, a "symbolic reparation" in itself,[345] a means of reclaiming "a country's history" and opening "it for public review."[346] It also provides a "road map" towards social development,[347] i.e., recommendations, which may further impact collective memory indirectly – for example, leading to an official apology by a representative of the state[348] – or directly – by proposing the creation of various memorialisation projects.[349] In addition to the final report, the archives of a truth commission, such as the aforementioned archives of an international tribunal, may also become an important carrier of memory,[350] as well as various memory projects created in a commission's work wake,[351] thus allowing for further harmonisation[352] of collective memory and its ultimate reconstruction, which in turn may prevent further atrocities in the future.[353]

339 Bakiner, *supra* note 275 at 73.
340 Lanegran, *supra* note 309 at 120.
341 Brants and Klep, *supra* note 143 at 37.
342 Laplante, *supra* note 288 at 441.
343 Humphrey, *supra* note 302 at 173.
344 Bakiner, *supra* note 275 at 67.
345 Humphrey, *supra* note 302 at 180.
346 Hayner, *supra* note 278 at 25.
347 Webster, *supra* note 272 at 10.
348 Hayner, *supra* note 278 at 26.
349 Garcia-Godos, *supra* note 263 at 82.
350 Joel A. Blanco-Rivera, "Truth Commissions and the Construction of Collective Memory: The Chile Experience" in Jeannette A. Bastian and Ben Alexander (eds), *Community Archives: The Shaping of Memory* (London: Facet, 2009) 133 at 135.
351 Katrien Klep, "Tracing Collective Memory: Chilean Truth Commissions and Memorial Sites" (2012) 5:3 Memory Studies 259 at 260.
352 Blanco-Rivera, *supra* note 350 at 136–137.
353 Hayner, *supra* note 278 at 29.

As noted earlier, it is the collective memory shift initiated by the work of truth commissions that may have a particularly strong impact, influenced both by the uncovered truth encompassed in the aforementioned commission's archives and final report[354] and the "shifting attitudes toward the other" in its wake.[355] This in turn may even lead to modifications of the initial official narrative established by the truth commission in question,[356] in a way that officially cements the changes to the collective memory of a society.

However, the impact of truth commissions on collective memory, rather successful in terms of raising social awareness and acceptance of a difficult past,[357] may come at a high cost: following a mechanism observed in Chapter 3, in the section concerning transitional justice, a commission's proceedings may lead to a certain deconstruction of a victim's individual memory, with various discrepancies in testimony coming into light,[358] potentially leading to re-traumatisation. Importantly, collective memories uncovered by the commission may prove problematic not only for the victims: akin to the passing of collective trauma-memories to future generations I remarked upon in Part I of the book, the commission members themselves, as well as members of the press covering a commission's proceedings, may become traumatised by their work, in most cases not receiving any psychological support.[359]

At the same time, focusing on particular events and narratives, and not others in the final report, may lead to the exclusion of certain, sometimes even commendable behaviours of parts of the population,[360] which are in a way sacrificed at the altar of the politically influenced[361] "national (re)imagination,"[362] hastening particular collective identity,[363] and in some cases even propagating official narratives of the past which never took place,[364] ultimately leading to collective forgetting. The questions of collective forgetting – often linked to amnesty, which, as noted earlier, may be an element of the truth commissions' framework – are the focus of the next section, devoted to the first hard legal institution of memory, legal amnesia.

354 Cynthia E. Milton, "The Truth Ten Years on: The CVR in Peru" in Eugenia Allier-Montaño and Emilio Crenzel (eds), *The Struggle for Memory in Latin America Recent History and Political Violence* (New York, NY: Palgrave Macmillan, 2010) 111 at 128.

355 Ervin Staub, *Overcoming Evil: Genocide, Violent Conflict, and Terrorism* (Oxford/New York, NY: Oxford University Press, 2011) at 454.

356 Lessa, *supra* note 314 at 129.

357 Grunebaum, *supra* note 313 at 98.

358 Hayner, *supra* note 278 at 148–149.

359 Hayner, *supra* note 278 at 145–146, 149–152.

360 Garcia-Godos, *supra* note 263 at 80–81.

361 Lanegran, *supra* note 309 at 113.

362 Bakiner, *supra* note 275 at 80.

363 Lanegran, *supra* note 309 at 120.

364 Andrews, *supra* note 269 at 58.

Hard Institution I. Law Repressing Memory: Legal Amnesia between Amnesty and Collective Forgetting

Collective forgetting, as noted in one of the previous chapters, is a major element of social perceptions of the past, directly linked to legal amnesia, and, as such, a vital part of the law and memory intersections. As I will demonstrate here, this oldest (next to perhaps material reparations) legal institution of memory (or rather, a legal institution of forgetting) is also the most nebulous one, in a way both casting and hiding in the shadows of the other institutions analysed earlier. As it has been remarked before, whenever law decides upon matters concerning the past, thus establishing a new official narrative, some collective memories will inadvertently not make it, leaving them to be collectively forgotten.

At the same time, legal amnesia may also be distinguished as the first hard legal institution of memory, not only having a major impact on a society's collective memory but also being directly constructed as such through law itself. Whereas previous legal institutions of memory had different goals, with the influence on collective memories being one, often secondary among the others, legal amnesia – just like memory laws, analysed in the next section – has as one of its main goals, if not the main one, the shift in law's – and thus society's – approach towards the past so that reconciliation may be achieved. Manifestations of legal amnesia, a natural element of law's "institutional memory,"[365] may be observed in the very "contingent and mercurial nature of law,"[366] with Goodrich, in his law as a literature genre argument, proposing to understand it "through the very act of forgetting, through the denial, the negation or the repression by means of which it institutes its identity, its life, its fictive forms," consigning "its sources, its languages, its judges and legislators" into oblivion in the hopes of assuming "the modern character and quality of the discourse of fate."[367] As such, legal amnesia is noticeable in a number of legal constructs (statues of limitations[368] or rehabilitation,[369] for example), and particularly in common law, with the precedent ultimately based on collective forgetting, as law's practice, "its presence and its violence," becomes "displaced into the abstract formulation of the necessity and normativity of its practice."[370] Legal amnesia is most visible, however,

365 Peter Goodrich, *Law in the Courts of Love: Literature and Other Minor Jurisprudences* (London/New York, NY: Routledge, 1996) at 114.

366 Marouf A. Hasian Jr., *Legal Memories and Amnesias in America's Rhetorical Culture* (Boulder, CO: Westview Press, 2000) at 2.

367 Goodrich, *supra* note 365 at 112.

368 Adam Czarnota, "Między polityką a prawem, czyli o sprawiedliwości okresu przejściowego" ["Between Politics and Law, or About Transitional Justice"] (2015) 27 Acta UnIversitatis Lodziensis. Folia Philosophica. Ethica Aesthetica Practica 13 at 19.

369 Czarnota, *supra* note 167 at 124.

370 Goodrich, *supra* note 365 at 124.

when taking the very direct form of amnesty laws, which will be the focus of this analysis following a more general introduction of this legal institution of memory.

As Suleiman notes, where forgive and forget often appear as a pair in the "ethical and individual" dimension, on the "juridical and collective" level, so do "amnesty and amnesia."[371] This is one of the reasons why amnesty often becomes part of the truth commissions' framework, which I noted earlier. Notably, the "desired" legal amnesia should mean holding "the past in reserve," but "forgetting without amnesia" and "forgiving without effacing the debt one owes to the dead,"[372] in a way realising the aforementioned Levinasian concept that law needs to be grounded in ethics influenced by collective memories of past difficulties.

Interestingly, this theoretical ideal was in a way established at the moment of legal amnesia's introduction as an institution of law: while amnesties also appeared earlier in ancient Greece, it was the Athenian amnesty of 403 BC that became the model.[373] Following the period of oligarchs' rule and a civil war, a "reconciliation agreement" was reached based on the concept of civil amnesia (an *a-mnēsteia*) being imposed on the collective trauma-memories of the period of conflict in the hopes of bringing the society together.[374] Importantly, the agreement, asking for *me mnesikakein* ("not to remember past wrongs"),[375] did not prohibit remembering the events in question *per se* (unlike some memory legislation belonging to the third category, analysed further in this chapter) but rather forbade "bringing legal prosecutions for crimes committed during this period," thus banning legal memory.[376] As such, the Athenian "legal system" turned into an "organ of memory for a city that wills itself to forget the past,"[377] guaranteeing social unity, but in a negative way, "by adhering to a litany of prohibitions"[378] (unlike soft and medium legal institutions of memory introduced earlier), which is the key to understanding why I propose to understand legal amnesia as a hard legal institution of memory.

Importantly, the "model" Athenian legal amnesia was based on keeping the collective memories of the civil war alive (also by memorialising its

371 Susan R. Suleiman, *Crises of Memory and the Second World War* (Cambridge, MA: Harvard University Press, 2006) at 216–217.

372 *Ibid.* at 232.

373 Andrew Wolpert, *Remembering Defeat: Civil War and Civic Memory in Ancient Athens* (Baltimore, MD: Johns Hopkins University Press, 2002) at 76–77.

374 Victoria Wohl, *Law's Cosmos: Juridical Discourse in Athenian Forensic Oratory* (Cambridge/New York, NY: Cambridge University Press, 2010) at 204.

375 Wolpert, *supra* note 373 at 76.

376 Wohl, *supra* note 374 at 204.

377 Wohl, *supra* note 374 at 205.

378 Wolpert, *supra* note 373 at 81.

heroes),[379] as "reconciliation was" – and in a way always is – "renegotiable," based on the "consent" and "continual vigilance" of all parts of society.[380] Thus, ideal legal amnesia should lead not to collective forgetting but rather to "mindful forgetfulness," with the perception of reconciliation shifted "from a symbol of compromise into a symbol of victory" alongside amnesty, now seen "as promoting, not complicating, justice."[381] As such, legal amnesia in the form of an amnesty allowed the city's community to maintain the illusion of social, political, and legal continuity with the period before the crisis,[382] not unlike Latvia's decision to reinstate its 1922 constitution following what was called not a regaining but a "*de facto* renewal" of independence in 1990,[383] pushing the previous 50-year period of communism into legal amnesia.

This ideal of limiting legal amnesia's impact to civil amnesia might have worked in the sheltered realities of the Athenian *polis* and may still be applied in the case of legal fictions such as the Latvian one; most often in contemporary times, however, legal amnesia leads to a certain degree of collective forgetting. As I have already noticed in this section and in the more minute details of the analysis of the four previous legal institutions of memory, when a particular memory enters the official narrative through law and becomes collective memory, those not included will ultimately be lost to a certain degree, potentially becoming counter-memories in the process of "selection and rejection,"[384] but forgotten nonetheless for large parts of society, particularly in the case of global memories. Thus, as I also remarked upon earlier, some atrocities (e.g., Rwandan genocide) become enshrined as genocide, while others slide into collective oblivion, living on only in the collective (counter-)memory of the affected group.

Moreover, as Simpson poignantly observes, "the moment of juridical remembrance" may itself constitute "a moment of amnesia," noting that the Nuremberg Tribunal's charter was "signed the day before the bomb on Nagasaki was dropped" and how the Holocaust itself was "obscured" by the complexity of international law during the IMT's proceedings.[385] Most importantly, in some cases law discards the Athenian "ideal" on its own, asking members of a society to collectively forget: the Roman institution of "*damnatio memoriae*" meant a complete eradication from the public space

379 Wolpert, *supra* note 373 at 87–90.
380 Wolpert, *supra* note 373 at 77, 80.
381 Wolpert, *supra* note 373 at 87.
382 Wolpert, *supra* note 373 at 84.
383 Jānis Pleps, "The Continuity of the Constitutions: The Examples of the Baltic States and Georgia" (2016) 6:2 Wroclaw Review of Law, Administration and Economics 29 at 35–36.
384 John Frow, "'From toute la mémoire du monde': Repetition and Forgetting" in Michael Rossington and Anne Whitehead (eds), *Theories of Memory: A Reader* (Baltimore, MD: Johns Hopkins University Press, 2007) 150 at 154.
385 Simpson, *supra* note 133 at 101–103.

of certain memories,[386] during the *restauration* in France, for example, the Charter of 1814 explicitly told the "courts and citizens" to forget the revolutionary period;[387] and, also in France, it is prohibited today to "allude to someone's past if those activities fall under a law of amnesty,"[388] additionally limiting archive access in such cases, even for researchers and journalists.[389]

As such, amnesties, the often dubious element of truth commissions' framework (I will answer the question as to why in greater detail here), remain the most blatant example of legal amnesia[390] and merit closer investigation. Following ancient Greece, amnesties became a staple of peace treaties,[391] as memorialised in the Roman maxim "*in amnestia consist substantia pacis*," which kept its validity well into the early modern period,[392] including the "birth of the modern state" with the adoption of the Peace of Westphalia in 1684,[393] implicitly demanding in one of its points that the memory of the atrocities taking place during the Thirty Years' War "shall be bury'd in eternal Oblivion."[394]

This changed in the 20th century. Already in the wake of World War I, the amnesty provisions were conspicuously missing from the Versailles treaty; later, following the 1928 Kellogg-Briand Pact and the prohibition of "the use of force" in international relations, the amnesty lost its place as a typical element of peace treaties. Similarly, it was not widely used after World War II, with amnesties implemented only for those who took part in the war on the side of the Allies, permanently turning the legal institution of memory from a general legal provision introduced in the wake of a conflict into a political tool.[395]

386 Burkhard Schäfer, "'Sometimes You Must Be Kind to Be Cruel': Amnesty Between 'publicae laetitiae and damnatio memoriae'" in Emilios A. Christodoulidis and Scott Veitch (eds), *Lethe's Law: Justice, Law and Ethics in Reconciliation* (Oxford/Portland, OR: Hart Publishing, 2001) 17 at 32.

387 Czarnota, *supra* note 368 at 26–27.

388 Anne Whitehead, *Memory* (Oxon: Routledge, 2009) at 155–156.

389 Suleiman, *supra* note 371 at 218.

390 Kieran McEvoy and Louise Mallinder, "Amnesties in Transition: Punishment, Restoration, and the Governance of Mercy" (2012) 39:3 Journal of Law and Society 410 at 414.

391 Paolo Coroli, "Behind the Rhetoric: The Implications of Prohibiting Amnesties" (2018) 13:1 The Journal of Comparative Law 95 at 95.

392 Maurus Reinkowski, "'Let Bygones Be Bygones': An Ottoman Order to Forget" (2003) 93 Wiener Zeitschrift für die Kunde des Morgenlandes 191 at 199.

393 Gabriela Della Morte, "International Law Between the Duty of Memory and the Right to Oblivion" (2014) 14 International Criminal Law Review 427 at 428.

394 Scott Veitch, "The Legal Politics of Amnesty" in Emilios A. Christodoulidis and Scott Veitch (eds), *Lethe's Law: Justice, Law and Ethics in Reconciliation* (Oxford/Portland, OR: Hart Publishing, 2001) 33 at 33.

395 Faustin Z. Ntoubandi, *Amnesty for Crimes Against Humanity Under International Law* (Leiden/Boston, MA: Martinus Nijhoff Publishers, 2007) at 19–21.

Perceived as "more subtle" than the amnesties of the yesteryear, today's amnesties are at a law-politics-memory crossroads, ordering law to look both at the past and the future,[396] not only an *ad hoc* instrument of peace but also a way of allowing a peaceful transition from an oppressive regime to democracy[397] in a number of cases, as noted in the previous section, introduced as an element of truth commissions. They are still introduced through a legislative process, with their effect being an "immunisation" of certain people from legal liability for certain acts (or the annulment of those sentences already ordered);[398] however, they are used instrumentally (as a "necessary bargaining chip" between the old and new regime)[399] and should be strictly limited to avoid their abuse as a legal instrument.[400]

Nota bene, amnesties should not be confused with a similar-on-the-surface but inherently different mechanism of legal amnesia, which is the pardon – where amnesty has a legislative basis, pardon is rather "an executive act granted by the Head of State."[401] Moreover, where pardon in most cases can take place only following a conviction, amnesties often take place before the beginning of any legal procedure.[402] This is why Greenawalt argues that when a pardon is granted before the course of justice has even begun, it should be regarded rather as an individualised act of amnesty[403] – keeping in mind that in general amnesties are collective acts and pardons individual ones.[404] This means that only amnesties may be considered social rituals in the Durkheimian sense unless part of a larger strategy, whereby pardons are used on such a scale or without individualisation that they become a *de facto* amnesty (as in the case of the Vietnam War draft resisters following President Carter's blanket pardon).[405] Finally, and perhaps most importantly, where a pardon is an act of "official forgiveness," amnesty is an act of "official forgetting."[406]

396 Veitch, *supra* note 394 at 34.
397 Ntoubandi, *supra* note 395 at 12.
398 Mohamed Bennouna, "Truth, Justice and Amnesty" in Lal Chand Vohrah, Fausto Pocar, Yvonne Featherstone, Olivier Fourmy, Christine Graham, John Hocking, and Nicholas Robson (eds), *Man's Inhumanity to Man: Essays on International Law in Honour of Antonio Cassese* (The Hague/London/New York, NY: Kluwer Law International, 2003) 127 at 131.
399 Ntoubandi, *supra* note 395 at 34.
400 Peter Krapp, "Amnesty: Between an Ethics of Forgiveness and the Politics of Forgetting" (2005) 6:1 German Law Journal 185 at 194.
401 Ntoubandi, *supra* note 395 at 10.
402 Suleiman, *supra* note 371 at 218.
403 Kent Greenawalt, "Amnesty's Justice" in Robert I. Rotberg and Dennis F. Thompson (eds), *Truth v. Justice: The Morality of Truth Commissions* (Princeton, NJ: Princeton University Press, 2000) 189 at 189–190.
404 Norman Weisman, "A History and Discussion of Amnesty" (1972) 4:2 Columbia Human Rights Law Review 529 at 530.
405 See: David Shichor and Donald R. Ranish, "President Carter's Vietnam Amnesty: An Analysis of a Public Policy Decision" (1980) 10:3 Presidential Studies Quarterly 443.
406 Suleiman, *supra* note 371 at 218.

The two main goals of amnesty are: the aforementioned hope for a peaceful transition to democracy, one providing stability to the new authorities, whether for fear of reprisals by the members of the previous regime or due to a focus on the future;[407] and, directly linked to it, "reconciliation and reunification" of a society, in the hopes that they lead to permanent peace[408] and, similarly to other legal institutions of memory, help bolster human rights[409] and democracy[410] within the society in question. Importantly, amnesties' success in achieving their goals for the large part rests on their implementation along with other legal institutions of memory,[411] such as truth commissions or international law tribunals introduced earlier.

Amnesties may be classified in different ways: as general (granting "immunity for all wrongful acts" committed during a conflict) and limited (granting "immunity only for specific offences or special groups"); internal (granted by the authorities of the country in question) and external (granted in a post-conflict international treaty);[412] if internal, introduced by the legislature, the executive, or the country's constitution;[413] adopted following a conflict on an international or local scale, and/or as a part of a political transition;[414] automatic or requiring petition for being granted;[415] conditional (provided on a case-by-case basis if the applicant in question agrees to supply certain information – most often the truth about the atrocities they committed) and non-conditional;[416] guaranteeing continued government employment or not;[417] affecting both criminal and civil liability or only the former;[418] involving victims and community participation at a local level or not;[419] and as self-amnesties (implemented by their own beneficiaries) and those established by the proceeding authorities.[420] I argue that this variety of amnesties is a

407 Laura M. Olson, "Provoking the Dragon on the Patio. Matters of Transitional Justice: Penal Repression vs. Amnesties" (2006) 88:862 International Review of the Red Cross 275 at 284.

408 Bennouna, *supra* note 398 at 132–133.

409 Heinz Klug, "Amnesty, Amnesia, and Remembrance: International Obligations and the Need to Prevent the Repetition of Gross Violations of Human Rights" (1998) 92 American Society of International Law Proceedings 316 at 317.

410 Weiffen, *supra* note 155 at 91.

411 Tricia D. Olsen, Leigh A. Payne, and Andrew G. Reiter, "Conclusion: Amnesty in the Age of Accountability" in Francesca Lessa and Leigh A. Payne (eds), *Amnesty in the Age of Human Rights: Accountability Comparative and International Perspectives* (Cambridge: Cambridge University Press, 2012) 336 at 343.

412 Ntoubandi, *supra* note 395 at 12.

413 Bennouna, *supra* note 398 at 132.

414 Ntoubandi, *supra* note 395 at 24.

415 Greenawalt, *supra* note 403 at 195.

416 Bennouna, *supra* note 398 at 131.

417 Klug, *supra* note 409 at 316.

418 Greenawalt, *supra* note 403 at 195.

419 McEvoy and Mallinder, *supra* note 390 at 432.

420 Della Morte, *supra* note 393 at 432.

testament to their long history, their flexibility, and their widespread perception as a valuable legal and political tool.

In spite of their popularity, however, amnesties are not free from controversy, and in recent years, the number of their opponents has been growing,[421] as these instruments of legal amnesia have become heavily scrutinised by the members of both the directly affected national and the international community in general.[422] As Coroli notes, there has been a shift from "a presumption of the legitimacy of amnesty" to "a presumption of its illegality" taking place in both the doctrine and practice of law,[423] due to their increasingly widespread perception as an instrumental way of achieving political goals by committing another injustice:[424] letting the perpetrators go free. In a way, the issues concerning amnesties lay in the law itself, given that they disrupt the traditional temporality of law, "re-writing" the events in question, as well as their "legal significance."[425] When an amnesty is implemented, "law acts but acts as if it is not," which is perceived as a particular social reminder that "law and right are not synonymous" and law, as any cultural product, is "contingent" upon the majoritarian social interest at a particular moment, thus – in this case – breaking its promises of *aequitas*[426] and guaranteeing accountability.[427]

Here, international law comes to help, providing the basis for the disregarding of amnesties concerning crimes that violate international humanitarian law,[428] particularly following the establishment of the ICC, which is not bound by a country's amnesty legislation.[429] That is not to say that amnesties are prohibited under international law[430] or that every amnesty will be disregarded and will lead to a case before the ICC – the Court is not to intervene if pursuing a case was not "in the interests of justice,"[431] and the Rome Statute does not refer to amnesties at all[432] – however, it is possible that

421 Max Pensky, "Amnesty on Trial: Impunity, Accountability, and the Norms of International Law" (2008) 1:1–2 Ethics and Global Politics 1 at 6.

422 McEvoy and Mallinder, *supra* note 390 at 415.

423 Coroli, *supra* note 391 at 100.

424 Greenawalt, *supra* note 403 at 191.

425 Veitch, *supra* note 394 at 36.

426 Erik Doxtader, "Easy to Forget or Never (Again) Hard to Remember? History, Memory and the 'Publicity' of Amnesty" in Erik Doxtader and Charles Villa-Vicencio (eds), *The Provocations of Amnesty: Memory, Justice, and Impunity* (Trenton, NJ: Africa World Press, 2003) 121 at 129–130.

427 Pensky, *supra* note 421 at 21.

428 Olson, *supra* note 407 at 285.

429 Pensky, *supra* note 421 at 13.

430 Coroli, *supra* note 391 at 96.

431 Declan Roche, "Truth Commission Amnesties and the International Criminal Court" (2005) 45:4 The British Journal of Criminology 565 at 568.

432 Coroli, *supra* note 391 at 97.

the ICC's Prosecutor will choose to pursue at least some cases in spite of an amnesty.[433] Similarly, a particular state may choose to disregard an amnesty of an individual on the basis of its universal jurisdiction obligations under international law.[434]

In addition to the questions of compatibility with international law, the obvious role of amnesties as political tools means that an amnesty will not necessarily be able to act as a true instrument of reconciliation.[435] The present-day "mistrust of amnesty," symptomatic of "a general mistrust of political power,"[436] thus becomes another element of the struggle for authority, an important part of which is also the power over the interpretation of the past, as remarked upon after Foucault in Chapter 2. This mechanism becomes particularly visible when amnesties are employed by truth commissions, disrupting collective memories: given their politicisation, it is not the actual truth that is the result of the truth-telling process before a commission, but rather "the fulfilment of an expectation of a legal memory that could not have had an original correspondent legal truth" and whose goal is reconciliation, which requires a rereading of the period of atrocities through the current political lens.[437]

Amnesties, as instruments of legal amnesia, in general have a particular relationship with collective memory. While being as much about forgetting (legally) as remembering (socially), in the present day, amnesties – be that intentionally in some cases and unintentionally in others – favour oblivion.[438] Their relationship with collective memory "is one of negation," and as such will ultimately lead to some level of collective forgetting,[439] given that every amnesty invariably brings about "an instrumentalized amnesia."[440] While a society may (and does) still remember, what is remembered following an implementation of an amnesty "is no longer available as a justification or reasonable cause for action"[441] and as such may become easily forgotten given that, in a way, the memory agents (victims of the previous regime) lose a powerful carrier of memory (lawsuit) with which they might have mobilised the collective memories of the rest of society.

Importantly, when paired with the truth commissions' "one narrative" strategy I have noticed in the previous section, amnesty's role as a legal institution of collective forgetting is particularly amplified and "brings a

433 Roche, *supra* note 431 at 575.
434 Bennouna, *supra* note 398 at 134–135.
435 Della Morte, *supra* note 393 at 433.
436 Coroli, *supra* note 391 at 103.
437 Veitch, *supra* note 394 at 41–42.
438 Della Morte, *supra* note 393 at 433.
439 Doxtader, *supra* note 426 at 122.
440 Krapp, *supra* note 400 at 190.
441 Doxtader, *supra* note 426 at 127.

risk that the choice to remember will be reduced to an abstract and timeless imperative."[442] At the same time, however, a lack of an amnesty may seriously hinder reconciliation,[443] given that, when in place, they allow for a social reintegration of the perpetrators,[444] and not only the victims, potentially even leading to the dissolving of the identity of those collective actors (e.g., guerrillas, terrorist organisations) which based their singularity precisely in the conflict for which an amnesty has been granted[445] – thus cementing reconciliation.

It also needs to be stressed that complete collective forgetting induced by legal amnesia following a period of atrocity is untenable in the long run. While amnesties will lead to collective forgetting, as I have remarked several times before, if a society is to truly move forward into the future, it first needs to deal with the collective trauma-memories of its past,[446] and as such, amnesty-induced collective forgetting may itself become a part of a countermemory.[447] Ultimately, this may mean that amnesties will not always stand the test of time due to a future shift in public opinion and needs – with the victims of an atrocity in certain instances requiring ample time to become ready for restorative justice[448] – as well as changes to legal consensus,[449] with a potential for accountability following many years after a transition.

Despite their issues and their contestation, as noted earlier, amnesties remain a useful political tool and should be regarded "in terms of a larger picture,"[450] all the more so that they, "lest we forget," as Scott Veich notes, "are here to stay."[451] Not only was there an average of 12.25 amnesties implemented each year between 1979 and 2010, but their number increased after 1989.[452] In each case, both national and international communities need to weigh the short- and long-term costs of implementing amnesties, as well as the cost of speaking against them: while there is certainly a danger of an amnesty locking a society in a *circulus vitiosus* of an "almost reconciliation" due to its prescriptive forgetting, a concept introduced in one of the

442 Doxtader, *supra* note 426 at 125.
443 Weisman, *supra* note 404 at 539.
444 McEvoy and Mallinder, *supra* note 390 at 434.
445 Schäfer, *supra* note 386 at 31.
446 Czarnota, *supra* note 368 at 28.
447 Suleiman, *supra* note 371 at 224.
448 Adam Crawford, "Temporality in Restorative Justice: On Time, Timing and Time-Consciousness" (2015) 19:4 Theoretical Criminology 470 at 481.
449 Olsen, Payne, and Reiter, *supra* note 411 at 349.
450 Weisman, *supra* note 404 at 538.
451 Veitch, *supra* note 394 at 33.
452 Louise Mallinder, "Amnesties' Challenge to the Global Accountability Norm? Interpreting Regional and International Trends in Amnesty Enactment" in Francesca Lessa and Leigh A. Payne (eds), *Amnesty in the Age of Human Rights: Accountability Comparative and International Perspectives* (Cambridge: Cambridge University Press, 2012) 69 at 79.

previous chapters on the one side, and rising counter-memories on the other, I would argue that in the case of a potential for a prolonged conflict – and only in such a case – it is a danger worth taking, as long as what is implemented is a well-designed legal amnesia, one echoing the Athenian one, providing legal forgetting but collective remembering, and thus giving the society in question a real chance at reconciliation.

Hard Institution II. Law Forcing Memory: Memory Legislation

Legal amnesia may be considered the opposite of the second hard legal institution of memory, memory legislation: where one asks for (at least some level of) collective forgetting, another proscribes it, in a very particular way. While collective remembering induced by memory legislation will undoubtedly lead to some level of collective forgetting on its own (as noted earlier, legal amnesia may be found in the shadows of all legal institutions of memory), fundamentally, their vectors are opposite.

Memory legislation is the youngest of the legal institutions of memory, appearing only in the 1980s and 1990s and becoming more widespread in the first and second decades of the 21st century, most often known under the name of memory laws[453] (as I presented it in the case study of France earlier in the book). As such, its field of study is still being demarcated, as the following analysis will show, and given that, I will propose a slightly different approach to their understanding than the one most established at present.

As a legal institution of memory, memory legislation concerns those acts of law that have as their main goal a direct impact on collective memory, the creation of one official narrative regarding certain events of the past. In some instances, the narrative is simply proclaimed, as in the case of parliamentary resolutions (non-punitive memory legislation); in others, the legally induced collective memories are protected by criminal law (punitive memory legislation). In both cases, their main goal is the protection of "the national unity and cultural coherence"[454] through the guarding of "the dominant narrative of the national" – and in certain instances international – "past against delegitimising views."[455]

453 Nikolay Koposov, *Memory Laws, Memory Wars: The Politics of the Past in Europe and Russia* (Cambridge: Cambridge University Press, 2017) at 25.

454 George Soroka and Félix Krawatzek, "Nationalism, Democracy, and Memory Laws" (2019) 30:2 Journal of Democracy 157 at 157.

455 Yifat Gutman, "Memory Laws: An Escalation in Minority Exclusion or a Testimony to the Limits of State Power?" (2016) 50:3 Law and Society Review 575 at 584.

Punitive memory legislation, adopted in 33 countries as of this writing,[456] may be perceived as a "natural progression" from cultural heritage protection law,[457] safeguarding particular memories instead. It first appeared as a way to combat the growing Holocaust denial in 1980s Germany and is still directly linked to the question of Shoah in particular, which stands behind the contemporary Western historical conscience and the desire to protect it against not only distortions but also doubts.[458]

Memory legislation, however, has soon departed from this niche, which in itself represents a shift in focus of the different societies around the world to "concrete historical events" as an "anchor" for their collective memories in recent years.[459] As a result, the Holocaust's unique status among collective trauma-memories has become questioned over the years,[460] and its legal protections have begun to be applied to various, not-Shoah-related instances. Today, memory legislation may be introduced whenever the majoritarian collective memory of a group becomes contested by the appearance of various, also untrue, counter-memories present within society.[461] Memory laws are thus implemented in the hopes of conveying "a moral message to" both the denialists and the rest of society,[462] thus achieving "at least a shift in perception" and potentially also the limitation of "all future reconstruction of the past" to "the official paradigm."[463] In addition to the protection of collective memories and the sealing of the official narrative, memory laws' secondary goals include the broadening of support for democracy and human rights,[464] protection of "social harmony,"[465] fostering of reconciliation, and improvement of international relations.[466]

456 Nikolay Koposov, "Historians, Memory Laws, and the Politics of the Past" (2020) 5:1 European Papers 107 at 110.

457 Lucas Lixinski, *Legalized Identities Cultural Heritage Law and the Shaping of Transitional Justice* (Cambridge/New York, NY: Cambridge University Press, 2021) at 179.

458 Nikolay Koposov, "Sur Les Lois Mémorielles: Histoire et typologie" ["On the Protection of Memory Laws: History and Typology"] (2018) 201:2 Le Débat 163 at 168.

459 Koposov, *supra* note 453 at 59.

460 Koposov, *supra* note 456 at 113.

461 Gutman, *supra* note 455 at 602.

462 Paul Behrens, "Why Not the Law? Options for Dealing with Genocide and Holocaust Denial" in Paul Behrens, Nicholas Terry, and Olaf Jensen (eds), *Holocaust and Genocide Denial: A Contextual Perspective* (Oxon/New York, NY: Routledge/Taylor and Francis, 2017) 230 at 231.

463 Brian F. Havel, "Public Law and the Construction of Collective Memory" in M. Cherif Bassiouni (ed.), *Post-Conflict Justice* (Ardsley, NY: Transnational Publishers, 2002) 383 at 393.

464 Ilya Nuzov, "The Dynamics of Collective Memory in the Ukraine Crisis: A Transitional Justice Perspective" (2017) 11 International Journal of Transitional Justice 132 at 147.

465 Lixinski, *supra* note 457 at 178.

466 Nuzov, *supra* note 464 at 136.

A certain debate exists as to the extent of what the term "memory laws" actually encompasses. Gutman proposes a classification of non-punitive and punitive memory laws, further dividing the second category into positive and negative memory laws, with the former concerning the maintenance of "a negative memory of a violent history" (e.g., laws banning genocide denial) and the latter aiming "to fortify a positive memory of such history" (laws which establish a positive official narrative of a difficult past).[467] This categorisation, while useful to a certain degree, does not include certain aspects of memory legislation, and as such, I propose to develop it further here.

In turn, Belavusau and Gliszyńska-Grabias, in their fundamental *oeuvre* for law and memory studies,[468] along with associated researcher Baranowska,[469] argue that any influence of the authorities on society's collective memories that uses law, be that through the type of regulations I introduced earlier as memory legislation or laws establishing national commemorations, school textbooks, and public monuments, should be branded as a memory law.

I disagree with this classification, finding it too encompassing. While all of these could be perceived as laws concerning memory, what should be regarded as memory laws proper – one of the legal institutions of memory – are those instances where law and collective memory do not merely intersect (as, for example, in the case of a legal text becoming a carrier of memory, and thus also a memory law[470]) but intersect in such a way that law has as its explicitly stated main goal a shift in collective memory through the process of repressive erasure, to use a concept introduced in Chapter 1. Moreover, in most cases, the location and form of monuments, the contents of the textbooks, the form of public commemorations, etc., are decided through various administrative decisions and, in general, not dedicated memory laws. (As I remarked earlier, when not implemented directly by the state, memorialisation initiatives may also appear as a part of international tribunals' community outreach projects or truth commissions' recommendations.) Thus, I propose the use of the term already introduced, memory legislation, to distinguish it from other legal acts concerning memory. As such, while laws establishing public commemoration

467 Gutman, *supra* note 455 at 575–576.

468 Uladzislau Belavusau and Aleksandra Gliszczyńska-Grabias, "Introduction" in Uladzislau Belavusau and Aleksandra Gliszczyńska-Grabias (eds), *Law and Memory: Towards Legal Governance of History* (Cambridge: Cambridge University Press, 2016) 1 at 1.

469 Grażyna Baranowska and Aleksandra Gliszczyńska-Grabias, " 'Right to Truth' and Memory Laws: General Rules and Practical Implications"(2018) 47 Polish Political Science Yearbook 97 at 99.

470 Paula Henrikson, "Scania Province Law and Nation-Building in Scandinavia" in Dirk van Hulle and Josep Leerssen (eds), *Editing the Nation's Memory: Textual Scholarship and Nation-Building in Nineteenth-Century Europe* (Amsterdam/New York, NY: Rodopi, 2008) 91 at 94; Barbara A. Misztal, "Legal Attempts to Construct Collective Memory: The Necessity and Difficulties of Aiming for Both Truth and Solidarity" (2011) 133 Polish Sociological Review 61 at 61.

and proper memory laws may be considered "stages of the same process" of establishing the official narrative and the creation of collective memories,[471] only the latter, tasked with the criminalisation of "certain statements about the past or," at least formulating "their official interpretation,"[472] should be perceived as a legal institution of memory (thus leaving, for example, the earlier-introduced act of the French parliament commemorating the Armenian genocide outside of the scope of the term "memory legislation" but including the prohibition of denial of this atrocity).

Using their broad understanding of memory laws as a starting point, Belavusau and Gliszyńska-Grabias recognise five interconnected "streams" of modern memory laws: (1) those connected to the denial of the Holocaust; (2) those linked to a protection against denial of the atrocities which took place before the Genocide Convention was introduced; (3) those addressing the fall of various 20th-century dictatorships; (4) those linked to decommunisation; and (5) those regarding the various mass atrocities around the world which took place following the recognition of the crime of genocide.[473]

Once again, I find their concept unhelpful to my analysis. Instead of this unclear, Western-centred, semi-geographic, semi-political division, I propose a categorisation of memory laws based on the underlying reasons behind their adoption, following Löytömäki, who acutely observes that what distinguishes memory laws is their background, as these legal institutions of memory are particularly politicised.[474]

Thus, I would argue for the division of memory legislation into three groups, focusing on the rationale behind their adoption, into: (1) those attempting to set one narrative in order to prevent an event from repeating itself (Gutman's positive punitive memory-laws, as well as the relevant non-punitive memory laws); (2) those attempting to set one narrative in order to work through collective trauma-memories of the society in question; and (3) those attempting to set one narrative in order to hide, outrun, or escape from the past (Gutman's negative punitive memory laws, as well as the relevant non-punitive memory laws).

In my perspective, there is no point in separating memory laws regarding genocides and other mass atrocities into two separate categories, since they share the same purpose: making sure that what happened is remembered correctly so that it does not take place again. The role of the Holocaust is vital for the rationale behind the first category of memory legislation,[475] and in some countries, bans on Holocaust denial are the only memory laws proper

471 Gutman, *supra* note 455 at 582.

472 Nikolay Koposov, "Populism and Memory: Legislation of the Past in Poland, Ukraine, and Russia" (2022) 36:1 East European Politics and Sciences 272 at 272–273.

473 Belavusau and Gliszyńska-Grabias, *supra* note 468 at 12–14.

474 Stiina Löytömäki, *Law and the Politics of Memory: Confronting the Past* (Oxon/New York, NY: Routledge, 2014) at 94.

475 Soroka and Krawatzek, *supra* note 454 at 160–161.

in place.[476] But other countries, as noted earlier, have expanded memory legislation to also include – as in the case of French article 24 bis – or to focus solely on other atrocities. Thus, I propose that all these memory laws should be recognised together as belonging to the first group.

Similarly, there is no point in separating the memory legislation into those resulting from a post-communist transition and those originating from other transitions, be that post-authoritarian, post-totalitarian, post-colonial, or related to a non-transitional reckoning with the past. In spite of the different circumstances, those memory laws are implemented to address similar questions, at least symbolically righting the wrongs of the past by providing a new narrative, one commemorating the victims and damning the oppressors of yesteryear, allowing the society in question to settle the accounts with the past. Thus, my second category would encompass, among others, both the memory laws recently adopted in the post-Maidan Ukraine in order to decommunise various aspects of its society and free it from post-Soviet, Russian influences,[477] and the French post-colonial law recognising slavery as a crime against humanity.

Ultimately, the third category of memory laws would encompass those regulations, the main purpose of which is to sweep certain difficult historic events under the carpet of collective memory, simplifying them by providing their whitewashed version so that they can be collectively celebrated without dwelling on any potentially unflattering details. Particularly good examples of such a memory law are the aforementioned French law on teaching about the country's colonial past in a positive light, and the Israeli Nakba laws putting the Jewish majority collective memories to the forefront and those of the Palestinian minority to the background of the official narrative.[478]

In addition to issues with classification, memory legislation, in particular punitive memory laws, is considered to be controversial,[479] both at the national and international levels. This, as I already noticed, highly politicised legal institution of memory, with various prominent agents of memory acting in its background,[480] has been criticised as limiting freedom of speech[481] and of research[482] and promoting censorship;[483] instrumentalising law for a role it

476 Koposov, *supra* note 458 at 165.
477 Nuzov, *supra* note 464 at 147–148.
478 Yifat Gutman and Noam Tirosh, "Balancing Atrocities and Forced Forgetting: Memory Laws as a Means of Social Control in Israel" (2021) 46:3 Law and Social Inquiry 705 at 724.
479 Soroka and Krawatzek, *supra* note 455 at 157.
480 Soroka and Krawatzek, *supra* note 455 at 164.
481 Gutman, *supra* note 455 at 583.
482 Koposov, *supra* note 456 at 109.
483 Robert A. Kahn, "Does It Matter How One Opposes Memory Bans? A Commentary on Liberté Pour L'Histoire" (2016) 15 Washington University Global Studies Review 55 at 69.

is not supposed to take,[484] of a "balm to appease moral suffering,"[485] turning judges into judges of history in the process;[486] contrarian to its own secondary goals of promoting social solidarity and democracy;[487] furthering social unity over truth regarding the past;[488] a redundant addition to the already existing hate speech provisions;[489] an unnecessary response to a non-discrete human rights issue (i.e., denialism);[490] raising problematic questions over the incompatibility of historical facts, collective memory, and law;[491] promoting competitive victimhood between different social groups;[492] and infringing on the counter-memories of minorities.[493] Moreover, they are perceived as a primarily Western concept, outside of Europe present only in several countries, such as Israel and Rwanda,[494] and a largely unnecessary one given that, memory laws critics argue, it is possible to counter "false historical claims" on their merits.[495]

Furthermore, on the international level, memory laws are not only perceived as a danger to cooperation between different nations,[496] but they have also been the focus of interest of several tribunals, with most recently the ECtHR finding Swiss memory legislation banning the denial of Armenian genocide unnecessary due to, *inter alia*, geographical and temporal distance,[497] a case that I analyse in greater detail in Part III of the book. (*Nota bene*, international organisations, such as the European Union, have

484 Eran Fish, "Memory Laws as a Misuse of Legislation" (2021) 54:3 Israel Law Review 324 at 326.
485 Robert Badinter, "Fin des Lois Mémorielles?" ["End of Memory Laws?"] 171:4 Le Débat 96 at 97.
486 Emanuela Fronza, "The Criminal Protection of Memory: Some Observations About the offense of Holocaust Denial" in Ludovic Hennebel and Thomas Hochmann (eds), *Genocide Denials and the Law* (Oxford/New York, NY: Oxford University Press, 2011) 155 at 172.
487 Gutman, *supra* note 455 at 602.
488 Misztal, *supra* note 470 at 67.
489 Gutman, *supra* note 455 at 575–578.
490 Eric Heinze, "Theorizing Law and Historical Memory: Denialism and the Pre-Conditions of Human Rights" (2018) 13:1 The Journal of Comparative Law 43 at 48.
491 Misztal, *supra* note 470 at 72.
492 Soroka and Krawatzek, *supra* note 454 at 161.
493 Igor Lyubashenko, Christian Garuka, Grażyna Baranowska and Vjeran Pavlaković, "The Puzzle of Punitive Memory Laws: New Insights into the Origins and Scope of Punitive Memory Laws" (2020) 35:4 East European Politics and Societies and Cultures 996 at 1000.
494 Koposov, *supra* note 458 at 166.
495 Michael Salter, "Holocaust Denial in Relation to the Nuremberg Trials" in Paul Behrens, Nicholas Terry, and Olaf Jensen (eds), *Holocaust and Genocide Denial: A Contextual Perspective* (Oxon/New York, NY: Routledge/Taylor and Francis, 2017) 21 at 32.
496 Soroka and Krawatzek, *supra* note 454 at 170.
497 Fish, *supra* note 484 at 335.

themselves encouraged the adoption of a "cosmopolitan" official memory, but only related to the Holocaust.[498])

In recent years, critics of memory legislation have particularly stressed the dangers presented by memory laws belonging to the third group, which, they argue, may "give legal protection to typically populist self-congratulatory national narratives,"[499] promoting "exclusivist interpretations of the past"[500] as a result. More generally, all punitive memory legislation has raised questions about the limits of banning particular visions of the past[501] and was accused of turning "court and trial" into "a space for building and imposing a memory."[502]

Its problems notwithstanding, memory legislation has a particularly strong and direct relationship with collective memory, given that it is its "custodian,"[503] having reawakened "the notion of the sacred in our societies," which in turn may "generate and legitimise an emotional need for suppressing opinions commonly assessed as blasphemous,"[504] bringing us once again close to the concepts of Durkheim, who, as noted earlier, proposed that law and its rituals (in this case prosecution for breaking of a memory legislation) have replaced those of religion, thus giving us a potential rationale behind the punitive aspect of some memory laws.

Memory legislation's impact on collective memory in general may be illustrated particularly well, however, with the return to Bergson's idea of a cone of memory introduced in Chapter 2: with this legal institution of memory, law directly adds a "scoop" of strictly limited collective memory into the cone, which will not stay on top of it but, while "melting," also disturbs the lower layers. It is highly debatable as to what actual impact this "melting" will have on collective memory: on the one hand, "the use of public law" in such cases carries "the enormous advantage of endurance,[505] turning memory into "a fixed object" – official memory – among the many different counter-memories present,[506] which, once in place, certainly protects it from the tendency of debates "about denial bans" becoming "arguments about genocides" themselves.[507]

498 Emanuela Fronza, *Memory and Punishment Historical Denialism, Free Speech and the Limits of Criminal Law* (The Hague: TMC Asser Press/Berlin: Springer, 2018) at 31; Koposov, *supra* note 472 at 273.
499 Koposov, *supra* note 472 at 280.
500 Soroka and Krawatzek, *supra* note 454 at 158.
501 Kahn, *supra* note 483 at 70.
502 Fronza, *supra* note 486 at 176.
503 Emanuela Fronza, "The Punishment of Negationism: The Difficult Dialogue Between Law and Memory" (2006) 30:3 Vermont Law Review 609 at 620.
504 Koposov, *supra* note 472 at 290.
505 Havel, *supra* note 463 at 387.
506 Havel, *supra* note 463 at 393.
507 Kahn, *supra* note 483 at 89.

On the other hand, memory legislation has been noticed to "strip" collective memory of its constituent functions, trying to entrap it in its place.[508] This is *de facto* not feasible, given that memory laws instigate vocal and widely publicised discussions about precisely those issues the memory of which it was supposed to regulate in the first place, undermining the social solidarity and stability it was also meant to cement,[509] and ultimately becoming a mere "gesture, a symbol that takes a position on a series of ethical and political"[510] issues, but not so much on the questions of law or truth. Furthermore, even when judicial decisions have been reached on the basis of a punitive memory law, while "powerful in the short run," they cannot be considered helpful in sustaining legally induced collective memory in the long term.[511] Moreover, as Dworkin notes, memory legislation will not stop denialists from spreading their lies, and conversely, the lack of it is not going to exponentially increase the risk of social conflicts,[512] as the members of the denial movement tend to perceive themselves "as resisting the 'conformist conspiracy' of the mainstream history,"[513] impervious to the potential effects of a memory law.

Perhaps, ultimately, memory legislation is not so much about affecting denialists. Perhaps it is also not so much directed at the various counter-memories proposed by the different minorities present within a society. Perhaps it is rather directed at the majority of the collectivity, establishing, rightfully or not, what is perceived as acceptable in this society, reassuring it while also creating a strong indication of what one should remember, at least publicly, if they are to become the full-fledged members of the society in question, thus clearly fostering, if not establishing in practice, social unity. As such, memory legislation should be considered not only in terms of the negative but rather, given its hidden potential for reconciliation, as another legal institution of memory that has been "used in practice for collective memory construction" in recent years.[514] Importantly, memory legislation's interplay with other institutions, if designed correctly, can also bring positive results, as in the case of France, where a person whose crimes were protected by legal amnesia (both amnesty and statute of limitations) but who was successfully prosecuted as a war-crime apologetic on the basis of a memory law and whose trial by itself reawakened collective trauma-memories of the Algerian war,[515] dormant due to legal amnesia. To fully comprehend the interplay

508 Fronza, *supra* note 498 at 74.
509 Gutman, *supra* note 455 at 602.
510 Fronza, *supra* note 503 at 622.
511 Fronza, *supra* note 486 at 177.
512 Ronald Dworkin, "The Unbearable Cost of Liberty" (1995) 3 Index on Censorship 43 at 45.
513 Behrens, *supra* note 462 at 249.
514 Gutman, *supra* note 455 at 583.
515 Löytömäki, *supra* note 474 at 1.

between various legal institutions of memory, however, they also need to be analysed in the context of memory politics and the right to memory, two additional factors that further impact the law and memory intersections that I introduce in the next chapter. First, however, I would like to reflect on the analysis undertaken in this chapter.

Conclusion: Legal Institutions of Memory as a Basis of the Understanding of Law and Memory Intersections

This chapter's journey through the six legal institutions of memory took us through their various particularities but also unveiled some of their similarities, which brings us, at its end, where it started: to a definition of legal institutions of memory, one enriched by these investigations.

In the introduction, I proposed an understanding of legal institutions of memory as particularly active legal carriers of memory (akin to the media, semi-carriers, semi-agents of memory), which actively employ law's mechanisms, institutions, and prestige to influence society's in-question collective memories. This initial definition may now be expanded to include several observations that may be made on the basis of this chapter's analysis.

First, all legal institutions of memory can be considered (at least in their most typical manifestation) as a Durkheimian ritual, proving his thesis that law has replaced religion within the society as the space of storage of common beliefs and social acumen. We may see this role in the repentance aspect of reparations, the universality of justice aspect of trials before international institutions, the open reckoning with the past proposed by lustration, the *catharsis* power of publicly telling one's story and uncovering the social truth in the process through truth commissions' work, the inconspicuous power of legal amnesia which gives a chance to collectively forget and remember at the same time, and the blatant force of memory legislation, clearly steeping into religion's role of deciding what is socially permitted, and what is forbidden.

Second, my analysis supports Foucault's argument of the major impact political power exerts on collective memories. While they may have been motivated by various factions in local or global society, legal institutions of memory are always a top-to-bottom mechanism introduced either by national authorities or the international community.

Third, while having different main and secondary goals, all legal institutions of memory are tasked with the settling of certain collective memories (most often collective trauma-memories following an atrocity), establishing a new narrative and influencing collective memory, as well as bolstering the support for social unity, democracy, and human rights within the society in question. They all also open the possibility for reconciliation, if not immediately, than at least in the future and are often, but not always, related to transitionary processes – unless, of course, employed nefariously, as in some cases analysed in Part III of the book.

Finally, whether intentionally or not, in the process of establishing the official narrative, they always inflict some degree of collective forgetting, as it is neither possible nor beneficial for social unity to include all counter-memories present within a society. This is only one of the large number of issues each legal institution of memory generates, showing that whenever law has an impact on collective memory, it also brings up various problems as a result.

Keeping these general observations in mind, I would like now to narrow down the particularities of the different legal institutions of memory and their categories, once again stressing that they are ordered depending on the level of intensity of law and memory's intersections in each case (which is illustrated in Figure 4.1).

Soft legal institutions of memory, reparations, and international tribunals are not directly concerned with collective memory, and their impact on it is not their main goal or often even a secondary goal. They are both rather a means of rendering justice to societies following some kind of atrocity, which in the process has a major impact on collective memory through the changes or resetting of the official narrative initiation and the beginning of the path to reconciliation; however, not one exerted directly, relying heavily on other legal institutions of memory to make a meaningful shift in the sphere of collective memory.

In that, reparations are a material or symbolic way of atoning for past atrocities committed either internally or externally in the hopes that, in lieu of the impossibility of the return to *status quo ante*, compensation or an apology will allow the society in question to work through their collective trauma-memories and move forward. In turn, international tribunals provide a possibility for a reckoning on the global stage with the legacy of an atrocity when the involved groups cannot or are unwilling to do it themselves. However, their narrative, while effective internationally, often fails to make a change on the local level.

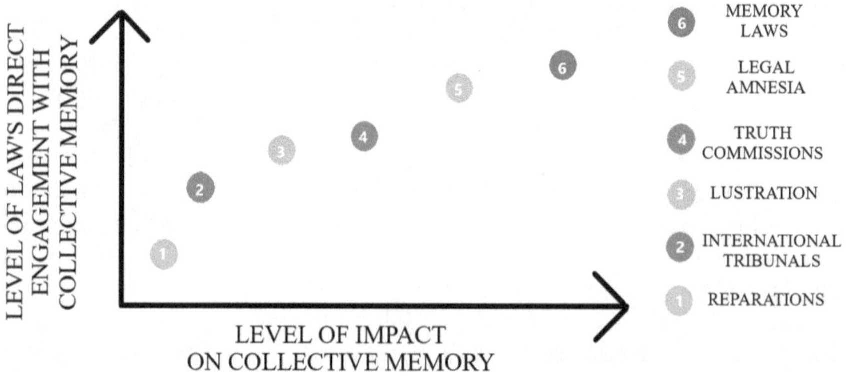

Figure 4.1 A sketch of law and memory intersections

Source: Author.

Medium legal institutions of memory, lustration and truth commissions, are concerned with collective memory; however, their main interest lies in a sort of reckoning with the past, which will allow them to re-unite society, be that former victims or perpetrators, while also strengthening the structure of the state, and as such, their relationship with collective memory is semi-direct. Importantly, their approaches to strengthening social bonds are quite different and could be regarded as complementary rather than contrary.

Lustration is an institution of administrative justice, focused on protecting the newly established regime by screening parts of society to a varying degree in case a particular person should have ties to the previous authorities. They use this process to reconceptualise the past and collective memories regarding it through the strengthening of a new official narrative. In turn, truth commissions are particularly concerned with the place of former victims in society and about uncovering the truth about the past on the basis of their testimony, which will then be distilled into one official narrative.

Ultimately, it is the hard legal institutions of memory, legal amnesia and memory legislation, that have collective memory as their main concern. While their other focus involves the question of social unity, which they use as the rationale for their introduction, as well as the different secondary goals, hard legal institutions of memory have as their forefront aim a direct impact on collective memory.

In principle, the two are opposed in terms of influencing collective memory. Legal amnesia, through instruments such as amnesty, aims to instigate legal forgetting and collective remembering at the same time by using the former as a basis for a new official narrative that will in turn influence the latter but ultimately foment collective forgetting. Memory legislation, for its part, attempts to reinforce the official narrative by defining it through law, thus introducing it to the legal realm so that in most cases, particular majoritarian collective memories are properly protected, in some cases employing criminal law for that purpose.

Such is the tripartite fundament of the law and memory framework for the understanding of their intersections I am proposing in this book, a fundament laid on the idea that legal institutions of memory are ultimately not so much focused on the past but rather are a testament to how societies "imagine possible futures"[516] – and that any meaningful future requires changes to collective memory that may take place only through law.[517] For their full comprehension and assessment of success in achieving the goals of law and memory intersections, however, as I have previously mentioned, questions of memory politics and the contended right to memory need to be introduced in the next chapter.

516 Tileagă, *supra* note 251 at 153.
517 Czarnota, *supra* note 197 at 183.

Chapter 5

The Hidden Power of Law and Memory Intersections

From Memory Politics to a Right to Memory

Introduction

The search for an understanding of law and memory's intersections has taken us first through sociology, philosophy, and theory of law and then through the various legal institutions of memory. To fully comprehend the relationship between the two, however, I propose to take a step back and look also in a slightly different direction: to the question of power and politics. These issues have already been touched upon earlier in the book, particularly in the section on Foucault's thoughts on power-memory relations, but they need to be analysed in greater detail, given that it is through their lens that the theoretical and conceptual of the previous chapters is brought into practice. Legal institutions of memory may be Durkheimian rituals; however, they need to be perceived as more than performative acts of social unity – also "as political projects whose goal is to cultivate and promote specific understandings of the past as part of an on-going political agenda"[1] – and analysed as such.

Thus, this chapter will focus on two additional power-related factors that need to be taken into account in my investigations but are often missing from legal research in a way that remains hidden: the issue of politics of memory, working both on a socio-political and political-institutional level; and the concept of a right to memory. I will then propose a way to include them in the initial model of law and memory intersections introduced in the previous chapter, completing the establishment of a framework for the investigation of the seven selected case studies in the following chapters.

At the Crossroads of Memory and Power: The Politics of Memory

In his case study of Gaullist France and its official narrative of World War II, as noted earlier in the book, Foucault remarked upon the broad influence a

1 Victor Roudometof, "Introduction: Beyond Commemoration: The Politics of Collective Memory" (2003) 31:2 Journal of Political and Military Sociology 161 at 162–163.

DOI: 10.4324/9781003461548-9

government's control over the official narrative has on a society's collective memories. This power authorities and other social actors (agents of memory) hold – and use – over social perceptions of the past has come to be known as politics of memory, memory politics, or historical politics.[2] It should not be confused with memory policy, an element of memory politics employed through different memory programmes[3] to transform selected collective memories to achieve particular goals.[4]

As Adam notes, collective memory mirrors collective identity, which is in turn – and thus they both are – influenced by memory politics,[5] understood as those aspects of politics whereby various agents of memory infuse the past "with their specific interests and meanings," which then "compete for dominance" within society in the hopes that, on the one hand, the establishment of particular collective memories will "lead to the creation or affirmation of common values as a foundation for social or political communities,"[6] and, on the other hand, have an impact on social "attitudes, behaviours, choices and decisions."[7] Regarding collective memory instrumentally[8] as a "legitimising symbol," various agents of memory "fight over"[9] it, using memory politics to further their particular objectives through collective memory in ways that are never free from at least some level of manipulation.[10] To put it succinctly, politics of memory are instrumental expressions of power over collective memory by various memory agents, not necessarily but often belonging to the government, who intend to influence social perceptions of the past to further particular political and/or social goals.

While it could be argued that collective memory belongs to the people and not the authorities – and that is certainly the case of, for example, familial collective memories – the various non-political collective memories are

2 Eugeniusz Ponczek, "Polityka wobec pamięci *versus* polityka historyczna: Aspekty semantyczny, aksjologiczny i merytoryczny w narracji polskiej" ["Memory Politics *Versus* Historical Politics: Semnatic, Axiological and Substantive Aspects"] (2013) 2 Przegląd Politologiczny 7 at 8.

3 Sarah Gensburger and Sandrine Lefranc, *Beyond Memory: Can We Really Learn from the Past?* (Cham: Palgrave Macmillan, 2020) at 16.

4 *Ibid.* at 3–6.

5 Heribert Adam, "Divided Memories: Confronting the Crimes of Previous Regimes" (2000) 118 Telos 87 at 88.

6 Aline Sierp and Jenny Wüstenberg, "Linking the Local and the Transnational: Rethinking Memory Politics in Europe" (2015) 23:3 Journal of Contemporary European Studies 321 at 322–323.

7 Joanna Marszałek-Kawa and Patryk Wawrzyński, "Remembrance, Identity Politics and Political Transitions" (2016) 45 Polish Political Science Yearbook 11 at 12.

8 Peter J. Verovšek, "Collective Memory, Politics, and the Influence of the Past: The Politics of Memory as a Research Paradigm" (2016) 4:3 Politics, Groups, and Identities 529 at 529.

9 Geneviève Zubrzycki and Anna Woźny, "The Comparative Politics of Collective Memory" (2020) 46 Annual Review of Sociology 175 at 186.

10 Ponczek, *supra* note 2 at 15–16.

rendered political "once they have worked their way through the sluices that link the formal and informal public spheres,"[11] as the "mnemonic power relations determine" the presence and survival of particular collective memories within society as a whole.[12] Putting memory politics into practice, agents of memory use law as a major reinforcing,[13] legitimising, and consolidating factor in the matters of collective memory,[14] employing different legal institutions of memory analysed in the previous chapter (ultimately, it depends on the politics of memory which ones are going to be used and to what extent), as well as different elements of cultural policy[15] (museums, school curricula, or institutes of memory, introduced in this chapter) and the various "forms of mediated memory" (places of memory, media, public commemorations),[16] all in order to support, create or recreate the official narrative.

It is this question of an official narrative that is the key to understanding memory politics processes. Having already used the term earlier in the book, I would now propose defining official narrative as a direct result of memory politics, a narrative established on the basis of carefully selected collective memories of past events that have received some level of official recognition – the higher the recognition, the more powerful it will be – most often from the state and its institutions (including legal institutions of memory), but potentially also from other various influential actors of civil society (e.g., vocal victim groups) or the international community.

As such, memory politics may be distinguished in all regimes, democratic, non-democratic, and those in transition, however working differently in each circumstance. In stable democracies, memory politics are characterised by "stasis," as both the establishment and social habits inhibit changes to collective memory, with the "forward-looking narratives flow[ing] logically from past events."[17] Thus, politically influenced social perceptions of the past "play a stabilising, conservative role" in a democracy.[18] In such a regime,

11 Verovšek, *supra* note 8 at 536.
12 Berthold Molden, "Resistant Pasts Versus Mnemonic Hegemony: On the Power Relations of Collective Memory" (2016) 9:2 Memory Studies 125 at 129.
13 Brianne McGonigle Leyh, "Imperatives of the Present: Black Lives Matter and the Politics of Memory and Memorialization" (2020) 38:4 Netherlands Quarterly of Human Rights 239 at 244.
14 Peter J. Verovšek, "Memory, Narrative, and Rupture: The Power of the Past as a Resource for Political Change" (2020) 13:2 Memory Studies 208 at 214.
15 Rafał Riedel, "Authoritarian Populism and Collective Memory Manipulation" in Michael Oswald (ed.), *The Palgrave Handbook of Populism* (Cham: Springer Nature, 2022) 195 at 203.
16 Simona Mitroiu, "Life Writing and Politics of Memory in Eastern Europe: Introduction" in Simona Mitroiu (ed.), *Life Writing and Politics of Memory in Eastern Europe* (Houndmills: Palgrave Macmillan, 2015) 1 at 19.
17 Verovšek, *supra* note 14 at 209.
18 Peter J. Verovšek, *Memory and the Future of Europe: Rupture and Integration in the Wake of Total War* (Manchester: Manchester University Press, 2020) at 27.

memory politics is most often occasional, discreet, and free of conflict, but still necessary, a *condicio sine qua non* of conducting politics.[19] Importantly, democratic regimes leave space for counter-memories to be heard,[20] with non-state memory agents potentially also powerful enough to "impose" specific collective memories on the public discourse.[21] An example of this is the media (a particular agent-carrier of memory, as noted earlier in the book), involved, along with many other agents in the private sector, in commercialisation of the social perceptions of the past to further their own goals.[22]

Politics of memory is a particularly evident element of non-democratic regimes, which, using various cultural institutions,[23] use collective memory to further selective social perceptions of the past, restricted to perceived harms against the nation, ones coming from the outside (be that from abroad or from parts of society perceived as foreign), and at the same time fostering collective forgetting of atrocities perpetrated by the regime itself. Nevertheless, even such memory politics may allow a society to work through some collective trauma-memories,[24] a task that becomes particularly important for transitional memory politics.

In the case of societies in transition, politics of memory are central to the political processes taking place,[25] with the official narrative employed and used "as a political asset"[26] to legitimise the new authorities.[27] Transitional memory politics are also directly connected with the recent collective trauma-memories, which now need to be "reinterpreted and assumed anew."[28] As such, politics of memory in these circumstances should allow for their working through,[29] as well as for a transformation of the political culture,[30] paving the way for democratisation[31] (both of which are some

19 Ponczek, *supra* note 2 at 12, 19.

20 Dalia Báthory, "Authoritarian and Post-Authoritarian Practices of Building Collective Memory in Central and Eastern Europe" (2015) 6 History of Communism in Europe 11 at 13.

21 *Ibid.* at 13.

22 Michael Schudson, "Dynamics of Collective Memory" in Daniel L. Schacter (ed.), *Memory Distortion: How Minds, Brains, and Societies Reconstruct the Past* (Cambridge, MA/London: Harvard University Press, 1995) 346 at 354.

23 Báthory, *supra* note 20 at 14.

24 Eric Langenbacher, "Collective Memory as a Factor in Political Culture and International Relations" in Eric Langenbacher and Yossi Shain (eds), *Power and the Past: Collective Memory and International Relations* (Washington, DC: Georgetown University Press, 2010) 36–37.

25 Stiina Löytömäki, *Law and the Politics of Memory: Confronting the Past* (Oxon/New York, NY: Routledge, 2014) at 6–7.

26 Marszałek-Kawa and Wawrzyński, *supra* note 7 at 15.

27 Gabor Rittersporn, "Skeptical Remarks on 'Divided Memories'" (2000) 188 Telos 109 at 111.

28 Báthory, *supra* note 20 at 14.

29 Mitroiu, *supra* note 16 at 5.

30 Marszałek-Kawa and Wawrzyński, *supra* note 7 at 13.

31 Alexandru Gussi, "Political Uses of Memory and the State in Post-communism" (2013) 4 Studia Politica: Romanian Political Science Review 721 at 721.

of the aims of legal institutions of memory when employed in transitional contexts, as noted in the previous chapter, proving their interrelation with memory politics). Importantly, to achieve these goals, transitional politics of memory – and, more broadly, politics of memory in general[32] – should ensure the presence of various counter-memories in the newly established official narrative,[33] as well as balance collective remembrance and collective forgetting,[34] and collective evoking.[35]

Memory politics may also be divided into internal and external. In the case of the former, it is conducted to support a particular identity and collective memory that has come to be perceived as correct and even desirable at a current moment by those in power, who impose changes on the already existing, as well as the newly established places of memory, all directly linked to the modifications to the official narrative.[36] In turn, external memory politics involve foreign relations with particular countries or groups and may result in the polarisation of international relations through its influence on *raison d'état*, as particular memory agents can choose to engage in extremely selective and or inflammatory politics of memory.[37] *Nota bene*, it needs to be noted that memory politics are the domain not only of local (including both a traditional internal and, increasingly in recent years, an external focus with the rise of so-called city diplomacy[38]) and national, but also of regional and international memory agents, who may also influence collective memories of a particular group,[39] as exemplified strongly by the official narratives created since the beginning of the European integration process, which have been aimed at establishing a collective "European memory" – and thus "a common identity."[40]

32 Maria P. Nascimento Araújo and Myrian Sepúlveda dos Santos, "History, Memory and Forgetting: Political Implications" (2009) 1 RCCS Annual Review: A Selection from the Portuguese Journal Revista Crítica de Ciências Sociais 77 at 92.
33 Mitroiu, *supra* note 16 at 17.
34 Marszałek-Kawa and Wawrzyński, *supra* note 7 at 15.
35 Agnieszka Łuczak, "The Pendulum of Memory: The (Lack of) Knowledge About German War Crimes" (2020), online: Przystanek Historia <przystanekhistoria.pl/pa2/tematy/english-content/62430,The-pendulum-of-memory-The-lack-ofknowledge-about-German-war-crimes.html>.
36 Ponczek, *supra* note 2 at 9.
37 Ponczek, *supra* note 2 at 9, 13.
38 See, e.g., Martijn Klem and Georg Frerks, "How Local Governments Contribute to Peace-Building" in Arne Much et al. (eds), *City Diplomacy: The Role of Local Governments in Conflict Prevention, Peace-Building, Post-Conflict Reconstruction* (The Hague: VNG International, 2008) 47 at 71; Greta Bertolucci, *City Diplomacy: The New Role of Cities in International Relations* (Rome: Luiss Guido Carli University, 2019) at 76.
39 Verovšek, *supra* note 8 at 537.
40 Sierp and Wüstenberg, *supra* note 6 at 324.

While as already noted in the case of the external one, memory politics in general often leads to conflict,[41] either creating new animosities or exacerbating the already existing ones within the society in question,[42] there is no running away from it: while postulated by some memory politics critics, its absence would also be a way of conducting politics of memory, as it could lead to collective forgetting, potentially also a political goal,[43] for example of memory abnegators, a category of agents of memory introduced in the first part of the book. Moreover, memory politics can also achieve positive, constructive results,[44] such as a transformation of a society's moral consciousness[45] or reconciliation between previously warring groups.[46] As such, memory politics should limit the manipulation of memory to a minimum and rather "be grounded in the honest effort to integrate" collective memory,[47] but for social and national and not purely political benefit.

Its actual goals notwithstanding, the potential for success of memory politics, whether conducted by the state, civil society, or the international community, rests on the memory agents' level of prestige[48] and competency in selecting what to collectively remember and what to collectively forget, all while "maintaining the illusion of a stable, representative, and consensual collective memory,"[49] as well as "on the social audibility and power of the voices that promote it to penetrate and determine the hegemonic set of specific memories that form" collective memory.[50] There is always danger, however, in memory agents overplaying memory politics, which may lead to "memory disorder," i.e., a "radical revision" of social perceptions of the past with potentially destabilising consequences[51] on the one hand, or to the authorities losing all credibility in the matters of collective memory[52] on the other. Interestingly, both are some of the criticisms that institutes of

41 Löytömäki, *supra* note 25 at 5.
42 Dovilė Budrytė, "Memory Politics and the Study of Crises in International Relations: Insights from Ukraine and Lithuania" (2021) 24 Journal of International Relations and Development 980 at 983.
43 Ponczek, *supra* note 2 at 14–15.
44 Verovšek, *supra* note 18 at 42.
45 Paul Gottfried, "On the Politics of Memory: A Reply to Adam" (2000) 118 Telos 115 at 117.
46 Riedel, *supra* note 15 at 208.
47 Jonathan Boyarin, "Space, Time, and the Politics of Memory" in Jonathan Boyarin (ed.), *Remapping Memory: The Politics of TimeSpace* (Minneapolis, MN: University of Minnesota Press, 1994) 1 at 27.
48 Schudson, *supra* note 22 at 359.
49 Zoltan Dujisin, "A Field-Theoretical Approach to Memory Politics" in Jenny Wüstenberg and Aline Sierp (eds), *Agency in Transnational Memory Politics* (New York, NY/Oxford: Berghahn Books, 2020) 24 at 40.
50 Molden, *supra* note 12 at 140.
51 Riedel, *supra* note 15 at 205.
52 Gussi, *supra* note 31 at 727.

memory, the state institutions of memory politics that I analyse in the following section, face in the course of their functioning.

Politicisation of Memory in Practice: Institutionalising Remembrance

Institutes of memory, institutes of remembrance, or memory institutes, recognisable thanks to their Orwellian name, but ultimately state institutions of memory politics "not of the Orwellian type,"[53] are created in a way against collective forgetting,[54] established in particular to deal with the aftermath of communism in Central and Eastern Europe (CEE), especially the archives of the secret police, remarked upon in Chapter 4, in the section regarding lustration, as Foucauldian heterotopias of deviation. Over the years, however, institutes of memory have become much more than means of conducting lustration, soon turning into the "militant arm" of the state politics of memory. Despite the fact that I do not recognise them as a legal institution of memory – as to why, I provide an answer later in this section – they merit a closer investigation as also laying at the intersections of law and memory politics. They are, in a way, politics of memory in practice.

While similar institutions were created in Western Europe following World War II,[55] memory institutes took their present-day shape after 1989, with the first one created in 1991 in Germany as the Federal Office for the Files of the State Security Service of the Former GDR (BStU[56] or Gauck-Birthler Institute[57]). Over the years, institutes of memory have become a ubiquitous element of the CEE memory politics landscape, with the Polish Institute of National Memory (IPN, also known in English as the Institute of National Remembrance, INR), the Slovakian Nation's Memory Institute (UPN), the

53 Dariusz Stola, "Poland's Institute of National Remembrance: A Ministry of Memory?" in Maria Lipman and Alexei Miller (eds), *The Convolutions of Historical Politics* (Budapest/New York, NY: Central European University Press, 2012) 45 at 54.

54 Anatoly M. Khazanov and Stanley G. Payne, "How to Deal with the Past?" (2008) 9:2–3 Totalitarian Movements and Political Religions 411 at 416.

55 Valentin Behr, "The Ministry of Memory" (2014), online: Books and Ideas <booksandideas.net/The-Ministry-of-Memory.html> 1 at 2.

56 Sara Jones, "Cross-Border Collaboration and the Construction of Memory Narratives in Europe" in Tea Sindbæk Andersen and Barbara Törnquist-Plewa (eds), *The Twentieth Century in European Memory: Transcultural Mediation and Reception* (Leiden/Boston, MA: Brill, 2017) 27 at 33.

57 From the names of its first directors – Federal Commissioners: Joachim Gauck and Marianne Birthler. See: Stola, *supra* note 53 at 47–48. In 2021 the BStU was disbanded and its archives incorporated in the Federal Archives (Bundesarchiv), however continuing its research work and retaining the open access policy for victims. See: Deutsche Welle, "Stasi Records Agency Disbanded but Files Live On" (2021), online: DW <dw.com/en/germany-disbands-stasi-records-agency-but-saves-files/a-57941839>.

Lithuanian Genocide and Resistance Research Centre (LGGRTC),[58] the Czech Institute for the Study of Totalitarian Regimes (USTR),[59] the Romanian National Council for the Study of the Securitate Archives (CNSAS), the Bulgarian Committee on Disclosing of Documents and Announcing Affiliation of Bulgarian Citizens to the State Security and the Intelligence Services of the Bulgarian National Army (CRDOPBGDSRSBNA),[60] and the Ukrainian Institute of National Memory (UINM)[61] following the German example. Importantly, a number of countries in the region have more than one single institution that we might call an institute of memory. In Germany, in addition to the now dissolved Gauck Institute, state memory politics has been realised by the Gedenkstätte Berlin-Hohenschönhausen, a museum in a former Stasi prison.[62] In Poland, next to IPN, there also exists a network of highly influential in the politics of memory museums and smaller research centres.[63] In Hungary, the former secret police archives are managed by the Historical Archives of State Security (ÁBTL),[64] whereas the government conducts its memory politics mainly through the Terror House, the Veritas Historical Research Institute, the Research Institute and Archives for the Study of the Regime Change, and the Committee of National Remembrance.[65] And in Latvia, alongside the Government Commission for KGB Research, there

58 Maciej Górny and Kornelia Kończal, "The (Non-)Travelling Concept of Les Lieux de Mémoire: Central and Eastern European Perspectives" in Małgorzata Pakier and Joanna Wawrzyniak (eds), *Memory and Change in Europe: Eastern Perspectives* (New York, NY/ Oxford: Berghan, 2015) 59 at 66–67.

59 Zoltan Dujisin, "A History of Post-Communist Remembrance: From Memory Politics to the Emergence of a Field of Anticommunism" (2021) 50 Theory and Society 65 at 86.

60 Georges Mink, "Institutions of National Memory in Post-Communist Europe: From Transitional Justice to Political Uses of Biographies (1989–2010)" in Georges Mink and Laure Neumayer (eds), *Politics in Central and Eastern Europe: Memory Games* (Houndmills/New York, NY: Palgrave Macmillan, 2013) 155 at 161–163.

61 Lina Klymenko, "Forging Ukrainian National Identity Through Remembrance of World War II" (2020) 22:2 National Identities 133 at 133.

62 Sara Jones, "Memory Competition or Memory Collaboration? Politics, Networks, and Social Actors in Memories of Dictatorship" in Christina Kraenzle and Maria Mayr (eds), *The Changing Place of Europe in Global Memory Cultures: Usable Pasts and Futures* (Cham: Palgrave Macmillan, 2017) 63 at 70.

63 Michał Łuczewski, Paulina Bednarz-Łuczewska, and Tomasz Maślanka, "The Politics of History in Poland and Germany" in Elena Rozhdestvenskaya, Victoria Semenova, Irina Tartakovskaya, and Krzysztof Kosela (eds), *Collective Memories in War* (Oxon/New York, NY: Routledge, 2016) 11 at 16.

64 Michal Kopeček, "In Search of 'National Memory': The Politics of History, Nostalgia and the Historiography of Communism in the Czech Republic and East Central Europe" in Michal Kopeček (ed.), *Past in the Making: Historical Revisionism in Central Europe After 1989* (Budapest: Central European University Press, 2008) 75 at 90.

65 Dujisin, *supra* note 59 at 76–80.

also exists a number of state museums engaged in memory politics.[66] *Nota bene*, it needs to be stressed that Russia has never established a memory institute, as the possibility of such a decentralisation of memory politics is perceived as weakening the authorities' direct influence on the social perceptions of the past.[67]

Importantly, while the German Gauck Institute, as historically the first, was the initial model for memory institutes in CEE, it was the Polish IPN that soon became perceived "as a laboratory of best and worst practices for keen regional observes."[68] It also needs to be noted that a number of memory institutes from the region have joined forces internationally, also with other similar organisations, in a number of different configurations: of the International Holocaust Remembrance Alliance (IHRA) established in 1998, of the European Network Remembrance and Solidarity (ENRS) established in 2005, of the European Network of Official Authorities in Charge of the Secret-Police Files (ENOA) established in 2008, and of the Platform of European Memory and Conscience (Platform) established in 2011.[69] This internationalisation allowed memory institutes to collectively "reach into politics, academia, and the Eurocracy"[70] – today, the Platform, for example, is composed of 62 influential state and NGO members.[71]

As Dujsin notes, these in-principle "anti-communist" institutions represent "the rise of a novel power arrangement, one that regulated the transactions between politics and historiography"[72] – and thus collective memory, connected to the appearance of an "activist-historian," an academic who uses their status as a researcher to further particular narratives.[73] Stemming on the one hand from a widespread perception of an "unfinished revolution" throughout the CEE and from the most often inefficient attempts at lustration in the 1990s on the other, memory institutes assumed the political role

66 Filip Cyuńczyk, *Narodowe instytuty pamięci i ich miejsce w prawnospołecznej rzeczywistości państw postkomunistycznych w Europie Środkowej i Wschodniej* [*National Institutes of Memory and Their Place in the Socio-Legal Reality of Post-Communist Countries in Central and Eastern Europe*] (Warszawa: Uniwersytet Warszawski, 2018), online: depotUW <depotuw.ceon.pl/bitstream/handle/item/3342/2200-DR-PR-340114.pdf?sequence=1> at 102.

67 Tomasz Stryjek, "Why Does Russia Not Have an Institute of National Remembrance and Does It Lose Because of This? Russian Politics of Memory Regarding World War II in the Second Decade of the 21st Century" in Przemysław Adamczewski and Wojciecj Łysek (eds), *Poland, Soviet Union, Russia: From Past Through Memory to Politcs* (Warszawa: Instytut Studiów Politycznych Polskiej Akademii Nauk, 2020) 159 at 161.

68 Dujisin, *supra* note 59 at 84.

69 Jones, *supra* note 56 at 29.

70 Dujisin, *supra* note 59 at 87–88.

71 Dujisin, *supra* note 59 at 89.

72 Dujisin, *supra* note 59 at 67.

73 Mink, *supra* note 60 at 163.

of working through collective trauma-memories,[74] in a way establishing a "regional" set "of rules and norms for managing" them.[75] While memory institutes' work comes under heavy scrutiny, as I outline further in this section, they have become "firmly ensconced" in their respective societies,[76] playing a major "role in the public debates" over the past in the region, succeeding in "shaping the language and content-driven, as well as emotional setting, in which 'memory' is referred to,"[77] in a way entrenching the official narrative along the lines which they themselves draw.

This "CEE memory institute model" includes a diverse, tightknit network of "experts and decision-makers, victims and executioners, police investigation services, recruitment agencies and 'agents,' and crystallised around this configuration is a wide range of routine behaviours and shared representations."[78] The model translates into an extremely particular legal and political status: memory institutes are "a part of public administration and enjoy . . . status equal to a ministry but independent from the government and any other political organ,"[79] but at the same time have been granted only a "fiction of independence" from politicians, as they remain under a certain amount of influence from the authorities, particularly due to their state-granted budget and state-appointed administration[80] and the lack of legal guarantees of internal pluralism.[81] Ultimately, memory institutes, as Cyuńczyk acutely remarks, act "in the name and on commission of the state," establishing an official narrative for its use and then operating that narrative to influence collective memory.[82]

While the range of activities each memory institute is tasked with varies, in the case of the most far-reaching one – Polish IPN – it includes the redress of the Nazi and communist wrongs against the nation[83] and the preservation of national memory as the "primary vocation," which is achieved through

74 Dujisin, *supra* note 59 at 83.
75 Mink, *supra* note 60 at 157.
76 Idesbald Goddeeris, "History Riding on the Waves of Government Coalitions: The First Fifteen Years of the Institute of National Remembrance in Poland (2001–2016)" in Berber Bevernage and Nico Wouters (eds), *The Palgrave Handbook of State-Sponsored History After 1945* (London: Palgrave Macmillan, 2018) 255 at 258.
77 Górny and Kończal, *supra* note 58 at 66.
78 Mink, *supra* note 60 at 157.
79 Stola, *supra* note 53 at 47.
80 Filip Cyuńczyk, "Public Memory Sphere and Its Legal Petrification: Few Remarks on the Legal Framework of the Institutes for the National Remembrance Functioning in Poland and Ukraine" (2019) 69 Visnyk of the Lviv University 3 at 5.
81 Cyuńczyk, *supra* note 66 at 111.
82 Cyuńczyk, *supra* note 66 at 112.
83 Rafał Reczek, "Rola Instytutu Pamięci Narodowej w procesie przywracania pamięci" ["The Role of National Institute of Memory in the Process of Memory Evoking"] (2015) 3 Środkowoeuropejskie Studia Polityczne 221 at 222.

lustration and a gradual granting of a broader access to archives, public education, prosecution of crimes against the nation (in the Polish case, both Nazi and communist crimes),[84] participation in public commemorations, and searching for the resting places of the broadly considered fighters against totalitarianism.[85] To fulfil their duties, memory institutes typically have a considerable budget, but one varying from country to country, ranging from 92 million euros in the case of Poland[86] and 90 million euros in the case of Germany, to 4 million euros in the case of Romania and 2.5 million euros in the case of Bulgaria.[87]

While their activity related to lustration and archival work most often draws attention and is considered the most important goal of memory institutes,[88] I would argue that it is actually their research and public education role that is particularly important in their general function as an instrument of memory politics. Perceived as highly "significant for the symbolic transformation" after years of communism,[89] it is through these actions that the memory institutes aim to "slowly build historical consciousness," or collective memory, of their own and neighbouring nations.[90] To use the Polish example of IPN once again, this collective memory shift is being undertaken not only with the more typical research activities, such as the organisation of conferences and seminars,[91] preparation of publications regarding the years 1939–1989 (several thousands of which came out during only IPN's first 15 years of existence), or the publication of research journals, but also through the development of newspaper editions, documentaries, an online channel, various model school lessons, exhibitions, and even board games. The Institute also has a permanent presence in the Polish memory landscape with its Educational Centre in Warsaw and different History Clubs throughout the country, and it organises various commemorative actions (including with the National Barrister Association, aimed at the ensuring of the rights of former political prisoners), which also engage in collective evoking,[92] as well as outdoor events such as picnics or games.[93] In addition to the Polish IPN, Ukrainian's UINM merits closer attention in its public outreach initiatives, given that

84 Behr, *supra* note 55 at 2.
85 Cyuńczyk, *supra* note 80 at 5.
86 Frances Millard, *Transitional Justice in Poland: Memory and the Politics of the Past* (London: I. B. Tauris, 2021) at 128.
87 Mink, *supra* note 60 at 161–162.
88 Kopeček, *supra* note 64 at 87.
89 Marta Kurkowska-Budzan, "Power, Knowledge and Faith Discourse: The Institute of National Remembrance" in Aleksandra Galasińska and Dariusz Galasiński (eds), *The Post-Communist Condition: Public and Private Discourses of Transformation* (Amsterdam: John Benjamins Publishing Company, 2010) 167 at 168.
90 Reczek, *supra* note 83 at 226.
91 Stola, *supra* note 53 at 51.
92 Reczek, *supra* note 83 at 227–232.
93 Goddeeris, *supra* note 76 at 259–260.

since 2014, it has been – uniquely for the region's memory institutes – directly tasked with distancing the country from Russia and bringing it closer to the European Union,[94] which was conducted by establishing a new official narrative and wide-ranging changes to public commemorations, including the putting together of new vocabulary with regards to the past.[95]

Never free from media attention, in a way also due to the enduring importance of issues they deal with,[96] memory institutes are not free from criticism. Accused of having a potentially chilling effect on counter-memories,[97] they are labelled ineffective bureaucracies[98] whose underscoring of the experience of communist atrocities puts them on a collision course with the European policy stressing the "uniqueness of the Holocaust,"[99] and whose lustration investigations may often lead to ambiguous and even untrue results, with those whose rights were infringed successfully bringing a number of cases before the ECtHR.[100] Over the years, memory institutes have also become increasingly influenced by various agents of memory, who "confront and compete with each other,"[101] engaging in manipulation of collective memory through memory politics.[102] As such, while thanks to their generous budgets, institutes of memory provide historians with increased funding, job availability, and media access, they often allow for less research autonomy,[103] with their internal "historical policy" often "subject to the immediate political context"[104] and their research in general considered to be too reliant on the archives[105] and too narrowly focused.[106] Moreover, while initially established as a means of dealing with collective trauma-memories, it seems that memory institutes have not led to reconciliation, keeping up the contentious debate about the past alive instead,[107] ultimately revealing their "hybrid nature,"[108] one "blurring" the lines between "history, identity and memory."[109]

94 Klymenko, *supra* note 61 at 134.
95 Klymenko, *supra* note 61 at 135–140.
96 Stola, *supra* note 53 at 48.
97 Kopeček, *supra* note 64 at 90.
98 Stola, *supra* note 53 at 54.
99 Dujisin, *supra* note 59 at 89–90.
100 Mink, *supra* note 60 at 163.
101 Mink, *supra* note 60 at 163–164.
102 Jones, *supra* note 62 at 70.
103 Behr, *supra* note 55 at 2.
104 Georges Mink, "Is There a New Institutional Response to the Crimes of Communism? National Memory Agencies in Post-Communist Countries: The Polish Case (1998–2014), with References to East Germany" (2017) 45:6 Nationalities Papers 1013 at 1021.
105 Millard, *supra* note 86 at 137.
106 Goddeeris, *supra* note 76 at 261–262.
107 Mink, *supra* note 60 at 157.
108 Mink, *supra* note 104 at 1024.
109 Millard, *supra* note 86 at 140.

This failure, even a disinterest in leading to social *katharsis* at least on some level, is one of the main reasons why I do not include memory institutes in my concept of legal institutions of memory, despite certain similarities: a disjunction with transitional justice concepts, as a number of memory institutes were created long after 1989;[110] participation in the establishment of a new official narrative; and being an element of memory politics. Unlike legal institutions of memory, however, memory institutes fail to directly engage with law, rather being its passive products; and, while they may be involved in activities considered Durkheimian rituals (e.g., lustration, public commemoration), these are only some of their functions, which, in fact, are much broader.

Thus, rather than a legal institution of memory, or, as Mink perceives them, a place of memory[111] – in the case of memory institutes, this memory carrier role is played out by the archives they house, which indeed are a place of memory, a Foucauldian heterotopia, as proposed earlier – I would argue that memory institutes are actually memory agents in their own right. In spite of being an instrument of politics of memory, as evidenced by their research and education activities, memory institutes play a major and active role in the shaping of collective memories of the communist and Nazi past throughout the CEE region.

Last, it needs to be remarked that the high-level institutionalisation of memory politics – and thus of collective memory – these politics of memory in practice in which memory institutes engage – has far-reaching repercussions, if not in paving a straight road, then at least in opening the door leading to a recognition of the right to memory, the concept which I introduce in the next section.

The Right to Memory: Between Conceptualisation and Unacknowledged Presence in Law and its Mechanisms

In her poignant essay on the need for inclusion of the memory of slavery into the widely shared collective memory, Christiane Taubira argued that:

> memory is a right. One which flows from an abuse of the law. An abuse of *ius gentium* in those instances when legislation does not provide a ban on torture, deportations, genocide, war crimes, crimes against humanity. From a violation of positive law in those instances when the formulation of these crimes and their penalisation are codified. This right to memory precedes and transcends the obligation to memory,[112]

110 Mink, *supra* note 60 at 167.

111 Mink, *supra* note 104 at 1014.

112 Christiane Taubira, "Le droit à la mémoire" ["The Right to Memory"] (2006) 25 Cités 164 at 164.

Taubira added that "the right to memory is not a sectorial right. It is not the pickings of the victims, of their relatives or of their descendants. This right is universal in that it concerns and involves the whole of society."[113] Her remarks in a way open up the question of the potential for the formulation of a legally enforceable right to memory.

The concept of the right to memory has increasingly appeared in the field of human rights beginning in the 1990s. It has been argued that memory itself is "a human right given that in its absence is responsible, for the large part, for the prolonging or repeating of acts of violence, . . . the most atrocious of human rights violations."[114] The potential right to memory has been proposed as "the right to a symbolic representation of the past embedded within a set of interventions and practices,"[115] as well as the "acknowledgement of the otherness of the past made present and future through various symbolic and cultural acts, gestures, utterances and expressions."[116] It has also been sketched out as "a fundamental right of all human beings that goes to the heart of human dignity, of political and sociocultural identity, and, therefore, of democracy," one affirming and protecting those collective memories that "ensure the physical survival and moral well-being of a people,"[117] allowing it to "establish itself as a political being," an equal participant in the political democratic process.[118]

At the same time, the French Council of State argued in a 2009 decision that while "a solemn duty of memory exist[s] and persist[s]," it remains a question of memory politics conducted by the state and not necessarily a legal issue.[119] Similarly, Huyssen asserts that a right to memory "is not legally or socially enforceable," unless it becomes possible to alter a person's individual memories at some point in the future[120] – choosing to ignore that our collective memories, as noted in the previous section, are constantly influenced by memory politics. This allows for the possibility, however, that a right to memory might function as a part of cultural rights.[121]

113 *Ibid.* at 166.

114 Fernanda Frizzo Bragato and Luciana Araújo de Paula, "A Memória Como Direito Humano" (2011) 2011 Relatório Azul 129 at 137.

115 Anna Reading, "Gender and the Right to Memory" (2010) 2 Media Development 11 at 11.

116 Anna Reading, "Identity, Memory and Cosmopolitanism: The Otherness of the Past and a Right to Memory?" (2011) 14:4 European Journal of Cultural Studies 379 at 380.

117 Philip Lee, "Towards a Right to Memory" (2010) LVII:2 Media Development 3 at 9–10.

118 Bragato and de Paula, *supra* note 114 at 140.

119 Vivian Grosswald Curran, "History, Memory and Law" (2011) 16:1 Roger Williams University Law Review 100 at 105.

120 Andreas Huyssen, "Historical Justice and Human Rights: A New Constellation" in Klaus Neumann and Janna Thompson (eds), *Historical Justice and Memory* (Madison, WI: University of Wisconsin Press, 2015) 27 at 34, 39–40.

121 *Ibid.* at 40.

In spite of the many different viewpoints on its shape and viability, however, certain dimensions of the right to memory, Lee remarks, may already be traced within different international law conventions, such as: the 1948 Universal Declaration of Human Rights, whose various provisions, including the freedom to participate in the cultural life of the community, cannot be "enjoyed to the full without access to collective memory"; the 1948 Convention on the Prevention and Punishment of Genocide, which also concerns mental harm committed on the members of the group, which may include harms to collective memory; the 1966 International Covenant of Economic, Social and Cultural Rights, the 1969 Declaration on Social Progress and Development and the 1986 Declaration on the Right to Development, which confirm manifold rights linked to collective memory; the 1994 International Covenant on Civil and Political Rights, which focuses on the protection of the rights of minorities, also oftentimes connected to a *de facto* protection of collective memory; the 2005 Convention on the Protection and Promotion of the Diversity of Cultural Expressions, which calls for the establishment of safe environments for the creation of culture; and the 2007 Declaration on the Rights of Indigenous Peoples, which grants them the protection of their collective memory (although still failing to address it as such).[122] It has also been in the context of indigenous peoples' rights that the concept of the right to memory appeared within the works of the Brazilian National Truth Commission as one "favouring a consolidation of human rights and citizenship of these [related to the questions of memory] social subjects."[123]

To this already extensive list of the right to memory's traces in legal texts, Reading adds the work undertaken by UNESCO and the Working Group on Archives and Human Rights within the International Council on Archives,[124] whereas Hearty includes in the rights to memory already present in the legal realm also the various United Nations (UN) policy reports on reparations, as well as truth commissions' recommendations, and the jurisprudence of the Inter-American Court of Human Rights (IACtHR), along with some domestic jurisdictions, ultimately following Jimeno's argument that a *de facto* "right to remember has latently emerged within transitional justice."[125] This thought might be complemented with Viejo-Rose's remark that "the prevalence of

122 Lee, *supra* note 117 at 8–9.

123 Valdir J. Morigi and Ana M. Giovanoni Forno, "Direito à memória: A Comissão Nacional da Verdade brasileira e as narrativas dos povos indígenas na construção da cidadania" ["Right to Memory: The Brazilian National Truth Commission and Narratives of Indigenous Peoples in the Construction of Citizenship"] (2020) 30:2 Informação & Sociedade: Estudos 1 at 2–3.

124 Reading, *supra* note 115 at 11.

125 Kevin Hearty, "Problematising Symbolic Reparation: 'Complex Political Victims,' 'Dead Body Politics' and the Right to Remember" (2020) 29:3 Social and Legal Studies 334 at 335.

legal language and ideas" which has "been downloaded from an international discourse" has as such "infiltrated memorial practice with claims of memorial rights."[126] Additionally, as I noted elsewhere, the questions of cultural heritage and the intricate national and international network establishing its protection are directly linked to collective memory, most visible in the case of World Heritage lists, which establish certain cultural objects, be that material or immaterial, as the heritage of all humanity[127] – elements, as Reading notes,[128] of global collective memory.

In my earlier research,[129] I proposed a different perspective on the right to memory from the one proposed by most researchers, also taking another direction in its conceptualisation than the one to be found in international law, basing it on the study of law and collective memory's interactions within the cityscape and the question of memory politics. As such, I put forward a proposal of the right to memory as a Janus, two-faced right, actually composed of a pair of opposite rights which need the other to function, being two sides of the same "memory coin": one connected to evoking (with two similar, but separate rights, the right to remember and be remembered) and another to disremembering (also with two similar, but separate rights, the right to forget and be forgotten). Thus, in the remainder of this chapter, I elaborate on this initial analysis, taking it out of the cityscape and following Levinas, whose idea of the diachronic ethics laying "in the face of the other" and at the basis of all law, including human rights law, remarked upon earlier, as Bragato and de Paula also note, may be directly linked to a right to memory[130] – arguing for a universal, internationally recognised right to memory.

The Right to Remember

The first component of the right to memory in my understanding is the right to remember. Perceived as a right oriented from the group or an individual towards society, it concerns the right for particular collective memories, notably counter-memories, to be represented within society through inclusion in

126 Dacia Viejo-Rose, "Memorial Functions: Intent, Impact and the Right to Remember" (2011) 4:4 Memory Studies 465 at 473.

127 Mirosław M. Sadowski, "Heritage Strikes Back: The Al Mahdi Case, ICC's Policy on Cultural Heritage and the Pushing of Law's Boundaries" (2022) 2 Undecidabilities and Law – The Coimbra Journal for Legal Studies 99.

128 Reading, *supra* note 116 at 387.

129 Mirosław M. Sadowski, "City as a Locus of Collective Memory: Streets, Monuments and Human Rights" (2020) 40:1–2 Zeitschrift für Rechtssoziologie – The German Journal of Law and Society 209 at 231.

130 Bragato and de Paula, *supra* note 114 at 140–142.

the official narrative and becoming a part of collective rituals such as public commemorations.

The right to remember may be linked to the concept of a "duty to remember," which emerged first after World War II as a duty to remember crimes of that period,[131] and then later in the 1980s, proposing that by remembering the difficult past, future atrocities may be prevented.[132] Developed over the years, the duty to remember comes particularly close to my understanding of the right to remember as proposed by Louis Joinet, who in his capacity as the special Rapporteur to the Sub-Commission on Prevention of Discrimination and Protection of Minorities, prepared a Set of Principles for the Protection and Promotion of Human Rights through Actions to Combat Impunity, arguing that "a people's knowledge of the history of its oppression is part of its heritage and, as such, must be preserved by appropriate measures in fulfilment of the State's duty to remember," explicitly stressing that said "measures shall be aimed at preserving the collective memory from extinction and, in particular, at guarding against the development of revisionist and negationist arguments."[133]

Importantly, in post-conflict situations, as noted by Lee and in the earlier part of my book concerning symbolic reparations, resurrecting or rehabilitating "a people's memory" is "the first step on the road to restitution,"[134] given that returning counter-memories to their rightful place in the official narrative is "an act of justice,"[135] allowing for the building of "a narrative of the future" on the basis of the revised collective memory[136] and changing power relations within the society in question.[137] A right to remember is needed, González and Ferreira note in a similar vein, given that "when the past is assumed with the value of being 'ours'" and where there is a willingness only to "highlight a set of memories of a society which considers them to belong to the whole," while actually excluding various groups within said society, "it becomes difficult to continue strengthening democracy when . . .

131 Ali Moussa Iye, "From the Duty to Remember to the Right to Remember" (2006) LVIII International Social Science Journal 187 at 187.

132 Lea David, "Against Standardization of Memory" (2017) 39 Human Rights Quarterly 296 at 301.

133 Louis Joinet, *Set of Principles for the Protection and Promotion of Human Rights Through Actions to Combat Impunity* (E/CN.4/Sub.2/1997/20/Rev.1) at 17.

134 Lee, *supra* note 117 at 6.

135 Lee, *supra* note 117 at 10.

136 Eliana Jimeno, "Historical Memory as Symbolic Reparation Limitations and Opportunities of Peace Infrastructures as Institutional Designs" in Fabio A. Díaz Pabón (ed.), *Truth, Justice and Reconciliation in Colombia: Transitioning from Violence* (Oxon/New York, NY: Routledge, 2018) 136 at 138.

137 Elazar Barkan, *The Guilt of Nations: Restitution and Negotiating Historical Injustices* (New York, NY/London: W. W. Norton & Company, 2000) at 343.

a present is built on a past that has not healed."[138] It needs to be stressed that the right to remember may also be exercised in general, and not only in transitory situations, "as a justification of minority rights, which in turn requires the broader society" to bring the minority's in question counter-memories into the official narrative.[139]

While theoretically rather straightforward, putting the right to remember into practice may see major challenges, intrinsically linked to the question of official narrative and public commemorations in effect "standardising memory"[140] and reinforcing "selective interpretations of the past through commemoration and memorialisation"[141] with the whole system of collective remembering working this way, e.g., not only museum exhibits in general but also a prevalent post-Holocaust concept of a museum dedicated to past atrocities.[142] Additionally, it may prove to be particularly difficult to include counter-memories in the official narrative when it remained unchallenged for long periods of time, potentially putting the groups in question at odds with their neighbours.[143] Even should they succeed in incorporating them, the new elements of the official narrative may still be silenced by other elements present in it due to memory politics, as I remarked upon earlier in the book.

Moreover, arguments of "competitive victimhood" and "joint responsibility" are often raised with regard to the right to memory,[144] while in the case of internal conflicts, the issue of honouring the victims on both sides of the right to remember divide may prove to be an arduous task,[145] one made more difficult due to memory politics but potentially rewarding as leading to a chance for reconciliation.[146] At same time, exercising the right to remember might also mean recovering but limiting access to certain collective memories for non-group members to protect them from globalisation[147] or implementing

138 Ana M. Sosa González and Maria L. Mazzucchi Ferreira, "Derecho de memoria y búsqueda de la verdad: Un estudio comparativo entre Brasil y Uruguay" ["The Right to Memory and Search of the Truth: A Comparative Study on Brazil and Uruguay"] (2012) 16:3 Diálogos 873 at 894.

139 Patrick Macklem, "Rybná 9, Praha 1: Restitution and Memory in International Human Rights Law" (2005) 16:1 The European Journal of International Law 1 at 15.

140 David, *supra* note 132 at 318.

141 Hearty, *supra* note 125 at 336, 346.

142 Sheila Watson, "Introduction to Part Four" in Sheila Watson (ed.), *Museums and their Communities* (Oxon/New York, NY: Routledge, 2007) 375 at 376–377.

143 Richard N. Lebow, "The Future of Memory" (2008) 617 Annals AAPSS 25 at 27.

144 Iye, *supra* note 131 at 188.

145 Viejo-Rose, *supra* note 126 at 469.

146 Hearty, *supra* note 125 at 348–349.

147 Reading, *supra* note 116 at 384–385.

the legal institution of memory of memory legislation to protect particular collective memories.[148]

The Right to Be Remembered

Also as a part of the right to evoking, I propose the right to be remembered as a rereading of the right to truth that emerged in the jurisprudence of the IACtHR. Perceived as a right oriented from society towards the individual or a group, it concerns the necessity of collective memories regarding particular people or groups to be returned to their rightful place within society through the process of breaking legal and social silences and establishing truth about their fate.

Over the years, the right to truth has become "one of the most important issues in Latin America,"[149] emerging "in response to the state's failure" to resolve questions concerning violations of international humanitarian law and of human rights, soon becoming "one of the pillars of the mechanisms of transitional justice,"[150] allowing us to "fill . . . a gap in History"[151] – and in collective memory. The right to truth was initially connected with the question of forced disappearances,[152] i.e., those instances of human rights violations when the victim is imprisoned by "state officials or groups acting in collaboration with the state, while the information" concerning their fate remains a secret but has since been developed as a more general right to information regarding major atrocities.[153]

In response to these violations of human rights, the right to truth appeared within the IACtHR's jurisprudence as "the duty to take all measures necessary to investigate and, where appropriate, punish those responsible and to make fair and adequate reparations to the victim's next of kin" as a response to these crimes.[154] In addition to the regional recognition of the General Assembly of American States, the right to truth has also been acknowledged

148 Kalliopi Chainoglou, "The Right to Historical Truth and Historical Memory Versus Historical Revisionism and Denialism: A Human Rights Analysis" in Kalliopi Chainoglou, Barry Collins, Michael Phillips, and John Strawson (eds), *Injustice, Memory and Faith in Human Rights* (Oxon/New York, NY: Routledge, 2018) 136 at 139.

149 Juan E. Mendez, "An Emerging 'Right to Truth': Latin-American Contributions" in Susanne Karstedt (ed.), *Legal Institutions and Collective Memories* (Oxford: Hart Publishing, 2009) 39 at 54.

150 IACHR, *The Right to Truth in the Americas* (OEA/Ser.L/V/II.152) at 21.

151 Sévane Garibian, "Ghosts Also Die Resisting Disappearance Through the 'Right to the Truth' and the *Juicios por la Verdad* in Argentina" (2014) 12:3 Journal of International Criminal Justice 515 at 538.

152 IACHR, *supra* note 150 at 27.

153 Grażyna Baranowska, "The Right to the Truth" (2017), online: Republica <publica.pl/teksty/baranowska-the-right-to-the-truth-62691.html>.

154 IACHR, *supra* note 150 at 29.

by various UN instruments,[155] as well as the work of the European Court of Human Rights (ECtHR) and the International Court of Justice (ICJ).[156]

Importantly, the right to truth as established by the IACtHR is two-dimensional, consisting not only of "the right of the victims and their family members to know the truth about the events that led to serious violations of human rights," as well as "the right to know the identity of those who played a role in those violations," but also granting such a right to the whole society,[157] in the hopes that it will help the reconciliation process.[158] It is directly connected to the work of two legal institutions of memory: truth (and reconciliation) commissions, and international tribunals.[159] However, the former's work cannot be considered sufficient to fulfil the state's duty to implement the right to truth[160] – and it may be an element of the process of granting amnesties,[161] which, as noted earlier, may require the applicant to provide some information about the events of which they were a part.

However, the right to truth in its present shape has severe limitations: IACtHR has considered the right to truth as an autonomous right in only one case,[162] and the right itself "remains a kind of 'pointer to the crime,'" authorising "a shift from law that effaces it (amnesty laws) to law that reveals it (trials for the truth)."[163] At the same time, when employed by the ECtHR and the ICJ, the right to truth has been understood as having a temporal limit beginning with the establishment of the two institutions.[164]

While known as the right to truth, I propose to consider it as a right to be remembered, given that it "is closely linked at its inception to the notion of a victim,"[165] following Huyssen in arguing that it is ultimately the victims, "the dead," who "have a right to remembrance,"[166] and it is only on the

155 Eduardo Ferrer Mac-Gregor, "The *Right to the Truth* as an Autonomous Right Under the Inter-American Human Rights System" (2016) IX:1 Mexican Law Review 121 at 124–125.
156 William A. Schabas, "Time, Justice, and Human Rights: Statutory Limitation on the Right to Truth?" in Nanci Adler (ed.), *Understanding the Age of Transitional Justice: Crimes, Courts, Commissions, and Chronicling* (New Brunswick, NJ: Rutgers University Press, 2018) 37 at 37.
157 IACHR, *supra* note 150 at 25.
158 Yasmin Naqvi, "The Right to the Truth in International Law: Fact or Fiction?" (2006) 88:862 International Review of the Red Cross 245 at 249.
159 Monique Crettol and Anne-Marie La Rosa, "The Missing and Transitional Justice: The Right to Know and the Fight Against Impunity" (2006) 88:862 International Review of the Red Cross 355 at 362.
160 Garibian, *supra* note 151 at 526.
161 Naqvi, *supra* note 158 at 272.
162 Mac-Gregor, *supra* note 155 at 125.
163 Garibian, *supra* note 151 at 518.
164 Schabas, *supra* note 156 at 52.
165 Naqvi, *supra* note 158 at 249.
166 Andreas Huyssen, "International Human Rights and the Politics of Memory: Limits and Challenges" (2011) 53:4 Criticism 607 at 611.

basis of this right to be remembered that their families and the whole society establish their claims for truth, which may also be considered a claim for the victims' return to collective memory.

Importantly, I am not alone in considering the right to truth – the right to be remembered – as a component of the right to memory. As Morigi and Forno note, "the right to memory consists of a subjective right of the victims and the whole society to receive truthful (or as close to the truth as possible) information (or a memorial narrative) regarding" the causes and circumstances of the atrocities in question,[167] a process which "involves cross-networks established between social actors, artefacts and carriers of information, as they help in the promotion of human rights and the construction of citizenship."[168] As such, the right to be remembered – the right to truth – needs to be recognised as an element of a broader right to memory.

The Right to Forget

Linking it to collective forgetting, I propose the right to forget as the third element of the right to memory. Perceived as a right oriented from society towards an individual or a group, it concerns the right to let collective memories concerning particular groups or individuals slide into oblivion, either due to their status as a victim or an amnesty.

Importantly, in a number of cases, it is the victims themselves who choose to invoke a right to forget, given that oftentimes they are unable to speak about their experiences, all the more so when there is no social space that would allow them "to couch their personal experiences within a collective narrative of events,"[169] such as a truth commission. Public commemoration only, the exercise of their – and society's – right to remember, may prove to be insufficient for the victims to work through their collective trauma-memories, as in many instances they are the ones "who must continue a daily existence in the environments where atrocities occurred," which puts them at odds with the pressure on commemoration.[170]

These issues prove to be particularly difficult with regard to the spaces constructed as a place for social rituals of remembering, particular places of memory, as wishes of the victim groups may be ignored for the benefit

167 Morigi and Forno, *supra* note 123 at 4.

168 Morigi and Forno, *supra* note 123 at 19.

169 Erika Apfelbaum, "Halbwachs and the Social Properties of Memory" in Susannah Radstone and Bill Schwarz (eds), *Memory: Histories, Theories, Debates* (New York: Fordham University Press, 2010) 77 at 86–87.

170 Shannon Davis and Jacky Bowring, "The Right to Remember: The Memorials to Genocide in Cambodia and Rwanda" in Shelley Egoz, Jala Makhzoumi, and Gloria Pungetti (eds), *The Right to Landscape Contesting Landscape and Human Rights* (Oxon/New York, NY: Routledge, 2016) 211 at 211.

of the international community, whose predominantly Western notions of evoking[171] are often very different from the local religious beliefs and acts of mourning.[172] As Reading remarks, non-Western rituals of remembering and forgetting may involve "modalities that do not involve museums, archives and monuments that name the dead," as they can "maintain social cohesion through particular rituals of forgetting or through the conscious not-naming of people or events."[173] In such instances, the victims and their families' right to forget should most definitely be respected over the global society's right to remember.[174]

Another dimension of the right to forget may involve leaving one's group behind and, as such, renouncing their collective memories through the process of not amnesia but rather "re-socialisation" in the new environment.[175] While this has been the *leitmotiv* of American culture since its inception, requiring immigrants to leave their old identity behind to adopt a new one, thus becoming a part of a united nation,[176] when applied to post-conflict situations, this aspect of the right to forget may be linked to the aforementioned question of legal amnesia through amnesty. If in place, a former oppressor may invoke a right to forget on the basis of amnesty and, even though not punished, demand to be allowed to become a full member of general society, despite the collective trauma-memories attached to their persona remaining unresolved. While potentially beneficial for social cohesion, as I noted earlier, such instances of the application of the right to forget can prove to be particularly inflammatory, clashing with the right to remember and to be remembered.[177]

The Right to Be Forgotten

The final component of the right to memory in my conceptualisation is the right to be forgotten. Perceived as a right oriented from the individual or a group towards society, I propose it as a rereading of the right to be forgotten that has appeared in the jurisprudence of the European Union (EU),

171 *Ibid.* at 215–216.
172 *Ibid.* at 219.
173 Reading, *supra* note 115 at 13.
174 Davis and Bowring, *supra* note 170 at 222.
175 Gregory W. Streich, "Is There a Right to Forget? Historical Injustices, Race, Memory, and Identity" (2002) 24:4 New Political Science 525 at 527–528.
176 Michael Medved, "You Must Remember This: What's Right with American Culture" (1995) 71 Policy Review 45 at 50–51.
177 Susana Kaiser, "The Struggle for Urban Territories: Human Rights Activists in Buenos Aires" in Clara Irazábal (ed.), *Ordinary Places, Extraordinary Events: Citizenship, Democracy and Public Space in Latin America* (Abingdon/New York, NY: Routledge, 2008) at 179.

understanding it as a right concerning the removal of certain collective memories from the general collective memory of a particular group.

The right to be forgotten first came to be a challenge to "the eternal memory of the internet,"[178] standing in contradiction to the traditional ways of building up collective memory, which includes high levels of collective forgetting.[179] In contrast, in the present day, there exists an "ever-expanding public sphere of memory with its irrepressible quest of archiving everything," where virtually everything is remembered, including events that would have naturally passed into oblivion before the arrival of the internet.[180]

The EU's right to be forgotten (RtbF) has appeared as a legal answer to this issue provided by the European Court of Justice (ECJ), which, basing its decision on the 1995 Date Protection Directive, put on every search engine a previously unrecognised[181] "obligation to remove certain personal information from its search results upon the data subject's demand."[182] If such a demand is granted – following an untransparent process – the information in question "is still available on the internet," but "it cannot be found through a search for the subject's name,"[183] which means those looking for said information are virtually transported "from the computer age back to the micro-fiche age on a search-by-search basis."[184] As few searchers will "have the patience" to undertake "potentially multiple searches on multiple platforms,"[185] when exercised, the right to be forgotten means that particular information will disappear, "be forgotten" from collective memory – which, Rusu argues, in a way "humanises" the digital memory, now induced judicially to forget,[186] giving the opportunity, de Mars and O'Callaghan note, to regain "some degree of control over various information flows that shape our identities."[187] Importantly, the RtbF continues to be further developed within the EU's legal system, as evidenced by the adoption of the 2018 General Data

178 Simon Wechsler, "The Right to Remember: The European Convention on Human Rights and the Right to Be Forgotten" (2015) 49:1 Columbia Journal of Law and Social Problems 136 at 136.

179 Mihai S. Rusu, "From the Will to Memory to the Right to Be Forgotten – a Paradigm Shift in the Culture of Remembering" (2015) 20:2 Philobiblon: Transylvanian Journal of Multidisciplinary Research in Humanities 384 at 407.

180 *Ibid.* at 407–408.

181 Christopher Rees and Debbie Heywood, "The 'Right to Be Forgotten' or the 'Principle That Has Been Remembered'" (2014) 30 Computer Law and Security Review 574 at 578.

182 Wechsler, *supra* note 178 at 136–137.

183 Wechsler, *supra* note 178 at 137–138.

184 Michael J. Kelly and David Satola, "The Right to Be Forgotten" (2017) 2017:1 University of Illinois Law Review 1 at 4.

185 *Ibid.* at 4.

186 Rusu, *supra* note 179 at 404.

187 Sylvia de Mars and Patrick O'Callaghan, "Privacy and Search Engines: Forgetting or Contextualizing?" (2016) 43:2 Journal of Law and Society 257 at 283.

Protection Regulation (GDPR), granting the right to demand "data deletion, as well as requiring data controllers to process erasure requests and inform third-party data processors about these requests."[188]

While the RtbF may be considered "a tool that gives society members better control over their identity creation,"[189] a broader right to be forgotten, one allowing the people and groups in particular to be able to once again build collective memory of themselves, might be needed in the current era of "gaining perfect mastery over memory"[190] through archiving large amounts of data online, following the right to be forgotten that already exists in relation to state archives, preventing most information from being freely accessed even when available through public repository.[191] As such, the right to be forgotten could allow for freedom of "being forced to recall what otherwise" would never be recalled without one's consent, as well as for freedom from "any use of information . . . which causes harmful effects"[192] – in a way "a manifestation of a broader right to be in charge over one's memory,"[193] making it possible "to erase, limit, or alter past records that can be misleading, redundant, anachronistic, embarrassing, or contain irrelevant data" in the hopes that "those past records do not continue to impede present perceptions of that individual"[194] – or of a collective.

In its present form, the right to be forgotten already "creates a chance" for collective forgetting to take place and "has a symbolic function signalling that interests in forgetting/being forgotten are of fundamental value."[195] As Tirosh postulates, a proper right to be forgotten should pertain both to the individuals and groups; should regard the act of forgetting as a "part of a bigger cultural memory process that contains both remembering and forgetting"; and should acknowledge "the role of memory in both individual and collective processes of identity building and self-determination."[196] Returning once again to post-conflict situations, one can exemplify such a legal amnesia as induced by the closing of the archives upon request of those whose files

188 Elizabeth Stainforth, "Collective Memory or the Right to Be Forgotten? Cultures of Digital Memory and Forgetting in the European Union" (2022) 15:2 Memory Studies 257 at 265.

189 Noam Tirosh, "Reconsidering the 'Right to Be Forgotten' – Memory Rights and the Right to Memory in the New Media Era" (2017) 39:5 Media, Culture and Society 644 at 652.

190 Rusu, *supra* note 179 at 404.

191 Eric Ketelaar, "The Right to Know, the Right to Forget? Personal Information in Public Archives" (1995) 23:1 Archives and Manuscripts 8 at 11–12.

192 Kiyoshi Murata and Yohkho Orito, "The Right to Forget/Be Forgotten" (2011), online: Academia.edu <academia.edu/31620676/The_Right_to_Forget_Be_Forgotten> 1 at 11.

193 Tirosh, *supra* note 189 at 645.

194 Kelly and Satola, *supra* note 184 at 3.

195 Patrick O'Callaghan, "The Chance 'to Melt into the Shadows of Obscurity': Developing a 'Right to Be Forgotten' in the United States" in Ann E. Cudd and Mark C. Navin (eds), *Core Concepts and Contemporary Issues in Privacy* (Cham: Springer, 2018) 159 at 162.

196 Tirosh, *supra* note 189 at 656.

may be found there, a move contrary to the legal institution of memory of lustration, but one, the institutions' critics say – as noted above – that could lead to reconciliation. At the same time, the right to be forgotten carries a danger that certain groups or individuals, and even countries as a whole,[197] may use it to "cleanse their image" following an atrocity,[198] resulting in "the inability to maintain a successful public record for historical purposes."[199] This puts it in a clash with the right to be remembered, given that, even when exercised by an individual, it affects the collective memory of a whole group.

What Right to Memory?

In one of my earlier works, I posed the question of whether there can be a legally enforceable right to memory.[200] Returning to this question several years later, following the previous analysis, I am now leaning towards an affirmative answer to this question, provided that a comprehensive right to memory is implemented, one balancing the evoking needs of individuals and the collectivities with those concerning disremembering. Only the right to memory pertaining to both individuals and collectivities, composed of the right to remember and be remembered and the right to forget and be forgotten, can achieve a much-needed balance within collective memory (see Figure 5.1).

Despite the fact that the right to be remembered has already been recognised as the right to truth within Latin America and the right to be forgotten – to a certain extent – as RtbF within the European Union, the two remain mostly regionally centred, while the right to remember is not explicitly pronounced, the right to forget is most often ignored, even when it may harm the victims of an atrocity. At the same time, the different aspects of the right to memory intersect with various legal institutions of memory: the right to remember with reparations and memory laws; the right to be remembered with international tribunals, truth (and reconciliation) commissions, and legal amnesia; the right to forget with legal amnesia; and the right to be forgotten with lustration. This observation only further confirms that the right to memory already exists, although it needs to be broadly construed and internationally recognised.

At the same time, the concept of the right to memory is not free of challenges. As noted earlier, both the right to forget and be forgotten clash with the right to remember and be remembered in different contexts. As such, when applied – like other human rights – its various aspects would need to be

197 Yekaterina Kuznetsova, "Dirty Secrets: How the Government Is Trying to Take Away Our Right to Remember" (2016) 68:17 The Current Digest 8 at 8.

198 Kelly and Satola, *supra* note 184 at 51.

199 Lawrence Siry, "Forget Me, Forget Me Not: Reconciling Two Different Paradigms of the Right to Be Forgotten" (2014) 103:3 Kentucky Law Journal 311 at 343.

200 Mirosław M. Sadowski, "Law and Memory: The Unobvious Relationship" (2017) 16:2 Warsaw University Law Review 262 at 287.

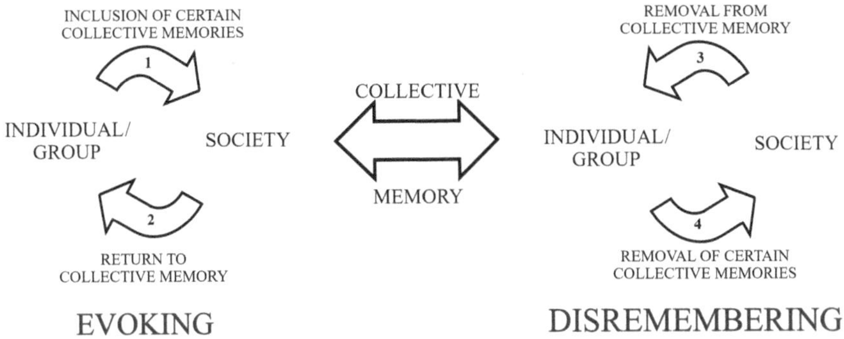

Figure 5.1 A schema of the right to memory, perceived as a Janus right balanced between evoking and disremembering: remembering – **1** the right to remember, **2** the right to be remembered; disremembering – **3** the right to forget, **4** the right to be forgotten

Source: Author.

properly weighed against one another. The right to memory, however, is first and foremost a chance to ultimately regulate the law and memory intersections: as Chainoglou notes, "the existing human rights instruments may not be the appropriate ones for resolving issues concerning claims to historical memory, and the existing human rights bodies may not consistently address denials of historical facts."[201] It is only through conceptualising, implementing, and exercising the two-dimensional right to memory that a proper treatment of law and memory intersections may be ensured.

Implementing it as proposed in this section of the book would potentially allow us to resolve a number of conflicts between law and collective memory. It would permit, on the one hand, the group to mindfully choose what and how to respect – to some degree, free in a way from memory politics – while at the same time respecting the victims' various sides of the right to memory and, on the other hand, ensuring that in the case of various legal processes involving past atrocities, "the side whose story has greater 'fit' with existing rules would no longer win hands-down on that account, for fit must be weighed against other values, especially those of robust public deliberation and memory-practice."[202] Only a right to memory will ensure that social solidarity is maintained when resolving collective trauma-memories[203] and thus lead to reconciliation.

201 Chainoglou, *supra* note 148 at 150.

202 Mark Osiel, *Mass Atrocity, Collective Memory, and the Law* (Oxon/New York, NY: Routledge, 2017) at 296.

203 Barbara A. Misztal, "Legal Attempts to Construct Collective Memory: The Necessity and Difficulties of Aiming for Both Truth and Solidarity" (2001) 133 Polish Sociological Review 61 at 63.

After all, as noted by González and Ferreira, "between the game of memory and oblivion, between the search and the right for memory and the truth, a past returns that oscillates between a spectre of itself and the appeasement of a time without peace,"[204] stressing why the properly conceptualised right to memory should be recognised as a part of human rights law.

Conclusion: Law and Memory Intersections Between Memory Politics and the Right to Memory

Following the previous chapter, which established the basis for the analysis of law and memory intersections through the conceptualisation of six legal institutions of memory, this one added two other layers for their comprehension, consisting of the politics of memory and the right to memory.

As I stressed previously, when approaching the intersections of law and memory, one needs to be aware of the influence of memory politics on each and every legal institution of memory on the one hand, but on the other also of the potential these institutions have for the exercise of the right to memory either by individuals or collectivities, hoping to take control over collective memory concerning them in some way. It could be argued that while memory politics are, in general, a top-to-bottom exercise of the power over memory, the right to memory is, in principle, a bottom-to-top exercise of the power over memory. It is only through the acknowledgement that legal institutions of memory do not operate in a vacuum, free from political or social influences, that we may fully understand them. As Knutsen remarks, "the focus must not only be on learning histories" – through collective memories – "but also on how they are used selectively in politics and democracy."[205]

Last, it also needs to be noted that employing law through memory politics or the right to memory will always lead to some of the "complexity" of collective memory being lost, given that law "provides affirmation for simplified binary categorisations"[206] – as I have pointed out in my review of legal institutions of memory – but at the same time grants those collective memories selected for the official narrative or designated for collective forgetting – even if only apparent – a level of universality and objectivity, legitimacy, and official recognition that history by itself never could.[207] This is why memory politics continues to be used as a tool within law and memory intersections, potentially also including the broadly conceptualised right to memory in the coming years.

204 González and Ferreira, *supra* note 138 at 894.

205 Ketil Knutsen, "Strategic Silence Political Persuasion Between the Remembered and the Forgotten" in Alexandre Dessingué and Jay Winter (eds), *Beyond Memory Silence and the Aesthetics of Remembrance* (Oxon/New York, NY: Routledge, 2016).

206 Löytömäki, *supra* note 25 at 129.

207 Löytömäki, *supra* note 25 at 130.

Conclusion to Part II: A New Law and Memory Framework

When law is called upon to deal with the issues of the past, it aims at a "transformation of hearts and minds," being both a tool in this transformation and "a stable base opening up some closed doors."[1] As this second part of my book shows, law truly is an instrument of such a transformation, in the form of legal institutions of memory; however, it is not always clear whether it may actually act as a stable base in such a process of legal reckoning with the past, given that its metaphorical waters are muddled with memory politics and a lack of acknowledgement and proper formulation of a right to memory. As a result, law and memory intersections often lead to "unsuccessful, uncertain, and inconsistent" experiences on the part of victims.[2]

What has become clear following this conceptual and, earlier, the theoretical analysis is the unsuitableness of the idea of transitional justice for a more general investigation of law and memory intersections – to repeat my argument, legal institutions of memory continue to shape the collective memory long after the transition from one regime to the other has been completed and have also been implemented in places that have not undergone a political or a legal transformation.

This need for a more general approach towards the questions of law and memory had already been noticed by Teitel in 2000, when she argued that her conceptualisation of transitional justice "should have import beyond periods of political flux, shedding new light on contemporary questions concerning human rights law's potential for responding to international conflict, and core understandings of the relation politics bears to justice."[3] Also noticing the internal limitations of the transitional justice concept, Collins proposed

1 Adam Czarnota, "Decommunisation and Democracy: Transitional Justice in Post-Communist Central-Eastern Europe" in Sven Eliaeson, Lyudmila Harutyunyan, and Larissa Titarenko (eds), *After the Soviet Empire: Legacies and Pathways* (Leiden: Brill, 2016) 165 at 183.

2 Ana Luleva, "Collective Memory and Justice Policy: Post-Socialist Discourses on Memory Politics and Memory Culture in Bulgaria" (2011) 15 Ethnologia Balkanica 125 at 140.

3 Ruti G. Teitel, *Transitional Justice* (Oxford/New York, NY: Oxford University Press, 2000) at 214.

DOI: 10.4324/9781003461548-10

Table 1 Framework for the understanding of law and memory intersections. Scores: 1–3 (1 the lowest, 3 the highest); +, ~, – (+ yes, ~ possibly, – no)

	Reparations	*International Tribunals*	*Lustration*	*Truth (and Reconcilation) Commissions*	*Legal Amnesia*	*Memory Legislation*
DIRECT IMPACT OF LAW	1	2	2	2	3	3
IMPACT ON COLLECTIVE MEMORY	1	1	2	3	3	3
POLITICISATION OF MEMORY	1	1	3	2	2	3
RECONCILIATION IMPACT	+	~	~	+	~	~
TRANSITIONAL PROCESSES APPLICATION	~	+	+	+	+	–
NON-TRANSITIONAL PROCESSES APPLICATION	~	+	–	~	–	+
CHANGE TO THE OFFICIAL NARRATIVE	~	~	~	+	~	+
HUMAN RIGHTS LAW INFLUENCE	–	+	–	+	–	–
INTERNATIONAL LAW INFUENCE	+	+	–	–	–	–
RIGHT TO REMEMBER	+	–	–	–	–	+
RIGHT TO BE REMEMBERED	–	+	–	+	+	–
RIGHT TO FORGET	–	–	–	–	+	–
RIGHT TO BE FORGOTTEN	–	–	+	–	–	–

Source: Author.

the idea of a Latin American–specific post-transitional justice, applicable to those situations whereby unresolved legal questions persist, although a transition from one regime to another has ended. This proposed type of post-justice focuses on sustaining democracy; challenges unresolved legal questions regarding past atrocities; includes a number of different memory agents; is fuelled by mostly bottom-to-top actions undertaken by non-state memory agents; involves various politics of memory; and has a more international effect.[4] However, it still fails to respond to the broader issues with transitional justice as a concept.

Importantly, the law and memory framework proposed in this part of the book and illustrated in Table 1 goes further than Teitel's and Collins's respective ideas. It not only acknowledges the importance of collective memory in transitional processes but also is applicable to all the cases of law and memory intersections, be that international, local, or regional, involving national or global collective memories, and takes place immediately following a transition, many years after a political change, and, perhaps most crucially, when no transformation occurs at all.

It is my personal hope that such a conceptualisation of law and memory intersections will allow for a better comprehension of legal processes involving collective memory, shedding light on their minute details, and potentially allowing for an increased awareness in the future instances of application of legal institutions of memory. To continue my discussions with Teitel once again, yes, "there is no single correct response to a state's repressive past"[5] – but there is and can be an informed one. In Part III of the book, the tripartite law and memory framework as proposed here – with legal institutions of memory basis and infused with awareness of memory politics and the right to memory – will be tested through its application to seven case studies: six corresponding to one legal institution of memory each, and the seventh of a country where four institutions may be distinguished, in the hopes of uncovering new meanings of law and memory intersections taking place in the last several decades in different legal, political, social, and cultural contexts.

4 Cath Collins, *Post-Transitional Justice Human Rights Trials in Chile and El Salvador* (University Park, PA: Pennsylvania State University Press, 2010) at 21–22.

5 Teitel, *supra* note 3 at 219.

Part III

The Practice

Reviewing Law and Memory's Intersections

Introduction to Part III

In the previous parts of the book, I first established a theoretical basis for my investigations, resting on three fundaments – sociological, philosophical, and theory of law – and later I distinguished six models of legal institutions of memory, proposing a new law and memory framework for their analysis. In this part of the book, I propose to test this new framework in practice, applying it to selected cases, six international and a localised one of a single state whereby four different legal institutions of memory may be found – Poland.

In all three chapters devoted to soft, medium, and hard legal institutions of memory, respectively, the case studies follow a similar pattern. After a brief factual introduction, a legal analysis is conducted, which is then complemented by investigations from the viewpoint of collective memory using the framework proposed in the previous part of the book. Such an organisation of the two chapters will allow for a proper comparison between the results of my research of the international legal institutions of memory and those functioning in Poland, with all the similarities and differences remarked upon in the conclusion to this part in an attempt to uncover certain similarities and differences in the analysed intersections of law and memory.

Importantly, the choice of case studies was not random. While in all instances of law and memory, intersections do not take place in a vacuum but rather are put into effect in particular social, legal, and political conditions in various countries around the world, only certain among them gain particular recognition – most often those implemented immediately following a transition. At the same time, other manifestations of the relationship between law and memory remain in the background, with Western and Eurocentric manifestations typically most visible in academic research.

DOI: 10.4324/9781003461548-11

As such, material reparations are most often analysed on the example of Germany in the aftermath of World War I,[1] with symbolic ones in the cases of Canada and Australia;[2] the effect of the ICTY's decisions on the matters of memory and truth is particularly investigated;[3] the question of lustration has been largely researched with regard to the whole region of Central Europe, and Czechia in particular;[4] truth (and reconciliation) commissions' research is centred around the case of South Africa;[5] Spanish amnesty post-Franco has come to epitomise all instances of legal amnesia;[6] and France came to be known as the land of memory laws, as remarked upon in the Prologue.

1 See, e.g., Kenneth K. Mwenda, "Legal Aspects of Payment of War Reparations" in Wolfgang Fischer (ed.), *German Hyperinflation 1922–23: A Law and Economics Approach* (Lohmer/Cologne: Eul Verlag, 2010) at 29; Albrecht Ritschl, "Reparations, Deficits, and Debt Default: The Great Depression in Germany" in Nicholas Crafts and Peter Fearon (eds), *The Great Depression of the 1930s: Lessons for Today* (Oxford: Oxford University Press, 2013) at 110; Paulina Matera, "The Question of War Debts and Reparations in French-American Relations After WWI" (2016) XXI:23 Humanities and Social Sciences 133.

2 See, e.g., Melissa Nobles, "Revisiting the 'Membership Theory of Apologies': Apology Politics in Australia and Canada" in Mihaela Mihai and Mathias Thaler (eds), *On the Uses and Abuses of Political Apologies* (Houndmills: Palgrave Macmillan, 2014) at 114; Jason A. Edwards, "Apologizing for the Past for a Better Future: Collective Apologies in the United States, Australia, and Canada" (2010) 75:1 Southern Communication Journal 57; Jeff Corntassel and Cindy Holder, "Who's Sorry Now? Government Apologies, Truth Commissions, and Indigenous Self-Determination in Australia, Canada, Guatemala, and Peru" (2008) 9 Human Rights Review 465.

3 See, e.g., Gorana Ognjenovic and Jasna Jozelic (eds), *Nationalism and the Politicization of History in the Former Yugoslavia* (Cham: Palgrave Macmillan, 2021); Orli Fridman, "'Too Young to Remember Determined Not to Forget': Memory Activists Engaging with Returning ICTY Convicts" (2018) 28:4 International Criminal Justice Review 423; Michel-André Horelt and Judith Renner, "Denting a Heroic Picture: A Narrative Analysis of Collective Memory in Post-War Croatia" (2008) 16:2 Perspectives 5 at 27.

4 See, e.g., Roman David, *Lustration and Transitional Justice Personnel Systems in the Czech Republic, Hungary, and Poland* (Philadelphia: University of Pennsylvania Press, 2011); Jiří Přibáň, "Oppressors and Their Victims: The Czech Lustration Law and the Rule of Law" in Alexander Mayer-Rieckh and Pablo de Greiff (eds), *Justice as Prevention: Vetting Public Employees in Transitional Societies* (New York, NY: Social Science Research Council, 2007) at 308; Kieran Williams, "Lustration as the Securitization of Democracy in Czechoslovakia and the Czech Republic" (2003) 19:4 Journal of Communist Studies and Transition Politics 1.

5 See, e.g., Mia Swart and Karin van Marle (eds), *The Limits of Transition: The South African Truth and Reconciliation Commission 20 Years on* (Leiden: Brill, 2017); Heidi Grunebaum, *Memorializing the Past: Everyday Life in South Africa After the Truth and Reconciliation Commission* (Oxon/New York, NY: Routledge, 2017); David Dyzenhaus, *Judging the Judges, Judging Ourselves: Truth, Reconciliation and the Apartheid Legal Order* (Oxford: Hart Publishing, 1998).

6 See, e.g., Michael Humphrey, "Law, Memory and Amnesty in Spain" (2014) 13 Macquarie Law Journal 25; Madeleine Davis, "Is Spain Recovering Its Memory? Breaking the *Pacto del Olvido*" (2005) 27:3 Human Rights Quarterly 858; Andrew Rigby, "Amnesty and Amnesia in Spain" (2000) 12:1 Peace Review 73.

In turn, I propose to apply the new law and memory framework in the chapters of this part to the less-often-studied but not less-worth-investigating cases of law and memory intersections from across the historical, geographical, and cultural global "board": Japan's material and symbolic reparations stretching over 70 years; ECtHR's jurisprudence regarding the questions of memory; Iraq's "lost" lustration; Brazil's truth commission convened over 20 years following the transition to democracy; Portugal's forgotten amnesia; and Rwanda's genocide denial memory legislation. As mentioned earlier, these analyses, taking legal institutions of memory from various continents, different cultural contexts, and divergent time frames, are simultaneously contrasted with those present only in one country, where four out of six legal institutions of memory may be distinguished.

Thus, to complement international studies, Poland is put in the spotlight here as a particularly interesting case from the perspective of collective memory due to its peculiar relationship with the past. As noted by Davis in the 1980s,

> Poles look to the past with special fondness. And the more distant past the better. Poland's rich history can provide them with both encouragement and consolation, with a storybook for escape from depressing reality, and with guidelines for action in their present predicament [the communist dictatorship]. Of course, everybody uses history in this way, for it is the storehouse of our collective memory and experience. But in Poland's case, the exercise is particularly intense, the sentiments are particularly strong. For Poles guard their national history with a fervour that to outsiders might look slightly ridiculous.[7]

However, "the more distant past the better" sentiment over the course of the years began overshadowing the more recent additions to Polish collective memory, with, for example, the 18th-century partition of the country – doubtless, an event of major importance – being used to explain the shape of various present-day social behaviours, the country's post-1989 transition, its voting patterns, etc.[8] While not necessarily ignoring contemporary memory influences on collective memory, the stress in Poland has clearly been on the collective memories at the top of the Bergsonian cone, rather than more recent ones, which, also of major importance, merit a closer investigation proposed in Chapter 8.

7 Norman Davis, "Poland's Dreams of Past Glory" (1982) 32:11 History Today 23 at 23.

8 Mirosław M. Sadowski, "Collective Memory and Historical Determinacy: The Shaping of the Polish Transition" in Balázs Fekete and Fruzsina Gárdos-Orosz (eds), *Central and Eastern European Socio-Political and Legal Transition Revisited: The CEE Yearbook*, vol. 7 (Frankfurt am Mein: Peter Lang, 2017) 175 at 178–179.

While this is by no means an attempt to provide an extensive study of Polish collective memory in general or a comprehensive analysis of the law and memory relationship in Poland in particular, I engage with four examples of legal institutions of memory in the country: the public apology in the form of the Letter of Polish to German Bishops; the case of the Katyń massacre heard by the ECtHR; the Polish take on lustration after 1989; and the country's most recent, 2018 memory legislation.

These case studies come with several absences and caveats. As Central and Eastern European countries, with, perhaps, the exception of Romania,[9] did not establish truth and reconciliation commissions, the absence of the second medium legal institution of memory in the case of Poland is not surprising. Poland also did not pay out material reparations (conversely, as of this writing, it is petitioning Germany for payment of post–World War II reparations),[10] and, as such, the focus here is only on the symbolic ones (compared to Japan, in the case of which both symbolic and material reparations are present). Additionally, while the country established a tribunal to judge Nazi war criminals after World War II, the Chief Commission for Investigation of German Crimes in Poland (which, following its various incarnations, ultimately became a part of the aforementioned Institute of National Memory, now tasked with investigating also the communist crimes),[11] it was by no means an international tribunal, and thus the effect of this legal institution of memory on the country's collective memory will be analysed with regard to a particularly impactful ECtHR decision.

Importantly, following the fall of communism, the country did not engage in legal amnesia on a major scale. The May 29, 1989, amnesty, which encompassed both the oppositions and those who broke the law on behalf of the communist regime in the process of disrupting strikes or demonstrations,[12] was of little consequence to the later processes of law and collective memory, as lustration became the main means of administering justice in the aftermath of the transition. In turn, the 2001 public apology of President Aleksander Kwaśniewski for the Jedwabne massacre and its aftermath[13] would require an analysis as an element of a larger debate on the Polish collective memories

9 Monica Ciobanu, "Criminalising the Past and Reconstructing Collective Memory: The Romanian Truth Commission" (2009) 61:2 Europe-Asia Studies 313.

10 Mieczysław Stolarczyk, "Reparacje wojenne dla Polski od Niemiec w latach 1945–2020" ["War Reparations for Poland from Germany in the Years 1945–2020"] (2020) 2 Krakowskie Studia Międzynarodowe – Krakow International Studies 171.

11 Nikolay Koposov, *Memory Laws, Memory Wars: The Politics of the Past in Europe and Russia* (Cambridge: Cambridge University Press, 2017) at 151.

12 Andrzej Municzewski, "Amnestie a legislacja" ["Amnesties and Legislation"] (1994) LVI:4 Ruch Prawniczy, Ekonomiczny i Socjologiczny 97 at 98–99.

13 Pierre-Frédéric Weber, "O przemianach pamięci oficjalnej w Europie po 1989 roku: Państwo a pamięć w Polsce i we Francji" ["On Changes of Official Memory in Europe After 1989: State and Memory in Poland and in France" (2014) 2 Przegląd Zachodni 59 at 66.

of World War II, and thus remains outside the scope of this book. Similarly, an in-depth investigation of the wide array of Polish memory laws,[14] many of which cannot be considered as memory laws proper, despite potential legal implications,[15] would take this study too far from its intended focus. As such, I propose to focus only on the most pertinent memory legislation, which established a particular system of legal protection of the Polish collective memory.

Together, through the application of the earlier proposed framework, the case studies analysed in ten sections will shed a particular light not only on the seven respective societies, but also on the intersections of law and memory in general.

14 Marcin Tomczak, "Memory Laws – definiowanie oraz współczesne występowanie praw pamięci" ["Defining and Describing the Contemporary Memory Laws"] (2019) XXXVI:3 Sensus Historiae 69 at 77–80.

15 See, e.g., Mirosław M. Sadowski, "City as a Locus of Collective Memory: Streets, Monuments and Human Rights" (2020) 40:1–2 Zeitschrift für Rechtssoziologie – The German Journal of Law and Society 209 at 223–225.

Chapter 6

Placing Soft Legal Institutions of Memory Within the New Framework

Introduction

This chapter brings into focus soft legal institutions of memory, putting the earlier proposed framework to work in the analysis of reparations and international tribunals. In regard to the first institution, I begin with the case of Japan, studying its material and symbolic reparations, keeping in mind the circumstances of their introduction, and being particularly interested in their social reception and changing attitudes over the years, both in and outside of Japan, showing the general perseverance of collective memories. This international case study is then contrasted with Polish symbolic reparations in the form of a 1965 Letter of Polish to German bishops, which, while today perceived as a cornerstone in the reconciliation between the two nations, was seen as an oddity, thus demonstrating the potential for an evolution of social perceptions of the past.

Moving on to the second soft legal institution of memory, both the study from an international and a national perspective focus on the European Court of Human Rights (ECtHR), looking at three different cases, all related to the question of genocide and the protection of its memory. In the international section, the *Perinçek* case is contrasted with the *Vasiliauskas* and *Drėlingas* cases, speaking to the limits of law in regard to cultivating the memory of the past. In turn, the *Katyń (Janowiec)* case in the Polish section relates to the larger issue of the recognition of communist crimes in European cultural contexts. Together, the different case studies shed an instructive light on soft legal institutions of memory.

Soft Institution I in Practice: Between Material and Symbolic Reparations in the Case of Japan

Following World War II, as noted earlier in the book, Japan became one of two countries – next to Germany – that saw an international tribunal convened to judge their crimes during the war, i.e., the International Military Tribunal for the Far East in Tokyo (IMTFE Tokyo). The Tokyo Tribunal,

DOI: 10.4324/9781003461548-12

however, was not the only legal institution of memory with which Japan engaged in the 20th century, the other being reparations, both material and symbolic.

Material Reparations in Japan

In regard to the issue of material reparations, their question was raised even before the end of the war: on the basis of the 1945 Potsdam Declaration, Japan was allowed to maintain at least such a level of industry which would allow the country to keep a stable economy and pay out "just reparations in kind."[1] One of the key goals of reparations was supposed to be the change of balance in the economic power of Japan with regard to the rest of Asia, as well as the removal of its war potential.[2] Later that year, the Far Eastern Commission (FEC) was established as a policy authority with regard to the American occupation of Japan, composed of the "Big Four" – the United States, the USSR, the United Kingdom, and China – as well as Australia, Canada, France, India, the Netherlands, New Zealand, and the Philippines, with Burma (present-day Myanmar) and Pakistan joining later.[3] In the following years, several American missions were sent to ascertain the number of reparations, but they came to different conclusions as to how to calculate it.[4]

While the exact matter of reparations was not resolved quickly, up to $3 billion (by the 1949 estimate) was acquired by the Allies on the basis of confiscated Japanese industrial and military property overseas, mainly in Korea, Formosa (present-day Taiwan), and Manchuria (present-day China and Russia).[5]

Additionally, in 1946, the FEC proposed an interim programme, known as the "obvious excess" programme, with different elements of Japanese industry (e.g., factories, machinery) chosen to be sent to various countries as reparations; however, failure to agree on allocation to specific countries considerably slowed the process of reaching a final decision. This has been used by the Japanese government and the country's industrialists, who, using the possibility to take active plants off the reparation list, attempted to put as many idle factories "into operation on some basis, even at a fraction of capacity" as possible.[6] At the same time, the Japanese government has also used the volatile economic situation, pursuing "a deliberate policy of low production and high inflation" to reduce the burden of reparations and

1 W. I. Petrie, "Reparations Since the Surrender: Changes in the Attitude Towards Japanese" (1950) 4:1 Australian Journal of International Affairs 51 at 51.
2 Joseph Z. Ready, "Reparations from Japan" (1949) 18:13 Far Eastern Survey 145 at 146.
3 J. L. Vellut, "Japanese Reparations to the Philippines" (1963) 3:10 Asian Survey 496 at 496.
4 Ready, *supra* note 2 at 148–149.
5 Ready, *supra* note 2 at 145.
6 Ready, *supra* note 2 at 147.

motivate the Allies to rebuild the country instead of focusing on compensation for the war, which coincided with and contributed to the changing view of the United States with regard to Japan, which I analyse here.[7]

Nevertheless, in 1947, the US government proposed an advance reparations programme directed to the most damaged countries during the war, later approved by the FEC, based on 30% of the objects available under the obvious excess programme, with half going to China and the rest "to be divided equally among the United Kingdom and Dutch Far Eastern territories [present-day Indonesia] and the Philippines." While also slowly advancing,[8] this programme allowed for $45 million worth of goods to be transferred by 1950.[9]

However, as soon as 1949, the American position on the issue of reparations began to change, with the country announcing a halt of reparation deliveries from Japan, as well as a vocal opposition to "any attempt on the part of the other Allies to impose a reparations programme on Japan" – despite upheaval among the other countries that were FEC members[10] – allowing for only 30% of reparations granted under the advance programme to be transferred.[11] This was due to several reasons, both local and geopolitical. As the American fear of the Soviet Union grew,[12] fuelled by mainland China's takeover by a communist regime,[13] the dire state of the Japanese economy was also increasingly becoming a costly burden for the United States.[14] As such, instead of reparations, "a policy of recovery and rehabilitation" was postulated,[15] with such a "reverse course" being a "part of a larger policy aimed at aligning Japan with the American-led camp in the Cold War confrontation in Asia."[16]

Ultimately, the matter of Japanese reparations was resolved in the 1951 San Francisco Peace Treaty, which stipulated in article 14 that the Allies, "except as otherwise provided in the present treaty, . . . waive all reparations claims," including those of "their nationals" affected by Japan, stressing that the country needs to "enter into negotiations with Allied Powers, so desiring, whose present territories were occupied by Japanese forces and damaged by Japan with a view to assisting to compensate those countries for the cost

7 Petrie, *supra* note 1 at 60.
8 Ready, *supra* note 2 at 147–148.
9 Tetsuo Ito, "Japan's Settlement of the Post-World War II Reparations and Claims" (1994) 37 Japanese Annual of International Law 38 at 49–50.
10 Petrie, *supra* note 1 at 55–56.
11 Ito, *supra* note 9 at 51.
12 Petrie, *supra* note 1 at 57.
13 Harry N. Scheiber, "Taking Responsibility: Moral and Historical Perspectives on the Japanese War-Reparations Issues" (2002) 20 Berkeley Journal of International Law 233 at 243.
14 Ito, *supra* note 9 at 41–42.
15 Benjamin J. Cohen, "Reparations in the Postwar Period: A Survey" (1967) 82 Banca Nazionale del Lavoro Quarterly Review 268 at 273.
16 Scheiber, *supra* note 13 at 243.

of repairing the damage done," however in a way "so as not to throw any foreign exchange burden upon Japan."[17] The treaty provisions clearly limit the scope of the Japanese reparations, restricting them to only "repairing the damage," and not harms inflicted on various peoples during the war,[18] failing to admit the responsibility of Japan for the war.[19]

Following the Peace Treaty, most countries decided to renounce their claims regarding reparations from Japan, notably Taiwan, the People's Republic of China (PRC),[20] India, and the Soviet Union,[21] with only several Asian countries arguing for them: Burma, Cambodia, Indonesia, Laos, the Philippines, South Korea, South Vietnam, and Thailand.[22] As such, Japan proceeded to sign two different types of agreements with these countries in the following years, considering either "direct reparations in the form of goods and services" or "economic aid with no compensation," including grants. Indonesia, the Philippines, and South Vietnam received reparations of the former kind,[23] and Burma was the only country to receive reparations of both kinds. In total, nine agreements were signed between 1955 (with Burma) and 1965 (with South Korea), amounting to $1.5 billion.[24] Later, Japan also provided reparations in the form of economic aid to Singapore, Malaysia, and Micronesia,[25] although in the case of the latter, aid was provided jointly by the United States and Japan and did not satisfy Micronesian demands.[26] The question of material reparations was to return once again in bilateral relations at the beginning of the 21st century, during Japanese talks with North Korea regarding the normalisation of mutual relations.[27]

17 Treaty of Peace with Japan, *Conference for the Conclusion and Signature of the Treaty of Peace with Japan, San Francisco, California, September 4–8, 1951: Record of Proceedings* (Washington, DC: Department of State, 1951).

18 Scheiber, *supra* note 13 at 236–238.

19 Ito, *supra* note 9 at 45.

20 Yolanda Alfaro Tsuda, "Notes of the 50th Year of the Normalization of Japan-Philippine Diplomatic Relations and the Postwar Reparations Agreement (1956–1986)" (2006) 53:2 Kobe College Studies 165 at 170.

21 Ito, *supra* note 9 at 55.

22 Cohen, *supra* note 15 at 273.

23 Ryo Fujikura and Mikiyasu Nakayama, "Origins of Japanese Aid Policy – Post-War Reconstruction, Reparations, and World Bank Projects" in Hiroshi Kato, John Page, and Yasutami Shimomura (eds), *Japan's Development Assistance Foreign Aid and the Post-2015 Agenda* (Houndmills: Palgrave Macmillan, 2016) 39 at 42.

24 Cohen, *supra* note 15 at 273–274.

25 Fujikura and Nakayama, *supra* note 23 at 43.

26 Wakako Higuchi, "Japan and War Reparations in Micronesia" (1995) 30:1 The Journal of Pacific History 87 at 88–90.

27 See Mark E. Manyin, "North Korea-Japan Relations: The Normalization Talks and the Compensation/Reparations Issue" (2002), online: CRS Report for Congress <globalsecurity.org/military/library/report/crs/RS20526.pdf>.

The reparation issue has also been raised a number of times by individuals from the so-called "detached territories," such as Korea, Taiwan,[28] and Micronesia, who were citizens of the Japanese empire before the war and who lost their status permanently following the 1951 Peace Treaty, with Japan, however, maintaining that only present-day Japanese citizens were eligible for any kind of such "internal" compensation[29] and that, in general, all claims had been realised either by the Treaty or the respective treaties with the countries in question.[30] As such, Japan has given "humanitarian considerations" to those peoples only on several occasions.[31]

Due to the negative experiences regarding cash reparations following World War I (in particular with regard to Germany),[32] Japan was allowed to fulfil its obligations "in kinds" or "in services" instead, through "mutual consultation and consent" between the interested parties.[33] This meant that reparations were merely "a very light burden" on the country's economy, with no "significant adverse effects on domestic costs or prices."[34] Rather paradoxically, the payment of reparations strengthened the Japanese economy, allowing the country access to foreign markets in Asia which otherwise, due to persistent collective-trauma memories of the war, would have been unavailable to them for decades, with the form of reparations (in kind) only accelerating trade relations, as the different Asian states came to be increasingly dependent on Japanese products,[35] and their elites forged close ties with Japan,[36] often profiting from the reparations at the expense of the larger population of their countries.[37]

In a way, the reparations programme allowed Japan to step into the role voided by the former colonial metropoles as a major provider of goods to the region, using geographical proximity to its advantage,[38] despite the post-colonial, anti-European collective memories often being considered less traumatic than the post-war anti-Japanese memories in formerly occupied countries.[39] Ultimately, the Japanese reparations programme came to be regarded "less as

28 Ito, *supra* note 16 at 59–62.
29 Higuchi, *supra* note 26 at 95.
30 Ito, *supra* note 9 at 38.
31 Ito, *supra* note 9 at 62–63.
32 Yoichi Itagaki, "Reparations and Southeast Asia" (1959) 6:4 Japan Quarterly 410 at 411–412.
33 Asia Kyokai Study Group, "Japan's War Reparations – Achievements and Problems" in Wolf Mendl (ed.), *Japan and South East Asia: Vol. II. The Cold War Era 1947–1989 and the Issues at the End of the Twentieth Century* (London/New York, NY: Routledge, 2001) 18 at 18.
34 Cohen, *supra* note 15 at 277.
35 Cohen, *supra* note 15 at 278–279.
36 Tsuda, *supra* note 21 at 173.
37 Vellut, *supra* note 3 at 503–504.
38 Tsuda, *supra* note 21 at 167–168.
39 Higuchi, *supra* note 26 at 87–88.

'punishment' or 'sanctions,' " and more as "cooperation for further economic development" of the respective countries.[40] The programme became the basis for Japan's aid operations in the following years, ones based on the principle of "non-intervention into domestic issues" of the recipient countries and a prioritisation of Asia, both stemming from the particular character of the initial reparations.[41]

Symbolic Reparations in Japan

While the matter of material reparations is closed according to the Japanese government, its stance leaves the door open to the possibility of symbolic reparations. Japan has engaged in various official and semi-official public acts of contrition since an expression of remorse in the 1972 Sino-Japanese declaration on the restoration of mutual relations, and these have continued throughout the 1980s to this day.[42] However, despite their significant number, Japan's symbolic reparations have left various Asian countries, most notably China and Korea, dissatisfied,[43] and as such merit closer investigation.

In the early 1990s, international pressure was mounting on Japan to openly confront its difficult past and remedy the victims of its atrocities.[44] Some of the main questions that invigorated the global debate on Japanese crimes were the Nanking Massacre, with up to 300,000 people killed by the invading forces in China during the winter of 1937–1938 (regarded by the Japanese as only an "Incident"),[45] and the issue of the so-called "military comfort women," i.e., between 50,000 and 200,000 women forced into prostitution and transported between various countries and battlefields through the "comfort system" "in order to maintain the soldiers' morale and, thus, make the process of occupying local areas smooth and efficient for the Imperial Japanese Military"[46] in the years 1931–1945.[47] The women in question

40 Itagaki, *supra* note 32 at 413.

41 Fujikura and Nakayama, *supra* note 23 at 43–44.

42 Ria Shibata, "Apology and Forgiveness in East Asia" in Kevin P. Clements (ed.), *Identity, Trust, and Reconciliation in East Asia: Dealing with Painful History to Create a Peaceful Present* (Cham: Palgrave Macmillan, 2018) 271 at 287–291.

43 Torsten Weber, "Apology Failures: Japan's Strategies Towards China and Korea in Dealing with Its Imperialist Past" in Berber Bevernage and Nico Wouters (eds), *The Palgrave Handbook of State-Sponsored History After 1945* (London: Palgrave Macmillan, 2018) 801 at 801–802.

44 Shibata, *supra* note 42 at 272.

45 Weber, *supra* note 43 at 802.

46 Mariko Izumi, "Asian-Japanese: State Apology, National Ethos, and the 'Comfort Women' Reparations Debate in Japan" (2011) 62:5 Communication Studies 473 at 473–474.

47 Joseph P. Nearey, "Seeking Reparations in the New Millennium: Will Japan Compensate the Comfort Women of World War II" (2001) 15:1 Temple International & Comparative Law Journal 121 at 121.

most notably included Koreans; however, they also came from China, Taiwan, the Philippines, the Netherlands, and Japan itself.[48]

The Japanese government has tried to ignore this issue, with extremely restricted access to the archives permitting only some documents to be revealed to the public by a historian in the early 1990s,[49] proving, however, direct involvement of the Japanese military in the operation of "comfort stations."[50] In addition to institutional obstruction, social processes of collective forgetting of this atrocity were only reinforced by the fact that most of its victims came from Confucian societies, ones that have not experienced democracy following the war, and as such, it took over 40 years for the question of "comfort women" to overcome local and national limitations and resurface in the public debate.[51] Proving once again the unique relationship between the trial and collective memory, this collective evoking process took place through the attempts at suing the Japanese authorities for reparations, including symbolic ones; these attempts were unsuccessful due to the aforementioned stance of the Japanese government that all material reparations claims were settled with the respective treaties.[52] Bowing to international pressure, the government established the Asian Women Fund for the victims;[53] however, it designated it as private, not public, thus stressing the lack of any legal responsibility on its part.[54]

In turn, the government offered a number of symbolic reparations. Beginning in the 1990s, consecutive Japanese politicians and officials have offered various acts of public contrition: "deep regret" with regard to the Japanese acts in Korea (Emperor Akihito);[55] "sincere remorse and apology for Japanese past actions" in Korea (Prime Minister Miyazawa);[56] an apology for Japan's "aggressive acts" and "colonial rule" which caused "intolerable pain and suffering" (Prime Minister Hosokawa);[57] "remorse" and "heartfelt apology" for Japan's "colonial rule and aggression" (Prime Minister Murayama, albeit in a private statement due to a lack of support for an official act in the

48 Tetsuro Kobayashi, Atsushi Tago, Kyu S. Hahn, and Yuki Asaba, "When Will Japan's Apology Lead to Reconciliation with South Korea?" in Tetsuro Kobayashi and Atsushi Tago (eds), *Japanese Public Sentiment on South Korea: Popular Opinion and International Relations* (Oxon/New York, NY: Routledge, 2022) 32 at 32.

49 Won Soon Park, "Japanese Reparations Policies and the 'Comfort Women' Question" (1997) 5:1 Positions 107 at 115.

50 Nearey, *supra* note 47 at 140.

51 Park, *supra* note 49 at 122–123.

52 Izumi, *supra* note 46 at 477–478, 481.

53 Kobayashi et al., *supra* note 48 at 32.

54 Nearey, *supra* note 47 at 140.

55 Weber, *supra* note 43 at 803.

56 Weber, *supra* note 43 at 805.

57 Shibata, *supra* note 42 at 278.

parliament);[58] "sincere apologies and remorse" towards the former "comfort women" (Chief Cabinet Secretary Yohei Kono);[59] "heartfelt apology" to the Chinese victims (Prime Minister Koizumi);[60] "deep remorse," "apology," and a promise never to "resort to any form of the threat of force" (Prime Minister Shinzo Abe).[61] Moreover, four prime ministers of Japan sent apology notes to the surviving victims of "comfort stations,"[62] and following the 2015 governmental meeting, the South Korean government was tasked with the establishment of the Reconciliation and Healing Foundation, with Japan pledging ¥1 billion as aid to the victims of forced prostitution and their families (which, however, was dissolved by Korea three years later due to political tensions between the two countries).[63]

Nevertheless, as noted earlier, there are countries that "argue that Japan 'has never apologized'," focusing "on the lack of a parliamentary resolution of apology,"[64] as well as the varying wording (apology, remorse, regret) and status (official, private) of the different acts of contrition.[65] Additionally, a certain "nullification" effect has been remarked upon with regard to the Japanese apologies, with the continuing visits of various prominent politicians to the Yasukuni Shrine, a place of rest for the souls of 2.5 million Japanese soldiers, as well as the wartime Prime Minister Hideki Tojo and other politicians sentenced by the Tokyo Tribunal.[66] Furthermore, parts of the media and academia, as well as different politicians, most notably former Prime Minister Shinzo Abe, have encouraged revisionist narratives, for example, arguing that while ultimately Japan "took the wrong course," the country's imperialism was "an act of self-defence against Western imperialism," having "a positive contribution to the liberation of Asia from this Western imperialist oppression," to quote the latter.[67]

Japanese Reparations at the Intersections of Law and Memory

Behind the legal language of the different treaties regarding material reparations and the administrative aspects of the various public apologies, the collective memory of both Japan and its respective neighbours becomes plainly

58 Shibata, *supra* note 42 at 281.
59 Shibata, *supra* note 42 at 283.
60 Weber, *supra* note 43 at 808.
61 Shibata, *supra* note 42 at 293.
62 Kobayashi et al., *supra* note 48 at 32.
63 Kobayashi et al., *supra* note 48 at 33.
64 Shibata, *supra* note 42 at 282.
65 Weber, *supra* note 43 at 804.
66 Shibata, *supra* note 42 at 285.
67 Weber, *supra* note 43 at 802–803.

visible and almost palpable. The question of reparation shows how Japan established its post-war identity and put it into practice, using various official narratives and collective memories. As mentioned earlier, the Tokyo Tribunal's judgement (towards which the Japanese hold ambiguous views) was employed to promote a particular, peaceful image of the country on the global stage. This viewpoint was only fuelled by the 1951 Peace Treaty, considered to be, rather than a symbol of defeat, an "instrument of reconciliation and trust,"[68] together with the bombings of Hiroshima and Nagasaki[69] fostering the *mokusatsu* ("to kill with silence") spirit among the Japanese after the war with regard to their difficult past.[70]

This approach is particularly noticeable in regard to material reparations, treated by the Japanese as if they could equate "moral responsibility with legal responsibility."[71] This stance clearly advances collective forgetting, ignoring the fact that different countries affected by their aggression may have divergent needs and expectations: while "the amount of reparation payments may be the same, the . . . feeling of satisfaction on the part of the recipient countries is not necessarily the same."[72]

Importantly, the case of Japanese reparations shows the increasing effect of outside factors on a country's official narrative in modern times: it was the shift in the American approach towards Japan at the end of the 1940s, cleverly exploited by the Japanese government, that contributed to the fostering of "a deliberate forgetfulness"[73] in the country. Ultimately, the American policies during the occupation failed to help the Japanese understand their role in the war, also creating a sense of "bitterness and anger with regard to how Japan had been treated so favourably" compared to other countries that were part of the Allies during the war.[74] The role played by the United States also impacted the Japanese post-war global hierarchy – "West (U.S.), Japan, and Asia, ordered from top to bottom," with a certain distancing itself from their own region, which may also be noted with regard to Japanese symbolic reparations, sometimes perceived as a means of "apology diplomacy," i.e., an instrumental use of public acts of contrition for immediate political goals.[75]

68 Kisaburo Yokota cited in Ito, *supra* note 9 at 43.
69 Izumi, *supra* note 46 at 483–484.
70 Scheiber, *supra* note 13 at 241, 247.
71 Kunihiko Yoshida, "Reparations and Reconciliation in East Asia as a Hot Issue of Tort Law in the 21st Century: Case Studies, Legal Issues, and Theoretical Framework" (2011) 11 Journal of Korean Law 101 at 116.
72 Itagaki, *supra* note 32 at 419.
73 Steven C. Clemons, "Recovering Japan's Wartime Past and Ours" (2001), online: New York Times <nytimes.com/2001/09/04/opinion/recovering-japan-s-wartime-past-and-ours.html>.
74 Scheiber, *supra* note 13 at 247.
75 Izumi, *supra* note 46 at 479–480.

While all countries of the region instrumentalise collective memories of the war,[76] the Japanese government in particular has been noted to apologise "as if the apology pays off its historical debts."[77] Such acts as the officials' visits to the Yasukuni Shrine dilute the effect of symbolic reparations and have been compared to a Dr Jekyll and Mr Hyde behaviour,[78] or a *hansei-zaru*, i.e., "a trained monkey that repeatedly performs a posture of self-reflection and regret at another's demand without knowing the actual meaning of this performance."[79]

Importantly, while the different acts of public contrition – to a certain degree, understandingly – fail to achieve the desired effect in the neighbouring countries,[80] in Japan itself, a veritable "apology fatigue" may be observed, a "growing sense of frustration that Asian neighbours fail to see Japan's nuanced memory context."[81] As such, in a 1990s survey, 50% of the respondents favoured a governmental response towards new reparations claims and 37% opposed it,[82] and similarly, in 2000, 50% of those surveyed noted that the Japanese "must, personally, bear responsibility for historical offenses," with 27% disagreeing.[83] Fifteen years later, 81% of respondents concurred that the "Japanese prime ministers have apologised enough to China and South Korea,"[84] a sentiment confirmed by a 2019 survey, in which 80% of the respondents agreed "that Japan did not need to apologise further regarding the issue of comfort women," with only 11% disagreeing.[85]

Looking into Japanese reparations, both material and symbolic, from the perspective of a legal institution of memory, one may ask whether they have fulfilled their intended role. While the introduction of reparations clearly determined Japan's responsibility, it is difficult to say if they managed to vindicate the victims and repair psychological abuse – given continued calls for increased material and symbolic acts of contrition on their part, it becomes clear that not all of the intended functions of reparations were realised. Likewise, when analysing reparation goals, while the victims were re-recognised as human beings by the Japanese, civic trust and solidarity were not rebuilt due to the transactional and instrumental approach of Japan to reparations. Even if the victims' counter-memories were ultimately taken to the forefront

76 Weber, *supra* note 43 at 811.
77 Izumi, *supra* note 46 at 479.
78 Kazuya Fukuoka, "Japanese History Textbook Controversy at a Crossroads? Joint History Research, Politicization of Textbook Adoption Process, and Apology Fatigue in Japan" (2018) 30:3 Global Change, Peace & Security 313 at 328.
79 Izumi, *supra* note 46 at 479.
80 Kobayashi et al., *supra* note 48 at 49.
81 Fukuoka, *supra* note 78 at 329.
82 Higuchi, *supra* note 26 at 97.
83 Fukuoka, *supra* note 78 at 329.
84 Fukuoka, *supra* note 78 at 330.
85 Kobayashi et al., *supra* note 48 at 33.

of the debate, it seems that the only major collective memory shift that took place was that amongst the Japanese themselves. It may now be postulated that they established a new official narrative in which they have already atoned enough for their wartime sins – many of which have been recast as a fight against imperialism on behalf of the colonised peoples. For them, their neighbours' collective memories should follow.

Nevertheless, while Japanese reparations encountered the various issues that I remarked upon when providing the model of this institution – the impossibility of achieving complete satisfaction of claims, the reinforcement of selective narratives, lack of implementation along other, more impactful institutions (as noted earlier, the Tokyo Tribunal only contributed to the failure of Japanese reparations to affect reconciliation) – their analysis proved the "soft" character of reparations as a legal institution of memory but nonetheless a legal institution of memory.

Their contrite aspect establishes reparations as a Durkheimian ritual, a top-to-bottom mechanism (lawsuits against the Japanese government for reparations have all failed), one creating a new narrative and influencing collective memory (although in ways not necessarily bringing it closer to historical accuracy) and involving a certain degree of collective forgetting. They also have a direct relationship with international law (in the case of material reparations) and may take place both in transitional (Japanese material reparations in the years following the war) and non-transitional (symbolic reparations employed many years after the war) circumstances. Furthermore, reparations are clearly an instrument of memory politics, one which, having the potential to realise the right to remember, inadvertently grants the reformed narrative a certain degree of legitimacy and objectivity – after all, despite apology fatigue and narrative distortion, also in the case of Japan, the society needed to integrate certain counter-memories into its collective memory. As such, it is particularly interesting to see how the Japanese experiences with symbolic reparations compare with the Polish ones, adopted in a very different historical and political context.

Soft Institution I in Practice Again: A Very Particular Public Apology, or the Letter of Polish to German Bishops

The 1965 Letter or Missive which the Polish bishops sent to their German counterparts at the end of the Second Vatican Council, taking the form of a public apology, is considered the first crucial element of the Polish-German reconciliation. It needs to be stressed that the letter came at a particularly difficult time in the relations between the two peoples (and three countries, as Germany was then divided into the Western Federal Republic of Germany [FRG] and the Eastern German Democratic Republic [GDR]).

On the one hand, in Poland, the collective trauma-memories of the German aggression of World War II were still omnipresent: during the war, due to both German and Russian actions, the country lost 5.2 million to 5.3 million people (15% of the whole population, the highest percentage of all countries affected by the war),[86] with a deliberate plan by both occupiers to destroy the Polish intelligentsia, with deaths of "39% of doctors, 33% of teachers, 30% of scientists and university scholars (approximately 700 university professors were killed), 28% of priests, and 26% of lawyers".[87] The material destruction of Warsaw alone amounted to 54.6 billion US dollars by a 2005 count.[88]

On the other hand, a number of Germans had grievances against Poland, as during the 1945 Potsdam Conference, the Allied powers agreed on granting the Eastern parts of pre-war Germany (which came to be known as the Recovered Lands) as compensation for Polish areas annexed by the USSR, conceiving a plan to deport 3.5 million Germans living there, with the resettlement carried out by the army and encouraged by propaganda.

The mutual relations were further complicated by the anti-German propaganda of the Polish post-war communist authorities, as well as their different attitudes towards the two German states: while the GDR was considered to be a brotherly communist nation, one free of war baggage, and signed a 1950 treaty acknowledging the post-1945 borders, Poland had only trade and economic relations with FRG, and no diplomatic relations, until 1972.[89] As such, in 1965, any rapprochement between the two nations seemed possible only in the distant future.

The Adoption and Contents of the 1965 Letter

It was in such a state of relations with Germany that the delegation of Polish bishops, headed by prelate cardinal Stefan Wyszyński, took part in the Second Vatican Council (1962–1965), convened under the concept of *aggiornamento*, or the renewal of the Catholic Church. As the end of the Council coincided with the preparations for Polish celebrations of the 1,000-year anniversary of statehood – dated to 966, the year Poland was officially baptised – the Polish Episcopate decided to send 56 letters to various religious officials from around the world, inviting them for the 1966 celebrations

86 Mateusz Gniazdowski, "Szkody wyrządzone Polsce przez Niemcy podczas II wojny światowej" ["Damages Inflicted on Poland by the Germans During the Second World War"] (2006) 6:34 Polski Przegląd Dyplomatyczny 13 at 39.

87 Mirosław M. Sadowski, "Collective Memory and Historical Determinacy: The Shaping of the Polish Transition" in Balázs Fekete and Fruzsina Gárdos-Orosz (eds), *Central and Eastern European Socio-Political and Legal Transition Revisited: The CEE Yearbook*, vol. 7 (Frankfurt am Mein: Peter Lang, 2017) 175 at 185–186.

88 Gniazdowski, *supra* note 86 at 41.

89 Adam Wójcik, "Orędzie biskupów polskich do biskupów niemieckich jako krok do unormowania stosunków polsko-niemieckich" ["The Missal of Polish Bishops to the German Bishops as a Step to the Normalisation of Polish-German Relations"] (2021) XX:1 Miscellanea Historico-Iuridica 121 at 122–128.

in Poland. This presented an opportunity "for the Church to attempt to do what the State would not" – a reconciliation with Germany.[90]

As such, on request by cardinal Wyszyński, the letter to the German Episcopate was drafted by (later cardinal) Bolesław Kominek, then archbishop of Wrocław, one of the major cities in the Recovered Lands. He was chosen for the task due to his family's background in Germany, his knowledge of the language, history, and customs of the country, and his long-term engagement in matters of possible reconciliation between Poland and Germany.[91] The letter was originally written in German,[92] with 83% of its ultimate version authored by abp. Kominek,[93] and its most notable part, "we forgive and ask for forgiveness," already present in the initial version.[94] While not all the bishops were sympathetic to the idea of the letter, cardinal Wyszyński's authority prevailed,[95] and it was ultimately signed by him, two archbishops and 36 bishops, i.e., all Polish representatives at the Council.[96]

Entitled *The Missal of Polish Bishops to Their German Brothers in Christ's Pastoral Service*, the letter was sent (or rather submitted) to the German side on November 18, 1965. It was not only of religious importance (despite later assertions remarked upon further in this section) but also of political importance, with apb. Kominek noting in the following years that the letter "was supposed to break open the doors to Europe"[97] for Poland, as it was written "not only to the German nation but also to ours [Polish]."[98] It should be

90 Piotr H. Kosicki, "*Caritas* Across the Iron Curtain? Polish-German Reconciliation and the Bishops' Letter of 1965" (2009) 23:2 East European Politics and Societies 213 at 215.

91 Józef Pater, "Rola kardynała Bolesława Kominka w przygotowaniu orędzia biskupów polskich do biskupów niemieckich" ["The Role of Cardinal Bolesław Kominek in the Preparation of the Missal of Polish Bishops to German Bishops"] (2007) 15:1 Wrocławski Przegląd Teologiczny 65 at 70–77.

92 Jan Rydel, "Nowe elementy mozaiki Nieznane niemieckie dokumenty dyplomatyczne o Liście Biskupów z 1965 roku" ["New Elements of the Mosaic: Unknown German Diplomatic Documents About the Letter of Bishops from 1965"] (2011) 627 Więź 101 at 103.

93 Wojciech Kucharski, "Rękopis orędzia biskupów polskich do biskupów niemieckich autorstwa ABPA Bolesława Kominka" ["The Manuscript of the Missal of Polish Bishops to German Bishops by ABPA Bolesław Komnek"] (2019) 3 Przegląd Zachodni 129 at 132.

94 Wojciech Kucharski, "Jak powstało orędzie biskupów polskich do biskupów niemieckich z 18 listopada 1965 roku" ["How the Missal of Polish to German Bishops from November 18, 1965 Was Created"] (2019) 2 Pamięć i Sprawiedliwość 502 at 517.

95 Wójcik, *supra* note 89 at 129.

96 Pater, *supra* note 91 at 65.

97 Bartłomiej Noszczak, "Nobel za Orędzie? List o. Stanisława Wawryna SJ do prymasa Stefana Wyszyńskiego w sprawie możliwości przyznania Episkopatowi Polski Pokojowej Nagrody Nobla za wystosowanie Orędzia do biskupów niemieckich" ["Nobel for a Missal? The Letter of Father Stanisław Wawryn SJ Do Primate Stanisław Wyszyński Regarding the Possibility of Granting the Polish Episcopate the Nobel Peace Prize for Sending the Missal to German Bishops"] (2017) 2 Pamięć i Sprawiedliwość 482 at 482–483.

98 Jerzy Myszor, "Orędzie biskupów polskich do niemieckich z 18 XI 1965 r.: Z perspektywy czasu" ["The Missal of Polish Bishops to the German Ones from 18 November 1965 from the Perspective of Passing Time"] (2006) 39:1 Śląskie Studia Historyczno-Teologiczne 172 at 174.

noted that in spite of the existence of two German states, there was only one German Episcopate, to which the letter was addressed.[99]

In addition to its religious arguments, the letter proposed a different understanding of Polish history and collective memory from the one presented by communist authorities, stressing close ties with the West in general and the different German states in particular, acknowledging the various legal, political, artistic, and religious involvement of Germans in Poland over the years and seeing it as an integral element of Polish culture. These positive bilateral experiences were contrasted with negative ones, drawing a direct line from the Teutonic Knights to Frederick the Great to Hitler as the main sources of neighbourly discord. The letter, however, once again balanced the negative with the positive – the acknowledgement of the suffering of those Germans opposed to the regime during World War II on the one side, and of those who were resettled from the Recovered Lands after the war on the other – while firmly stating that the decisions on the border changes were made without Polish representatives and may not be reversed, as the new territories, which have had a long history of often direct ties with Poland, became a vital part of the country after the war following the loss of its Eastern territories.[100]

Most importantly, however, the letter brought up the issues of collective forgetting and reconciliation, as the Polish bishops were "reaching out their hands" to the German Episcopate, both "granting forgiveness and asking for it," which soon became the most notable element of the missal, best known under the paraphrase "we forgive and ask for forgiveness,"[101] meaning that the letter was also a public apology. As such, while being "an ecclesiastical and religious document, it simultaneously became a text with a political dimension and played a special – dual – role."[102]

The Letter's Immediate Aftermath

The letter was not sent in a vacuum. It was part of a longer process that was initiated in the 1950s and then continued in the early 1960s involving close

99 Winfred Lipscher, "Ewangelia czy polityka? Wymiana listów pojednania biskupów polskich i niemieckich w roku 1965 oraz jej następstwa" ["The Gospel or Politics? An Exchange of Letters of Reconciliation Between Polish and German Bishops in 1965 and Its Consequences"] (2006) 1 Przegląd Zachodni 133 at 134.

100 Zbigniew Mazur, "Kampania propagandowa PZPR po orędziu biskupów polskich do biskupów niemieckich (województwo wrocławskie)" ["Propaganda Campaign of the Polish United Workers' Party (PZPR) Following the Address of the Polish Bishops to the German Bishops (Wrocław Region)" (2007) 1 Przegląd Zachodni 135 at 136–139.

101 Rydel, *supra* note 92 at 102.

102 Karolina Wigura, "Alternative Historical Narrative: 'Polish Bishops' Appeal to Their German Colleagues' of 18 November 1965" (2013) 27:3 East European Politics and Societies and Cultures 400 at 401.

contacts between German and Polish bishops,[103] including, as mentioned earlier, the work of abp. Kominek. However, the reaction of the German Episcopate to the Polish letter, sent on December 5, 1965, was rather cautious[104] and focused only on uncontroversial issues, ignoring the question of the border, and while acknowledging the importance of the Recovered Lands for Poland, it stressed their prominence for the exiled Germans. Most importantly, the German letter did not offer forgiveness towards the Poles.[105]

The FRG's government was informed about the existence of the letter only on November 30, 1965,[106] and ultimately did not take a public stance on the letter, most likely due to the border issue. The German Evangelical Church, despite an earlier positive attitude towards reconciliation, also did not react to the letter publicly, perceiving it as not a real chance at a change in bilateral relations between Poland and FRG. From the German side, ultimately, only the FRG press responded in a somewhat positive way.[107] All in all, as Rydel argues, both the German Episcopate and the country's authorities underestimated the vital role of the Church in Poland and the political clout of cardinal Wyszyński, failing to recognise the importance of the will for reconciliation expressed in the letter for future bilateral (the letter did not mention the existence of GDR) relations between Poland and Germany, only realising the missal's potential following the Polish authorities' and the USSR's[108] and GDR's nervous responses following its publication, with the latter perceiving it as undermining its sovereignty, considering the act an attempt at normalisation of the Polish relations with the FRG.[109]

In turn, the Polish communist authorities were aware of the letter some time in advance of its publication, thanks to a close-knit network of secret service collaborators, including some priests from Wyszyński's circle; however, they remained in the dark in regard to its more minute details.[110] As

103 Theo Mechtenberg, "Porozumienie i pojednanie z Polską w NRD" ["Agreement and Reconciliation with Poland in the GDR"] (2006) 1 Przegląd Zachodni 141 at 142–146.

104 Dariusz Wojtaszyn, "Wschodnioniemiecka recepcja wymiany listów między polskimi i niemieckimi biskupami w 1965 roku" ["East German Reception of the Exchange of Letters Between Polish and German Bishops in 1965"] (2017) 16:1 Pamięć i Sprawiedliwość 94 at 94.

105 Sylwia Dec-Pustelnik, "List biskupów" ["Bishops' Letter"] (2014), online: Interakcje. Leksykon komunikowania polsko-niemieckiego <polska-niemcy-interakcje.pl/articles/show/2>.

106 Rydel, *supra* note 92 at 104.

107 Dec-Pustelnik, *supra* note 105.

108 Rydel, *supra* note 92 at 107–108.

109 Piotr Łysakowski, "Glosa do listu biskupów polskich do biskupów niemieckich z 18 listopada 1965 roku w dokumentach Instytutu Pamięci Narodowej" ["A Gloss to the Echo, in the Documents of the Institute of National Remembrance, of the Polish Bishops' Letter of 18 November 1965 to the German Bishops"] (2009) 17 Rocznik Polsko-Niemiecki 114 at 119.

110 Wojciech Kucharski, "Prawdziwa bomba: Jak powstawało Orędzie biskupów polskich do biskupów niemieckich" ["A Real Bomb: Arose as the Message of the Polish Bishops to the German Bishops"] (2010) 615 Więź 123 at 123–126.

such, the public opinion in Poland was informed about the letter only on December 10, possibly due to previously ongoing consultations with the USSR on how to respond following the missal's publication.[111] The regime then engaged in a major propaganda campaign against the Church under the slogan "we cannot forget and we will not forgive,"[112] using all means available, in particular the media, also disrupting Catholic celebrations[113] and organising provocations.[114] The regime accused the Episcopate of involvement in politics and revisionism with regard to the post-war shape of the Polish-German border, taking advantage of the fact that Polish society did not know the whole text of the letter, only decontextualised parts published in the state media.[115] In the later declassified documents, it became clear, however, that in 1966, the Polish regime realised the magnitude of the letter, acknowledging its impact on the Polish-German dialogue and motivating not only Catholics.[116] *Nota bene*, it needs to be noted that the communist authorities' reaction was seen as beneficial for the FRG, with its government perceiving the Polish authorities' attack on the letter as showing the country negatively on the international scene, as an enemy of peace.[117]

Given the still-widespread collective trauma-memories of World War II at that time, it does not come as a surprise that the state propaganda was initially well received by the majority of Polish society.[118] According to the (clearly biased and unrepresentative) results of research conducted by the communist authorities, the majority of the Polish population did not approve of the latter, with the least amount of support among factory workers, more moderate attitudes among farmers, and lukewarm attitudes among teachers, bureaucrats, and teenagers.[119] Nevertheless, there were some public acts of defiance, such as by Zofia Kossak-Szczucka, a notable author and organiser of clandestine help for the Jews during World War II, who rebuffed a state award granted to her at that time, citing the authorities' behaviour towards the Church as the reason.[120]

111 Pater, *supra* note 91 at 66.
112 Kosicki, *supra* note 90 at 213–214.
113 Adam Lepa, "Sygnatariusz orędzia biskupów polskich do biskupów niemieckich" ["The Signatory of the Missals of the Polish to German Bishops"] (1993) 2 Łódzkie Studia Teologiczne 47 at 50–51.
114 Kosicki, *supra* note 90 at 227.
115 Lipscher, *supra* note 99 at 134–135.
116 Łysakowski, *supra* note 109 at 120.
117 Piotr Madajczyk, "Orędzie biskupów polskich w ocenie niemieckiego MSZ" ["The Polish Bishops' Letter of Reconciliation to the German Bishops, as Assessed by the German Foreign Office"] (2011) 19 Rocznik Polsko-Niemiecki 73 at 84.
118 Pater, *supra* note 91 at 67.
119 Mazur, *supra* note 100 at 152.
120 Lepa, *supra* note 113 at 52.

As such, within the atmosphere of growing animosity, the planned celebrations of the 1,000 years of Polish statehood – which, as mentioned earlier, were the inspiration for sending the letter in the first place – changed into a competition between the Church and the communist authorities. Whereas the Episcopate sacralised Polish history, putting the religious upfront, hoping to strengthen not only the people's faith but also national identity, the regime focused on the state aspects of the past, hoping to increase its support and stress its power over all domains of the public life apart from the religious. As such, due to the 1965 letter, the central point of the celebrations was not the anniversary itself, but rather the question of the relations between the Church and the state, between the Poles and the Germans, and the broader issue of the shape of the Polish identity.[121] Ultimately, however, the communist authorities refrained from escalating the conflict with the Church, perceiving the conducted actions as sufficient.[122]

In regard to the reaction of the Polish Episcopate to the aftermath of their letter, the bishops were clearly disappointed with the German response and did not hesitate to state that publicly in the German media.[123] As cardinal Wyszyński later remarked, "we received from Germans everything we wanted to, but not from those we wanted. The borders were recognised by an SPD [German socialist party] government and the Evangelical Church, and we wanted it to have been the Christian-democratic party CDU and the Catholic Church."[124]

Internally, the Church attempted to counteract communist propaganda, with cardinal Wyszyński stressing already on December 12, 1965, that the regime clearly distorted the sense of the letter. Also that month, the Episcopate issued a statement stressing the non-political character of the missal[125] (in that it was not completely true with regard to its intentions), while the then abp. Karol Wojtyła (later cardinal and Pope John Paul II) explained the deeper idea behind the attempt at reconciliation, stressing that the apology on the part of the Polish Episcopate – the asking for forgiveness – was thought to be an overture for their German counterparts so that they could

121 Mazur, *supra* note 100 at 135.

122 Tomasz Gajowniczek, "Urząd do spraw Wyznań wobec kościelnych prób pojednania polsko-niemieckiego w latach 1965–1966" ["The Office for the Faith Affairs on the Church Attempts at Polish-German Reconciliation in the Years 1965–1966"] in Karolina Tybuchowska-Hartlińska (ed.), *Oblicze olsztyńskiej politologii. Tom IV: Studia i szkice politologiczne: W kręgu problemów polskiej polityki* [*The Faces of Pathology in Olsztyn. Vol. IV: Political Science Studies and Sketches. Amongst the Questions of Polish Politics*] (Olsztyn: Wyd. INP UWM, 2011) 39 at 49.

123 Dec-Pustelnik, *supra* note 105.

124 Myszor, *supra* note 98 at 175.

125 Pater, *supra* note 91 at 67.

do the same.[126] In turn, in an enthusiastically received sermon in January 1966, abp. Kominek called state propaganda surrounding the missal "a slap in the face of the real Polish *raison d'état*"[127] (in so doing, perhaps inadvertently, acknowledging the letter's political aspects). The Episcopate also sent an open letter to all Polish Catholics in March 1966, further explaining its intentions behind the missal.[128]

It was only after the celebrations of the 1,000 years of statehood, however, that the social sentiments began to calm down, as symbolically, during the anniversary mass in Częstochowa (a place of pilgrimage in Poland of major importance), Wyszyński explained the ideas behind reconciliation, and, asking thrice "do you forgive?," he each time received an answer from the crowds "we forgive!"[129] While this did not mean that the social attitude towards the letter in particular or the Germans and Germany in general immediately changed, it shows that the explanation of the real motives behind the letter was sufficient for the social situation to de-escalate.[130]

Polish Symbolic Reparations at the Intersections of Law and Memory

While the magnitude of the letter was immediately noted internationally, with the possibility of granting the Nobel Peace Prize to the Polish Episcopate discussed in 1966 (ultimately, the prize was not awarded at all that year),[131] and a German Catholic think tank, Bensberger Kreis, in 1968 preparing a memorandum on Polish-German reconciliation published two years later, signed by then Professor Joseph Ratzinger (later Pope Benedict XVI),[132] it was only in the following years that the letter became of major importance for Polish collective memory, turning into a symbol for Polish-German reconciliation. As remarked by Lipski already in the 1980s, "the reaching out by

126 Henryk J. Muszyński, "Przebaczenie i pojednanie pomiędzy Polakami i Niemcami jako dar i zadanie. W 50 lat po wymianie listów biskupów polskich i niemieckich" ["Forgiveness and Reconciliation Between the Poles and the Germans as a Gift and a Task: 50 Years After the Exchange of Letters Between Polish and German Bishops"] (2016) 1 Paedagogia Christiana 139 at 144.

127 Pater, *supra* note 91 at 68–69.

128 Radosław Ptaszyński, "Przebaczenie pod lupą Służba Bezpieczeństwa wobec listu Episkopatu Polski z 10 lutego 1966 r" ["Forgiveness Under the Surveillance of the Ministry of Public Security"] (2018) 6 Polish Biographical Studies 209 at 210.

129 Henryk J. Muszyński, "Wkład biskupów Polski i Niemiec w proces pojednania naszych narodów i budowania jedności Europy" ["The Contribution of Polish and German Bishops in the Process of Reconciliation of Our Nations and Building the European Unity"] (2017) 19 Acta Cassubiana 399 at 401.

130 Muszyński, *supra* note 126 at 147.

131 Noszczak, *supra* note 97at 485–486.

132 Rydel, *supra* note 92 at 109–110.

the Polish Episcopate to the German Episcopate was the boldest and the most farsighted action undertaken in the post-war history of Poland."[133]

Soon, the letter's long-term effects became increasingly visible, as it is thought to have been a "major impulse" behind the FRG's ultimate recognition of the Polish border in 1970.[134] It was followed by other gestures, both symbolic – the kneeling of Willy Brandt before the Warsaw Ghetto Monument in 1970, the 1989 sign of peace made between FRG Chancellor Helmut Kohl and Tadeusz Mazowiecki (the first non-communist Polish prime minister after World War II) during the mass in Krzyżowa (Kreisau), the 1996 meeting of John Paul II with Kohl under the Brandenburg Gate – and legal – the 1972 full recognition of Polish Church administration on the Recovered Lands by Pope Paul VI, the 1990 Polish-German treaty confirming the post-1945 border, and the 1991 treaty on good neighbourly relations between the two countries.[135]

Over the years, the letter retained its value as the fundament of the Polish-German reconciliation, with an increasingly future-focused understanding of the document on the 20th anniversary of its signing,[136] followed by joint statements of the Polish and German bishops on its 30th[137] and 40th anniversaries,[138] and major celebrations of the 50th anniversary. In addition to the traditional joint statement of the two countries' Episcopates, public exhibitions took place in Poland and in Germany, as well as lectures, concerts and conferences, a commemorative resolution of the Polish Senate,[139] and a joint statement of Polish and German presidents.[140] However, in this process of acknowledgement of the importance of the letter, a certain amount of collective forgetting regarding its initial reception took place[141] – as remarked upon by Kosicki, back in the day, "the letter may indeed have been [considered] un-Polish, if to be 'Polish' is to give priority to the past."[142] As its

133 Jan J. Lipski, *Dwie ojczyzny, dwa patriotyzmy* [*Two Motherlands, Two Patriotisms*] (Warsaw: Otwarta Rzeczpospolita, 2008) at 18–19.
134 Wójcik, *supra* note 89 at 133.
135 Muszyński, *supra* note 126 at 151.
136 Sylwia Dec-Pustelnik, "Kilka słów o mediatyzacji pamięci, czyli jak 'Polityka' oraz 'Tygodnik Powszechny' budowały narrację o pojednaniu polsko-niemieckim w latach 1965–1989/90" ["A Few Words on the Mediatisation of Memory, or How 'Polityka' and 'Tygodnik Powszechny' Were Building a Narrative on the Polish-German Reconciliation in the Years 1965–1989/90"] (2017) 16 Political Preferences 153 at 161.
137 Muszyński, *supra* note 129 at 403–404.
138 Lipscher, *supra* note 99 at 138–139.
139 Sylwia Dec-Pustelnik, "List biskupów polskich do biskupów niemieckich z perspektywy 50 lat" ["The Letter of Polish to the German Bishops from the Perspective of 50 Years"] 185 24 Niemcoznawstwo at 185–191.
140 Muszyński, *supra* note 129 at 408.
141 Dec-Pustelnik, *supra* note 136 at 162.
142 Kosicki, *supra* note 90 at 226.

future understanding took hold of the Polish official narrative, a certain phenomenon of secularisation of the collective memory of the letter over the years may also be observed, as rather than an initiative of religious representatives, it came to be considered an initiative of representatives of Polish society.

While in 1965 the Episcopate was, naturally, not a political representative of the country, the letter clearly broke the Polish communist authorities' monopoly in the field of international relations.[143] Given its stature and authority among Polish society, with the Church considered to be "closer to the nation than to the state," and the perceived lack of legitimacy of the communist authorities,[144] the Episcopate may most surely be regarded as able to have delivered a public apology on behalf of the Poles. As noted by Jackowska, with the 1965 letter, the Church took upon itself the role of a "non-political authority showing a possible exit out of the labyrinth,"[145] one possibly leading to reconciliation. As a soft legal institution of memory, it was "not a breakthrough, but a U-turn and the beginning of the dialogue and of the process which led to mutual rapprochement."[146]

Looking at the letter as a form of symbolic reparation, it clearly consisted of all three aforementioned elements required for it to take effect (the verdictive, the attributive, and the participatory), recognising the past harms and asking for forgiveness, however, in an innovative way – along with the suffering of Germans (as it would be in a typical apology), that of the Poles was also stressed. In that, the Episcopate engaged in memory politics, presenting the Polish viewpoint on the history of neighbourly relations between the two countries, as such providing their German counterparts with a template for their public apology, one that they would only need to deliver. While this did not happen back in the day, it cannot be said that the letter failed to achieve its goals as a public apology, ultimately succeeding in transforming the relationship between Poland and Germany and reaffirming the values and to a point shifting collective memories of Polish society (regarding the post-war exiles), thus rendering the missal a quality of a Durkheimian ritual, one acknowledging the right to remember of both groups and not just one. Thus, such a form of public apology could be replicated in those instances when both collectivities have suffered, even as disproportionately as in the case of Poland with regard to Germany. To use another, somewhat similar example from this book in one of the next chapters, should Tutsi ask for

143 Wójcik, *supra* note 89 at 130.

144 Myszor, *supra* note 98 at 175–176.

145 Natalia Jackowska, "Protagoniści i spadkobiercy: Rola Orędzia biskupów z 1965 roku w dialogu konfesyjnym i europejskim" ["Protagonists and Heirs: The Role of the Address of Polish Bishops of 1965 in Confessional and European Dialogue"] (2006) Przegląd Zachodni 93 at 113.

146 Muszyński, *supra* note 126 at 141.

forgiveness for their war crimes committed during and after the civil war on Hutu, rather than removing them from the public discourse, reconciliation in Rwanda could be at a very different stage from what it is right now. In any case, reparations, be they material or symbolic, remain a major legal instrument, in certain instances linked with the rulings of international tribunals, the focus of the next two sections of this chapter.

Soft Institution II in Practice: ECtHR – Conflicting Memories, Singular Narratives

The European Court of Human Rights (hereinafter the ECtHR, the Court), like other international tribunals, in certain cases needs to decide upon matters laying at the intersections of law and memory. As such, I propose to focus on three such instances that not only are regarded as debatable but also demonstrate certain particularities existing within the Council of Europe's human rights system, as well as the more general issues concerning international tribunals as legal institutions of memory.

The Court, the Memory, and the Law

The first law and memory question the ECtHR is often called upon to deal with concerns memory laws proper, which various member countries have introduced in recent years, leading to a number of cases in which the costs and benefits of free speech protection need to be weighed in recently. Of particular importance in deciding such cases are articles 10 and 17 of the European Convention of Human Rights (hereinafter the Convention, the ECHR). Article 10, "Freedom of speech," states that:

1. Everyone has the right to freedom of expression. This right shall include freedom to hold opinions and to receive and impart information and ideas without interference by public authority and regardless of frontiers. This Article shall not prevent States from requiring the licensing of broadcasting, television or cinema enterprises.
2. The exercise of these freedoms, since it carries with it duties and responsibilities, may be subject to such formalities, conditions, restrictions or penalties as are prescribed by law and are necessary in a democratic society, in the interests of national security, territorial integrity or public safety, for the prevention of disorder or crime, for the protection of health or morals, for the protection of the reputation or rights of others, for preventing the disclosure of information received in confidence, or for maintaining the authority and impartiality of the judiciary.[147]

147 Article 10 of the European Convention of Human Rights.

In its jurisprudence, the ECtHR established a three-step test that each regulation must pass in order not to be found in violation of the limitations of free speech allowed to be introduced under the Convention: the restriction must be stated by law; its goal needs to be justified; and, most importantly, it has to be "necessary in a democratic society and proportionate to the legitimate aim pursued."[148]

In turn, the ECHR's article 17, "Prohibition of abuse of rights," prevents the nefarious use of protections guaranteed by the Convention (e.g., the freedom to deny a genocide), stating that:

> Nothing in this Convention may be interpreted as implying for any State, group or person any right to engage in any activity or perform any act aimed at the destruction of any of the rights and freedoms set forth herein or at their limitation to a greater extent than is provided for in the Convention.[149]

Cases regarding memory laws proper (concerning genocide denial prohibition, in most instances that of the Holocaust) rested first solely on article 10 of the Convention, with all circumstances surrounding the freedom of speech limitations reviewed individually in each case. The article has been used, for example, as the basis of two Shoah-related cases originating in Germany, whereby ECtHR confirmed that the anti-abortion and anti-animal cruelty activists, speaking publicly about the "Babycaust" and "the Holocaust on your plate," respectively, could have been found guilty of banalising Shoah, as the German law on the basis of which they were convicted does not breach the Convention.[150]

In some denialism cases, the ECtHR also invoked article 17, taking advantage of its abuse clause (known as the guillotine effect).[151] The Court clearly stated in the 1998 *Lehideux* case that negating "clearly established historical facts – such as the Holocaust – . . . would be removed from the protection of

148 Paolo Lobba, "Testing the 'Uniqueness': Denial of the Holocaust vs Denial of Other Crimes Before the European Court of Human Rights" in Uladzislau Belavusau and Aleksandra Gliszczyńska-Grabias (eds), *Law and Memory: Towards Legal Governance of History* (Cambridge: Cambridge University Press, 2016) 109 at 112.

149 Article 17 of the European Convention of Human Rights.

150 Uladzislau Belavusau, "Memory Laws and Freedom of Speech: Governance of History in European Law" in András Koltay (ed.), *Comparative Perspectives on the Fundamental Freedom of Expression* (Budapest: Wolters Kluwer, 2015) 537 at 545.

151 Monica Spatti, "Denying the Armenian Genocide in International and European Law" in Flavia Lattanzi and Emanuela Pistoia (eds), *The Armenian Massacres of 1915–1916 a Hundred Years Later: Open Questions and Tentative Answers in International Law* (Cham: Springer International Publishing, 2018) 237 at 243.

Article 10 by article 17,"[152] thus venturing into the intersections of law and memory further than ever before (until the *Perinçek* case analysed in the next subsection).[153]

The use of article 17 gave the Court more freedom in their judgement, since, unlike in the cases where only article 10 was invoked, no individual circumstances needed to be analysed.[154] The Court simply argued that negating the Holocaust is directly linked to Nazism, an ideology most definitely not compatible with the Convention.[155] However, as Lobba notes,[156] article 17's guillotine effect was later narrowed in the *Garaudy* judgement.[157] The Court explained that in its understanding, the denial of Shoah has nothing to do with looking for historical truth and is not compatible with the Convention because of its result – negationism leads to discrimination and hate crimes, infringes on human rights, and is underlyingly anti-Semitic or antidemocratic.[158]

The second instance of law and memory issues with which the ECtHR engages concerns the question of the crime of genocide and its definition in the local and international legal provisions within the Council of Europe's system of protection of human rights. While countries may extend the scope of the understanding of genocide in their legislation with regard to the one proposed in the Convention on the Prevention and Punishment of the Crime of Genocide (hereinafter the Genocide Convention, UNCG), it may be applied only in consideration of future cases and not retroactively.[159] In deciding whether retroactivity takes place, the Court needs to consider article

152 ECtHR, *Lehideux and Isorni vs France* (Appl. No. 24662/94), 23 September 1998, para 47.

153 Carmelo D. Leotta, "Criminalizing the Denial of 1915–1916: Armenian Massacres and the European Court of Human Rights: *Perinçek* v *Switzerland*" in Flavia Lattanzi and Emanuela Pistoia (eds), *The Armenian Massacres of 1915–1916 a Hundred Years Later: Open Questions and Tentative Answers in International Law* (Cham: Springer International Publishing, 2018) 251 at 257.

154 Spatti, *supra* note 151 at 243.

155 Leotta, *supra* note 153 at 259.

156 Lobba, *supra* note 148 at 115.

157 ECtHR, *Garaudy vs France* (Appl. No. 65831/01), 24 June 2003.

158 Michał Balcerzak, "Prawa człowieka a negowanie Holocaustu i innych zbrodni przeciwko ludzkości oraz aktów ludobójstwa" ["Human Rights and Denial of Holocaust and Other Crimes Against Humanity and Acts of Genocide"] (2019), online: Uczyć się z historii <uczycsiezhistorii.pl/artykul/prawa-czlowieka-a-negowanie-holocaustu-i-innych-zbrodni-przeciwko-ludzkosci-oraz-aktow-ludobojstwa/>.

159 Tomasz Lachowski, "Sowieckie ludobójstwo i prawo międzynarodowe: Litewskie zmagania ze zbrodniami ZSRS w świetle orzeczenia Europejskiego Trybunału Praw Człowieka w sprawie Drelingas" ["Soviet Genocide and International Law: Lithuanian Struggle with the Crimes of the USSR in the Light of the European Court of Human Rights Judgment in the Case of Drelingas" (2021) 19 Rocznik Instytutu Europy Środkowo-Wschodniej 237 at 244.

7 of the Convention ("No punishment without law"), which, establishing the *nulla poena sine lege* rule, states that:

1. No one shall be held guilty of any criminal offence on account of any act or omission which did not constitute a criminal offence under national or international law at the time when it was committed. Nor shall a heavier penalty be imposed than the one that was applicable at the time the criminal offence was committed.
2. This Article shall not prejudice the trial and punishment of any person for any act or omission which, at the time when it was committed, was criminal according to the general principles of law recognised by civilised nations.[160]

In its jurisprudence, the ECtHR clarified that the second paragraph of article 7 allows for the prosecution of World War II crimes under the Convention, thus opening the possibility of prosecution of other criminal acts on the basis of international law.[161] Furthermore, the Court established a test of legality based on two "qualitative requirements": accessibility, i.e., the criminal law in question needs to be "sufficiently accessible," and foreseeability, i.e., one's ability "to understand 'from the wording of the relevant provision . . . what acts and omissions will make him criminally liable.' "[162]

Additionally, when assessing the cases concerning the validity of particular genocide laws, the ECtHR bases its decisions on the UNCG, focusing in particular on articles II and III:

Article II. In the present Convention, genocide means any of the following acts committed with intent to destroy, in whole or in part, a national, ethnical, racial or religious group, as such:

(a) Killing members of the group;
(b) Causing serious bodily or mental harm to members of the group;
(c) Deliberately inflicting on the group conditions of life calculated to bring about its physical destruction in whole or in part;
(d) Imposing measures intended to prevent births within the group;
(e) Forcibly transferring children of the group to another group.

160 Article 7 of the European Convention of Human Rights.
161 Dovilė Sagatienė, "The Debate About Soviet Genocide in Lithuania in the Case Law of the European Court of Human Rights" (2021) 49:4 Nationalities Papers 776 at 784.
162 Gustavo Minervini, "The Principle of Legality and the Crime of Genocide: *Drelingas vs Lithuania*" (2020) 20 Human Rights Law Review 810 at 815.

Article III. The following acts shall be punishable:

(a) Genocide;
(b) Conspiracy to commit genocide;
(c) Direct and public incitement to commit genocide;
(d) Attempt to commit genocide;
(e) Complicity in genocide.[163]

As I note in the subsections that follow, these articles are particularly scrutinised, both by the court and by academics, with often divergent conclusions as to what considers genocide, and the ECtHR supposedly broadening its understanding of the crime in the analysed cases.

ECtHR and the Perinçek Case

I turn my analysis first to the most recent judgement on denialism as of this writing, as it pertains to the larger debate on the hierarchy of collective trauma-memories and the uniqueness of the Holocaust among other genocides. Given the limitations of this case study, I will focus only on the second, Grand Chamber judgement,[164] which was not only a clear departure from the earlier judicial decisions but also pulled the Court deeper into law and memory debates.

In the *Perinçek* case, the applicant, Doğu Perinçek, was a Turkish lawyer and politician affiliated with the Talât Pasha Committee, a negationist think tank named after the alleged architect of Armenian genocide.[165] Hoping to "test" the genocide denial laws in Switzerland, protecting the memory of the Armenian genocide,[166] during his 2005 visit to the country, Perinçek gave several public speeches arguing that the 1915 massacre of the Armenians was not a genocide,[167] postulating that such views are "an international lie" and "a conspiracy against Turkey."[168] After some deliberation of whether Swiss law penalising genocide denial applied to this case, the country's courts concluded that the categorisation of the 1915 massacre as a genocide was generally agreed upon by historians and thus found Perinçek not only guilty of breaking the law but also of being racist in his statements.[169]

163 Articles I and II of the in the Convention on the Prevention and Punishment of the Crime of Genocide.
164 ECtHR, *Perinçek vs Switzerland* (Appl. No. 27510/08), 15 October 2015.
165 Başak Ertür, "Law of Denial" (2019) 30 Law and Critique 1 at 5.
166 *Ibid.* at 6.
167 Belavusau, *supra* note 150 at 545.
168 Balcerzak, *supra* note 158.
169 Vivian Grosswald Curran, "Evolving French Memory Laws in Light of Greece's 2014 Anti-Racism Law" (2014) 41 Legal Studies Research Paper Series 1 at 12.

When the judgement was upheld two times by the Swiss courts, Perinçek appealed to ECtHR with several claims, arguing, *inter alia*, that his right to freedom of expression, guaranteed by article 10 of the Convention, had been violated. In 2013, the Court's Second Chamber found in favour of Perinçek, but upon Switzerland's request, the case was to be ultimately decided by the Grand Chamber.[170]

As I mentioned earlier, in its 2015 judgement, the Court, finding in favour of the applicant, departed from its reasoning established in earlier cases. ECtHR may have used article 17 to dismiss the application as aiming to protect actions prohibited under the Convention. The Grand Chamber argued, however, that the article's guillotine effect is applicable only to those actions the aim of which is leading to hatred or violence – and Perinçek's statements could not have been clearly classified as such.[171]

The Grand Chamber argued that the protection from denial granted to Shoah lies less on it's being an established historical fact and more on several other issues, such as antidemocratic and anti-Semitic connotations of denial, as well as a specific historical context of the countries in which its penalisation had been introduced.[172] This argument, as Leotta acutely notes, represents a shift from the Court's focus on a statement's content (as in earlier cases) to a judgement of its values.[173]

Additionally, when applying the aforementioned three-point article 10 test to this particular case, the Court found that Swiss law passed the first two (being stated by law and being justified) but failed the third (being needed in a democratic society). Here, the Court was hoping to find a balance between article 8 of the Convention (the Right to respect for private and family life), protecting Armenians from having their suffering denied, and article 10. Importantly, the Grand Chamber acknowledged the Armenian collective memory of the massacre, admitting that their national identity was centred around this event.[174]

Ultimately, the ECtHR proposed seven criteria to examine the interplay between articles 8 and 10 in this case: the nature of statements; the context of interference; the extent of statements affecting the rights of the Armenians; the existence of a consensus regarding this question among countries-parties to the ECHR; international law obligations; Swiss courts' justification of their decision; and the severity of the interference. Ultimately, the Court found that Switzerland did not sufficiently explain why the freedom of expression needed to be so severely restricted in the country's particular context, and thus, it was unnecessary to protect the Armenians in this way in a democratic society.[175]

170 Ertür, *supra* note 165 at 6.
171 Lobba, *supra* note 148 at 117.
172 Leotta, *supra* note 153 at 263.
173 Leotta, *supra* note 153 at 263.
174 Ertür, *supra* note 165 at 15.
175 Leotta, *supra* note 153 at 263–268.

ECtHR and the Vasiliauskas *and* Drėlingas *Cases*

Similar to the *Perinçek* case, the 2015 *Vasiliauskas*[176] and 2019 *Drėlingas*[177] cases also involved the question of the understanding of genocide, which was analysed as not touching the memory of the crime through the validity of memory laws, but rather the crime itself. Both cases concerned the eradication of the Lithuanian partisans during the second Soviet occupation of the country (1944–1990), which saw 85,000 Lithuanians killed or rendered dead (including 20,000 partisans and over 1,000 of their supporters) and 132,000 deported further into the Soviet Union,[178] amounting to over 10% of the country's population at that time.[179] Among those were members not only of armed resistance and their accolades but also of Lithuanian intelligentsia and other active social and political communities: civil servants, state officials, "public figures, intellectuals and the academic community, farmers, priests, and members of the families of those groups,"[180] considered to be "the backbone of pre-war Independent Lithuania."[181]

Both cases included applicants who used to be employed in Soviet security services (MGB-KGB) and who were involved in the capture and death of armed resistance-members (active, in the *Vasiliauskas* case, and inactive in the *Drėlingas*),[182] with the former implicated in a 1953 operation to capture two partisans in hiding, which resulted in their death,[183] and the latter taking part in a 1956 operation to capture the head of the all-partisan organisation (LLKS Council) Adolfas Ramanauskas ("Vanagas") and his wife Birute Mazeikatie ("Vanda"), who were later tortured and sentenced to death ("Vangas") or deportation ("Vanda").[184] Importantly, Drėlingas was a

176 ECtHR, *Vasiliauskas vs Lithuania* (Appl. No. 35343/05), 20 October 2015.

177 ECtHR, *Drėlingas vs Lithuania* (Appl. No. 28859/16), 12 March 2019.

178 Minervini, *supra* note 162 at 811.

179 Lars Berster, "The Soviet Crackdown on Lithuanian Partisan Movements (1946–1956): A Genocide? Background Deliberations on the ECHR Judgment in *Drėlingas vs. Lithuania*" (2021) 7:2 International Comparative Jurisprudence 125 at 143.

180 Sagatienė, *supra* note 161 at 780.

181 Justinas Žilinskas, "Drėlingas vs Lithuania (ECHR): Ethno-Political Genocide Confirmed?" (2019), online: Blog of the European Journal of International Law <ejiltalk.org/drelingas-v-lithuania-echr-ethno-political-genocide-confirmed/>.

182 Justinas Žilinskas, "Non-Protected Groups within Protected Groups: A New View to the Genocide in Drėlingas vs Lithuania (ECHR) Case" in A. P. Hetman (ed.), *Збірник тез доповідей та наукових повідомлень учасників ювілейної XX міжнародної науково-практичної конференції молодих учених* [*A Collection of Abstracts of Reports and Scientific Reports of Participants of the Jubilee 20th International Scientific and Practical Conference of Young Scientists*] (Kharkiv: Yaroslav the Wise National University of Law, 2020) 35 at 35.

183 Sagatienė, *supra* note 161 at 778.

184 Minervini, *supra* note 162 at 812.

prison guard in "a partisan detention operation" and as such was considered to have been "only" complicit in the genocide.[185]

In both cases, the applicants were sentenced on the basis of Lithuanian legislation introduced following the post-1989 transition, article 99 of the Criminal Code, which broadens the definition of genocide with regard to the Genocide Convention by including political and social groups in the protected catalogue. This became the key legal issue to be decided by the ECtHR: while the USSR signed the UNCG in 1949 and ratified it in 1954, such an extended understanding of protected groups raised the questions of legality with respect to retroactivity of the Lithuanian prosecutions.[186]

Importantly, in 2014, the Lithuanian Constitutional Court itself found parts of article 99 incompatible with the Lithuanian constitution, finding the country's legislation to be in breach of article 7 of the convention by a retroactive introduction of the political and social groups categories as protected from genocide. It did, however, state that given the nature and intent of Soviet crimes in Lithuania, these atrocities may be considered genocide, provided that the affected communities were such a vital part of a national or an ethnic group that their eradication had destructive consequences on the whole Lithuanian society. As such, the country's courts followed the Constitutional Court's reasoning in future cases.[187]

The *Vasiliauskas* case, however, had been decided before Lithuanian courts earlier, and thus, the ECtHR found Lithuania in the 2015 decision (split nine to eight) in breach of Article 7 of the Convention. The ECtHR argued that the basis for prosecution was not foreseeable in 1953,[188] as the broader definition of the crime of genocide was not yet in place at the time; that the fact that partisans were only a part of the group intended for destruction did not match the reasoning of the crime of genocide in 1953 (although it was later broadened in international law practice); and that Lithuania failed to demonstrate the importance of the affected group for the rest of society.[189]

In turn, in the 2019 *Drėlingas* case, the different reasoning of domestic Lithuanian courts allowed for the ECtHR to agree (in a five-to-two decision)[190] on the foreseeability of the applicant's conviction, as it took place after the ratification of the Genocide Convention by the USSR.[191] The Court also concurred with the view that the partisans were a vital element of the national and ethnic group responsible for the protection "of national identity, culture and national self-awareness," arguing that not only may

185 Sagatienė, *supra* note 161 at 785–787.
186 Lachowski, *supra* note 159 at 244–245.
187 Lachowski, *supra* note 159 at 247–248.
188 Sagatienė, *supra* note 161 at 778.
189 Žilinskas, *supra* note 181.
190 Žilinskas, *supra* note 181.
191 Sagatienė, *supra* note 161 at 785.

genocide "target a group of people belonging to several protected groups," but the groups themselves also "might be interchangeable," as such accepting the broader-than-earlier-accepted definition of the crime of genocide.[192] Later that year, the Grand Chamber rejected the request to refer the case, meaning the earlier decision became final.[193]

ECtHR at the Intersections of Law and Memory

The three cases demonstrate different aspects of the international tribunals' role as a legal institution of memory, proving that in the cases involving the matters of collective memory, identity, and history, there are no uniform solutions. In regard to the *Perinçek* case, by taking a different path from that in the previous decisions – and in the Second Chamber judgement – the Grand Chamber seemed to have hoped to avoid accusations of being "judges of history" (the fact that seven judges presented a dissenting opinion, arguing that a genocide is self-evidentiary, notwithstanding).[194] Quite contrarily, it was pulled into another intersection of law and memory, with a different controversial issue arising: the question of potentially larger protection from denial granted to the Holocaust than to other genocides within the countries-parties to the Convention.[195]

Linking the possibility of introducing the penalisation of genocide denial not only with its main goal – hatred – but also with its context, the Court established a geographical distinction, arguing that countries that were in some way implicated in Shoah may penalise negationism, whereas countries with no links to the Armenian 1915 massacre cannot set one narrative about the atrocity.[196] Looking from the perspective of collective memory and the interplay between memories functioning on different levels – local, national, global – the Court seems to have shut the door for any other genocide to reach the level of protection that the Holocaust has from denial in most, if not all, European countries. Additionally, it could be imagined that a potential Irish or Portuguese Holocaust denier could now raise an argument before the Court that since neither country had a direct connection to Shoah, they should not be penalised for negating it under any memory laws.

Moreover, by focusing on Switzerland having no links with the Armenian genocide, the Court ignored a number of third-party applicants who raised

192 Carola Lingaas, "Conceptualizing the National Group for the Crime of Genocide: Is Law Able to Account for Identity Fault Lines?" (2021) 49:2 Nationalities Papers 240 at 249.
193 Minervini, *supra* note 162 at 814.
194 Lobba, *supra* note 148 at 126.
195 Aleksandra Gliszczyńska-Grabias, "Memory Laws or Memory Loss? Europe in Search of its Historical Identity Through the National and International Law" (2014) XXXIV Polish Yearbook of International Law 161 at 171.
196 Spatti, *supra* note 151 at 244.

the issue of how Perinçek's statements resonate in the Turkish anti-Armenian climate. The Grand Chamber focused solely on the fact that Switzerland did not raise this argument during Perinçek's original trial. As a result, today Turkey distorts the ECtHR's judgement to foster their narrative about the Armenian genocide.[197]

The Court also needs to be criticised for its investigation of, among other factors, the question of time that has passed since the Armenian massacre. As Leotta poignantly notes,[198] penalisation of genocide denial protects not only the victims of this crime but also all the members of the group that was supposed to be exterminated – by taking such a perspective, the Court clearly ignored the way unresolved collective trauma-memories may pass between generations, becoming a major element of a group's identity. The unintended effect of using this argument may be an application to reinvestigate the need for Holocaust denial penalisation in a world with no Shoah survivors left, which is bound to come in the near future.

The ECtHR's 2015 judgement in the *Perinçek* case demonstrates how difficult cases laying at the intersections of law and memory are: by trying not to decide upon a legal qualification of a historical event, the Court opened a different Pandora's box. However, I must stress that I disagree with the viewpoint that the Grand Chamber's decision gives the Holocaust a larger level of protection from denial than to other genocides. In contrast, it seems that the judgement endangers the memory of Shoah itself, opening up the possibility of protection against genocide denial being forced into the narrow confines of a freedom of expression box, which protects all but the victims and their descendants.

While the decision in the *Perinçek* case was limiting for the protection of collective trauma-memories laying at the basis of a group's identity, the judgement in the *Drėlingas* case opened new avenues for their preservation. As Lachowski acutely notes, it was the first case in which a Soviet-conducted genocide was recognised on an international level – even though the only direct and legal responsibility for the crime was borne by the applicant.[199]

By allowing a broader definition of the crime of genocide, that of an "ethno-national-political genocide,"[200] to stand in court, it challenged the perspective that crimes committed by the USSR, as conducted on a political and social basis and not a national and ethical one, could not have constituted genocide.[201] Such a viewpoint taken by the Court has been met with considerable dissent, with critics calling into question the Soviet intent and

197 Ertür, *supra* note 165 at 16–17.
198 Leotta, *supra* note 153 at 269–270.
199 Lachowski, *supra* note 159 at 250.
200 Lachowski, *supra* note 159 at 251.
201 Žilinskas, *supra* note 181.

motivation to commit genocide due to their focus on different characteristics of the group members than purely national, ethnic, racial, or religious,[202] those other factors (national and ethnic) being considered rather a "weak 'co-motive.' "[203]

Indeed, this case was the first instance of such a qualification of Soviet atrocities[204] motivated by the goal of establishing a new *homo sovieticus* in lieu of pre-existing "free and separate" nations[205] and represents a more general shift in categorising such crimes, given that in the International Criminal Court's (ICC) Rome Statue, the crime of genocide does not include social and political groups, which technically are protected under the crimes against humanity distinction that, however, fails to include the eradication of active-duty partisans.[206]

Importantly, it is from the viewpoint of law and memory that the reason for the different verdicts in the *Vasiliauskas* and the *Drėlingas* cases becomes more understandable. Once the Lithuanian courts clarified their legal argument, stressing the vitality of the partisans for the survival of the whole ethnic group, the genocidal intent became clearly visible: through the eradication of collective memory agents, the destruction of a group's identity becomes possible, even if the percentage of those killed is not necessarily substantial.

It also needs to be noted that Lithuania's success in the *Drėlingas* case empowers the "victims to challenge ongoing efforts to whitewash the Soviet history of brutal and massive repressions in the former Soviet occupied nations," allowing for "at least symbolic justice to the victims of Soviet genocide," and putting these counter-memories on the global stage.[207] In general, as Caroli remarks, the question of categorisation of a crime as genocide reverberates through not only criminal prosecutions but also collective memories, having the potential to exacerbate memory politics.[208] This became clearly visible in the Russian response to the decision – in the *Vasiliauskas* case, the country even intervened as an *amicus curiae*[209] – which was highly critical and needs to be regarded as an element of broader negationist politics conducted by Russia in recent years,[210] the culmination of which is the narrative surrounding their 2022 invasion of Ukraine.

202 Berster, *supra* note 179 at 138–143.
203 Berster, *supra* note 179 at 144.
204 Paolo Caroli, "Drelingas v Lithuania (N. 28859/16): The ECtHR Acknowledges the Lithuanian Ethno-Political Genocide" (2020), online: International Law Blog <internationallaw.blog/2020/03/18/drelingas-v-lithuania-n-28859-16-the-ecthr-acknowledges-the-lithuanian-ethno-political-genocide/>.
205 Lachowski, *supra* note 159 at 252.
206 Žilinskas, *supra* note 182 at 36–37.
207 Sagatienė, *supra* note 161 at 788.
208 Caroli, *supra* note 204.
209 Lachowski, *supra* note 159 at 247.
210 Lachowski, *supra* note 159 at 250–251.

The three ECtHR decisions confirm the earlier observations regarding international tribunals as extraordinary intersections of law and collective memory. The cases heard were limited in scope. The Court remained resistant to singular country narratives (be that Switzerland, Turkey and Armenia, or Lithuania and Russia) but at the same time was unable to change them (both Turkey and Russia continue their politics of memory distortion) – which establishes it as a soft legal institution of memory – failing to lead to reconciliation, however allowing, at least in the *Drėlingas* case, for a certain vindication of the victims by succeeding in the shift in official narratives and collective memories with the first official recognition of the Soviet genocide having a particularly strong impact. At the same time, the aforementioned individualisation of guilt takes place in front of an international tribunal, which was demonstrated once again in the *Drėlingas* decision, although, given the Russian stance on its past crimes, the rehabilitating effect of the perpetrators' society is unlikely to happen in this case. In turn, in the *Perinçek* case, the Court's decision clearly showed the difficulties posed by the intrinsically limited process of the establishment of legal truth, having potentially far-reaching consequences for the matters of both law and memory in its aftermath, leading to some degree of collective forgetting.

Looking into the ECtHR further as a legal institution of memory, one also notices different similarities with other international tribunals: the role of a trial before them as a Durkheimian ritual, their being top-to-bottom mechanisms of power, with the potential to realise the right to be remembered (successfully in the *Drėlingas* case and unsuccessfully in the *Perinçek* case), taking place in non-transitional situations (in all three cases, the proceedings took place many years following the Armenian and Lithuanian genocides, respectively), confirming the role of non-criminal international tribunals as influential places of intersection between law and memory. In the next section, I look further into this legal institution of memory, studying ECtHR once again using a different case laying at the intersections of law and memory.

Soft Institution II in Practice Again: Opportunity Missed, or the *Katyń* Case before ECtHR

In March 1940, the NKVD (USSR's interior ministry at that time) proposed to Joseph Stalin an "examination" of the cases of 14,700 Polish prisoners of war in camps, as well as a further 11,000 present in the western parts of Belarus and Ukraine, arguing that the capital punishment should be applied "without summoning those under arrest and without presentation of the accusation." These mass executions came to be later known as the Katyń Massacre, after first exhumations took place in that area following its fall under the German occupation in 1943, with the final count of those killed, as per a 1965 note to Khrushchev, amounting to 21,857 people executed in the Katyń forest, Ostashkovo, and Starobels camps, and other camps and prisons in the western parts of the USSR.[211] It needs to be stressed that those killed belonged to the Polish intelligentsia: they were officers and reservists of the Polish army, including policeman, teachers, academics, doctors, members of the civil service, lawyers, engineers, priests, artists, businesspeople, and social workers.[212] Furthermore, the families of those executed were subject to deportations: among over 300,000 Polish citizens deported far into the USSR, approximately 59,000 were relatives of Katyń Massacre victims.[213]

In spite of the fact that the evidence uncovered by the Germans clearly attributed the crime to the Russians, the USSR denied any responsibility and later blocked, with the help of the Allies, any attempts by the Polish government-in-exile to set up an independent commission to investigate the matter, instead creating several commissions of their own, which found Nazi Germany responsible, ultimately even (unsuccessfully) attempting to prosecute Germans for this crime during the IMT proceedings in Nuremberg. It was only in the early 1950s through the work of the US Congressional Madden Committee (Select Committee to Conduct an Investigation of the Facts, Guidance, and Circumstances of the Katyn Massacre) that the truth about Russian responsibility was acknowledged internationally, but not locally, with any mentions of Katyń censored by the communist authorities in Poland, with severe punishments for those violating it.[214]

The USSR, still denying its involvement in the Massacre, engaged in perpetrating the so-called Katyń lie, going to great lengths to keep up its façade of innocence, destroying the documentation relating to the executed Poles in 1959 while sealing other files for a number of years. Despite the fact that Russia ultimately acknowledged responsibility, opening an investigation into the matter that took place between 1990 and 2004, it was not only discontinued "on the grounds that all alleged suspects were dead," but out of the 183 case volumes, 36 were classified as "top secret" and 8 as "for internal use only," thus permanently barring access to them for the Massacre victims' families. Attempting to gain permission to see these and other documents, as well as to be recognised as next-of-kin, and also asking for a legal rehabilitation of their relatives by the Russian authorities, in the years

211 Thomas R. Langtry, *The Katyn Massacre: Causes and Consequences of Russian Impunity* (San Francisco, CA: Golden Gate University School of Law, 2020) at 1–6.

212 Zuzanna Maciejczak, Marlena Modzelewska, Rafał Wiśniewski, Roch Dąbrowski, Maksymilian Olenderek, Tadeusz P. Rutkowski and PBS, *Pamięć o zbrodni katyńskiej w Polsce: Raport z badania ilościowego i jakościowego* [*Memory of the Katyń Massacre in Poland: A Report on the Basis of Qualitative and Quantitative Research*] (Warsaw: Narodowe Centrum Kultury, 2018) at 4.

213 Ireneusz C. Kamiński, "The Katyń Massacres Before the European Court of Human Rights: From Justice Delayed to Justice Permanently Denied" (2015) 29:4 East European Politics and Societies and Cultures 784 at 786.

214 Langtry, *supra* note 211 at 1–6, 10.

2003–2009, some of the families lodged a number of complaints, requests, and suits before various institutions in Russia. However, these efforts were to no avail – the country denied all claims, arguing that it was impossible to establish the fate of the applicants' family members as their bodies were not among those exhumed.[215]

The Case of Janowiec (and Others) *v.* Russia[216] *Before the ECtHR*

Given that Russia became a party of the ECHR in 1998, the aforementioned lack of developments motivated several family members of those murdered in the Katyń Massacre to lodge a complaint against Russia before the ECtHR. The applicants stipulated that: the 1990–2004 investigation was "not efficient as required by the Convention," which violated its article 2; that the way in which their requests were denied by the Russian institutions "amounted to denigrating and inhuman treatment," which violated article 3 of the Convention; and that "the refusal of the Russian government to disclose documents from the Russian investigation into the massacre, which the Court had requested," could amount to a violation of article 38, obliging parties to cooperate with the ECtHR.[217] The applicants were later joined by the Polish government as a third party and six NGOs *amicis curiae*: Open Society Justice Initiative, Public International Law and Policy Group, Amnesty International, European Human Rights Advocacy Centre, the Human Rights Centre "Memorial," and Essex Transitional Justice Network, with the latter three acting jointly.[218]

The Chamber of the Court delivered its judgement on April 16, 2012; however, unsatisfied with the verdict, the applicants appealed to the Grand Chamber, which agreed to hear the case, ultimately deciding *in peius* (which is permitted under the Convention) on October 21, 2013. In that, the Grand Chamber confirmed only two of the Chamber's findings, the violation of article 38 and a lack of violation of article 2, contrarily, not finding that article 3 was violated with regard to the victims' family members.[219]

215 Gabriella Citroni, "*Janowiec and Others vs Russia*: A Long History of Justice Delayed Turned into a Permanent Case of Justice Denied" (2013) XXXIII Polish Yearbook of International Law 279 at 280–281.

216 ECtHR, *Janowiec and Others vs Russia* (Appl. No. 55508/07 and 29520/09), 21 October 2013.

217 Ireneusz C. Kamiński, "Answers to the Questions for the Hearing in the Case of Janowiec and Others vs Russia (Joint Cases nos. 55508/07 and 29520/09) Strasbourg, 6 October 2011" (2011) XXI Polish Yearbook of International Law 409 at 409.

218 Kamiński, *supra* note 213 at 792, 798.

219 Marina Eudes, "L'affaire Katyn devant la Cour européenne des droits de l'homme – Addendum" ["The Katyń Case Before the European Court of Human Rights – an Addendum"] (2013) LIX Annuaire français de droit International 319 at 319–320.

In regard to article 38 of the ECHR, the Grand Chamber unanimously found Russia in violation of cooperation with the Court rule, as the country continuously refused to submit the national decision closing the 1990–2004 investigation of the Massacre,[220] stating that the Russian courts did not conduct any factual analysis as to why the documents were classified as secret.[221] As such, the ECtHR confirmed that even in those cases when it finds itself incompetent to judge a case on its merits, the states are required to submit all requested materials and information.[222]

The Grand Chamber also confirmed in a 13–4 decision the Chamber's judgement in the part relating to a lack of *ratione temporis* competence to investigate a violation of article 2,[223] remarking that the main aspects of all investigations of the Katyń Massacre on the Russian part took place before 1998 (when Russia became a party to the Convention).[224] In analysing that aspect of the case, the Court proposed that in order to be admissible, a case would need to pass both the "new elements test," i.e., the "discovery of new and sufficiently important material after the critical date of ratification as triggering a fresh procedural obligation under Article 2," which may be applied to only those cases where no more than ten years passed between the event and the ratification of the Convention; and the "Convention values test," i.e., that "the required connection for the Court's jurisdiction may be found to exist if the triggering event is of a larger dimension than an ordinary criminal offence, and amounts to the negation of the very foundations of the Convention" – however, it may be passed by only those occurrences which took place after November 4, 1950.[225] The *Katyń* case clearly did not pass either of the tests. As such, while acknowledging that there exist examples of successful prosecutions of temporally distant crimes, the Grand Chamber argued that such actions are only prerogatives of the respective states and are not obligatory under the Convention.[226]

Importantly, where the Chamber recognised the violation of article 3 with regard to some of the victims' family members,[227] in a 12–5 decision, the Grand Chamber did not find such a violation, arguing that the case law relating to this article refers only to instances of forced disappearances, whereas after a certain period of time, and most surely since 1998, those

220 *Ibid.* at 321.

221 Witold Kulesza, "Zbrodnia katyńska przed Europejskim Trybunałem Praw Człowieka – refleksje nad wyrokiem z 21 października 2013 roku" ["The Katyń Massacre Before the European Court of Human Rights – Reflections on the Judgement of 21 October 2013"] (2017) XLIII Nowa Kodyfikacja Prawa Karnego 349 at 351–352.

222 Citroni, *supra* note 215 at 361.

223 Kamiński, *supra* note 213 at 800–802.

224 Eudes, *supra* note 219 at 323–324.

225 Kamiński, *supra* note 213 at 800–804.

226 Citroni, *supra* note 215 at 286.

227 Citroni, *supra* note 215 at 287.

who disappeared in the Katyń Massacre, even if their fate was not confirmed by exhumations, may only be considered dead,[228] and as such, the applicants' emotions did not "reach the necessary threshold" of degrading and inhuman treatment[229] in light of "the pronouncements of the Russian courts that withheld acknowledgement" of the killings.[230]

Last, it needs to be noted that also contrary to the Chamber, the Grand Chamber did not recognise the Katyń Massacre as a war crime, "refusing to enter in any such considerations."[231]

The Katyń Case at the Intersections of Law and Memory

Leaving the ECtHR judgement aside for a moment, the collective trauma-memory of the Katyń Massacre remains of major importance to Poles, not only to those whose family members were killed but also to society in general, which regards it as another example of the occupier's attempts at the destruction of Polish society through the eradication of its intelligentsia – after 1989, the memory of Katyń became part of the official narrative, passed on by a variety of state and non-governmental memory carriers and agents.[232] The importance of Katyń in the Polish collective memory was only augmented following the 2010 Smoleńsk plane catastrophe, which saw the Polish delegation flying to the commemorative celebrations of the Katyń Massacre there, headed by then President Lech Kaczyński, die alongside all other 95 passengers, in a way "echoing" the 1940 events.[233]

As such, even before the Russian occupation of Crimea in 2014 and the 2022 invasion of Ukraine, the bilateral relations with Poland were tense. The *Katyń* case and associated collective memories were a major source of discord between the two countries, stemming also from the fact that Russia does not even recognise it as a war crime, whereas for Poles, the Massacre amounted to the crime of genocide,[234] as the USSR's goal "was to eliminate the entire

228 Eudes, *supra* note 219 at 321–322.
229 Citroni, *supra* note 215 at 289.
230 Kamiński, *supra* note 213 at 803–804.
231 Eudes, *supra* note 219 at 322–323.
232 Maciejczak et al., *supra* note 212 at 5–7.
233 Marina Eudes, "L'affaire *Katyn* dans le prétoire de la Cour européenne des droits de l'homme: L'un des plus grands crimes de l'histoire enfin jugé" ["The Katyń Case in the Courtroom the European Court of Human Rights: One of the Biggest Crimes in History Finally Judged"] (2012) LVIII Annuaire français de droit international 679 at 679–680.
234 Adrian Szumski, "Wyrok Europejskiego Trybunału Praw Człowieka z 16 IV 2012 r. w 'Sprawie Katyńskiej' (Sprawa Janowiec i inni przeciwko Rosji) – aspekty prawne i znaczenie dla relacji polsko-rosyjskich" ["The Judgement of the European Court of Human Rights from 16 April 2012 in the 'Katyń Case' (Janowiec and Others vs Russia) – Legal Aspects and Its Meaning for the Polish and Russian Relations)"] (2013) 1 Dyplomacja i Bezpieczeństwo 123 at 123–124.

officer corps in order to rob Poland of its intellectual and military elite, necessary for the formation of a viable independent post-war Poland."[235] As noted by Kulesza, the ECtHR's decision in the *Janowiec* case was a "confirmation of the procedural efficacy of a consistent strategy of that country [Russia] negating international justice with regard to its own actions," one dating to the Nuremberg Tribunal.[236] The case represented perhaps the last possibility of bringing Russia to justice, as the country recently ceased to be a party of the ECHR in the wake of its invasion of Ukraine.[237]

Importantly, in the *Janowiec* case, the ECtHR proposed a very different approach to events taking place before the adoption of the Convention than the IACtHR with regard to the IACHR. The latter court in a number of cases found the state parties in violation of the obligation to investigate atrocities, including those occurring "well before the critical date" of ratification"[238] – such an argumentation is the fundament of the aforementioned right to truth, proposed in this book as the right to be remembered.

Thus, as Kulesza argues, with the Katyń judgement, the Court "lost a chance to make an input and set out – in the category of human rights – the standard of protection of the legal good which in contemporary times is the collective memory," proposing that the degrading treatment against which article 3 of the Convention protects also relates to the instances of denying certain memories, as the ECHR was adopted in the aftermath of World War II,[239] and as such was, as noted earlier in the book, similar to many other acts of international and human rights law at that time influenced by the collective memories of the conflict. Overall, it becomes clear that the ECtHR ignored not only the right to be remembered of the victims, their families, and the broader Polish society, but also overlooked the very values on which the Convention and the Court itself were established.

Looking at the ECtHR once more from the perspective of a legal institution of memory, it needs to be noted that the *Janowiec* case confirmed that proceedings before non-criminal tribunals also deal with matters of collective memory, turning international tribunals into places of Durkheimian collective rituals. As a soft institution, it is unlikely that the judgement caused a collective memory shift in either Poland or Russia, most definitely not leading to reconciliation between the two countries; however, the Court's

235 Allan Gerson, "72 Years Later: Still Seeking Accountability for the Katyn Forest Massacre" (2012) 44:3 Case Western Reserve Journal of International Law 605 at 608.

236 Kulesza, *supra* note 212 at 366.

237 Committee of Ministers, "Russia Ceases to Be a Party to the European Convention on Human Rights on 16 September 2022" (2022), online: Council of Europe <coe.int/en/web/portal/-/russia-ceases-to-be-a-party-to-the-european-convention-of-human-rights-on-16-september-2022>.

238 Citroni, *supra* note 215 at 290–293.

239 Kulesza, *supra* note 212 at 371–372.

failure to recognise the Katyń Massacre as – at least – a war crime may have inadvertently given support to the Russian narrative of a regular crime, with the ECtHR again failing to escape memory politics in the pursuit of a solely legal memory.

Conclusion: Soft Legal Institutions of Memory in Practice

This chapter provided an analysis of two soft legal institutions of memory, each concerning different social, cultural, political, and legal circumstances, and each to a certain degree diverging from its respective model delineated in the previous part of the book. The Japanese reparations, both material and symbolic, have had an underlying political and economic agenda, while the letter of the Polish bishops to their German counterparts was a reciprocal public apology, one delivered not by the authorities, but rather by Catholic clergy, acting as representatives of Polish society. In a similar vein, the first analysed cases showed that the ECtHR failed to establish a singular approach to the questions of memory in its jurisprudence, while in the Katyń case, the Court case once again attempted not to be a judge of the past but still ended up creating a particular narrative of the Massacre.

At the same time, however, the case studies confirmed earlier observations that proposed legal institutions of memory as top-to-bottom, heavily politicised Durkheimian rituals, with a small level of direct influence of law on their shape and, in turn, their own divergent impact on collective memory, allowing for various aspects of the right to memory to be fulfilled when implemented, all while demonstrating their limitations, with only the Polish symbolic reparations being successful in leading to the Polish-German reconciliation. The next chapter will show whether these observations will correspond with the examined medium legal institutions of memory.

Chapter 7

Placing Medium Legal Institutions of Memory within the New Framework

Introduction

Moving on further into the application of the new law and memory framework, this chapter is focused on the analysis of medium legal institutions of memory. Beginning with the first one, lustration, I analyse the seemingly particular case of its implementation in Iraq, showing, however, that the problems it has faced are similar to those found in other places where vetting was implemented. This study is complemented by that of the Polish lustration, which, now spanning the course of over three decades, continues to have an impact on the country's politics, albeit somewhat diminished as years go by from the viewpoint of society.

The final section of this chapter turns to the second medium legal institution of memory, that of a truth (and reconciliation) commission. Using the case of the recent Brazilian truth commission, I demonstrate the difficulties of putting this institution into practice, since its use in South Africa came to be particularly associated with matters of law and memory. While this study is not complemented by a Polish equivalent, given that the country did not employ that particular institution, together, the three analyses deepen the understanding of the intersections of law and memory not only in the three countries but also more generally in regard to medium legal institutions of memory.

Medium Institution I in Practice: Leaving the Past Behind with the (A)Typical Lustration in Iraq

The 2003 military intervention in Iraq of the US-led coalition has had a number of implications on the country itself, as well as the whole region, some of which, pertaining to the matters of law and memory, are analysed in this section. It first needs to be noted that the ground for a regime change in Iraq was laid out much earlier; however, it was not until 9/11 and the ensuing war on terror that the US government took a particular interest in

DOI: 10.4324/9781003461548-13

not only Afghanistan but also Iraq,[1] where the Ba'athist regime (from the name of the main party, Ba'ath) of President Saddam Hussein was accused of committing atrocities against various ethnic groups (Kurds, Shia), as well as thought to harbour weapons of mass destruction, which ultimately prompted an invasion.[2]

One of the key goals of the intervention was the reconstruction of the country as a democratic society, free from the Ba'ath Party's influences.[3] As such, a process of lustration, one modelled on the post-1945 de-Nazification of Germany[4] (in spite of their intrinsic differences described earlier in the book) and the post-1989 Central and Eastern European decommunisation practices,[5] better known under the name of de-Ba'athification, was implemented. In the following analysis of this legal institution of memory, I propose to distinguish six phases: (1) pre-intervention planning and initial decisions made in the immediate aftermath of the invasion; (2) Paul Bremer's work as the head of the Coalition Provisional Authority (CPA); (3) the establishment and initial decisions of the Higher National De-Ba'athification Commission (HNDC); (4) the softening of de-Ba'athification during the period of governance of Prime Minister Ayad Allawi; (5) the return of de-Ba'athification and its entrenchment in the 2005 constitution and the 2008 Law of the Supreme National Commission of Accountability and Justice (or the Accountability and Justice Law, AJL); and (6) the process of de-Ba'athification becoming a natural element of Iraqi national life.

Lustration in Iraq

The first steps towards de-Ba'athification were taken in the planning phase of the 2003 invasion, most notable among them being: a long-standing American cooperation with various organisations comprising Iraqi exiles, such as the Iraqi National Congress (INC), headed by Ahmad Chalabi, and Iraqi National Accord (INA), with Ayad Allawi at the helm, as well as Kurdish opposition parties from the inside of Iraq; the adoption of the Iraq Liberation Act in 1998 which provided large financing to opposition groups;

1 Shamiran Mako and Alistair D. Edgar, "Evaluating the Pitfalls of External Statebuilding in Post-2003 Iraq (2003–2021)" (2021) 15:4 Journal of Intervention and Statebuilding 425 at 427.

2 Matthew A. George, *U.S. Army Civil Affairs and Political Transformation in Occupation: Lustration and Recasting Society* (Fort Leavenworth, KS: U.S. Army Command and General Staff College, 2017) at 95.

3 Shamiran Mako, "Subverting Peace: The Origins and Legacies of de-Ba'athification in Iraq" (2021) 15:4 Journal of Intervention and Statebuilding 476 at 476.

4 Aysegul Keskin Zeren, "From De-Nazification of Germany to De-Baathification of Iraq" (2017) 132:2 Political Science Quarterly 259 at 271.

5 Roman David, "From Prague to Baghdad: Lustration Systems and Their Political Effects" (2006) 41:3 Government and Opposition 347 at 349.

the organisation of the 1999 Dessert Crossing Seminar by the US Central Command (which criticised the viability of expat groups taking responsibility for the governance of Iraq); the creation of a joint task force of the State Department and a number of US federal agencies in order to establish the Democratic Principles Working Group of the Iraqi Opposition (which analysed de-Nazification and decommunisation);[6] the Future of Iraq Study project which, composed of exiled Iraqi elites meeting under the auspices of the State Department, produced an extensive report which was the first to propose the idea of de-Ba'athification; and the State Department memorandum "Reconstruction in Iraq – Lessons of the Past," advocating lustration as de-Saddamification, i.e., of only those responsible for atrocities and at the top of the state hierarchy.[7]

Following the 2003 invasion and the fall of Baghdad on April 9 to American forces, such a plan of a mild de-Ba'athification was implemented by General Tommy Franks, who abolished the Ba'ath Party in a message to the Iraqis,[8] and Lieutenant General Jay Garner, who became the head of the Office of Reconstruction and Humanitarian Affairs (ORHA).[9] During his tenure, ORHA was open to cooperation with former party members, provided that they renounced their affiliation and were not implicated in any atrocities.[10]

The US Iraq policy in the immediate aftermath of the invasion, however, was full of conflicting decisions, with the idea of Paul Bremer replacing Garner appearing in late April 2003. Initially, Bremer was supposed to share his duties with another person (Zalmay Khalilzad, a proposed "Muslim face" of the occupation); ultimately, though, he was to be sent alone, receiving "supreme authority over all Iraq,"[11] as the head of the Coalition Provisional Authority (CPA), established to replace the ORHA.[12]

Soon after his arrival, in May 2003, Bremer issued two decisions that were to shape the lustration policy in Iraq for years to come: CPA Order No. 1: De-Baathification of Iraqi Society and CPA Order No. 2: Dissolution of Entities. The former (No. 1) concerned the prohibition "of symbols and images glorifying Hussein and his party," and, most importantly, the removal of the

6 Mako, *supra* note 3 at 479–480.

7 Zeren, *supra* note 4 at 271–272.

8 Miranda Sissons and Abdulrazzaq Al-Saiedi, *A Bitter Legacy: Lessons of De-Baathifi cation in Iraq* (New York, NY: International Center for Transitional Justice, 2013) at 10.

9 Zeren, *supra* note 4 at 273.

10 W. Andrew Terrill, *Lessons of the Iraqi De-Ba'athification Program for Iraq's Future and the Arab Revolutions* (Carlisle, PA: Strategic Studies Institute, 2012) at 13.

11 James P. Pfiffner, "US Blunders in Iraq: De-Baathification and Disbanding the Army" (2010) 25:1 Intelligence and National Security 76 at 76–77.

12 Aysegul Keskin Zeren, "Iraq's Struggle with De-Ba'thification Process" (2017) 29:1 Global Change, Peace & Security 57 at 65.

Ba'ath "party members and collaborators from positions of responsibility," banning them from employment in the public sector in the future; the Order was applicable to those holding the four top layers of positions in the Ba'ath Party. In turn, the latter (No. 2) had even further reaching consequences, ordering the dissolution of Iraq's "army, air force, navy, air defence force, republican and special republican guards, emergency forces, al Quds force, and directorate of military intelligence," as well as the "ministries of defence, information, and state for military affairs," and several different elements of the state security and paramilitary organisations, cancelling all ranks and titles. Only non-senior party members could apply for termination payments, and in a similar vein, war widows and veterans could continue receiving pensions only if the original beneficiary was not a senior party member. Importantly, in regard to both Orders, Bremer and those assigned such power by him could grant exceptions.[13] Moreover, even those who were not party members but worked on one of the top three levels of public administration were required to be interviewed to determine their role in Hussain's regime.[14]

Nota bene, the precise origins of such an approach to lustration are unknown, with Douglas Feith (then US Under Secretary of Defense for Policy), Donald Rumsfeld (then US Secretary of Defense), and the White House and State Department supposedly all involved in the planning, making the decision against the judgement of Jay Garner, the military planners, and the senior CIA officer in Iraq, and without consultation with the Secretary of State, the National Security Advisor, or other officials.[15]

As such, following the introduction of the two Orders, in CPA Order No. 5, the Iraqi de-Ba'athification Council (IDC) was established,[16] reporting directly to Bremer,[17] and in the following week, the Accreditation Review Committees (ARCs) were created to realise the IDC's functions.[18] During this second phase of implementing de-Ba'athification, the investigations were conducted by US civilian staff, who, after a review process and considering all information available, were supposed to "make a factual finding" regarding one's party membership, also informing the person in question of the appeal process before the ARCs, which were composed of one military and two civilian members, one of whom was supposed to be an Iraqi, and had the power of granting exceptions.[19]

Later that year, in November 2003, the CPA transferred the responsibility for the de-Ba'athification process to the provisional government, with Iraqis

13 Zeren, *supra* note 4 at 274–275.
14 Terrill, *supra* note 10 at 14.
15 Pfiffner, *supra* note 11 at 78–80, 85.
16 Zeren, *supra* note 12 at 68.
17 Terrill, *supra* note 10 at 23.
18 Zeren, *supra* note 12 at 68.
19 Zeren, *supra* note 12 at 71.

at the head of all ministries (Iraqi Governing Council, IGC),[20] establishing the Higher National de-Ba'athification Commission (HNDBC). The new regulations stipulated that those dismissed under the Orders "should have been entitled to advance written notification, the opportunity to respond to the notification, and the right to appeal," following which, if verified positively, they would have been reinstated with back pay and, if verified negatively, would retain a right to a further review by the HNDBC.[21]

Unfortunately, these changes remained only "on paper," as Ahmad Chalabi, the aforementioned head of one of the expat organisations, INC, became the head of HNDBC, at the same time extending the scope of de-Ba'athification and making the whole lustration process less transparent. The Commission's power was used as a source of political blackmail,[22] fostering the atmosphere of paranoia in the country with regard to former party members, and undertaking decisions heavily criticised by Bremer.[23] The exception and reinstation procedures were particularly convoluted, with a general lack of due process protections,[24] as well as religious and ethnic politics, analysed in greater detail, a contributing factor in making the decisions.[25]

The situation changed temporarily in August 2004 when Chalabi lost the support of the US and Bremer, which allowed the interim government headed by Ayad Allawi, the head of INA, another exile association supported by the Americans mentioned earlier, to diminish and even revert the process of de-Ba'athification, which he perceived as "undermining the national unity,"[26] particularly at a time of growing insurgency.[27] He was hoping to begin a reconciliation process instead and permit those former party members who did not participate in any abuses of power to return to public administration, even succeeding in limiting the HNDBC's work,[28] but not in disbanding it, as he had hoped.[29]

When Allawi lost power following the 2005 elections, de-Ba'athification returned with force, with the Commission's "powers and pre-eminence . . . immediately reinforced" by the new government headed by Prime Minister Ibrahim al-Ja'afari.[30] Lustration also became enshrined in the new

20 Sissons and Al-Saiedi, *supra* note 8 at 12.
21 Zeren, *supra* note 4 at 275–276.
22 Zeren, *supra* note 4 at 276.
23 Terrill, *supra* note 10 at 24–25.
24 David Pimentel and Brian Anderson, "Judicial Independence in Postconflict Iraq: Establishing the Rule of Law in an Islamic Constitutional Democracy" (2013) 46 The George Washington International Law Review 29 at 46.
25 Zeren, *supra* note 4 at 72–74.
26 Zeren, *supra* note 12 at 276.
27 Sissons and Al-Saiedi, *supra* note 8 at 14.
28 Terrill, *supra* note 10 at 45–47.
29 Zeren, *supra* note 12 at 66.
30 Sissons and Al-Saiedi, *supra* note 8 at 14.

constitution, with article 7 banning the Ba'ath Party and article 135 reaffirming the power of the HNDBC but placing it under the control of the Council of Representatives.[31] It needs to be noted that the Constitutional Assembly and the elections were boycotted by the Sunni minority most affected by de-Ba'athification, as I note in the next subsection.[32]

Three years later, the parliament introduced the Law of the Supreme National Commission for Accountability and Justice, which established the Accountability and Justice Commission in HNDBC's place, with an attempt to make the lustration process more transparent and appealing easier, granting more protection to those exercising their right to do so – but the new law also made it more difficult to receive an exception or be reinstated.[33] Furthermore, the parliament failed to choose the new Commission members in time, allowing the HNDBC Board's members to retain their function, only now under the banner of AJC.[34]

In the following years, de-Ba'athification remained a political tool, becoming an organic part of Iraq's political landscape, used, for example, in an attempt to exclude 511 candidates and ban 15 political parties from running in the 2010 elections, at the same time as AJC members were candidates themselves,[35] or to remove the Iraqi Chief Justice in 2013, who, while later reinstated as a judge at a lower position, was used as an example of the Commission's power over judicial independence.[36] Thus, as Pavel notes, in the case of Iraq, it became difficult to imagine removing "the Feith-drafted, Rumsfeld-advocated, Bremer-initiated, Chalabi-orchestrated, al-Sadr-and-al-Maliki [Iraqi prime ministers following Allawi] revived" lustration process from the hands of the ruling elite,[37] even following Chalabi's ultimate departure from the AJC in 2011.[38]

De-Ba'athification at the Intersections of Law and Memory

Almost two decades after the de-Ba'athification process was initiated, Iraq remained a deeply divided country on social, ethnic, religious and political levels. Furthermore, the three main groups, Shiites, Sunnis, and Kurds, "are themselves fragmented into secular groups, royalists, traditional communities,

31 Zeren, *supra* note 12 at 70.
32 Terrill, *supra* note 10 at 47–48.
33 Zeren, *supra* note 4 at 277.
34 Terrill, *supra* note 10 at 49–50.
35 Sissons and Al-Saiedi, *supra* note 8 at 19–20.
36 Pimentel and Anderson, *supra* note 24 at 48.
37 Ryan Pavel, *The De-Baathification of Iraq: The Development and Implementation of an Ostensibly Necessary Vetting Policy That Turned into a Tool of Sectarianism* (Ann Arbor, MI: University of Michigan, 2012) at 74–75.
38 Sissons and Al-Saiedi, *supra* note 8 at 20–21.

and others," with further fractures added by Hussein's regime and the American occupation.[39]

Importantly, throughout most of its modern history, the different Iraqi governments pursued memory politics of fostering national unity, beginning during the period of monarchy that followed British colonial rule, starting in the 1930s, with the opening of the Museum of Arab Antiquities, set on the promotion of Arabism, and the Museum of National Costumes, linking the Iraqi's past to its present, as well as other cultural institutions (places of memory) with a particular identity-building agenda.[40] Once the monarchy had been toppled in 1958 and a new military regime headed by 'Abd al-Karim Quasim was installed, the national identity-building efforts continued with the initiation of a wide-ranging study of Iraqi folklore, the promotion of popular culture and new symbols based on the country's Mesopotamian past (which were added to the country's flag) and the establishment of "guidance centres" in various parts of Iraq, whereby "the populace was exposed to lectures, films, publications, photography exhibits, and speeches by Qasim himself."[41]

These efforts were continued by the new Iraqi authorities coming from the Ba'athist and Nasirist circles who organised a coup d'état in 1963, then only by the Ba'ath Party following their 1968 coup, and ultimately by Saddam Hussein's regime born in its aftermath since he became president in 1979. This period saw a number of new museums created and old cultural institutions reorganised to both "promote nationalist feelings among Iraqis" and "demonstrate the Ba'ath party's populist character," with an even greater support of popular culture, providing the society with "an ersatz version of Iraqi history and folklore."[42] Furthermore, Hussein endorsed a cult of his personality throughout the country, as his image "became ubiquitous across Iraq," deepened the supposed ties with the Mesopotamian and Islamic past, and, following the perceived win over Iran following the 1980s war, engaged in the construction of numerous monuments dedicated to this victory.[43] While this nation-building project "was accompanied by a vast network of coercive institutions," it nonetheless gave Iraq a common collective memory,

39 David, *supra* note 5 at 366.

40 Eric Davis, "The Museum and the Politics of Social Control in Modern Iraq" in John R. Gillis (ed.), *Commemorations: The Politics of National Identity* (Princeton, NJ: Princeton University Press, 2018) 90 at 94–95.

41 *Ibid.* at 96–97.

42 *Ibid.* at 97–99.

43 Benjamin Isakhan, "Targeting the Symbolic Dimension of Baathist Iraq: Cultural Destruction, Historical Memory, and National Identity" (2011) 4 Middle East Journal of Culture and Communication 257 at 261.

"which went at least some way toward uniting the people behind a cohesive national identity."[44]

De-Ba'athification, however, dramatically changed Iraq's official narrative. As noted earlier, along with lustration, CPA Order No. 1 also initiated the process of removal of symbols and monuments relating to the Ba'athist regime, which, following the initial phase of unstructured destruction – in some cases leading to controversies, as in the case of Iraq-Iran war monuments – was institutionalised in 2007 when the Iraqi government established the Committee for Removing Symbols of the Saddam Era.[45] Together, as a result of these changes, to cite Isakhan, "the entire web of symbolic nation building and the finely fabricated political rhetoric that the Baathist regime had been spinning for decades all but completely unravelled,"[46] also destroying the community ties forged during earlier regimes. As observed in Chapter 1, material carriers of memory are particularly vital in sustaining a group's identity; without them, there was nothing left to support the old official narratives.

The destructive social effect of the symbolic processes of de-Ba'athification was only exacerbated by the consequences of the practical one, with lustration fostering old ethnic and religious divides. While the pervasiveness of Ba'ath Party membership was different in various regions of the country, it was usually lower in Shia-majority areas and higher in Sunni-majority areas, which were "disproportionately represented in the party's patronage and cooptation networks," and as such, the Sunnis occupied "both rank-and-file and lower echelons of party ranks." This resulted in the lustration particularly affecting Sunnis,[47] who perceived it to be a de-Sunnification process,[48] given also that Shias were granted a larger number of exceptions than Sunnis.[49] Such an unearthing of the deeply rooted tensions led to a social separation of Sunnis from Shias and Kurds and their marginalisation in the new regime,[50] ultimately resulting in "widespread sectarian violence" throughout the country, later exacerbated by the rise of Daesh,[51] with ties between ISIS and ex-Ba'athist intelligence officers revealed in 2015.[52]

Importantly, the Iraqi lustration seemed to overlook the fact that party membership during the years of Hussain's regime was often a matter of a

44 *Ibid.* at 275.
45 *Ibid.* at 270–273.
46 *Ibid.* at 260–264.
47 Mako, *supra* note 3 at 482–483.
48 Zeren, *supra* note 4 at 276–277.
49 Terrill, *supra* note 10 at 32.
50 Toby Dodge, "Beyond Structure and Agency: Rethinking Political Identities in Iraq After 2003" (2020) 26 Nations and Nationalism 108 at 115.
51 Michael T. Hamilton, *Imposing Change: Analyzing Lustration Policies in Post-War Iraq and Germany* (Williamsburg, VA: College of William and Mary, 2016) at 77.
52 Zeren, *supra* note 12 at 57–58.

career choice rather than ideological conviction, as some better-paying and higher-level jobs were available only to Ba'ath members.[53] As such, in 2002, 16,5% of Iraqis were affiliated with the party,[54] which meant that the de-Ba'athification led to between 20,000 and 120,000 Iraqis losing their positions, including "doctors, teachers, and other technocrats," along with 500,000 soldiers,[55] which, given the lack of proper replacements, "effectively crippled the country's most important ministries and state institutions,"[56] resulting in 60–75% unemployment by October 2003.[57] At the same time, many Hussein supporters did not rise high in the party, and as such, their jobs were safe,[58] even though they may have been involved in various criminal activities on a lower level.[59]

As a result, no reconciliation could take place in an environment where de-Ba'athification was perceived to only foster "interethnic distrust of foreign-imposed democratisation, which heightened fractionalisation and exclusion at the onset of the transition," becoming rather "a jurisdictional tool for institutionalizing discrimination by previously excluded Shia and Kurdish expatriate elites and the neoconservative architects of the invasion," resulting in a "markedly impeded cross-communal cohesion and reconciliation."[60] As it has been acutely noted, while lustration was "a necessary surgery," with it taking the form of de-Ba'athification, "the patient [the country] died."[61]

Nota bene, one memory aspect of lustration has been noted by the Iraqi policymakers themselves, with a stipulation in article 3.6) of the 2008 Law of the Supreme National Commission for Accountability and Justice that one of the AJC's aims was to "serve the Iraqi memory through documenting the crimes and illegal practices of the elements of the Ba'ath Party," as well as to "provide a database about those elements to be accessible to the public in order to fortify future generations from falling into the clutches injustice, tyranny and oppression."[62] Unfortunately, the lawmakers failed to acknowledge the further reaching aspects of the process, which had such a profound impact on their society.

Looking at the Iraqi de-Ba'athification process from the viewpoint of legal institutions of memory, it certainly fulfilled the main goal of lustration: it

53 Terrill, *supra* note 10 at 20–21.
54 Dodge, *supra* note 50 at 115.
55 Mako, *supra* note 3 at 483–484.
56 Hamilton, *supra* note 51 at 76.
57 David, *supra* note 5 at 367.
58 Terrill, *supra* note 10 at 26.
59 Zeren, *supra* note 12 at 68.
60 Mako, *supra* note 3 at 477.
61 Zeren, *supra* note 12 at 58.
62 Article 16 of the Law of the Supreme National Commission for Accountability and Justice in Chibli Mallat and Hiram Chodosh, *Law in Iraq: A Document Companion* (Oxford/New York, NY: Oxford University Press, 2012) at 954.

ensured that the members of the former regime did not return to power. Introduced by the occupying forces but maintained by successive governments, it was a top-to-bottom mechanism *ad extremum*. Positioning itself as a Durkheimian ritual through its purification function, it had a broad scope and approached its subjects as perpetrators, although not necessarily criminally responsible.

At the same time, however, its use as a political instrument meant that instead of bringing more transparency, lending a *catharsis* effect onto Iraqi society, reinforcing the new regime through the promotion of particular values, and exercising the right to be forgotten on the part of those ex-party members who did not participate in atrocities, it succeeded only in destroying the previous official narrative – proving its role as a medium legal institution of memory. At the same time, it failed to present a viable alternative for the whole community, leaving the Iraqi collective memories at the mercy of various ethnic and religious groups currently in power, as the doctrine of a common national identity seemed to have been collectively forgotten. As I remark in the next section, the Polish lustration, while not taking place in such polarised circumstances, has thus far also failed to achieve its goals of reconciliation.

Medium Institution I in Practice Again: A Never-Ending Story, or the Case of Polish Lustration

The fall of communism in Poland, unlike in many other countries (GDR, Czechoslovakia, Georgia, Armenia, or the Baltic States), did not involve spectacular instances of Durkheimian rituals; as I noted elsewhere, given that the "revolutionary carnival of *Solidarność*" – the Polish "Solidarity" workers' opposition movement – took place in the early 1980s, and it did not happen again in 1989; rather, the changes took the form of a "refolution," a "half-reform, half-revolution," i.e., "a change from the above."[63]

In that, the opposition sat down with the communist authorities in the so-called roundtable negotiations, giving the Communist Party "an opportunity to present itself in a new light and to demonstrate its departure from ideological dogmatism," resulting in its formation of a social-democratic coalition immediately after the transition.[64] Following the astounding win of all but one available place in the first semi-free elections on June 4, 1989, the candidate of opposition, the aforementioned Tadeusz Mazowiecki, became prime minister,

63 Mirosław M. Sadowski, "Collective Memory and Historical Determinacy: The Shaping of the Polish Transition" in Balázs Fekete and Fruzsina Gárdos-Orosz (eds), *Central and Eastern European Socio-Political and Legal Transition Revisited: The CEE Yearbook*, vol. 7 (Frankfurt am Mein: Peter Lang, 2017) 175 at 187–188.

64 Susanne Y. P. Choi and Roman David, "Lustration Systems and Trust: Evidence from Survey Experiments in the Czech Republic, Hungary, and Poland" (2012) 117:4 American Journal of Sociology 1172 at 1184.

while the former head of the communist regime, General Wojciech Jaruzelski, became president. Soon, the disagreements within the Solidarity movement led to the establishment of various political parties on its basis, positioning themselves on different parts of the political scene, often in opposition to one another, with the so-called "war at the top" taking place following the election of Lech Wałęsa, one of the Solidarity leaders, as president in 1990.[65]

Importantly, the Mazowiecki administration did not want to engage with coming to terms with the communist past, focusing on the future, which came to be known as the politics of *gruba kreska* (a thick line), proposed in the speech by the prime minister with regard to the baggage of the economic legacy of the previous regime but later used symbolically to describe a collective forgetting approach adopted by his government.[66] This position, however, soon became untenable, with Poland ultimately settling, like other Central and Eastern European countries, on lustration as the legal institution of memory established to deal with collective trauma-memories.

A Bumpy Road Between Nowhere and Somewhere of Polish Lustration

Given the large number of different concepts and approaches proposed to lustration in the aftermath of the transition in Poland, whose detailed historical analysis remains outside the scope of this book, in this subsection I will focus only on the implemented legal solutions. Thus, I propose to distinguish four phases of the Polish lustration: (1) 1989–1997; (2) 1997–2006; (3) 2006–2015; and (4) 2015–present.

As noted earlier, the initial policy of a future-only focus implemented after 1989, at first supported by the work of the 1990 historians committee (the so-called Michnik commission), which recommended that the communist Ministry of Interior archives not be made publicly available,[67] resulted in the fact that proper vetting affected only the actual members of the former secret services. Out of the 24,000 members, 14,000 "were screened by verification commissions determining whether they were disqualified in the face of law violations or human rights infringements," with 10,349 verified positively and approximately 5,000 hired within the new intelligence services.[68]

65 Carl Tighe, "Lustration – the Polish Experience" (2016) 46 Journal of European Studies 338 at 342–344.

66 Spasimir Domaradzki, "Lustration in Poland" in Marcin Moskalewicz and Wojciech Przybylski (eds), *Understanding Central Europe* (Oxon/New York, NY: Routledge, 2018) 385 at 386.

67 *Ibid.* at 386.

68 Ireneusz P. Karolewski, "Memory Games and Populism in Postcommunist Poland" in Chiara De Cesari and Ayhan Kaya (eds), *European Memory in Populism: Representations of Self and Other* (Oxon/New York, NY: Routledge, 2020) 239 at 243.

The narrow focus of lustration was soon challenged, however, with the first actual attempt at vetting proposed in 1992. On January 31, *Sejm* (the lower chamber of the Polish Parliament) adopted a lustration resolution that bound the interior minister to prepare in a relatively short period of time a list of senior public officials who collaborated with communist secret services (UB, *Urząd Bezpieczeństwa*, and SB, *Służba Bezpieczeństwa*) in the years 1945–1990, including local governors, members of parliament, senators, judges, prosecutors, and councilpersons.[69] The compiled list (known as the Macierewicz List, after the name of the Minister of Interior responsible for its drafting, Antoni Macierewicz) consisted of the names of not only confirmed collaborators but also those only registered as such, including 64 members of parliament and of the government, as well as *Sejm*'s Speaker and then President Lech Wałęsa.[70] Ultimately, the government was dismissed a day later,[71] and the resolution itself was struck by the Constitutional Tribunal, which found it unconstitutional on June 28, 1992, stating that such a vital act should have taken the form of an act of parliament rather than a resolution.[72]

In the following years, a number of different lustration projects were proposed. However, the question gained particular momentum following the 1995 "Olin" Scandal (*afera "Olina"*), which saw then Prime Minister Józef Oleksy accused of having been a Russian spy, resulting in his resignation.[73] In its wake, the second phase of lustration may be distinguished, beginning with the adoption of the Lustration Act on April 11, 1997.[74]

The provisions of the 1997 Act affected approximately 30,000 people,[75] all senior state officials – the president, members of parliament and senators, high-level members of the civil service, judges, members of the Constitutional Tribunal, prosecutors, barristers, and the heads of the public media – requiring that they present an affidavit whether or not they worked or collaborated with the communist secret services between July 22, 1944, and

69 Cecylia Kuta, "Lustracja w Polsce na tle krajów Europy Środkowej" ["Lustration in Poland in Comparison with the Countries in Central Europe"] (2014) 5:11 Horyzonty Polityki 97 at 104–106.

70 Domaradzki, *supra* note 66 at 386–387.

71 Aleks Szczerbiak, "Explaining Late Lustration Programs: Lessons from the Polish Case" in Lavinia Stan and Nadya Nedelsky (eds), *Post-Communist Transitional Justice: Lessons from Twenty-Five Years of Experience* (Cambridge: Cambridge University Press, 2015) 51 at 54–55.

72 Kuta, *supra* note 69 at 105–106.

73 Domaradzki, *supra* note 66 at 387.

74 Ustawa z dnia 11 kwietnia 1997 r. o ujawnieniu pracy lub służby w organach bezpieczeństwa państwa lub współpracy z nimi w latach 1944–1990 osób pełniących funkcje publiczne [The Act of 11 April 1997 on the revealing of work or service with state security organs or collaboration with them in the years 1944–1990 by those holding a public function] Dz.U. 1997 nr 70 poz. 443.

75 Szczerbiak, *supra* note 71 at 56.

May 10, 1990. Collaboration was understood as conscious and secret cooperation with secret services, in which the person actually provided them with certain information. The affidavits would then be checked by the Lustration Court (which first was supposed to be a separate institution composed of 21 different judges, but due to issues with their election, its competences were granted to the Warsaw Court of Appeals, whereby a separate Division V was established to deal with lustration issues),[76] with the process initiated and supervised by the Public Interest Advocate (*Rzecznik Interesu Publicznego*, RIP), upon his analysis of the submitted affidavits as false. Should a person be found to have lied, they lost the right to hold public functions for ten years; however, they may have resigned from the position earlier, which led to a discontinuation of the proceedings, or "request to be recognised as people forced to cooperate under the threat of life or health."[77] Importantly, under the 1997 Act, there were no negative sanctions to those former collaborators who acknowledged their past other than in the court of public opinion.[78]

It is in this second phase of lustration that the aforementioned (in Part II of this book) Institute of National Memory (*Instytut Pamięci Narodowej*, IPN) appeared as an important actor. Established alongside the 1997 Lustration Act, it initially was tasked with guarding the former secret services' archives and regulating public access[79] to the larger number of documents (90 linear kilometres, including files on almost 100,000 collaborators) inherited from the previous regime.[80] As such, journalists, historians, and other researchers were granted unfettered access to the archives, with those who were victims of the secret services allowed to consult their own files.[81] IPN's role soon expanded, however, as the vetting process in Poland entered its next stage.

The third phase of lustration was prompted by the so-called 2002 Rywin scandal (*afera Rywina*), in which film producer Lew Rywin was recorded offering a bribe for arranging changes in the new media law favourable to "the 'group in power,' which wanted to remain anonymous but possibly included" the then-prime minster from the post-communist party. This and other scandals involving the socialist government "were felt to exemplify the corrupt and croneyistic network that had allegedly colonised Polish capitalism and led to calls for more radical lustration," influencing the 2005

76 Kuta, *supra* note 69 at 108–110.

77 Domaradzki, *supra* note 66 at 388.

78 Maciej Chmielewski, "Lustration Systems in Poland and the Czech Republic Post-1989: The Aims and Procedures of Political Cleansing" (2010), online: Theses.cz – Vysokoškolské kvalifikační práce <theses.cz/id/6655ba/104185-205175600.pdf> 1 at 31.

79 Karolewski, *supra* note 68 at 248–249.

80 Tighe, *supra* note 65 at 361–362.

81 Szczerbiak, *supra* note 71 at 56.

elections win by the conservative and liberal parties, which both supported the introduction of a new lustration law.[82]

Adopted on October 18, 2006, and entering into force several months later, the new act[83] proposed major revisions to the lustration process, closing the institutions of the Lustration Court and RIP, instead granting the competence of verifying the affidavits to the newly established lustration department of the IPN, which, in case of finding them inaccurate, would bring the case to a criminal court.[84] Importantly, instead of before the Court of Appeals in Warsaw, the proceedings now take place in the district proper for the domicile of the accused, who were also granted access to the secret chancellery of court in matters relevant to their defence.[85]

In its original version, the 2006 Act would have affected approximately 700,000 people.[86] However, it was severely limited by a 2007 amendment and a Constitutional Tribunal judgement in the same year, with further changes allowing for greater access to the files and modifying the procedure of the elections of IPN authorities introduced in 2010.[87] As such, the documents now made available to the general public include both the files of employees and collaborators of the communist secret services and are anonymised only by request of the victims of surveillance, as well as former employees and collaborators with regard to their sensitive data.[88]

Importantly, in its present form, the 2006 Act obliges those born before August 1, 1972, to submit a lustration affidavit regarding their work or collaboration with the communist secret service between July 22, 1944, and May 10, 1990, including, *inter alia*, the president, members of parliament and senators, holders of key public offices, members of the local government, lawyers, and candidates for these offices. The collaboration needed to have been conscious, secret, and actual. Those found to have lied in their statement would lose said function and the right to hold public functions for 3 to

82 Szczerbiak, *supra* note 71 at 57–58.

83 Ustawa z dnia 18 października 2006 r. o ujawnianiu informacji o dokumentach organów bezpieczeństwa państwa z lat 1944–1990 oraz treści tych dokumentów [The Act of 18 October 2006 on the revealing of information regarding the documents of state security organs from the years 1944–1990 and about the content of these documents] Dz.U. 2006 nr 218 poz. 1592.

84 Kuta, *supra* note 69 at 111–112.

85 Aleksandra Mężykowska, "Wykonywanie przez Polskę wyroków Europejskiego Trybunału Praw Człowieka dotyczących postępowań lustracyjnych" ["The Implementation of the European Court of Human Rights' Judgments by Poland"] (2012) 2 Ius Novum 153 at 154.

86 Chmielewski, *supra* note 78 at 32.

87 Domaradzki, *supra* note 66 at 390.

88 Michał Krotoszyński, *Lustracja w Polsce w świetle modeli sprawiedliwości okresu tranzycji* (Warsaw: Helsińska Fundacja Praw Człowieka, 2014) at 130.

10 years or, in the case of lawyers, be judged by the relevant autonomous bar associations' bodies.[89]

The last, fourth phase of lustration may be distinguished following the 2015 electoral win of the national-conservative Law and Justice (*Prawo i Sprawiedliwość*, PiS) Party – which also authored the 2006 lustration law while in government at that time – and should be regarded as a larger element of their memory politics, the major point of which is a broadly understood decommunisation, which I analyse in greater detail elsewhere.[90] These most recent changes, while not affecting the lustration act itself, impact a number of different legal bills in that they broaden the number of posts from which former security services collaborators are barred. Where previously they (as well as those who worked at UB and SB) were banned only from holding various positions at the IPN as well as in contemporary Polish secret services, following 2015 this catalogue was extended to dozens of other offices, ranging from Supreme Court justices, to university provosts and department heads, to all employees of the National Revenue Administration (*Krajowa Adminsitracja Skarbowa*, KAS), to members of the board of the National Hunting Association (*Polski Związek Łowiecki*, PZŁ), to give just a few examples. As such, in these instances, those admitting to having collaborated, unlike under the previous regulations, are sanctioned not only morally but also legally.[91]

In addition to state lustration, the Catholic Church engaged in lustration on its own, creating a Historical Commission in December 2006.[92] By June 2007, when it finished its term, the Commission found that 13 bishops and up to 15% of the priests were collaborators.[93] Additionally, the phenomena of a "game of dossiers"[94] (*gra teczek*, i.e., dossiers in which the files relating to collaboration were compiled) and of 'wild lustration' may be distinguished in Poland, whereby public accusations of collaboration are used "as a tool for ideological or political struggle, [with] the media uncontrollably exposing alleged 'collaborators' " over the years, affecting three prime ministers and two presidents.[95] The most notable example of this process was the so-called Wildstein list, prepared in 2004 by Bronisław Wildstein and

89 Michał Krotoszyński, "Ustawodawstwo lustracyjne wobec upływu czasu" ["Lustration Laws and the Passage of Time"] (2015) 6 Forum Prawnicze 83 at 91–94.

90 Mirosław M. Sadowski, "Law and Collective Memory in the Service of Illiberalism: Through the Looking-Glass: Transformation or a Reactionary Revolution?" (2021) 1 Krakowskie Studia Międzynarodowe – Krakow International Studies 107 at 118–122.

91 Marta Zięba, "To What Extent Is Lustration an Effective Mechanism of Transitional Justice and Democratic Consolidation? The Case of Polish Lustration Law" (2012) 23:2 Security and Human Rights 147 at 124–129.

92 Domaradzki, *supra* note 66 at 390.

93 Tighe, *supra* note 65 at 352.

94 Idalia Mirecka and Tomasz Sygut, "Medialna gra o teczki" ["The Media Game of Dossiers"] (2005), online: Tygodnik Przegląd <tygodnikprzeglad.pl/medialna-gra-o-teczki/>.

95 Zięba, *supra* note 91 at 150–151.

published online a year later. As a journalist, Wildstein had access to IPN documents and managed to compile a list of approximately 162,000 names on that basis; however, he failed to distinguish between actual collaborators and those people who were "for various reasons, persons of interests for the SB, but not actually recruited agents," thus causing major public outcry.[96]

The Polish Lustration at the Intersections of Law and Memory

As noted by Szczerbiak, "Poland is a case of late (and recurring) lustration."[97] The reason behind this phenomenon is that, much more so than the two previous legal institutions of memory analysed in this chapter, lustration – and the collective memory shift it brings – was particularly instrumentalised in the country, with the post-Solidarity parties more inclined towards its radical forms, whereas those involving former communists largely reserved towards it,[98] with successive governments adopting different approaches to the matters of lustration, ones fitting their larger political agenda.[99]

The issue became so politicised due to high levels of public support. While in Poland "lustration and file access did not, on their own, determine election outcomes,"[100] and in the early 1990s only 37% of Poles supported the removal of former party members from the involvement in public life,[101] ultimately, given that "within the Polish society an equivocal condemnation of the former system existed, which made lustration a rather natural and expected feature of the process of transition,"[102] the pro-transparency stance became more pronounced, with 68% of those surveyed in 1993 in favour of opening the archives of the communist secret services.[103] The support for more radical forms of lustration grew over the years, with 53% in 1999, 56% in 2005, 59% in 2006, and 62% in 2007 supporting the removal of former collaborators from high public offices.[104]

Importantly, Polish lustration is not free from criticism. The court decisions in different cases were noted to be "opaque, inconsistent, and

96 Karolewski, *supra* note 68 at 249.
97 Szczerbiak, *supra* note 71 at 51.
98 Karolewski, *supra* note 68 at 245.
99 Michał Krotoszyński, *Lustracja w Polsce po 2015 r: Zmiana modelu i problemy konstytucyjne* [*Lustration in Poland After 2015: A Change of the Model and Constitutional Issues*] (Warsaw: Helsińska Fundacja Praw Człowieka, 2014) at 133.
100 Szczerbiak, *supra* note 71 at 63.
101 Choi and David, *supra* note 64 at 1184.
102 Domaradzki, *supra* note 66 at 391.
103 Anna Krakus, "Men of Paper: Polish Lustration Law and Its Faulty? Biographical Basis" (2017) 29:3 Law & Literature 485 at 490.
104 Chmielewski, *supra* note 78 at 36–37.

contradictory,"[105] and in several instances, their proceedings were found not to be in accordance with the ECHR by the ECtHR, violating article 6, as the right to a fair trial was not guaranteed during lustration proceedings, with those accused not having enough time and facilities to prepare their defence in the eyes of the Court.[106]

Another major issue in the Polish lustration process is that of the accuracy of the secret services' files on which it is based. As acutely noted by Krakus, "Poland has crossed over Mazowieczki's 'thick line,' but it has brought the work of the SB out of the past and into the present."[107] Importantly, the model of lustration adopted in the country "requires two authentic sources of information – truthful confessions from current office holders, and valid records of earlier collaboration with the communist regime"; however, the communist security services not only "created some entries in the registry that were fake,"[108] but also worked diligently between August 1989 and February 1990 to destroy a number of files, in particular those relating to politicians and the Catholic Church.[109]

As a result, some of the files found in the archives are incomplete or inaccurate, which is most problematic given that their impact goes "beyond the realm of politics and employment law as their findings put personal reputations at stake."[110] Even if "claims of collaboration" are ultimately dismissed, "the alleged exposure of high-ranking officials often leaves an inerasable mark on the public collective memory of the past and creates rival historical accounts."[111]

Nevertheless, in spite of these issues, as Zięba remarks, the lustration process in Poland allowed to expose "the value of truth . . . in a society plagued by generations of denials, cover-ups and lies, where many have a paramount desire to establish exactly what happened," as, importantly, "for those affected by large-scale abuses by the communists, the demand for truth is often more critically felt than the desire for justice."[112] By putting truth on the pedestal, the Polish lustration came close to another legal institution of memory, that of a truth (and reconciliation) commission, rather focusing on uncovering what happened in the past for the whole of society, exercising its

105 Karolewski, *supra* note 68 at 244.
106 Mężykowska, *supra* note 85 at 153.
107 Krakus, *supra* note 103 at 502.
108 Ola Svenonius, Fredrika Björklund, and Paweł Waszkiewicz, "Surveillance, lustration and the Open Society: Poland and Eastern Europe" in Kees Boersma, Rosamunde Van Brakel, Chiara Fonio, and Pieter Wagenaar (eds), *Histories of State Surveillance in Europe and Beyond* (Oxon/New York: Routledge, 2014) 95 at 106.
109 Tighe, *supra* note 65 at 362.
110 Krakus, *supra* note 103 at 492.
111 Zięba, *supra* note 91 at 151.
112 Zięba, *supra* note 91 at 150.

right to be remembered more than the previous regime collaborators' right to be forgotten. Another similarity between the two institutions was noted by Choi and David, who, however, focused on a comparable mechanism of sanctions: only those unwilling to tell the truth and found to have lied will be punished under the Polish lustration system, as in some (e.g., South African) truth (and reconciliation) commissions.[113]

Additionally, with regard to the goal of strengthening the new regime, the Polish lustration, despite all its drawbacks, "provided a transparent, judicial instrument for rooting out those with a vested interest in dishonesty about their past (and instruments to appeal against such a judgment)."[114] However, in spite of the fact that the country's Constitutional Tribunal, as well as the ECtHR and other courts in a number of instances, remarked about a lack of a need for lustration laws in stable democracies, the Polish 2006 Act does not have such a limit.[115] As of June 30, 2021, the IPN received over 466,000 affidavits, of which it managed to analyse approximately 27%, with 111,656 truthful statements, 2,144 concluded court proceedings, and 1,446 affidavits found to be false.[116]

Looking at the Polish lustration from the viewpoint of legal institutions of memory, one may repeat after Svenonius et al. that it "is not only a way to reconcile with the past but also shows that the status of the 'past' itself is problematic. The past here intersects, reminds and disturbs the present and refuses a clear line to be drawn between then and now."[117] In spite of this law and memory chaos they cause, I would argue that lustration laws persist, as, in their role in Durkheimian rituals, they give society a certain sense of security with regard to its communist past, even while it is becoming increasingly distant.

However, following the 2016 uncovering of a number of files taken from the archives of the last communist minister of interior, among which was that of the collaborator "Bolek," i.e., Lech Wałęsa,[118] the social interest in the matters of lustration has diminished. As the discovery of the file seemed to put an end to the long debate as to whether Wałęsa was or was not a collaborator,[119] I would stipulate it also – paradoxically – had a *catharis* effect on the larger Polish society, which, after having its worst suspicions regarding the past confirmed in a symbolic way, while not achieving reconciliation *per se*, was ultimately able to move on from its difficult past, at least with regard to the collective trauma-memories of secret services' collaborators. In

113 Choi and David, *supra* note 64 at 1177.
114 Zięba, *supra* note 91 at 154.
115 Krotoszyński, *supra* note 89 at 95–98.
116 Krotoszyński, *supra* note 99 at 122–126.
117 Svenonius, Björklund and Waszkiewicz, *supra* note 108 at 107.
118 Sadowski, *supra* note 63 at 182–183.
119 Karolewski, *supra* note 68 at 251.

addition, in any case, once people born before August 1, 1972, will cease running for any of the listed positions, the issue of lustration will itself become mute. Nevertheless, the question of combining or replacing lustration with a truth commission in the early 1990s will forever haunt the Polish historiographers. It is on the example of Brazil that this institution of memory is analysed in the next section.

Medium Institution II in Practice: (Never) Too Late for Truth in the Case of Brazilian Commission

Brazil, alongside Bolivia,[120] remains the last of South American countries to engage in coming to terms with the difficult past by establishing a truth commission, *Comissão Nacional da Verdade* (National Truth Commission, hereinafter referred to as the Commission or CNV), with the longest temporal distance between its conception and the period of investigation in the region.[121] Created in 2011 following a long and arduous process, the most important elements of which I analyse in this section, it concluded its work with the publication of its final report in 2014.[122]

The Commission was set up to investigate the crimes of the Brazilian dictatorship (1964–1985), starting with a military coup and the deposition of President João (Jango) Goulart, which was conducted in response to social reforms negatively affecting parts of the middle class and the army,[123] who, in the midst of the Cold War, feared the changes were paving the way for a communist revolution in Brazil.[124] As such, the junta had the backing of the judiciary[125] as well as other vital parts of society, including major national and international capital, with such a high level of social support in certain strata

120 Emmanuel Frías Sampaio, *Politics of Memory of the Recent Past in Brazil: The Federal Government's Role in Constructing Collective Memory Between 2003 and 2016* (San Martín: Global Campus on Human Rights, 2019) at 85.

121 Anthony W. Pereira, "Progress or Perdition? Brazil's National Truth Commission in Comparative Perspective" in Timothy J. Power and Peter R. Kingstone (eds), *Democratic Brazil Divided* (Pittsburgh, PA: University of Pittsburgh Press, 2017) 152 at 157.

122 Janaína de Almeida Teles, "Overcoming the Legacy of the Military Dictatorship Through the National Truth Commission in Brazil: An Ongoing Debate" (2021) 37:1 Portuguese Studies 5 at 5.

123 Iasmin Goes, "Between Truth and Amnesia: State Terrorism, Human Rights Violations and Transitional Justice in Brazil" (2013) 99 European Review of Latin American and Caribbean Studies 83 at 87.

124 Alessandra Gasparotto, Renato Della Vechia, and Marília Brandão Amaro da Silveira, "A Criação Da Comissão Nacional da Verdade e a Luta por Verdade, Memória e Justiça no Brasil" ["The Creation of the National Commission of Truth and the Struggle for Truth, Memory and Justice in Brazil"] (2012) XIII:27 Espaço Plural 84 at 86–87.

125 Marcelo D. Torelly, "Assessing a Late Truth Commission: Challenges and Achievements of the Brazilian National Truth Commission" (2018) 12 International Journal of Transitional Justice 194 at 196.

that Gasparato et al. argue that the regime should be considered military-civil rather than just military dictatorship.[126]

The dictatorship succeeded in keeping up the façade of democracy by allowing the parliament to stay open, permitting a concessionary opposition party to function, conducting elections, and having various generals succeed one another as president of the country. Following the 1968 demonstrations, however, the façade crumbled, as the parliament was temporarily closed, the presidential prerogatives extended, and the *habeas corpus* suspended, followed by purges of various institutions from dissidents. As such, a number of those opposed to the regime turned to revolutionary armed struggle, conducting terrorist attacks and organising guerrilla movements. In turn, the government responded with a strategy of subduing the opposition with torture, killings, and forced disappearances, conducting a military operation against its opponents in the years 1972–1974, with the period later known as *anos de chumbo* (years of lead). At the same time, significant economic success resulted in the general public's continued support of the regime.[127]

Following the years of lead, a slow *distensão* (liberalisation) began, with the return of civil rights, less press censorship, and fewer human rights abuses. As the opposition's calls for amnesty for political prisoners increased, the regime seized this opportunity to pass an amnesty law in 1979, which concerned not only members of armed resistance against the government but also state agents responsible for committing the atrocities. Following major demonstrations in favour of direct presidential elections in 1983 and 1984, the regime agreed for a civilian president to be chosen by the electoral college in 1985, with a new constitution adopted in 1988 and a new, democratically elected president ultimately taking office in 1990.[128] However, given the negotiated nature of the transition, officials appointed by the military regime continued to occupy their posts for a number of years, with, for example, the last Supreme Federal Tribunal (STF, Brazilian Supreme Court) judge selected by the junta to retire only in 2003.[129]

The Long and Winding Road to a Truth Commission

As noted previously, Brazil had to wait for 21 years since a full transition to democracy for a truth commission to be established. This does not mean, however, that there were no earlier attempts at reworking its collective trauma memories. In 1985, a publication titled *Brasil: Nunca Mais* (*Brazil: Never*

126 Gasparotto, Della Vechia, and Amaro da Silveira, *supra* note 124 at 88.

127 Rebecca J. Atencio, *Memory's Turn: Reckoning with Dictatorship in Brazil* (Madison, WI: University of Wisconsin Press, 2014) at 9–10.

128 *Ibid.* at 10–14.

129 Torelly, *supra* note 125 at 197.

Again) emerged, proving on the basis of documents copied from the Supreme Military Court's Archives the systematic use of torture as "a state policy" during the years of the military regime.[130] Moreover, following the inauguration of the democratically elected president, the vast archives of *Departamento de Ordem Política e Social* (Department of Political and Social Order, DOPS) were transferred to their states of origin, and the discovery of a mass grave prompted exhumations that reverberated through Brazilian society.[131]

Soon afterwards, in 1992, the parliamentary *Comissão de Representação Externa de Busca dos Desaparecidos* (Commission of External Representation for the Search of the Disappeared, CREBD) was created, aiding family members of those killed and disappeared by the regime in the search for information about their fate for the next two years.[132] It was followed by the introduction of the Law of the Disappeared in 1995, which acknowledged the state's responsibility for 136 disappearances, granting their families a possibility of reparation, and created the *Comissão Especial sobre Mortos e Desparecidos Políticos* (Special Commission on Political Deaths and Disappearances, CEMDP) tasked with investigating the matter further,[133] ultimately granting reparations to over 500 people and presenting a final report, *Direito à Memória e à Verdade* ("Right to Memory and Truth") in 2007.[134] In addition to its publication, various memorialisation initiatives were proposed as part of "The Right to Memory and Truth" initiative, including a teachers' workshop, a touring exhibition, and construction of several new monuments.[135] It was followed by a 2009 project, *Memórias Reveladas* ("Uncovered Memories"), tasked with collecting the documents from the dictatorship period through the newly established *Centro de Referência das Lutas Políticas no Brasil* (Centre for the Testimomy of Political Struggle in Brazil), housed in the National Archives.[136]

130 Samantha Viz Quadrat, "The Historian's Role, Public History, and the National Truth Commission in Brazil" (2020) 3:2 International Public History 1 at 2.

131 Atencio, *supra* note 127 at 14.

132 Atencio, *supra* note 127 at 15.

133 Goes, *supra* note 123 at 90.

134 Marcelo D. Torelly, "Das Comissões De Reparação à Comissão da Verdade: contribuições da Comissão sobre Mortos e Desaparecidos Políticos (1995) e da Comissão de Anistia (2001) para a Comissão Nacional da Verdade" ["From Reparation Commissions to the Truth Commission: Contributions of the Commission on Political Deaths and Disappearances (1995) and of the Amnesty Commission (2001) to the National Truth Commission"] in Giuseppe Tosi, Lúcia de Fátima Guerra Ferreira, Marcelo D. Torelly, and Paulo Abrão (eds), *Justiça de Transição: Direito à Justiça, à Memória e à Verdade* [*Transitional Justice: The Right to Justice, to Memory and to Truth*] (João Pessoa: Editora da UFPB, 2014) 215 at 235.

135 Nina Schneider, "Breaking the 'Silence' of the Military Regime: New Politics of Memory in Brazil" (2011) 30:2 Bulletin of Latin American Research 198 at 206.

136 Gasparotto, Della Vechia, and Amaro da Silveira, *supra* note 124 at 91 n 20.

Another commission, *Comissão de Amnistia* (Amnesty Commission, CA), was established in 2001, tasked with providing moral and economic reparations to those who were professionally affected, banned, and exiled by the dictatorship, recognising 35,000 cases of political persecution,[137] establishing a considerable archive, and conducting one of the largest reparation programmes in the world during its tenure.[138]

Despite their relevance, the three commissions did not have a mandate to conduct a broad-scale investigation. This paved the way for the establishment of a proper truth commission, only fuelled by the gradual restriction of access to the archives, which took place first in 1991 and then again in 2002,[139] as well as a failure of an interministerial commission created to address the archival issue in 2006.[140] While various approaches towards the question of past atrocities were proposed in the 2000s,[141] with 137 "free conferences" organised on various state levels with 14,000 civil society members, the truth commission idea was ultimately conceptualised during the 2008 National Human Rights Conference[142] and became enshrined in the third National Plan of Human Rights (PNDH-III) in 2009.[143] As such, a committee was formed in 2010, including a representative of the CEMPD, tasked with the delimitation of the legal realms of such a commission.[144]

The establishment of the commission was also influenced by other internal issues, such as Brazil's STF 2010 decision to uphold the 1979 amnesty law as "legitimised by the democratisation process" – while at the same time calling for a new way of resolving the country's difficult past – as well as external factors, most notably the IACtHR decision in the *Gomes Lund* et al. case later that year, in which Brazilian amnesty law was found to be incompatible with the Inter-American system of human rights.[145]

While the first proposal of a truth commission was heavily criticised by various state bodies and organs (from the army to the judiciary to civil servants), a certain "dilution" allowed for the project to be ultimately approved

137 Torelly, *supra* note 134 at 223, 225.
138 Pereira, *supra* note 121 at 154.
139 Goes, *supra* note 123 at 91.
140 Teles, *supra* note 122 at 7.
141 Nina Schneider and Gisele Iecker de Almeida, "The Brazilian National Truth Commission (2012–2014) as a State-Commissioned History Project" in Berber Bevernage and Nico Wouters (eds), *The Palgrave Handbook of State-Sponsored History After 1945* (London: Palgrave Macmillan, 2018) 637 at 638.
142 Nina Schneider, "Truth No More? The Struggle Over the National Truth Commission in Brazil" (2011) 11:42 Iberoamericana 164 at 169.
143 Teles, *supra* note 122 at 11.
144 Torelly, *supra* note 134 at 220.
145 Ramon Rebouças Nolasco de Oliveira and Rafael Lamera Giesta Cabral, "National Truth Commission in Brazil: The Thread of History and the Right to Memory and Truth" (2021) 20 Opinión Juridica 113 at 117–118.

in 2011. The changes included the modification of such terms as "political repression" to "political conflict," as well as a reduction of the temporal and material scope (the seven-person Commission was supposed to investigate gross human rights violations committed in the years 1946–1988 in the period of two years).[146] It was also stressed that the Commission was not to have "a jurisdictional or persecutory character,"[147] thus denying it any punitive measures and putting it in line with other truth commissions. Importantly, to facilitate the commission's work, its establishment was passed along with the Freedom of Information Act (LAI), which declassified any documents relating to human rights violations.[148]

Brazilian National Truth Commission

Beginning its work on May 16, 2012,[149] the Commission was composed of seven members – five lawyers, a political scientist, and a psychoanalyst – with former victims and their family members excluded from sitting on the CNV. While the lack of historians was notable, the Commission soon established an agreement with the Brazilian National History Association (ANPUH), allowing for a number of researchers to collaborate in subgroups and in document management,[150] closely cooperating also with the Brazilian Bar (OAB).[151] Importantly, each of the Commission's 14 thematic groups, headed by at least one commissioner with support staff, was also allowed to liaise with other civil society organisations, to a certain degree operating independently.[152]

The CNV also collaborated with 27 local truth commissions out of over 100 established in its wake,[153] which were convened at trade unions, universities, and municipal and regional government bodies. This greatly aided its works,[154] as they often including former victims among their members[155] and were in a unique position to gather local collective memories as part of their truth-finding work.[156] It also needs to be noted that this phenomenon

146 Schneider and de Almeida, *supra* note 141 at 640.
147 De Oliveira and Cabral, *supra* note 145 at 124–125.
148 Schneider and de Almeida, *supra* note 141 at 641.
149 Goes, *supra* note 123 at 92.
150 Quadrat, *supra* note 130 at 5.
151 Ivo Canabarro, "Caminhos da Comissão Nacional da Verdade (CNV): Memórias em construção" ["The National Truth Commission's Paths: Memories in Construction"] (2014) 69 Seqüência (Florianópolis) 215 at 222.
152 Torelly, *supra* note 125 at 207.
153 Torelly, *supra* note 125 at 207.
154 Schneider and de Almeida, *supra* note 141 at 641–642.
155 Cristina Hollanda, "Brazilian Truth Commissions as Experiments of Representation: Between Impartiality and Proximity" (2019) 55:3 Representation 323 at 333.
156 Canabarro, *supra* note 151 at 223.

of "commissionism" was an unusual rereading of the truth commissions' paradigm,[157] one bringing the legal institution of memory much closer to the people on the ground than in the established model.

Soon after beginning its proceedings, the CNV decided to restrict its temporal scope to the military regime period, despite its broader mandate,[158] and to investigate only the dictatorship's and not the opposition's crimes.[159] Its main goals included the conducting of investigations, humanitarian activities (uncovering the location of bodies), integration activities (the providing of help to the victims of atrocities, as well as the promotion of justice), and forward-looking activities (the promotion of collective memory and "non-recurrence").[160] As such, its purpose related less to the assigning of guilt and more to the "rescue of facts, information, testimonies, and documents" regarding the time of military regime, a promotion of "memory recovery work against definitive oblivion."[161]

During its proceedings, the Commission operated on the basis of the archives of *Brasil: Nunca Mais*, the CEMDP, CA, as well as the 16 million documents declassified from the National Archive, with the facts established by the previous commissions accepted as true[162] – in spite of the fact that the CNV, unlike the previous commissions, did not operate under the assumption of truthful information, which resulted in it's having broader investigative powers.[163] At the same time, the CNV encountered major problems with regard to obtaining confessions from the perpetrators[164] as well as receiving documents from the army, which, despite LAI, always provided "superficial and occasionally contradictory or false" information.[165]

During over two years of operation (its mandate was extended by seven months),[166] the Commission managed to carry "out public meetings; travelled around many states in the country; visited former secret centres of detention, torture, and extermination; created social networks; and periodically released work-in-progress reports."[167] It heard over 1,000 victim testimonies,[168] but with a certain caveat: it treated them as subjective narratives, to a degree

157 Hollanda, *supra* note 155 at 324.
158 Schneider and de Almeida, *supra* note 141 at 640.
159 Henrique Furtado, "On Demons and Dreamers: Violence, Silence and the Politics of Impunity in the Brazilian Truth Commission" (2017) 48:4 Security Dialogue 316 at 326.
160 Sampaio, *supra* note 120 at 86.
161 De Oliveira and Cabral, *supra* note 145 at 133.
162 Torelly, *supra* note 134 at 227.
163 Torelly, *supra* note 134 at 226.
164 Canabarro, *supra* note 151 at 221.
165 Schneider and de Almeida, *supra* note 141 at 641.
166 Torelly, *supra* note 125 at 208.
167 Quadrat, *supra* note 130 at 5.
168 Sampaio, *supra* note 120 at 90.

tainted memories[169] (in a way echoing the Bergsoninan cone of memory analysed earlier in the book) and not documents, recognising the limitations and temporal distance from the investigated events.[170] *Nota bene*, this reliance on documents over testimonials was criticised as uncharacteristic for a truth commission and potentially limited its impact on collective memory.[171]

In addition to its work in uncovering the truth, the Commission also engaged in symbolic changes to the collective memory, including the amendment of the death certificate of Vladmir Herzog, a dissident journalist killed by the regime in 1975 who officially died by suicide[172] – thus exercising his right to be remembered – also conducting a programme to formally designate sites where atrocities were committed as places of memory.[173] The CNV also conducted investigations into the deaths of two pre-junta presidents, although it did not manage to confirm foul play on the part of the regime.[174]

While continuously promoting the results of its work online,[175] the Commission ultimately produced a final report at the end of 2014.[176] It counts 3,383 pages and is divided into three volumes. The first volume presented the history of the dictatorship, establishing beyond doubt a link between the crimes and senior state officials, including the presidents of the dictatorship period. The second volume was devoted to the crimes committed on minorities, such as women, the LGBT, and the rural and indigenous populations. The third volume catalogued crimes against the opposition, with a list of 434 killed or disappeared victims and 377 perpetrators,[177] in turn divided into three categories depending on their level of responsibility for atrocities (direct; politico-institutional; and for the control over procedures or knowledge and support of the systematic abuses).[178] A larger number of the perpetrators, however, remain unnamed due to a lack of sources.[179]

The report also made 29 recommendations, of which only 8 pertained to past atrocities and the others were prospective.[180] The propositions included the request for an official recognition of their responsibility in the crimes by

169 Canabarro, *supra* note 151 at 218.
170 Torelly, *supra* note 134 at 228.
171 Teles, *supra* note 122 at 24.
172 Goes, *supra* note 123 at 92.
173 Mauricio Lissovsky, "The Brazilian Dictatorship and the Battle of Images" (2015) 8:1 Memory Studies 22 at 33.
174 Torelly, *supra* note 125 at 209.
175 Schneider and de Almeida, *supra* note 141 at 642.
176 Colin M. Snider, " 'The Perfection of Democracy Cannot Dispense with Dealing with the Past': Dictatorship, Memory, and the Politics of the Present in Brazil" (2018) 62:1 The Latin Americanist 55 at 55.
177 Schneider and de Almeida, *supra* note 141 at 643.
178 Furtado, *supra* note 159 at 325.
179 Teles, *supra* note 122 at 26.
180 Pereira, *supra* note 121 at 168.

the army and the proposal to suspend the amnesty law, also linking the current violations of human rights with the unresolved issues of the past, proposing a number of changes to the functioning of the military and the police, concluding with a concept of "a body to oversee the implementation of the recommendations." '[181]

Brazil's National Truth Commission at the Intersections of Law and Memory

Over the years, two major memory narratives have appeared in Brazil with regard to the period of dictatorship: that of a revolution against leftist forces that were hoping to turn the country into a "new Cuba"; and that of a coup, an illegal taking of power by force that led to atrocities committed on the opposition members.[182] The latter was further reinforced by the 1979 amnesty, which linked reconciliation with impunity and fostered collective forgetting.[183] The Commission was supposed to produce one official narrative of the events, uncovering the truth for future generations.

In that, as Sampaio notes, it succeeded to a certain degree, having a major "memory component" through the consolidation of "its reports into a new state version of the recent past, which questioned the official versions (of the dictatorial State) up to that time, despite the refusal of military sectors to cooperate."[184] However, the CNV's report did not substantially contribute to the knowledge of the regime's crimes, which, along with a lack of references to the contemporary Brazilian historiography on the dictatorship, means that its direct historical impact will be moderate,[185] its spacious archives notwithstanding.

In contrast, it had a significant impact on collective memory, allowing the non-victimised generations to participate in the collective trauma-memories of the past, with the assembled archives opening the door to "a *sui generis* kind of remembrance of a past not lived, but, at the same time, present in the future by the inevitable historical projections, resulting from narratives which are always selective"[186] – with the process of collective forgetting noticeable in the Commission's official narrative based on, as Furtado poignantly notes, the demons (the military regime) and the dreamers (the opposition)

181 Schneider and de Almeida, *supra* note 141 at 644.

182 Erica S. Almeida Resende and Fabrício H. Chagas-Bastos, "Remembering the Coup, Celebrating the Revolution: Securitization of Memory and Mnemonical Disputes in Brazil" (2021) 7:2 Global Affairs 233 at 236.

183 Furtado, *supra* note 159 at 319.

184 Sampaio, *supra* note 120 at 89.

185 Schneider and de Almeida, *supra* note 141 at 645.

186 De Oliveira and Cabral, *supra* note 145 at 134.

dichotomy, which stretches historical truth, depoliticising the opposition's "practice of resistance as the nonideological defence of the rule of law."[187]

The Commission also successfully dispelled a number of "myths" regarding the junta period, definitively proving senior officials' involvement and confirming that the committed atrocities "were part of a systematic policy by the Brazilian state." However, it faced a number of problems with regard to the popularisation of this and other findings, as its report's dissemination thus far has been modest, all the more so as it did not include a summary and was written in technical legal language.[188]

Another major difficulty for the entrenchment of the CNV's findings in the Brazilian collective memory was the aforementioned "temporal distance" between the Commission and the events in question, which "diluted the political and symbolic impact that the commission could have had on the victims' relatives, on survivors, and, more broadly, on Brazilian society,"[189] given that it "allowed for a dearth of narratives and a subsequent conviviality of silence and conflicting memories" to already stabilise themselves among the general public throughout the years.[190]

This issue became acutely visible when discrepancies were noted between the work of one of the local and the national truth commissions, with the CNV disproving certain claims pertaining to the period of dictatorship but the local narrative holding on, thus showing how difficult it is even for medium legal institutions of memory to affect collective memories on the ground, given that "state-sponsored commissions may narrow the range of permissible lies," but "they may also reinforce long-held myths."[191] This process also shows that not only in the case of lustration, as noted earlier in the book but also in the case of truth commissions, medium legal institutions of memory have the most profound effects if they are implemented directly following a transition.

Nevertheless, at the beginning of its proceedings, which, as noted by Atencio, coincided with a premiere of a film concerning the period of Brazilian dictatorship, the Commission's impact on collective memory was considerable.[192] By 2014, however, the political atmosphere shifted, with, on the one hand, various social groups drawing parallels between the then Brazilian government and the dictatorship period, reinterpreting the images of police violence through the lens of collective memory;[193] and, on the other, growing calls for the rehabilitation of the military dictatorship from parts of the

187 Furtado, *supra* note 159 at 328.
188 Schneider and de Almeida, *supra* note 141 at 645.
189 Teles, *supra* note 122 at 23.
190 Sampaio, *supra* note 120 at 91.
191 Schneider and de Almeida, *supra* note 141 at 642.
192 Atencio, *supra* note 127 at 4–5.
193 Snider, *supra* note 176 at 60–61, 66.

public,[194] fuelled by the reissue of an anti-opposition publication from the 1980s.[195]

Furthermore, in the following years, Brazil failed to comply with the Commission's recommendations,[196] and the military failed to issue a public apology for their role in the atrocities.[197] Ultimately, with the inauguration of Jair Bolsonaro as president in 2019, memory politics regarding the diverging views of the period of dictatorship returned with full force,[198] putting the CNV's short-term legacy into question. It remains to be seen whether President Lula's current third administration will successfully reshape the official narrative. In any case, the Commission's work most definitely did not close the door on Brazil's difficult past, with a recent decision on the federal level to recognise an atrocity from the time of dictatorship as a crime against humanity,[199] only fuelling further debates.

Looking at the Brazilian National Truth Commission from the perspective of legal institutions of memory, while it established a new official narrative, as mentioned earlier, it cannot be said that it allowed Brazil to come to terms with its difficult past. As one of the most recent truth commissions, established a number of years after the events in question, it engaged in innovative practices such as collaboration with local commissions, thus diminishing its limitations as a top-to-bottom institution. At the same time, however, it valued documents over victims – perhaps in an attempt to evade some of the issues surrounding other truth commissions (the deconstruction of victims' memories, for example) – meaning that it lost some of the value of the truth commissions' most important asset with regard to collective memory building, i.e., the exposure of the larger population to haunting testimonies. As such, in the pursuit of truth, the CNV sacrificed some of its power as a social ritual.

While not as politicised at the time of its proceedings as some of its contemporaries, to a certain degree because the granting of amnesty did not rest on a perpetrator's appearance and truthful testimony before the Commission (as it did, for example, in South Africa), the CNV's report did not manage to shift the Brazilian political debate in any major way. It did, however, succeed in reaffirming the victims' right to be remembered, confirming the effectiveness of truth commissions as medium legal institutions of memory.

194 Quadrat, *supra* note 130 at 6.
195 Snider, *supra* note 176 at 63.
196 Schneider and de Almeida, *supra* note 141 at 646.
197 Pereira, *supra* note 121 at 158.
198 Almeida Resende and Chagas-Bastos, *supra* note 182 at 234.
199 De Oliveira and Cabral, *supra* note 145 at 138.

Conclusion: Medium Legal Institutions of Memory in Practice

Following this study of two medium legal institutions of memory, once again employed in very different socio-legal contexts, it should be noted that the previous observations have thus far been confirmed. In practice, each institution somehow diverged from the model: the goals of the Iraqi lustration were ultimately lost among political squabble, which, ironically, put it in the same line as those vetting processes that took place in Central and Eastern Europe, in spite of a very different context, as the next study of Poland showed. However, the latter, in its conciliatory approach, came close to the concept behind truth (and reconciliation) commissions, which in its own way distances it from the model, and the Brazilian Truth Commission, rather than providing a *catharsis* for the victims, worked mostly with documents, valuing them as evidence more than individual memories.

In spite of these differences from the model, which should be expected, the three analyses also proved medium legal institutions of memory to be Durkheimian rituals of law, with a medium level of direct influence of law on their shape, impacted by politics and others in positions of power, which, while making it possible for the various faces of the right to memory to be realised, are in fact rather limited in the realisation of their main goals. Neither in the case of Iraq nor in the cases of Poland and Brazil did reconciliation take place, while the success of vetting itself in the case of the two former ones remains debatable. The next chapter serves as a final check of whether the observations made in the previous parts of the book comport with the results of the analysis of hard legal institutions of memory.

Chapter 8

Placing Hard Legal Institutions of Memory within the New Framework

Introduction

In the closing chapter of Part III, I turn to the two hard legal institutions of memory, legal amnesia and memory legislation. Beginning with the former, I focus on the Portuguese quasi-amnesty following the 1974 Carnation Revolution and the later counter-revolution, which took an atypical form with long-lasting results. While, as mentioned in the Introduction to Part III, Poland did not have any impactful amnesty that would merit an analysis here, the Portuguese case by itself provides a number of insights into not only the legal institution of memory of legal amnesia, but also the intersections of law and memory in general.

In regard to memory legislation, I first analyse the legal framework present in Rwanda, which was introduced in the aftermath of the genocide to prevent its repetition but may be perceived as potentially counterproductive. It is complemented with memory legislation present in Poland, which, while initially following a traditional path, took a particular turn in recent years, with a unique civil law regime currently in place. Together, the three case studies serve as a final step in testing the new law and memory framework proposed in this book.

Hard Institution I in Practice: Forgetting and Evoking with Law, or the Case of Portugal's Legal Amnesia

For a large part of the 20th century, Portugal was ruled by António de Oliveira Salazar as a *Estado Novo* (New State) dictatorship. Salazar became a minister of finance in 1928 following a military coup that brought down the First Republic two years earlier and then assumed full power as prime minister in 1932, with the new regime institutionalised in the 1933 Constitution. He stepped down only in 1968 due to health reasons and died two years later.[1] He was replaced by Marcelo Caetano, who, despite his initial attempts

1 Filipa Perdigão and Alexandre Ribeiro, *The Discursive Construction of Portuguese National Identity in the Media Thirty Years After the 1974 Revolution* (Lancaster: Lancaster University, 2010) at 60–61.

DOI: 10.4324/9781003461548-14

at liberalisation,[2] governed through the period of increased social upheaval[3] until the April 25, 1974, Revolution, the so-called Carnation Revolution (*Revolução dos Cravos*).[4]

The *Estado Novo* regime was focused on fostering nationalist and traditional values of the Portuguese, basing its ideology on "a mythical idea of nation and national interest" with a goal of recreating the people and establishing a "new order" to "end the liberal century" in Portugal through the lack of political freedom (single-party regime), no freedom of expression (censorship), and presence of political police,[5] the infamous *Polícia de Informação e Defesa do Estado* (Information and State Defence Police, PIDE), since 1968 known as the *Direcção Geral de Segurança* (Directorate General of Security, DGS).[6] An important part of this ideological programme was maintaining the connection with the country's colonies, regarded as a vital component of the nation, and as such, the regime engaged in a major war effort to prevent them from gaining independence, starting with the war in Angola in 1961, soon followed by fighting in Guinea-Bissau and Mozambique.[7]

Importantly, in spite of political repression (over 30,000 political prisoners throughout the period of the dictatorship)[8] and economic difficulties that contributed to the mass emigration of up to 20% of the population in the years before the revolution, only fuelled by the 1973–1974 oil crisis,[9] it is the military conflict on "three fronts" that saw over 900,000 Portuguese drafted into the army[10] and 43% of the public finances dedicated to the

2 Guya Accornero, "'Everything Was Possible': Emotions and Perceptions of the Past Among Former Portuguese Antifascist Activists" (2019) 24:4 Mobilization: An International Quarterly 439 at 439.

3 Raquel da Silva and Ana Sofia Ferreira, "The Post-Dictatorship Memory Politics in Portugal Which Erased Political Violence from the Collective Memory" (2019) 53 Integrative Psychological and Behavioral Science 24 at 29.

4 Robert M. Fishman and Manuel Villaverde Cabral, "Socio-Historical Foundations of Citizenship Practice: After Social Revolution in Portugal" (2016) 45 Theory and Society 531 at 536.

5 da Silva and Ferreira, *supra* note 3 at 28.

6 See: Irene Flunser Pimentel, *O caso da PIDE/DGS: Foram julgados os principais agentes da Ditadura portuguesa?* [*The Case of PIDE/DGS: Were the Forefront Agents of the Portuguese Dictatorship Judged?*] (Lisbon: Temas e Debates-Círculo de Leitores, 2017).

7 Perdigão and Ribeiro, *supra* note 1 at 61–62.

8 Filipa Raimundo and António Costa Pinto, "From Ruptured Transition to Politics of Silence: The Case of Portugal" in Nico Wouters (ed.), *Transitional Justice and Memory in Europe (1945–2013)* (Cambridge: Intersentia, 2017) 173 at 175.

9 Charles Downs, *Revolution at the Grassroots: Community Organizations in the Portuguese Revolution* (Albany, NY: State University of New York Press, 1989) at 15.

10 Manuel Loff, "Coming to Terms with the Dictatorial Past in Portugal After 1974: Silence, Remembrance and Ambiguity" in Stefan Troebst (ed.), *Postdiktatorische Geschichtskulturen in Süden Und Osten Europas: Bestandsaufnahme und Forschungsperspektiven* [*Post-Dictatorial Historical Cultures in Southern and Eastern Europe: Catalogue and Research Perspectives*] (Göttingen: Wallstein Verlag, 2010) 55 at 109.

war effort.[11] This is considered to be the main reason as to why the 1974 Revolution broke out – as Schmitter notes, leaving the "impending" military defeat aside, the fall of the regime was not inevitable in that particular moment, with a lack of any major "mobilisation of civil society" before the transition.[12]

The legal and political changes in the years that followed merit a closer investigation, given that they were first revolutionary and then reactionary, with a major programme of legal amnesia and collective forgetting, in which various Portuguese governments have engaged up to this day, thus establishing a particular official narrative regarding the past. First, however, despite its influence on the breaking out of the Revolution, as well as a major impact the decolonisation process has had on Portuguese collective memory[13] – while itself becoming, paradoxically, collectively forgotten (as de Medeiros notes, "it is as if in the rush to put the past behind it, the nation had decided simply to forget the wound at the base of both its past and present conditions")[14] – it remains outside the scope of this section given that it is not directly connected with the legal institution of memory in question.

Legal Amnesia in Portugal Between Revolution and Reaction

While it is also not the point of this section to closely analyse the events of the 1974 Revolution, as it will be focused rather on its legal, political, and social ramifications, it nevertheless needs to be briefly introduced. The Carnation Revolution can be divided into four major periods: (1) April to September 1974, which started with the Revolution and ended with a resignation from the presidency of one of its more conservative leaders, António de Spínola, seeing first changes to the political (purges) and economic (nationalisations) systems of the country; (2) October 1974 to March 1975, which saw increased activity of a large number of both the previously clandestine and the newly established political parties, as well as an escalation of strikes calling for a major economic shift, ending with an unsuccessful coup of the right-wing military; (3) March to November 1975, which saw nationalisation of

11 Paulo de Medeiros, "Hauntings: Memory, Fiction and the Portuguese Colonial Wars" in Timothy G. Ashplant, Graham Dawson, and Michael Roper (eds), *Commemorating War* (New Brunswick, NJ: Transaction Publishers, 2009) 201 at 203.

12 Philippe C. Schmitter, "The Democratization of Portugal in Its Comparative Perspective" in Fernando Rosas (ed.), *Portugal e a Transição para a Democracia (1974–1976)* [*Portugal and Transition to Democracy*] (Lisbon: Edições Colibri/Fundação Mário Soares/Instituto de História Contemporânea da Faculdade de Ciência Socias e Humanas de Universidade Nova de Lisboa, 1998) 337 at 340–341, 360.

13 Loff, *supra* note 10 at 112.

14 de Medeiros, *supra* note 11 at 201.

major domestic companies in various economic sectors, free elections to the Constituent Assembly – won by moderate parties – and the completion of the decolonisation process, as well as an increased polarisation of the society, culminating in the so-called "hot summer" with a number of political clashes around the country, in turn resulting in the centre-left and right-wing parties joining forces to diminish the influences of the Communist Party; (4) and November 1975 to June 1976, beginning with a counter-coup on November 25 as the moderate government "went on strike" and demanded that the military establish the conditions for them to govern freely, which later succeeded in the calming of public moods. This was followed by parliamentary elections in April 1976, won once again by moderate parties, a new constitution, which entered into effect at that time, and, ultimately, the June presidential elections won decisively by one of the military leaders of the November coup, General António Ramalho Eanes.[15] A fifth, post-revolution period may also be distinguished, during the years 1976–1982, with further cooperation between moderate parties, also engaging in the official disbanding of some of the socialist and revolutionary legacies of the constitution, ending with its major revision in 1982.[16]

Of particular interest to my analysis is the question of purges, taking place with regard to the real and perceived members and supporters of the *Estado Novo* regime during the revolution, as well as their reversal through the acts of legal amnesia in the post-revolutionary period. Importantly, in 1974 and 1975, purges affected all parts of the country's life: the government, the military, the secret police, the civil service, the courts and public education, as well as the private sector, all taking different forms. This policy was then reversed in general after 1976, as the new governments instigated a process of "reconciliation and pacification,"[17] based not on typical broad amnesties but on a concept of reintegration or the return of those affected to public life.

The first dismissals, instigated by the National Salvation Committee (Junta da Salvação Nacional, JNS), i.e., the seven generals in power in the immediate aftermath of the revolution,[18] affected the regime's government – the president, prime minister and ministers, single-party leaders, civil governors, and members of parliament – through Law 1/74, Law 170/74, and Decree Law 172/74 of April 25, 1974, and Law 2/74 of May 14, 1974.[19] The most senior officials were allowed to go into exile with their families, first on the

15 Downs, *supra* note 9 at 16–33.

16 António Costa Pinto, "Coping with the Double Legacy of Authoritarianism and Revolution in Portuguese Democracy" (2010) 15:3 South European Society and Politics 395 at 403.

17 António Costa Pinto, "Authoritarian Legacies, Transitional Justice and State Crisis in Portugal's Democratization" (2006) 13:2 Democratization 173 at 191.

18 Raimundo and Costa Pinto, *supra* note 8 at 177.

19 Raimundo and Costa Pinto, *supra* note 8 at 178.

island of Madeira and then in Brazil,[20] while those who stayed in most cases faced only the loss of their political rights.[21]

Various institutions of the regime were dissolved, in some cases with political actions coming before appropriate legislation, with the National Assembly, the single party, the militia organisations such as the Portuguese Legion (Legião Portuguesa, LP) and Portuguese Youth (Mocidade Portuguesa, MP), the censor and the political tribunals, and the Corporatist Chamber among those affected.[22] Furthermore, in regard to the local government, one of the organisations linked to the Communist Party removed members of the former regime from their posts, taking over city councils. This was followed by more institutionalised nominations of provisional administrative commissions by the JSN later in 1974, who came from different political parties.[23]

Importantly, following the fall of the regime, Portuguese political life had to be established anew, with a particular concern that no one associated with *Estado Novo* was included in the political parties. Nevertheless, one of the right-wing parties was almost delegalised,[24] while those individuals with links to the regime on the local level were not allowed to stand in the first elections.[25] However, already in 1978, the former regime's dignitaries were permitted to return, with an unfreezing of accounts of its last president, who, unlike Marcelo Caetano, also given this opportunity, chose to come back from Brazil.[26] Ultimately, only one of the former interior ministers was sentenced to ten months in prison, while another was found innocent, and other government members who were initially detained were set free without a trial.[27]

In regard to the military, first purges were initiated by the *Movimento das Forças Armadas* (Armed Forces Movement, MFA), the organisers of the April coup; these affected 60 generals who publicly supported the *Estado Novo* regime in the build-up to the revolution, putting them on reserve.[28] Soon afterwards, special military commissions were put in charge of more institutionalised purges by Decree Law 775/74,[29] with 300 officers placed on reserve by the end of 1974, followed by a removal of those close to General Spínola

20 Costa Pinto, *supra* note 16 at 398.
21 Raimundo and Costa Pinto, *supra* note 8 at 178.
22 Costa Pinto, *supra* note 16 at 398.
23 Costa Pinto, *supra* note 17 at 181, 185.
24 Costa Pinto, *supra* note 17 at 177.
25 António Costa Pinto, "Settling Accounts with the Past in a Troubled Transition to Democracy: The Portuguese Case" in Alexandra Barahona De Brito, Carmen Gonzalez Enriquez, and Paloma Aguilar (eds), *The Politics of Memory and Democratization* (Oxford: Oxford University Press, 2001) 66 at 69.
26 Raimundo and Costa Pinto, *supra* note 8 at 188–189.
27 Pimentel, *supra* note 6 at 538–539.
28 Costa Pinto, *supra* note 17 at 176, 180.
29 Raimundo and Costa Pinto, *supra* note 8 at 179.

after the unsuccessful March 1975 right-wing coup, and ultimately also of those linked to the far left after the November 1975 moderate counter-coup (many of whom chose to leave the country for Angola and Mozambique, which were already socialist regimes by that time), with, ultimately, a new generation of officers taking higher offices in the army.[30]

In addition to the military, the question of the political police was of particular and symbolic importance. Following its dissolution in Portugal (it continued to exist in colonies under the name Military Information Police for some time), up to 1,000 former PIDE/DGS agents were arrested by the military through the Comando Operacional do Continente (Operation Command for Continental Portugal, COPCON),[31] while others left the country. To prosecute them, the new government established the *Comissão de Extinção da PIDE – DGS, MP* and *LP* (Commission for the Abolition of the Political Police, Portuguese Legion and Portuguese Youth, CEPML), which proceeded with the arrests and detained the police's collaborators.[32] Further institutionalisation of this issue came in July 1975, when Constitutional Law 8/75 criminalised PIDE/DGS,[33] establishing military tribunals that were to judge former political police agents, as well as members of government overseeing them, with no statute of limitations and sentences ranging from 2 to 12 years.[34]

Once the revolution reached its fourth stage, however, Law 18/75 ordered a release on parole of the former PIDE/DGS officers under arrest, giving those already sentenced by the military a right to an appeal to the Supreme Court. The trials of those who had not yet been sentenced began at the end of 1976, already in the "reconciliation period," and became known as show trials, given that they were "meant to silence the voices of those who demanded justice," instead of delivering actual justice. The judgements were reached on the basis of the time of employment, whether or not an agent worked in the colonies, and character letters, with much lighter sentences than initially prescribed under Law 8/75, varying from recognition of time served as punishment, to one month to two years of imprisonment, often further reduced by short-term pardons or following an appeal to the Supreme Court.[35] Of 344 identified as collaborators, most were sentenced to between two and four months of prison, with time served counted towards their punishment, or a loss of political rights.[36] By 1978, former PIDE/DGS agents who did

30 Costa Pinto, *supra* note 25 at 75.
31 Raimundo and Costa Pinto, *supra* note 8 at 182.
32 Costa Pinto, *supra* note 17 at 180.
33 Pimentel, *supra* note 6 at 535.
34 Costa Pinto, *supra* note 25 at 73.
35 Raimundo and Costa Pinto, *supra* note 8 at 185–186.
36 Pimentel, *supra* note 6 at 539–540.

not commit crimes even had their rights as public employees restored by relevant institutions.[37]

With regard to bureaucracy, in Decree 277/74, the new authorities created the *Comissão Inter-Ministerial de Saneamento e Reclassificação* (the Inter-Ministerial Purge and Reclassification Commission, CIMSR), which coordinated the spontaneous purges that had already taken place in some ministries and began new ones in others by establishing local purge commissions.[38] The civil servants were subject to punishment ranging from a transfer to another post to dismissal, with the harshest penalties affecting those closest to the regime as well as collaborators with the political police. However, the mechanism was uneven and varied from institution to institution: the least affected were the Ministries of Justice and of Foreign Affairs, while the Ministries of Labour and of Education were subject to the broadest purges.[39] In total, approximately 20,000 civil servants were subject to some kind of sanction.[40]

In regard to the judiciary, out of 500 judges, 42 were purged, either forcibly retired or dismissed. Some of them were returned to their positions in 1977, however, by CARSR (a general reintegration commission, which I introduce in greater detail later in this subsection), and two of these were later nominated to the Supreme Court.[41]

The education system was also subject to a purge process, with JSN removing those in managing positions at the universities from their functions, as well as creating purge commissions composed of notable professors, schoolteachers, and writers. In some cases, however, the changes were affected by a particularly mobilised student movement that would deny institutional access to some instructors, be that at a university or a secondary school level. This led a number of professors to emigrate to Brazil, whereas many others became involved in the establishment of private universities.[42]

In general, with regard to the civil service and education sector, in the post-revolution period, the role of purge commissions was taken on by *Conselho da Revolução* (Council of the Revolution, established in place of the JSN in 1975), which engaged in the process of rehabilitation and reconciliation, either returning the majority of those dismissed to their former posts (transferring them to different institutions in cases of social backlash; however, at some universities, reintegration did not begin until the early 1980s) or changing their dismissal to compulsory retirement, with seniority restored and lost payments returned.[43]

37 Raimundo and Costa Pinto, *supra* note 8 at 188.
38 Costa Pinto, *supra* note 17 at 181–182.
39 Costa Pinto, *supra* note 17 at 183–185.
40 Costa Pinto, *supra* note 25 at 74.
41 Costa Pinto, *supra* note 25 at 77.
42 Costa Pinto, *supra* note 17 at 184–185.
43 Raimundo and Costa Pinto, *supra* note 8 at 177, 188.

The private sector was also affected by the purges, with workers organised in the *Comissões de Trabalhadores* (Workers' Commissions),[44] particularly in large, basic industry companies, rallying against industrialists and managers. This especially affected "upper middle class owners and managers" working in the Lisbon area, who often emigrated, either on their own volition or as a consequence of being forced out of their jobs.[45] Ultimately, over 50% of industrialists in the largest companies, 43% of those in larger firms, and 15% of those in small enterprises left, with professional managers the most affected and owners the least affected.[46] Purges in the private sector became institutionalised only with Decree Law 52 from 1976, which gave two of a number of commissions legal status but put them under the competence of a main commission directing bureaucratic purges, which by then was already tasked with reintegration of those unjustly removed from their posts, resulting in the return of many industrialists from Brazil to Portugal in the years 1976–1980.[47]

Importantly, the reintegration process in general became institutionalised in Decree Law 471 in 1976, which was one in the series of legislation "designed to facilitate the return of exiles and business administrators who had been forced out by the purges," stating that illegal purges in both the public and private sectors "were legally null and void."[48] It was followed by the establishment of the *Comissão de Análise de Recursos de Saneamento e de Reclassificação* (Commission for the Assessment of Purge Appeals and Reclassification, CARSR) by Decree Law 117–1/76, which, working until the mid-1980s, rehabilitated "the vast majority of appellants."[49] As a result of this process, by 1995, a large number of *Estado Novo* government appointees and collaborators "returned to political and economic power."[50]

Portuguese Legal Amnesia at the Intersections of Law and Memory

Collective memory processes in Portugal following the dictatorship may be divided into two phases: the 1974–1976 period of memory evoking, where various counter-memories from the times of the regime, in particular of the

44 Costa Pinto, *supra* note 17 at 182.

45 Nancy Bermeo, "Redemocratization and Transition Elections: A Comparison of Spain and Portugal" (1987) 19:2 Comparative Politics 213 at 220–221.

46 Costa Pinto, *supra* note 16 at 400–402.

47 Costa Pinto, *supra* note 25 at 80.

48 Costa Pinto, *supra* note 17 at 192.

49 Raimundo and Costa Pinto, *supra* note 8 at 187.

50 Manuel Loff, "Dictatorship and Revolution: Socio-Political Reconstructions of Collective Memory in Post-Authoritarian Portugal" (2014) 3:2 Culture and History Digital Journal 1 at 6.

opposition towards it and its political repression,[51] came to light;[52] and the post-1976 period of fostering reconciliation, epitomised by the different acts of legal amnesia introduced during that time. It is the latter's continued influence that lays at the basis of what came to be known as the "double legacy" of contemporary democratic Portugal, built not only on the heritage of *Estado Novo*'s authoritarianism, but also of "the authoritarian threat of the left of 1974–1975,"[53] with the Revolution for years described as the main reason behind Portugal's economic problems by parts of the political elite.[54]

As such, while the current Portuguese official narrative was established around the "ritual commemoration" of the Revolution's anniversary, various political parties began stressing different events as the fundament of modern Portugal, ranging from the free April 1975 elections to the November 1975 counter-coup, but not, with the exception of the Communist Party,[55] the Revolution itself – with all political actors actively engaging in memory politics with regard to their respective electorates.[56] This meant that by the early 1990s, "there was a clear devaluation of the memory of resistance to the dictatorship, both regarding its peaceful and violent components."[57]

At the same time, the weakening of the collective memory of the Revolution depreciated Salazar's regime,[58] the memories of which were further softened "by the state, the media, and certain trends in historiography."[59] Ultimately, the discussions regarding the *Estado Novo* became intrinsically linked with debates on the Revolution, which fostered collective forgetting,[60]

51 Manuel Loff and Luciana Soutelo, "Dictatorship and Revolution Disputes Over Collective Memory in Post-Authoritarian Portugal" in Hugo García, Mercedes Yusta, Xavier Tabet, and Cristina Clímaco (eds), *Rethinking Antifascism: History, Memory and Politics, 1922 to the Present* (New York, NY: Berghan Books, 2016) 300 at 304.

52 Da Silva and Ferreira, *supra* note 3 at 35.

53 Costa Pinto, *supra* note 25 at 84.

54 Loff and Soutelo, *supra* note 51 at 306.

55 Costa Pinto, *supra* note 16 at 405.

56 Filipa Raimundo and Claudia Generoso de Almeida, "The Legacy of the Portuguese Transition to Democracy: April-Warriors Versus November-Warriors" in Maria Elena Cavallaro and Kostis Kornetis (eds), *Rethinking Democratisation in Spain, Greece and Portugal* (Cham: Palgrave Macmillan, 2019) 45 at 65.

57 da Silva and Ferreira, *supra* note 3 at 36.

58 Sónia Vespeira de Almeida and Sónia Ferreira, "Dictatorships and Revolutions in Portugal and Chile: Ethnography, Memory and Invisibilities" (2015) 26:5 History and Anthropology 597 at 607.

59 Joana Craveiro, "'A Living Museum of Small, Forgotten and Unwanted Memories': Performing Oral Histories of the Portuguese Dictatorship and Revolution" in Rina Benmayor, María E. Cardenal de la Nuez, and Pilar Domínguez Prats (eds), *Memory, Subjectivities, and Representation: Approaches to Oral History in Latin America, Portugal, and Spain* (Houndmills: Palgrave Macmillan, 2016) 207 at 221.

60 Loff, *supra* note 50 at 7, 10.

revisionism,[61] and even negationism, with attempts at rehabilitating the dictatorship.[62] Furthermore, while victims and oppositions of the regime ultimately became eligible for material and symbolic reparations,[63] remembrance in the public sphere remains slender and mostly symbolic, rather than a result of a structural policy, whether one looks into changes to the names of buildings, street names, or museums,[64] which further promotes collective forgetting.

An example of this phenomenon is the 1999 exhibition commemorating 25 years since the Revolution organised by the left-wing government, where while the regime of *Estado Novo* was meticulously portrayed, the events of the transition were conspicuously absent. As Costa Pinto notes, "it would have been very hard for an official exhibition to deal with the transitional period given the complex legacy of the first two years of the transition."[65] In a similar vein, the right-wing government organised the 30th anniversary of the revolution five years later under the slogan "April Means Evolution," which shifted the focus from commemorations to the debate as to whether the Revolution or the post-Revolution period should be recognised as the founding period of present-day Portugal.[66] It was only more recently that the symbols of the Revolution returned more broadly during anti-austerity protests;[67] however, with such levels of collective forgetting already present in the country, one needs to question their role as effective memory carriers.

Throughout the years, several events took place that had the potential for a collective memory shift, one of which could impact the official narrative. These included the 1992 scandal of granting a pension to former political police agents, while it was denied to some members of the resistance to the

61 Luciana de Castro Soutelo, *A memória pública do passado recente nas sociedades ibéricas: Revisionismo histórico e combates pela memória em finais do século XX* [*The Public Memory of the Recent Past in the Iberian Societies: Historic Revisionism and Fights for Memory at the End of the 20th Century*] (Oporto: Universidade do Porto, 2015) at 510.

62 Raquel Varela, "Conflito ou coesão social? Apontamentos sobre história e memória da Revolução dos Cravos (1974–1975)" ["Conflict or Social Cohesion? Notes on the History and Memory of the Carnation Revolution (1974–1975)"] in Raquel Varela (ed.), *Revolução ou Transição? História e Memoria da Revolução dos Cravos* [*A Revolution or a Trnsition? History and Memory of the Carnation Revolution*] (Lisbon: Bertrand Editora, 2012) 185 at 186–187.

63 Raimundo and Costa Pinto, *supra* note 8 at 191–193.

64 Pimentel, *supra* note 6 at 558.

65 Costa Pinto, *supra* note 16 at 407.

66 Varela, *supra* note 62 at 189.

67 Britta Baumgarten, "The Children of the Carnation Revolution? Connections Between Portugal's Anti-Austerity Movement and the Revolutionary Period 1974/1975" (2017) 16:1 Social Movement Studies 51 at 56–57.

Estado Novo;[68] the unseemingly 1994 TV debate that put together a former political prisoner turned historian, a revolutionist, and an ex-PIDE/DGS member;[69] the 2005 widely attended funeral of a historic Communist Party leader;[70] and the surprising results of the 2007 "Great Portuguese" TV show that saw Salazar not only make it to the final, where he was audaciously "defended" by a notable political scientist, but also win the contest.[71] However, none of these events "has been particularly divisive within Portuguese society,"[72] a testament to the degree to which memories of *Estado Novo* have become "diluted": although collective forgetting of the time of dictatorship "has not been complete, one can talk more of a memory shortage than an excess of memory."[73]

Importantly, the processes of collective forgetting were also strengthened by a lack of a single, potent official narrative regarding the period of the Revolution, only amplified by a myriad of individual memories of the event available in the public sphere in the form of biographies or documentaries, whose presence, in a way filling the official void of remembrance, resulted in a certain distancing of the Portuguese society from the events in question. As Ramos Pinto poignantly notes, most often in the case of the April 25 Revolution:

> the people appear as a victim (of poverty, of repression, of the war) in the name of which "the revolution is made." Even this grammatical articulation – that "the revolution is made" – using a verb without a subject shows us a past in which the collective appears nebulous, amorphic, merely vaguely related to the event that has done itself, by the hands of all and by the hand of no one. In this fog of memory, the same few figures who personalise the events reappear, overshadowing other subjects.[74]

68 Manuel Loff, "Estado, democracia e memória: Póliticas públicas e batalhas pela memória da ditadura portuguesa (1974–2014)" ["The State, Democracy and Memory: Public Politics and Battles for Memory of the Portuguese Dictatorship (1974–2014)"] in Manuel Loff, Filipe Piedade, and Luciana Castro Soutelo (eds), *Ditaduras e revolução: Democracia e políticas da memória* [*Dictatorships and Revolution: Democracy and Politics of Memory*] (Coimbra: Edições Almedina, 2015) 23 at 90–92.

69 *Ibid.* at 93–98.

70 Loff, *supra* note 10 at 105.

71 Loff, *supra* note 68 at 113–114.

72 Costa Pinto, *supra* note 16 at 408.

73 Pimentel, *supra* note 6 at 557.

74 Pedro Ramos Pinto, "'Onde estavas tu no 25 de abril, pá?' Revolucionários, movimentos sociais e cidadania quotidiana" ["'And Where Were You on the 25th of April, eh?' Revolutionaries, Social Movements and Everyday Citizenship"] in José Neves (ed.), *Quem faz a história: Ensaios sobre o Portugal contemporâneo* [*Who Makes History: Essays on Contemporary Portugal*] (Lisbon: Tinta-da-China, 2016) 49 at 49–51.

The phenomena of collective forgetting were likely influenced by the singularity of Portuguese society, whose "social cohesion and dynamic development," as de Sousa Santos notes, "is premised upon the reproduction of unstable equilibria between highly heterogenous and dissociated social, economic, political, and cultural processes, many of them inscribed in the history of the country."[75] As Lourenço argues, the Portuguese identity remains deeply rooted in the country's long-gone imperial past, the collective memory of which is considered "above all to explain why contemporary Portugal, and in particular that after April 25, has lived . . . without notorious historical and cultural trauma."[76] However, I would argue that they were also strengthened by the different instances of legal amnesia employed in the aftermath of the Revolution.

The importance of this legal institution of memory on the current shape of Portuguese collective memory cannot be overstated. As Pimental notes, "in the memory of that period of the majority of the Portuguese who lived through these events, there remains – and with good reason – the feeling that no member of the political police was arrested, tried or convicted."[77] I would argue, however, that the effect of various acts of legal amnesia acts reached much further than just with regard to the memory of the fate of the former PIDE/DGS agents. In fact, through reconciliation they initiated, they fostered major changes to collective memory of the *Estado Novo* regime, the tumultuous character of the Revolution, and the particularities of the decolonisation process.

The nature of Portuguese legal amnesia, which took the particular form of reintegration, is difficult to categorise. It clearly took the form of bans on the legal memory, ones re-writing the classification of the *Estado Novo* regime's crimes assumed during the Revolution. At the same time, these acts do not constitute an amnesty, as they were individual, often political decisions made by a variety of different state and military bodies in the process, also very different from that of lustration. They cannot be categorised as pardons either, given that they were a result of a general, *en masse* reconciliation policy pursued by consecutive governments since 1976, lending them a quality of a social ritual, which pardons notably lack, as mentioned earlier in this book. The Portuguese process of PTR (purge then reintegration) cannot also be easily categorised as reactionary, given that its focus was building a solid social basis for a democratic Portugal rather than the return of *ancien régime*.

75 Boaventura de Sousa Santos, "State and Society in Portugal" in Helena Kaufman and Anna Klobucka (eds), *After the Revolution: Twenty Years of Portuguese Literature, 1974–1994* (Lewisburg, PA/London/Cranbury, NJ: Bucknell University Press/Associated University Presses, 1997) 31 at 64.

76 Eduardo Lourenço, *Nós é a Europa ou as duas razões* [*We Are Europe, or the Two Reasons*] (Lisbon: Imprensa Nacional/Casa da Moeda, 1994) at 11.

77 Pimentel, *supra* note 6 at 542.

Importantly, the ensuing extensive process of collective forgetting – confirming the hard character of this legal institution of memory – promoted by the post-Revolution elites engaging in memory politics (aided in that by the general particularity of the country's identity), allowed the Portuguese legal amnesia to play a major role in not only an (ultimately) peaceful transition to democracy but also to lead to a permanent reunification of the society, one based both on the victims' right to be remembered, albeit mostly on the individual level, and the collectivity's right to forget the difficulties of the past. While the historical truthfulness of the Portuguese official narrative to a certain degree suffered as a result, the post-Revolution stability of the country is a testament to legal amnesia's effectiveness as a legal institution of memory. In that respect, the narratives surrounding the upcoming celebrations of the 50-year anniversary of the Revolution in 2024 are a case study particularly worth studying from the law and memory perspective. Unfortunately, the historical distortion cannot in any way be regarded positively in the case of the next country analysed as an example of the functioning of a hard legal institution of memory in practice: Rwanda.

Hard Institution II in Practice: Law Forcing Memory and What Comes Next in Rwanda's Memory Legislation

Rwanda, the scene of the last of four major genocides of the 20th century (following Armenian, Jewish, and Khmer),[78] has engaged in a particularly prolific process of introducing memory legislation with regard to its atrocities, in addition to constitutional provisions proposing several other acts that are supposed to set one official narrative of the events but are also used instrumentally by the country's government, as noted further in the analysis.

While it is not the place of this section to provide a detailed investigation of the Rwandan genocide, it needs to be noted here that it took place in the context of post-colonial ethnic tensions, with the former authorities first favouring the Tutsi minority elite for a number of years and then shifting their support to the Hutu working-class majority. This resulted in a political transition to Hutu rule in 1959, which, in turn, soon began a policy of ethnic discrimination towards the former establishment.[79]

As many Tutsi found refuge in Uganda and other countries of the region, it was there that the Rwanda Patriotic Front (RPF) and its military wing Rwanda Patriotic Army (RPA) were created, attacking Rwanda in 1990 in

78 Jean-Pierre Chrétien, "Le droit à la recherche sur les génocides et sur les négationnismes" ["The Right to Research on Genocides and Denials"] (2012) 15 Revue Arménienne des Questions Contemporaines, online: Open Edition Journals <journals.openedition.org/eac/463>.

79 Timothy Longman, *Memory and Justice in Post-Genocide Rwanda* (Cambridge: Cambridge University Press, 2017) at 39–41.

order to take political power in the country,[80] which triggered a brutal – with atrocities committed on both sides of the conflict[81] – three-year-long civil war, seemingly concluded following the signing of the 1993 Arusha Accords.[82]

However, after the 1994 plane crash caused by a rocket attack on the plane carrying the presidents of Burundi and Rwanda,[83] in which the RPF may have been involved,[84] the latter country's Hutu-dominated regime engaged in "one hundred days of genocide."[85] The mass killings took place between April 7 and July 1994, encompassing almost the whole state, with between 800,000 and 1,000,000 casualties,[86] 90% of which were civilian,[87] including ethnic Tutsi (of whom 75% perished[88]), as well as Hutu opposed to the regime's policies and foreigners.[89] It is also estimated that between 250,000 and 500,000 women were raped during that period.[90] The genocide was stopped only by the forcible removal of the former authorities by the Tutsi-dominated RPF,[91] which then engaged in revenge killings in Rwanda and neighbouring countries, claiming up to 40,000 victims.[92]

80 David Mwambari, "*Agaciro*, Vernacular Memory, and the Politics of Memory in Post-Genocide Rwanda" (2021) 120 African Affairs 611 at 617.

81 René Lemarchand, "Genocide, Memory and Ethnic Reconciliation in Rwanda" in Stefaan Marysse, Filip Reyntjens, and Stef Vandeginste (eds), *L'Afrique des grands lacs: Annuaire 2006–2007* (Paris/Anvers: Harmattan/Centre d'étude de la région des grands lacs d'Afrique, 2007) 21 at 23.

82 Stephen Brown, "The Rule of Law and the Hidden Politics of Transitional Justice in Rwanda" in Chandra Lekha Sriram, Olga Martin-Ortega, and Johanna Herman (eds), *Peacebuilding and Rule of Law in Africa: Just Peace?* (Hoboken, NJ: Taylor and Francis, 2010) 179 at 179.

83 Dominique E. Uwizeyimana, "Aspects and Consequences of the Rwandan Law of Genocide Ideology: A Comparative Analysis" (2014) 5:23 Mediterranean Journal of Social Sciences 2370 at 2371.

84 René Lemarchand, "The Politics of Memory in Post-Genocide Rwanda" in Philip Clark and Zachary D. Kaufman (eds), *After Genocide: Transitional Justice, Post-Conflict Reconstruction and Reconciliation in Rwanda and Beyond* (New York, NY: Columbia University Press, 2009) 65 at 68.

85 Denise Bentrovato, "Accounting for Genocide: Transitional Justice, Mass (Re)Education and the Pedagogy of Truth in Present-Day Rwanda" (2017) 53:3 Comparative Education 396 at 396–397.

86 Samantha Lakin, "Memory and Victimhood in Post-Genocide Rwanda Legal, Political, and Social Realities" in Sarah Federman and Ronald Niezen (eds), *Narratives of Mass Atrocity. Victims and Perpetrators in the Aftermath* (Cambridge/New York, NY: Cambridge University Press, 2022) 201 at 203.

87 Elisabeth King, "Memory Controversies in Post-Genocide Rwanda: Implications for Peacebuilding" (2010) 5:3 Genocide Studies and Prevention: An International Journal 293 at 296.

88 Jutta Helm, "Rwanda and the Politics of Memory" (2005) 23:4 German Politics and Society 1 at 1.

89 Sarah L. Steele, "Memorialisation and the Land of the Eternal Spring: Performative Practices of Memory on the Rwandan Genocide" (2006), online: Researchgate <researchgate.net/publication/228353861_Memorialization_and_the_Land_of_the_Eternal_Spring_Performative_Practices_of_Memory_on_the_Rwandan_Genocide> 1 at 2.

90 King, *supra* note 87 at 296.

91 Bentrovato, *supra* note 85 at 400.

92 Mwambari, *supra* note 80 at 617.

As a response to the violence in the country, a number of legal institutions were established: the International Criminal Tribunal for Rwanda (ICTR), created in 1994 by the UN to judge those responsible for the genocide and other violations of international humanitarian law; national prosecutions in Rwanda, since 1996 tasked with bringing those responsible for genocide and crimes against humanity to justice; and *gacaca* courts, created in the hopes of expediating justice on the community level, and responsible since 2005 for trying those involved in lesser violations of law.[93]

Throughout the whole post-genocide transition process and to this day, the RPF has continued to rule Rwanda, with President Paul Kagame[94] and the 15% Tutsi minority in power[95] governing as technically a democracy but with a partly elected, partly co-opted parliament,[96] further "legitimised and reinforced" by the international community,[97] propagating themselves "as pure heroes who stopped the genocide" – which means their crimes cannot be investigated,[98] with any such attempts by the ICTR blocked.[99] A major aspect of such an official narrative is the country's memory legislation.

Memory Laws Proper in Rwanda

It can be argued that the scene for Rwanda's memory legislation was set in the country's constitution. First adopted in 2003 and then revised in 2015, the Rwandan constitution already in the preamble commits the state to fight against "genocide negationism and revisionism."[100] This is clarified in article 10, compelling the authorities to prevent and punish "the crime of genocide," ordering them to fight "against denial and revisionism of genocide" and to eradicate "genocide ideology and all its manifestations," as well as to remove "discrimination and divisionism based on ethnicity, region or on any other ground," and to promote national unity.[101] While the freedom of press is

93 Brown, *supra* note 82 at 183–186.

94 Thomas A. Kelley III, "Maintaining Power by Manipulating Memory in Rwanda" (2017) 41:79 Fordham International Law Journal 79 at 80–81.

95 Brown, *supra* note 82 at 181.

96 Klaus Bachmann, Igor Lyubashenko Christian Garuka, Grażyna Baranowska and Vjeran Pavlaković, "The Puzzle of Punitive Memory Laws: New Insights into the Origins and Scope of Punitive Memory Laws" (2021) 35:4 East European Politics of Societies and Cultures 996 at 1001.

97 Brown, *supra* note 82 at 179.

98 Lakin, *supra* note 86 at 204–205.

99 Brown, *supra* note 82 at 187.

100 Preamble to the Constitution of the Republic of Rwanda of 2003 as Revised in 2015, online: Constitution Project <constituteproject.org/constitution/Rwanda_2015?lang=en>.

101 Article 10 of Constitution of the Republic of Rwanda of 2003 as Revised in 2015, online: Constitution Project <constituteproject.org/constitution/Rwanda_2015?lang=en>.

guaranteed in article 38, its limits are "determined by law."[102] Importantly, the Rwandan Supreme Court has not found the different elements of the legal framework concerning the matters of memory, analysed here, at odds with the country's constitution.[103]

The first piece of legislation that can be considered a memory law proper is the 2001 Law on Prevention, Suppression and Punishment of the Crime of Discrimination and Sectarianism. This law penalises all acts of discrimination "with the aim of denying one or a group of persons their human rights," as well as sectarianism, i.e., an act that leads to "conflict that causes an uprising that may degenerate into strife among people," under the punishment of a hefty fine and imprisonment between three months and two years (with higher penalties for government officials and members of various organisations).[104] Importantly, the thinly veiled purpose of the law is a ban on ethnic references ("except as narrowly approved by the government"),[105] a part of a larger collective memory strategy analysed further in the second part of this section.

In addition to the 2001 Law, in 2003, another memory law was introduced, Repressing the Crime of Genocide, Crimes Against Humanity and War Crimes. It recognises the crime of negationism of genocide, its minimisation or justification, but also of masterminding or helping "mastermind a plan to discriminate" under the punishment of between 10 and 20 years of imprisonment and the dissolution of any political and social entities should they be responsible for the act.[106] In a later case, the Rwandan Supreme Court clarified that the 2003 Law does not explain the crime of minimisation; however, it confirmed that a certain "a degree of intentionality is required" for it to be committed.[107]

In 2008, another memory legislation was introduced, the Law Relating to the Punishment of the Crime of Genocide Ideology,[108] a crime known as

102 Article 38 of Constitution of the Republic of Rwanda of 2003 as Revised in 2015, online: Constitution Project <constituteproject.org/constitution/Rwanda_2015?lang=en>.

103 Pietro Sullo, "Writing History Through Criminal Law: State-Sponsored Memory in Rwanda" in Berber Bevernage and Nico Wouters (eds), *The Palgrave Handbook of State-Sponsored History After 1945* (London: Palgrave Macmillan, 2018) 69 at 70.

104 Law 47/2001 on Prevention Suppression and Punishment of the Crime of Discrimination and Sectarianism in Lemarchand, *supra* note 81 at 25–26.

105 Kelley III, *supra* note 94 at 113.

106 Law No. 33bis/2003, Repressing the Crime of Genocide, Crimes Against Humanity and War Crimes in Sullo, *supra* note 103 at 73–74.

107 Sullo, *supra* note 103 at 80.

108 Law No. 18/2007 of 23 July 2008 in Sejal Parmar, "Reckoning with the Past? Rwanda's Revised Genocide Ideology Law and International Human Rights Law on Freedom of Expression" in Paul Behrens, Nicholas Terry, and Olaf Jensen (eds), *Holocaust and Genocide Denial: A Contextual Perspective* (Oxon/New York, NY: Routledge/Taylor and Francis, 2017) 94 at 94.

ingengabitekerezo ya jenoside in the local language.[109] Tasked with criminalising the loosely defined genocide ideology under very severe punishment (long imprisonment, high fines, severe penalties also for children, including the possibility of prison sentences for those above the age of 12),[110] it was widely criticised internationally.[111] As such, some of the provisions of the Genocide Ideology Law were amended in 2013.[112] A preambular stressing the links with international human rights law was added, and the main goal of the law was defined more clearly. The definition of genocide was linked to that of the 1948 Genocide Convention, with other UN-acknowledged genocides, in addition to that of Tutsi, recognised by the Law.[113] Furthermore, the law provides "a very detailed interpretation of Rwandan history, the contradiction of which raises criminal liability for genocide negation."[114]

Under the (still only "cosmetically"[115]) amended version, the crime of genocide ideology was defined as "any deliberate act committed in public," i.e., in the presence of at least two other people, "which may show that a person is characterised by ethnic, religious, nationality or racial-hatred with the aim to: (1) advocate for the commission of genocide; (2) support the genocide."[116] Other crimes recognised under the Law include "incitement to commit genocide," "negation of genocide," "minimisation of genocide," "justifying genocide," as well as those related to the destruction of evidence, human remains, or memorial sites connected to the genocide, and "violence against a genocide survivor." Importantly, the Law provides an extremely broad scope of "genocide memory-adjacent" acts which are considered to be criminal, ranging from statements claiming "that genocide is not genocide," to the deliberate misconstruction of the facts relating to the genocide, to the supporting of "a double genocide theory," i.e., that both Tutsi and Hutu were victims of that atrocity.[117] Furthermore, the amendment lessened some of the penalties under the Genocide Ideology Law, with the crime of genocide ideology and other related crimes punishable with five to nine years of imprisonment and a fine of 100,000 to 1,000,000 Rwandan francs.[118]

In general, the broadly defined crimes of the different memory laws provide "judges and prosecutors with an unfettered margin of appreciation

109 Uwizeyimana, *supra* note 83 at 2371.
110 Sullo, *supra* note 103 at 74–76.
111 Parmar, *supra* note 108 at 99.
112 Law No. 84/2013 of 11/09/2013, Law on the crime of genocide ideology and other offences, Official Gazette no. 43bis of 28/10/2013 in Parmar, *supra* note 108 at 95.
113 Parmar, *supra* note 108 at 100–101.
114 Sullo, *supra* note 103 at 81.
115 Sullo, *supra* note 103 at 82.
116 Parmar, *supra* note 108 at 101.
117 Parmar, *supra* note 108 at 101.
118 Parmar, *supra* note 108 at 113–114.

when applying the relevant provisions."[119] And while the laws, if taken literally, could potentially also be used to bring the members of the current regime to justice for their acts during and in the aftermath of the civil war,[120] the Rwandan government employs them against their opponents and critical journalists, with over 100 cases linked to the question of genocide ideology registered every year in the past decade,[121] a part of a larger strategy of propagating particular collective memories of the genocide.

Rwandan Memory Legislation at the Intersections of Law and Memory

To be properly understood, Rwanda's opulence of memory legislation needs to be analysed within the broader socio-political context, as only one of a number of instruments in the memory politics arsenal of the country's authorities, who aspire "to create national consciousness through the practice of genocide commemoration"[122] as the "legal, political, and social realities externally shape and define who is recognised as a victim" in Rwanda[123] – all with the goal of promoting "shared identity, unity and reconciliation."[124]

The fundament of this new official narrative – during the 1995 commemorations, both Tutsi and Hutu victims were recognised[125] – is the myth of a pre-colonial national unity,[126] built "at the expense of ethnic identities, now dismissed and effectively outlawed by the Rwandan government as colonial fabrications that divided society and ultimately underpinned the genocide,"[127] with, as such, any references to one's ethnic background removed from identification cards or textbooks,[128] and the new nation known as Banyarwanda.[129]

In spite of officially promoting unity, however, the authorities engage in the promotion of only singular victimhood, i.e., that of Tutsi,[130] which means that neither the memory of those Hutu "who saved Tutsi at their own

119 Sullo, *supra* note 103 at 76.
120 Lemarchand, *supra* note 81 at 26.
121 Parmar, *supra* note 108 at 114–116.
122 Lakin, *supra* note 86 at 202.
123 Lakin, *supra* note 86 at 206.
124 Julia Viebach, "Of Other Times: Temporality, Memory and Trauma in Post-Genocide Rwanda" (2019) 25:3 International Review of Victimology 277 at 281.
125 Lemarchand, *supra* note 84 at 65.
126 Longman, *supra* note 79 at 60.
127 Bentrovato, *supra* note 85 at 400.
128 Nico Edwards, "Post-Genocide Rwanda's Struggle to 'Never Forget' and Move on" (2021), online: E-International Relations <e-ir.info/2021/04/30/balancing-on-a-knifes-edge-post-genocide-rwandas-struggle-to-never-forget-and-move-on/>.
129 Lemarchand, *supra* note 84 at 65.
130 Lakin, *supra* note 86 at 205.

peril"[131] and of "Twa, or those of mixed Hutu and Tutsi background" who perished during the genocide nor of those killed in "other civil wars of 1990s in Rwanda and in the Democratic Republic of the Congo (DRC)" is officially remembered.[132] As Hearty notes, such an approach to the questions of collective memory may be considered "victors' justice" on the RPF's part, instrumentally imposing on a supposedly de-ethnicised society divisions along the lines of victims-perpetrators and winners-losers, which ultimately translate into Tutsi-Hutu,[133] thus confirming that the logic of ethnicity "is alive and well" in the country.[134]

In addition to legislation, the Rwandan official narrative has been imposed through the whole "bureaucratic infrastructure, right down to the village level," the country's media,[135] and various memory projects (both public and private rituals), some "compulsively practiced" for the benefit of the international audience. These include the construction of monuments and museums, the preservation of sites of genocide, and the production of various forms of art.[136]

The official narrative is also heavily promoted by the education sector, which engages in "mass (re)education" and "pedagogy of truth," fostering "an atmosphere of uncritical conformity and compliance along with a concomitant culture of silence and self-censorship."[137] As the government placed a moratorium on teaching history in schools, arguing that the "distorted historical narratives promulgated by the schools since the colonial era" were one of the driving forces behind the genocide,[138] its teaching became the responsibility of (re)education camps, either *ignado* (solidarity camps) established for new university students, civil society members, church leaders, judges, and politicians, or *itorero*, re-education camps for former soldiers, combatants, prisoners, *genocidaires*, street children, prostitutes, and "other undesirables."[139]

It is within such a socio-political environment, whereby "the genocide has been shamefully instrumentalised for the benefit of the regime,"[140] one which adopts a particular "we know genocide better" attitude,[141] that Rwanda's memory legislation operates. Its wide reach affects not only the internal

131 Lemarchand, *supra* note 84 at 73.
132 Mwambari, *supra* note 80 at 613.
133 Kevin Hearty, "Law, 'Presentist' Agendas, and the Making of 'Official' Memory After Collective Violence" (2022) 49:3 Journal of Law and Society 495 at 498, 510.
134 Lemarchand, *supra* note 81 at 25.
135 Kelley III, *supra* note 94 at 116.
136 Steele, *supra* note 89 at 2, 16.
137 Bentrovato, *supra* note 85 at 411.
138 Longman, *supra* note 79 at 34.
139 Kelley III, *supra* note 94 at 123.
140 Lemarchand, *supra* note 84 at 74.
141 Parmar, *supra* note 108 at 97.

opposition – such as the former President Pasteur Bizimungu, who was incarcerated and whose party was banned,[142] the former Prime Minister Faustin Twagiramungu, the regime's opponent in the 2004 presidential elections, whose political party was dissolved,[143] or Victoire Umuhoza, a candidate in the 2010 presidential elections, sentenced on the basis of the 2008 Law for "supporting a double genocide theory" (a sentiment she did not express, which was later recognised by the African Court on Human and Peoples' Rights, who in 2017 found Rwanda in violation of the African Charter on Human and Peoples' Rights).[144] It also affects those responsible for petty crimes in those cases when the alleged perpetrator is Hutu and the victim is a Tutsi survivor,[145] earnest witnesses before *gacca* courts (in one known case sentenced on the basis of the 2003 Law),[146] or even a journalist who made a mistake with regard to the terms "survivors" and "victims," incarcerated for three months before being acquitted, and a singer sentenced for ten years for lyrics recognising the victims of the genocide and of other atrocities in the same line.[147]

Foreign organisations were also affected by Rwanda's memory legislation, with BBC and Human Rights Watch (HRW) found guilty of "spreading genocide ideology,"[148] as well as individuals, with Peter Erlinder, who worked for the defence before the ICTR arrested him in Rwanda on the basis of the 2008 Law charges of genocide denial for his work before the Court, a clear violation of the presumption of innocence and the right to defence, rendering, as Behrens remarked, the country's justice system a "Kafkaesque (or Cardassian)" quality.[149]

As has been noted, such a form of memory legislation, looked into from the big picture perspective on the official narrative in Rwanda, is not only "unlikely to lead to meaningful peacebuilding" and reconciliation.[150] Contrarily, with the silencing of "the voices of Hutu, as well as Tutsi dissenters," the regime "trades present stability for future dangers,"[151] given that, as Lemarchand notes, "it is not unreasonable to suggest that with the passage

142 Brown, *supra* note 82 at 182.
143 Lemarchand, *supra* note 81 at 26.
144 Charles A. Khamala, "Genocide Denial and Freedom of Political Expression in the *Ingabire* Case" (2018) 2 African Human Rights Yearbook 481 at 457–459, 481–483.
145 Uwizeyimana, *supra* note 83 at 2372.
146 Sullo, *supra* note 103 at 74.
147 Kelley III, *supra* note 94 at 130–131.
148 Sullo, *supra* note 103 at 77.
149 Paul Behrens, "Why Not the Law? Options for Dealing with Genocide and Holocaust Denial" in Paul Behrens, Nicholas Terry, and Olaf Jensen (eds), *Holocaust and Genocide Denial: A Contextual Perspective* (Oxon/New York, NY: Routledge/Taylor and Francis, 2017) 230 at 238–239.
150 King, *supra* note 87 at 303.
151 Brown, *supra* note 82 at 195.

of time, as group identities become even more polarised under the impact of those very policies so loudly condemned by the Rwandan government," the various counter-memories will "coalesce into separate ethnic memories."[152]

Analysing Rwanda's memory legislation as a legal institution of memory, one finds that the country's different memory laws are not easily categorised. While they clearly fit into the first group, establishing an official narrative in order for an event – the genocide – not to repeat itself, their instrumental use means that they also belong to the third group, as through the designation of one collectivity as victims and another as perpetrators, they seek to hide the difficult RPF's past from the time during and after the civil war.

As such, the typical memory law limitations on free speech protecting the "sacred" memory from "blasphemy" through "ritualistic" prosecution – as noted earlier in the book – in the case of Rwandan memory legislation are extremely broad, and the instrumental use of law for immediate political goals in their case is particularly noticeable – instead of protecting the different victim groups' right to remember an atrocity, they were turned into tools diminishing their human rights. While still fulfilling their main goal, protecting the somewhat distorted collective memory of genocide, one needs to remark that in this case, the hard legal institution of memory is too difficult, with the possibility, as noted earlier, of achieving results contrary to those envisaged by the country's authorities, possibly leading to future conflict. While not as problematic, the Polish memory legislation analysed next also raises a number of questions as to the necessary limits to laws concerning the questions of memory.

Hard Institution II in Practice Again: Memory Politics of Civil Law, or Polish Memory Legislation

Poland, as noted in Chapter 6, experienced severe destruction during World War II, from the hands of both the USSR and Nazi Germany. It was the Third Reich that on the occupied territory established an extermination system of "concentration camps" (*Konzentrationslager*) and "annihilation camps" (*Vernichtungslager*), with the latter being "areas of continual executions of transported victims" from not only the territory of pre-war Poland but also the rest of Europe, in particular of Jewish origin.[153] In total, over 1,000,000 Polish citizens are thought to have died in camps, of which nine were placed in the present-day territory of the country: Auschwitz-Birkenau,

152 Lemarchand, *supra* note 81 at 29.

153 Piotr Mostowik and Edyta Figura-Góralczyk, "'Polish Death Camps' as an 'Opinion' of Which Expressing Is Protected by German Law? Questionable *Bundesgerichtshof's* Judgement of 19.7.2018" in Magdalena Bainczyk and Agnieszka Kubiak-Cyrul (eds), *State's Responsibility for International Crimes: Reflections upon the Rosenburg Exhibition* (Stuttgart: Franz Steiner Verlag, 2021) 91 at 94.

Bełżec, Groß-Rosen, Kulmhof, Majdanek, Sobibór, Stutthof, Treblinka, and Warsaw.[154]

Importantly, despite such attempts by the occupiers, no collaborative Polish authorities were established, "which was a phenomenon and an exception on a European scale"; also uniquely amongst other occupied territories, the provision of help to Jews was forbidden under the death penalty.[155] Given that, as well as the fact that the camps were established by the Nazi German authorities and that "the only element connecting these camps with Poland was their location on the territory of occupied Poland,"[156] there is "a great deal of sensitivity . . . in contemporary Poland . . . aimed at counteracting the falsification of history by using the word 'Polish' in context and connection to events related to crimes planned and organised by the invaders during" World War II on the overtaken areas.[157]

While it is sometimes asserted that the adjective Polish with regard to concentration and annihilation camps may only mean "a spatial specification,"[158] the phrase is nonetheless considered to be "somewhat denial-oriented."[159] Importantly, the first instance of a public use of the phrase "Polish death camps" dates to 1944, and the employment of this and similar "defective codes of memory" has since persisted in the international media and in statements made by politicians on a global stage. While the Polish Ministry of Foreign Affairs (hereinafter MFA) has conducted a large number of interventions in such cases over the years,[160] the country's government has established an intricate network of memory legislation to counteract the phenomenon, some of which were ultimately eliminated from the legal system, while others persist to this day.

The Wide Array of Polish Memory Legislation

Poland, similar to other European countries, banned denialism in 1998,[161] the prohibition of which may be found in Article 55 in relation to Article 1

154 Adam Strzelec, " 'Polish Camps . . .' in the Context of Amendment of the Law on the Institute of National Remembrance – Commission of Prosecution of Crimes Against the Polish Nation of 26 January 2018" in Magdalena Bainczyk and Agnieszka Kubiak-Cyrul (eds), *State's Responsibility for International Crimes: Reflections upon the Rosenburg Exhibition* (Stuttgart: Franz Steiner Verlag, 2021) 116 at 116.

155 Mostowik and Figura-Góralczyk, *supra* note 153 at 95.

156 Strzelec, *supra* note 154 at 116.

157 Mostowik and Figura-Góralczyk, *supra* note 153 at 95.

158 Jörg Hackmann, "Defending the 'Good Name' of the Polish Nation: Politics of History as a Battlefield in Poland, 2015–18" (2018) 20:4 Journal of Genocide Research 587 at 601.

159 Tomasz Cebulski, "Can History and Memory Heal Us? Thirty Years of Polish-Israeli Relations" (2021) 15:1 Israel Journal of Foreign Affairs 53 at 60.

160 Strzelec, *supra* note 154 at 117–119.

161 Kornelia Kończal, "Mnemonic Populism: The Polish Holocaust Law and Its Afterlife" (2020) 29:4 European Review 457 at 457.

of the 1998 Act on the Institute of National Memory (hereinafter in this section IPN Act).[162] It states that "who publicly and counterfactually denies the atrocities listed in Article 1 Point 1, is subject to a fine or imprisonment up to 3 years. The sentence is publicly pronounced." Said atrocities are enumerated and presently include the crimes committed between November 8, 1917, and July 31, 1990, on Polish citizens and nationals, such as Nazi and communist atrocities, as well as those committed by "the members of the Ukrainian units collaborating with the Third German Reich," and crimes against peace, war crimes, and crimes against humanity. Previously, the list also included atrocities committed by Ukrainian nationalists; however, it was struck in this part by the Constitutional Tribunal in 2019.

As noted by Pohl and Burdziak, the provisions of Article 55 may be translated into the following obligation: "everyone, at all times and in any place," is prohibited from intentionally, "publicly and contrary to the facts to the (objective) truth deny[ing] (and not just diminish[ing]) some or all of the crimes referred to in the (closed and ambiguous catalogue of)" Article 1 Point 1 of the IPN Act.[163] Importantly, in the Polish negationism ban, there is a specific focus only on crimes committed on Polish citizens and nationals, as only their collective memory is protected.

Kłak argues that the obligation for the state to create such a protection has its basis in article 5 of the Polish Constitution,[164] which states that:

> The Republic of Poland shall safeguard the independence and integrity of its territory and ensure the freedoms and rights of persons and citizens, the security of the citizens, safeguard the national heritage and shall ensure the protection of the natural environment pursuant to the principles of sustainable development.[165]

In this, the national heritage also includes collective memory, as "the distortion of history . . . may affect all members of the 'community.' "[166]

162 Ustawa z dnia 18 grudnia 1998 r. o Instytucie Pamięci Narodowej – Komisji Ścigania Zbrodni przeciwko Narodowi Polskiemu [The Act of December 18, 1998 on the Institute of National Memory – Commission for the Prosecution of Crimes Against the Polish Nation] Dz.U. 1998 nr 155 poz. 1016.

163 Łukasz Pohl and Konrad Burdziak, "Holocaust Denial and the Polish Penal Law – Legal Considerations" in Patrycja Grzebyk (ed.), *Responsibility for Negation of International Crimes* (Warsaw: Wydawnictwo Instytutu Wymiaru Sprawiedliwości, 2020) 123 at 131.

164 Czesław Kłak, "Odpowiedzialność karna z art. 55a ust. 1 i 2 ustawy o Instytucie Pamięci Narodowej – Komisji Ścigania Zbrodni przeciwko Narodowi Polskiemu" ["Criminal Responsibility According to Article 55a Paragraph 1 and 2 of the Institute of National Remembrance Act – Main Commission for the Prosecution of Crimes Against the Polish Nation"] (2017) 96 Przegląd Więziennictwa Polskiego 169 at 186.

165 The Constitution of the Republic of Poland of 2 April 1997, online: Sejm <sejm.gov.pl/prawo/konst/angielski/kon1.htm>.

166 Kłak, *supra* note 164 at 186–187.

Given the existence of a constitutional rule that may be interpreted as granting protection to the memory of the past, even before the introduction of specific civil law provisions, a particular approach to the safeguarding of collective memory has developed in Polish jurisprudence on the basis of articles 23 and 24 of the Civil Code,[167] which provide the means of safeguarding personal interests:

> Art. 23. Protection of personal interests. The personal interests of a human being, in particular health, freedom, dignity, freedom of conscience, name or pseudonym, image, privacy of correspondence, inviolability of home, and scientific, artistic, inventive or improvement achievements are protected by civil law, independently of protection under other regulations.
>
> Art. 24. Means of protection. § 1. Any person whose personal interests are threatened by another person's actions may demand that the actions be ceased unless they are not unlawful. In the case of infringement he may also demand that the person committing the infringement perform the actions necessary to remove its effects, in particular that the person make a declaration of the appropriate form and substance. On the terms provided for in this Code, he may also demand monetary recompense or that an appropriate amount of money be paid to a specific public cause.

On the basis of these provisions, a number of court cases relating to an infringement of memory were successfully adjudicated before the Polish courts in recent years, with a total of over 60 trials concerning the use of the phrase "Polish death camps."[168] The most notable among these was the 2016 case brought before the court by former Auschwitz prisoner Karol Tendera, a Polish citizen, against German television network ZDF, which in a 2013 website posting used the phrase "Polish extermination camps of Majdanek and Auschwitz." While this expression was corrected following a diplomatic intervention, on the same day, Mr. Tendera demanded not only a correction but also an apology on the network's website and in the press, as well as a specific payment to a charity. Following only a personal apology by ZDF and an exchange of letters, Mr. Tendera brought the matter to a Polish court in 2014. Before the beginning of the proceedings in 2016, the network provided a general apology on its website. Importantly, while the lawsuit was first dismissed on a technical basis, this decision was overturned by the Court

167 Kodeks cywilny z dnia 23 kwietnia 1964 r. [The Civil Code of 23 April 1964] in Ewa Kucharska (tr.), *The Civil Code – Kodeks Cywilny* (Warsaw: C. H. Beck, 2011) at 20–21.

168 Jan Kluza, "Cywilne środki ochrony dobrego imienia Rzeczypospolitej Polskiej na gruncie nowelizacji ustawy o IPN" ["Civil Measures to Protect the Good Name of the Republic of Poland on the Basis of the Amendment to the Act on the Institute of National Remembrance"] (2020) 33 Studenckie Prace Prawnicze, Administratywistyczne i Ekonomiczne 211 at 212.

of Appeal in Cracow, which for the most part sided with the plaintiff in a December 22, 2016, judgement, ordering the network to publish an apology on its website "on the main page, in a frame, with the bold font, size of 14 points and on their own cost (and maintaining it for a period of one month)" according to an ordered statement, finding that an infringement of personal interests took place, and previous apologies were not adequate.[169]

ZDF only partially complied with the judgement, according to the plaintiff; however, the ensuing proceedings to enforce it before the German courts remain outside of the scope of this book. Nevertheless, a similar judgement followed in 2021, where ZDF and another television producer lost against an organisation of the former Polish World War II partisans for portraying them as anti-Semitic in a TV series.[170]

In addition to the existing legal provisions, in 2018, the Polish parliament proposed a specific legal solution on the basis of civil law allowing for a collective protection of memory, adding to the IPN Act Chapter 6c,[171] entitled "Protection of the reputation of the Republic of Poland and the Polish Nation." It composed of three articles:

> Art. 53o. The provisions of the Act of 23 April 1964 – Civil Code (Journal of Laws of 2017, item 459, 933 and 1132) on the protection of personal interests shall apply accordingly to the protection of the reputation of the Republic of Poland and the Polish Nation. Action for the protection of the reputation of the Republic of Poland or the Polish Nation may be brought by a non-governmental organisation acting within the scope of its statutory goals. Any damages or compensation awarded shall be due to the State Treasury.
>
> Art. 53p. Action for the protection of the reputation of the Republic of Poland or the Polish Nation may also be brought by the Institute of National Remembrance. In such cases, the Institute of National Remembrance shall have the capacity to be a party to court proceedings.
>
> Art. 53q. The provisions of art. 53o and art. 53p shall apply irrespective of the governing law.

169 Mostowik and Figura-Góralczyk, *supra* note 153 at 96–97.

170 Mostowik and Figura-Góralczyk, *supra* note 153 at 98–108, 112.

171 Ustawa z dnia 26 stycznia 2018 roku o zmianie ustawy o Instytucie Pamięci Narodowej – Komisji Ścigania Zbrodni przeciwko Narodowi Polskiemu, ustawy o grobach i cmentarzach wojennych, ustawy o muzeach oraz ustawy o odpowiedzialności podmiotów zbiorowych za czyny zabronione pod groźbą kary [The Act of 26 January 2018 on the Change of the Act on the Institute of National Memory – Main Commission for the Prosecution of Crimes Against the Polish Nation, the Act on Tombs and War Cemeteries, the Act on Museums and the Act on the Responsibility of Collective Entities], online: Ministerstwo Sprawiedliwości <gov.pl/web/sprawiedliwosc/nowelizacja-ustawy-o-ipn-wersja-w-jezyku-angielskim>.

In extending the Civil Code articles 23 and 24 protections to the reputation of Poland and the country's nation in addition to the cases of their individual infringement,[172] Chapter 6c allows for various modes of protection, both financial (compensation paid to the State Treasury) and non-financial (a cease and desist demand or a claim to remedy an infringement).[173] Importantly, as Lankoroński argues, Poland and the Polish nation should be understood here on the basis of the country's current constitution, with the former relating to the current Republic of Poland based on the 1997 basic law (but potentially also extending to the "claims for defamation of the First [pre-1795] and Second [1918–1939/45] Republics, especially those of their traditions and legacies that remain extant and give shape to the Third Republic [since 1990] of today") and the latter encompassing all Polish citizens and potentially also the Polish diaspora.[174]

In turn, attempts at the establishment of criminal legal solutions to the question of memory distortion by the Polish government have generally remained unsuccessful. In 2006, two provisions to the criminal code were added:

> Art. 132a. Anyone who publicly accuses the Polish nation of participating in, organising or being responsible for communist or Nazi crimes shall be subject to a penalty of imprisonment of up to 3 years.
>
> Art. 112 subsection 1a. Regardless of the regulations in force at the place where the offence was committed, the Polish Criminal Law shall apply to a Polish citizen and a foreigner in the event of an offence of slander of the Polish Nation.

The articles were struck down by the Constitutional Tribunal in 2008,[175] not on the basis of their merits but due to issues surrounding the procedure of their adoption.[176]

172 Kluza, *supra* note 168 at 215.

173 Agnieszka Kubiak-Cyrul, "Protection of the Reputation of the Republic of Poland and the Polish Nation in the Law on the Institute of National Remembrance" in Magdalena Bainczyk and Agnieszka Kubiak-Cyrul (eds), *State's Responsibility for International Crimes: Reflections upon the Rosenburg Exhibition* (Stuttgart: Franz Steiner Verlag, 2021) 136 at 140–142.

174 *Ibid.* at 145.

175 Strzelec, *supra* note 154 at 119–121.

176 Mirosław Wyrzykowski, "Ustawa o Instytucie Pamięci Narodowej przed Trybunałem Konstytucyjnym" ["The Act on the Institute of National Memory Before the Constitutional Tribunal"] (2018) XL Gdańskie Studia Prawnicze 355 at 356–357.

Ten years later, in addition to the aforementioned civil law solutions, criminal legal provisions were added to the IPN Act:[177]

> Article 55a. 1. Whoever publicly and contrary to the facts attributes to the Polish Nation or to the Polish State responsibility or co-responsibility for the Nazi crimes committed by the German Third Reich, as specified in Article 6 of the Charter of the International Military Tribunal – Annex to the Agreement for the prosecution and punishment of the major war criminals of the European Axis, executed in London on 8 August 1945 (Journal of Laws of 1947, item 367), or for any other offences constituting crimes against peace, humanity or war crimes, or otherwise grossly diminishes the responsibility of the actual perpetrators of these crimes, shall be liable to a fine or deprivation of liberty for up to 3 years. The judgment shall be communicated to the public.
>
> 2. If the perpetrator of the act specified in section 1 above acts unintentionally, they shall be liable to a fine or restriction of liberty.
> 3. An offence is not committed if the perpetrator of a prohibited act set out in sections 1 and 2 above acted within the framework of artistic or scientific activity.
>
> Article 55b. Irrespective of the law applicable at the place of commission of the prohibited act, this Act shall be applicable to a Polish citizen as well as a foreigner in the event of commission of the offences set out in art. 55 and art. 55a.

Importantly, the provisions also established the criminalisation of an act if committed outside of Poland, regardless of the existence of adequate law in the foreign country where the offence took place.[178] Causing major international outcry, however, they were removed only several months later, as I will explain further.

Nota bene, in Polish law, there also exists a criminal provision protecting the various national symbols from being damaged or insulted under the punishment of a fine or imprisonment up to one year. Due to its particularity as protecting memory carriers rather than singular collective memories and official narratives, it remains outside of the scope of this book, but I analyse it elsewhere.[179]

177 Ustawa z dnia 26 stycznia 2018 roku, *supra* note 171.

178 Kłak, *supra* note 164 at 173.

179 Mirosław M. Sadowski, "Fluttering the Past in the Present: The Role of Flags in the Contemporary Society: Law, Politics, Identity and Memory" in Anne Wagner and Sarah Marusek (eds), *Flags, Color, and the Legal Narrative: Public Memory, Identity, and Critique* (Cham: Springer, 2021) 85 at 92–93.

Polish Memory Legislation at the Intersections of Law and Memory

Poland has a long history of legal provisions protecting the good name of the Polish nation or Poland itself, with the first Supreme Court judgements delineating the difference between an individual affront and that of the nation dating to 1934, with others following, for example, in 1946 and 1961.[180] It was the introduction of proper memory laws, however, that resulted in all Polish memory legislation, but the Civil Code provisions relating to personal interest protection were particularly scrutinised over the years.

In its current form, the penalisation of negationism (article 55 of the IPN Act) has been noted to be particularly limited (only protecting the memory of these events that were already established as facts) and with a potential for abuse by both the perpetrators, who may easily claim ignorance and thus lack intent, and the authorities, who may exploit the provision's vagueness.[181] I would also stress its limitation in having an application to only atrocities committed on Polish citizens and nationals, potentially meaning that negating the World War II genocides committed on other peoples could not be punished.

In regard to the civil provisions of the IPN Act (articles 55o–q) concerning the protection of the good name of Poland and the country's nation, Cyrul criticises the attribution "to the Republic of Poland and the Polish Nation personal rights analogous to those of legal persons," which results in their being recognised "as a kind of civil law entities with respect to the protection of their good name," which is in itself problematic and *a contrario* the established concepts in the Polish civil law, complicating "the identification of individual interests of the subject of the protected right in light of the provisions on the protection of personal rights."[182] In a similar vein, Machnikowski argues that article 58o creates a particular, public law rather than civil law obligation of respect towards Poland and the Polish Nation for foreigners, one which does not have a basis in typical social values, also stressing the vagueness of what exactly constitutes the infringement of said article.[183]

Issues with the international application of the law proscribed in article 53q were also raised,[184] as Chapter 6 provisions pose problems with regard to

180 Kłak, *supra* note 164 at 187–188.

181 Pohl and Burdziak, *supra* note 163 at 130.

182 Kubiak-Cyrul, *supra* note 173 at 143.

183 Piotr Machnikowski, "Badania nad totalitaryzmem – prawda historyczna i wolność indywidualna – prawo prywatne w służbie publicznej. Uwagi na tle 'cywilnoprawnych' przepisów ustawy o IPN" ["Studies on Totalitarianism – Historical Truth and Individual Freedom – Private Law in the Public Service: Remarks on the Basis of the 'Civil Law' Provisions of the IPN Act"] (2021) 43:3 Studia and Autorytaryzmem i Totalizmem 104 at 110–112.

184 Kluza, *supra* note 168 at 219.

the question of court jurisdiction, which will need to be established according to general rules of Polish, EU, and international law.[185] Additionally, questions of potential limitations to freedom of expression, artistic creation, and scientific research were raised.[186]

In regard to the now defunct criminal legal provisions, the Criminal Code 2006 addition was already heavily criticised at the drafting stage as vague and contrary to general rules of criminal law[187] as well as potentially limiting the public debate on contemporary Polish history.[188] As for the 2018 amendments, the most problematic issue with articles 55a and 55b was that of the question of intent, as susceptible to punishment were not only those who intentionally broke the law but also those ignorant of its existence who did not know that their public statements on certain historical events needed to be factually based when concerning certain moments from Polish history.[189] Also characterised as problematic were the provisions of article 55a point 1, given that the artistic or scientific activities that broke the law but were free from prosecution were not defined, thus posing a difficulty as to how broadly or narrowly they should have been understood.[190]

In addition to legal scrutiny, the legislation was also criticised for its optics. Introduced a day before the Holocaust Remembrance Day,[191] it was considered to be "aimed at shaping the memory about Polish attitudes towards Jews during World War II at home and abroad,"[192] another element

185 Bogusław Lanckoroński, "Safeguarding the Good Repute of the Polish State and Nation (Art. 53o–53q of the Act on the Institute of National Remembrance – Commission for the Prosecution of Crimes Against the Polish Nation)" in Patrycja Grzebyk (ed.), *Responsibility for Negation of International Crimes* (Warsaw: Wydawnictwo Instytutu Wymiaru Sprawiedliwości, 2020) 139 at 153–161.

186 *Ibid.* at 148.

187 Strzelec, *supra* note 154 at 119–120.

188 Wyrzykowski, *supra* note 176 at 356.

189 Paweł Bachmat, "Odpowiedzialność karna za przestępstwa z art. 55a ust. 1–2 oraz kontratyp z art. 55a ust. 3 ustawy o Instytucie Pamięci Narodowej – Komisji Ścigania Zbrodni przeciwko Narodowi Polskiemu" ["Criminal Liability Referred to in Article 55a Paragraphs 1–2 and Its Exclusion ("kontratyp") Article 55a Paragraphs 3 of the Act on the Institute of National Remembrance – Commission for the Prosecution of Crimes Against the Polish Nation"] (2018) 3 Zeszyty Prawnicze Biura Analiz Sejmowych Kancelarii Sejmu 111 at 121–122.

190 Kłak, *supra* note 164 at 203–207.

191 Katharina Geiselmann, "The Importance of Language in European Memory Politics: What the Discourse Around the Polish 'Holocaust Law' Reveals" in Janny de Jong, Marek Neuman, and Margriet van der Waal (eds), *Where Is Europe? Respacing, Replacing and Reordering Europe: Selected Papers Presented at Euroculture Intensive Programme 2018* (Groningen: Euroculture Consortium, 2019) 4 at 4.

192 Katarzyna Liszka, "Articles 55a and 55b of the IPN Act and the Dialogue About the Holocaust in Poland" (2019) 3 Archiwum Filozofii Prawa i Filozofii Społecznej. Journal of the Polish Section of IVR 81 at 89.

of memory politics of the aforementioned Law and Justice Party.[193] The fact that the changes were implemented at a time of elections in both Poland and Israel resulted only in a more heated debate regarding the law in both countries, with, ultimately, the removal of articles 55a and 55b on June 27, 2018, following US pressure and negotiations between the two parties.[194] The amendment of the IPN Act was followed by a joint statement of Israeli and Polish prime ministers who "cherished the new entente between their two countries and declared their commitment to truth and historical justice as well as their rejection of anti-Semitism and anti-Polonism."[195]

Overall, it seems that, thus far, Polish memory legislation, in particular the repealed penal provisions, has had an effect opposite to the intended one. As it has been noted, the introduction of the 2018 amendment led to an increase in the presence of the expression "Polish death camps" internationally, with the MFA intervening approximately 250 times a year, compared to *circa* 100 times beforehand.[196] As Strzelec argues, diplomatic action, together with educational programmes, seems to be more effective than specific memory legislation – in the four months that the 2018 penal legislation was in place, no prosecution was initiated, despite over 80 submissions.[197] It must also be observed that by 2021, there were no judgements on the basis of the civil law regulations introduced to the IPN Act in 2018.[198]

From the perspective of legal institutions of memory, the Polish memory legislation analysed in this section clearly falls into the first of three proposed categories, ensuring that the collective memory of the protected events is correct so that they do not repeat themselves. However, some researchers would place the now removed criminal legal provisions in the third group as attempts at setting one narrative in order to whitewash collective memory. Furthermore, in the analysis of the Polish case, the classification of memory legislation as a hard legal institution of memory becomes once again clearly visible – not only the now defunct criminal law but also civil law provisions attempt to directly shape the public debate (both locally and internationally), clearly delineating what is acceptable (historical facts) and what is not (counterfactual statements), but failing to see not only the potential grey area in the middle but also the widespread ignorance with regard to Polish history.

An object of memory politics, in the memory legislation regarding the protection of the reputation of Poland and the country's nation, the Durkheimian

193 Kończal, *supra* note 161 at 461–463.
194 Cebulski, *supra* note 159 at 59–60.
195 Marta Bucholc, "Commemorative Lawmaking: Memory Frames of the Democratic Backsliding in Poland After 2015" (2019) 11 Hague Journal on the Rule of Law (2019) 85 at 103.
196 Strzelec, *supra* note 154 at 128–129.
197 Strzelec, *supra* note 154 at 130–132.
198 Kubiak-Cyrul, *supra* note 173 at 146.

quality of this legal institution of memory becomes particularly visible: as the Polish right to remember is exercised, legal rituals protect a particular narrative against "blasphemy." At the same time, the different issues surrounding virtually all Polish memory legislation demonstrate the more general problems surrounding this legal institution of memory, also showing its slim potential for achieving results attempted by the legislature.

Conclusion: Hard Legal Institutions of Memory in Practice

The study of two hard legal institutions of memory, taken from three diverse socio-political, socio-legal, and historical situations, further demonstrated the suitability of the new law and memory framework to analyse their intersections. Despite the small discrepancies between their respective models and actual applications – Portuguese legal amnesia took an extraordinary form, defying the traditional amnesty-based approach to the questions of legal forgetting, while Rwandan memory legislation has become so instrumentalised that it may ultimately be counterproductive, and Polish memory legislation established a unique civil law regime of protection, linking the collectivity's memories with personal interest protections – they proved themselves to be significantly politicised rituals linked to the different aspects of the right to memory, with a high level of direct influence of law on their shape.

Similarly to the soft and medium legal institutions of memory, the study conducted in this chapter proved the limitations of legal institutions of memory. Only in the case of Portugal can one speak of a major and lasting impact on the social perceptions of the past, with Rwandan memory legislation hijacked for political purposes and the Polish remaining problematic, never able to achieve its goals. As this chapter completes the practical study of legal institutions of memory, a certain big picture look at the different aspects of legal institutions of memory is needed, bringing together the thoughts put forward here, which is the focus of the Conclusion to this final part of the book.

Conclusion to Part III: Applying the New Law and Memory Framework and What Happened

Throughout the course of this third part of the thesis, nine different examples of legal institutions of memory were analysed in ten case studies. These intersections opened up a space for not only a general comparative engagement, uncovering, for example, a similar relationship with history, memory, and identity in Portugal and in Poland, but also for a specific one with regard to four institutions: symbolic reparations (Japan and Poland), international tribunals (ECtHR with regard to Swiss, Lithuanian, and Polish cases), lustration (Iraq and Poland), and memory legislation (Rwanda and Poland).

In regard to the institution of symbolic reparations, where the many Japanese public apologies remain unsuccessful in leading to reconciliation between Japan and Korea and Japan and China, the Polish bishops' letter succeeded in being the driving force behind the rapprochement between Poland and Germany. Importantly, in the latter case, the process, once initiated by a single act, took years to bear fruit, while Japan has been issuing numerous public apologies for the past 30 years, thus far to no avail. It seems to be that the key to the realisation of true reconciliation through symbolic reparations was the openness of the Polish side to the issues of the other side, in spite of being its main victim, whereas Japanese apologies are perceived as insincere and, as such, fail to create a collective memory shift.

The ECtHR was analysed here as a legal institution of memory in four cases: *Perinçek*, *Vasiliauskas*, *Drėlingas*, and *Janowiec*. The latter two cases were of major importance to the collective memories of the Lithuanian and Polish societies, whereas the first one was rather relevant to the global collective memory of the Armenian genocide. Importantly, the Court failed to establish one standard in deciding cases laying at the intersections of law and memory, often using particular legal reasoning, different from that of other international human rights tribunals, in the hopes of circumnavigating its being called to be a judge of history. However, it still created a limited but meaningful impact on collective memory.

Both analysed cases of lustration showed its potential for politicisation. Whether in the case of Iraq, where the institution was set up by a foreign power, or in the case of Poland, which engaged in lustration on its own

DOI: 10.4324/9781003461548-15

volition, the vetting processes were hijacked by those in power to achieve singular political goals. While successful in removing and blocking certain groups of people from positions in power (in the case of Iraq) and, to a certain degree, of bringing the truth regarding the past to the present (in the case of Poland), in achieving these goals, the lustration processes also lost their reconciliation aims, which bears the question of their suitability as a means of settling the accounts of the past.

In turn, memory legislation in the case of both Rwanda and Poland demonstrates that the limits law may be taken to in the hopes of permanently changing collective memory, both nationally and on a global stage. Whether plainly contradicting the freedom of speech provisions (in the case of Rwanda) or attempting only to shape the debate on the past in a certain way (in the case of Poland), issues regarding the instrumentalisation of collective memory by law become plainly visible in the case of this legal institution of memory. Importantly, in forcefully pushing one narrative of the past, the authorities in both countries may actually have led to a larger dissemination of the memory narrative from which memory legislation was supposed to protect. This also, in the case of this legal institution of memory, raises the question of its appropriateness in the matters of law and memory, as it seems to be severely limited to only those instances when a single narrative to be protected is set and already widespread in society.

Last, while not attempting to be repetitive, it should be noted once again here that in the case of soft, medium, and hard legal institutions of memory, the main observations regarding legal institutions of memory were confirmed. While in practice the different institutions varied in various ways from the established models, they were all top-to-bottom instruments of memory politics, which, taking the form of Durkheimian rituals, to a certain (limited) degree succeeded in influencing social perceptions of the past. While being marred with a number of issues, most notably with regard to the legal rules laying at the basis of their creation, in the present day, they may be found in virtually all cultural and temporal contexts. Importantly, whether employed in transitory, post-transitory, or non-transitory circumstances, legal institutions of memory were always used in response to certain collective trauma-memories, but to achieve different goals: fostering reconciliation, collective forgetting, or collective evoking, propagating short-term political and/or economic objectives, or, in certain instances, just as some of the many cogs in the collective memory policy conducted by the authorities.

Conclusions: Intersections of Law and Memory – Remarks After the Inquiry

What About Law and Memory?

As the preceding chapters prove, law is a major instrument in the creation of collective memory – and, vice versa, in certain instances collective memory itself influences the law. To cite Christodoulidis and Veitch's poignant observation,

> law, like any template that makes meaning possible, must accommodate and institute memory in its own specific way, allow it to find expression in its pathways, in a representational space that may disclose and reveal it. Any accounting of the past cannot but be selective. In this selection process, aspects of the past will be actualised and repressed – and those actualised will in a crucial sense depend on what is repressed.[1]

While as remarked at the beginning of this book, every trial is itself of major importance for the social perceptions of the past, throughout humanity's history, various particular legal institutions have been established to address issues of yesteryear. Starting in antiquity with reparations and amnesty laws, it was the Nuremberg trials that ultimately, Misztal remarks, "brought the issue of collective memory and justice to the attention of the world."[2] In addition to international tribunals, other legal institutions of memory, also analysed in this study, were created more recently: truth and reconciliation commissions, memory laws, and lustration.

Although applied not only in transitional situations, institutions of memory are always "deployed" in response to the resurfacing or persistent presence of certain difficult issues from the past, be that more recent or more

1 Emilios Christodoulidis and Scott Veitch, "Reflections on Law and Memory" in Susanne Karstedt (ed.), *Legal Institutions and Collective Memories* (Oxford/Portland, OR: Hart, 2009) 63 at 63.

2 Barbara A. Misztal, "Memory and Democracy" (2005) 48:10 American Behavioral Scientist 1320 at 1324.

DOI: 10.4324/9781003461548-16

distant. My book proposed a departure from the more established transitional justice perspective, showing that law and memory processes, even when initiated during a transition (when they are most visible), may continue for many years, long after the society in question has moved on from not only the difficult past but also the transition itself, as the case studies of Japan, Portugal, Brazil, and Poland suggest. Nevertheless, the importance of transition as the great collective memory *spiritus movens* cannot be understated: as Karstedt observes, transitions "epitomise and in many ways bring to the fore the intricate relationship between legal institutions and collective memories."[3] It is in their aftermath that the collective memory inversion takes place, as the counter-memories of the former opposition become a part of the official narrative, whereas those of the previous authorities are turned into counter-memories themselves.

Nevertheless, it is often only after a certain amount of time has passed since the transition that the full picture of law and memory intersections becomes visible, as "the very situation of transition conceals from our captivated imagination how much and in how many realms of law collective memories are 'legalised' and how much of collective memory and history in modern societies is constructed following 'legal blueprints.'"[4] This book attempted to uncover these blueprints by analysing both theoretically and in practice the most vital legal institutions of memory, while acknowledging that there are a number of other instances of law and memory intersections that remain outside the scope of the proposed framework. These most notably include the question of administrative law regulations on street names and monuments, which are notoriously abused for political purposes.

The problem of the politicisation and instrumentalisation of the past through law has been one of the *leitmotivs* of this book. To follow Karsedt's observations once again, "in the process of coming to terms with the past, legal institutions are thoroughly implicated in the political process and concomitant social and cultural changes," which is inherent to them, as it is their very "objective of establishing a shared truth and common past that makes them particularly vulnerable to being captured by powerful forces."[5]

What renders my book particularly topical is that in recent years, collective memories have become "politicised as never before, and the question of what kind of historical narrative . . . a state chooses to promote has become a salient feature of both domestic and international politics."[6] As this study clearly shows, today perhaps more than ever, "the past is not fixed but is

3 Susanne Karstedt, "Introduction: The Legacy of Maurice Halbwachs" in Susanne Karstedt (ed.), *Legal Institutions and Collective Memories* (Oxford/Portland, OR: Hart, 2009) 1 at 2.
4 *Ibid.* at 2.
5 *Ibid.* at 13.
6 Thomas U. Berger, *War, Guilt, and World Politics After World War II* (Cambridge: Cambridge University Press, 2012) at 10.

subject to change: both narratives of events and the meanings given to them are in a constant state of transformation."[7] And it is the law that plays a major role in this process.

The State of Intersections of Law and Memory

To uncover the various aspects of law and memory's intersections, I proposed a different approach in every part of the book – theoretical, conceptual, and practical – analysing them through the lens of the law and humanities methodology. Beginning with a sociological, philosophical, and legal theoretical analysis, the first part of the study established the understanding of fundamental notions and ideas used throughout the book. First introducing the concept of collective memory, I analysed both its Halbwachsian origins, which remain the basis for all memory studies, and its more contemporary rereadings, reviewing the different approaches to the question of social perceptions of the past and dividing them into four non-exclusive groups. This analysis proved to be particularly fruitful with regard to uncovering the notion of global collective memory, i.e., those collective memories that are shared universally around the world, which later proved useful when approaching the institution of international tribunals.

The investigation conducted in the sociological section also allowed me to introduce other concepts not directly related to collective memory, such as its opposite, collective forgetting, a certain degree of which is always a result of the work of legal institutions of memory, as well as the idea of collective trauma-memory, which I propose to use to describe the persistent collective memories of past atrocities, and the notions of agents of memory (those actively engaged in the creation and dissemination of particular collective memory) and carriers of memory (the tangible and intangible socio-cultural objects that carry with them particular collective memories).

The sociological observations were complemented by philosophical ones, relating to four thinkers whose work I found to be most relevant to my study. Remaining in the realms of contemporary French philosophy, I first turned attention to Émile Durkheim, whose conception of law replacing religion in modern societies, as well as his remarks on the importance of social rituals, such as public commemorations, for the cohesion of a group, were particularly impactful for my later research. Next, I ventured into the analysis of the work of Henri Bergson, whose observations on the particularity of memory, which at first glance seemed irreconcilably different from those of

7 Katharine Hodgkin and Susannah Radstone, "Part I: Transforming Memory. Introduction" in Katharine Hodgkin and Susannah Radstone (eds), *Memory History Nation: Contested Pasts* (Oxon/New York, NY: Routledge, 2003) 23 at 23.

Halbwachs, upon closer investigation allowed me to deepen the proposed understanding of collective memory.

Then, I chose to focus on the thought of Emmanuel Levinas, whose proposed diachronic theory of ethics convincingly presents the links between law and memory on a more profound level, pertaining to the very essence of law and social relations. Finally, I moved to the research of Michel Foucault's observations on the question of power over memory, which provide an explanation as to why politicians and others in positions of authority attempt to exert control over official narratives. Foucault's concepts of counter-memories, i.e., those memories that appear in opposition to the official narrative, as well as of heterotopias also proved to be particularly useful when later analysing, respectively, the process of collective memory inversion, the question of secret police archives, and, more broadly, the institutes of memory housing them, which remain of major importance from the perspective of law and memory.

My theoretical deliberations are closed by an analysis of the relationship between the theory of law and collective memory or, more precisely, between human rights law, international law, and the concept of transitional justice. As I stipulated, human rights law intersects both directly (when memories of past violations motivate new regulations) and indirectly (during domestic trials concerning human rights violations that have the potential to shift established memories) with collective memory. In turn, with regard to international law, the interactions may be perceived as either everyday (when memories themselves become an object of international law) or extraordinary (during trials before international tribunals). Ultimately, I turned my attention to the presently overused concept of transitional justice, which I not only overviewed but also critically reviewed, pondering upon not only its goals, main ideological traits, and its (oftentimes unacknowledged) relationship with collective memory but also its potential for generating future conflict, as promises of reconciliation most often fall short of realisation (as noticed in most case studies later in the book).

As such, I closed the first part of the book with a departure from the transitional justice paradigm, also proposing a definition of collective memory from the perspective of law. I argued that collective memory should be perceived

> as a social memory. This social memory is not created or established solely individually but within various groups to which one belongs, in particular the local community and the nation, but today also the global society. As such, it is being influenced by those in power in order to further different goals, from social unison to the inclusion of diverse voices into the official narratives, using various means, among which law stands out as a particularly potent one. At the same time, collective memory influences various social products, including law, in a perpetual case of *circulus vitiosus*.

The settling of the question of the definition opened the way to Part II of the book, focused on the development of a conceptual approach to intersections of law and memory. To propose a new framework for their understanding, I introduced the idea of legal institutions of memory, those legal mechanisms that become carriers of memory, influencing it on a number of different levels. Dividing them into three categories (soft, medium, and hard) on the basis of the level of their directness in attempting to change collective memory, I distinguished six such institutions, proposing a model for each of them.

Beginning with the analysis of soft legal institutions of memory, I first turned my attention to reparations, i.e., material or symbolic remedies that the perpetrator provides the aggravated party with in hopes of normalisation of relations, restitution, or even reconciliation. Throughout this process, major shifts in the official narrative on the part of the victimiser may occur; however, changing collective memories locally usually proves a much more difficult task. A similar issue arises with regard to international tribunals, the second soft legal institution of memory – while trials before these institutions are social rituals of worldwide importance, establishing global collective memories, they often fail to initiate a shift in perspectives of the affected communities.

Next, I moved on to medium legal institutions of memory, both conceptualised in the second part of the 20th century. Starting my study with lustration, I remarked on the ways in which the various approaches to vetting tend to share similar problems, being based on former secret services archives – Foucauldian *heterotopias*, often becoming heavily instrumentalised by politicians to advance singular goals, leading to polarisation of collective memories and thus whole societies. In turn, I argued that the second medium legal institution of memory, that of a truth (and reconciliation) commission, while promising a "revolutionary catharsis" through an open discussion about the difficult past, aiming to bring back counter-memories to the forefront of the public debate through the establishment of the truth, may lead to a major shift in the general public's perceptions of the past but at the same time further alienate the former victims.

Last, I chose to focus on hard legal institutions of memory, beginning with legal amnesia, or collective forgetting institutionalised by law, most often, but not only, through amnesties. This institution, by deciding what to remember and what to forget, is potentially of major influence on collective memory but at the same time may foster not only persistent counter-memories, but also resentment among the former victims. In turn, the final legal institution of memory, that of memory legislation, institutionalises evoking, deciding what may be publicly remembered. Despite its noble origins as a means of protecting the memory of Shoah, it has major potential for instrumentalization and may prove to be extremely dangerous for social cohesion and international relations.

This conceptualisation of six models is complemented by a further investigation of the ways in which those in power use law in an attempt to turn collective memories into a political instrument. As such, I first explored the notion of memory politics, delineating the ways in which all regimes, both non-democratic and liberal, attempt to shape social perceptions of the past, showing both their internal (with regard to a single society) and external (directed towards foreign countries) dimensions. Then, I turned my attention to the question of institutes of memory, those public institutions that have as their goal the cultivation and propagation of the official narrative adopted by the authorities. The fact that they often house archives of former secret services renders them even more vulnerable to politicisation.

Ultimately, in an attempt to propose a way forward for the oftentimes difficult law and memory intersections, I postulated the recognition of a specific right to memory, which, while already existing in various international provisions, remains unacknowledged as a specific right. To reconcile its different aspects, I proposed the right to memory as a two-faced Janus right, composed of the right to evoking (the right to remember, to have certain collective memories in the official narrative, and the right to be remembered, to have certain – both positive and difficult – collective memories returned to their rightful place within society) and the right to disremember (the right to forget, to allow for certain collective memories to be eliminated from the official narrative, and the right to be forgotten, to have certain memories removed from the public discourse). Such a conceptualisation of the right to memory, I argued, would allow us to balance the often contradictory evoking and disremembering needs of a society, permitting us to assess the different collective memories through the same lens. It could also permit a better understanding of legal institutions of memory, whereby each can be linked to a different aspect of the right to memory.

It is on the basis of the six models and the analysis of the political dimension of law and memory intersections, as well as the earlier theoretical study, that I closed Part II of the book with my proposed new law and memory framework. Linking the various aspects of my research, the framework is based on a number of factors: the direct influence of law, its impact on collective memory, the level of politicisation of memory, the impact on reconciliation, the possibility of application in transitional and non-transitional situations, the impact on the official narrative, the influence of human rights law and international law on the institution in question, and, ultimately, the link between each institution and a different aspect of the right to memory.

Such a framework was put to the test in Part III, the final part of the book, focused on the analysis of the intersections between law and memory in practice, studying cases from various cultural, social, and legal contexts. Following the six distinguished legal institutions of memory, I put it to the test in three chapters, each devoted to, respectively, soft, medium, and hard legal institutions of memory. When it came to the former, I began with the analysis of reparations in Japan, which has used in particular its material but also to a certain degree symbolic reparations as a tool of economic diplomacy, expanding its dominance over South–East Asian markets at the same time as paying its dues, which may be one of the reasons why its public apologies have thus far fallen short of initiating a meaningful, long-term *détente* in relations with China and Korea. This study was complemented by that of the symbolic reparations in Poland, which took the form of the 1965 letter of Polish to German bishops. While not initially successful, it became the foundation of Polish-German reconciliation, demonstrating that in regard to the matters of collective memory, the long-term effects of legal institutions may be very different from the short-term ones.

Then, I turned to the analysis of the second soft legal institution of memory, researching the European Court of Human Rights (ECtHR) as an example of an international tribunal. My study of two cases heard before it showed that the Court has a major influence on the European collective memory but has thus far not adopted a single policy with regard to matters relating to the past and collective memory. It was complemented with an analysis of a Polish case before ECtHR, the *Janowiec* case, which once again showed the Court's lack of a coherent policy with regard to the matters of the past.

In the next chapter, focused on medium legal institutions of memory, I turned to lustration, analysing it on the seemingly atypical example of Iraq, which confirmed the model traits of this legal institution of memory. I showed that despite being initiated almost a decade later, the country's authorities not only repeated the mistakes of Central and Eastern Europe with regard to vetting, but actually amplified them, with devastating effects on social cohesion. This analysis was complemented by that of lustration in Poland, whereby the vetting process proved to be overtly politicised, as policies have continued to shift along with the governments and are in a way never-ending, with changes to its scope introduced as late as in the mid-2010s.

In turn, the example of the second medium legal institution of memory, a truth commission, researched in the case of Brazil, demonstrated the possibilities for innovation that this legal institution of memory provides in regard to the brining of counter-memories back to the public discourse. At the same time, however, this case also showed how vital for the impact on collective memory is the social willingness to adopt a different narrative, which was clearly lacking at the time the commission's report was published.

Ultimately, in the third chapter of the final part of the book, I turned to hard legal institutions of memory, first focusing on legal amnesia in the case of Portugal. While this country did not introduce a typical blanket amnesty for the members of the previous regime, its reintegration programme following the revolution, using a variety of different means, allowed Portuguese society to come to terms with their difficult past, however, at a price of widespread, if involuntary, collective forgetting.

In turn, Rwandan memory legislation ensures the propagation of a single narrative at the expense of historical truth, promoting a whitewashed version of events. In denying not only counter-memories but also any deviations from the narrowly established official narrative, it is sowing the seeds of potentially broad social discord. This case study was complemented by the analysis of Polish memory legislation, the extensive catalogue of which, while not necessarily always growing, seems to change every several years. Importantly, in addition to the typical European penal repercussions for those breaking certain elements of the official narrative, Poland also established a particular civil law system of collective memory protections, extending them to the good name of the country.

With these remarks, my argument in this book was completed, as I was able to compare and contrast the incidental uses of legal institutions of memory with those taking place in the same environment – Poland – which confirmed the relevance of the proposed framework, showing similarities in the effect the different institutions have on collective memory in spite of varying circumstances.

Thus, several more general observations on the inner workings of the legal institutions of memory can now be made: (1) they are always established as a response to either resurfacing or persistence of certain difficult issues from the past, whether or not in a transitional situation; (2) their short- and long-term effects may be very different, but they always require a certain openness to coming to terms with the past from the groups in question to be brought about; (3) despite the existence of certain models, each society applies a legal institution of memory in its own particular way, often, however, facing similar difficulties in their application, regardless of unique circumstances; (4) they are always politicised to a certain degree, and as such, not only certain truths but also the reconciliation process in general may be blocked; (5) they show the limits of law's potential in having a meaningful impact on collective memory, with their effectiveness largely depending on the underlying socio-political issues already in place within a group; and (6) while focusing on the past, they are future-oriented, and only through their better understanding – as proposed here, with the concept of the right to memory – they can lead to social cohesion rather than more conflict in the days to come.

Furthermore, the intersections of law and memory are paradoxical in a number of ways. While it is an individual who remembers, the society, through its different cultural products, including the law, to a certain degree successfully, influences what about and how the past is remembered, and what is forgotten; while both law and memory are intangible, when they intersect, they often do so in space, with a certain spatial situatedness quality to them, be that an object of material reparation, a publicly declared act of apology or an amnesty, a courtroom, an archive, or a meeting of a commission; and ultimately, that while one of the main reasons as to why legal institutions of memory are established is the need to deal with certain collective trauma-memories of the past, at the same time they exist in order to (among other goals) shift these collective memories, in that not always helping the societies to work through their difficult past, but always, in the search of remembering, leading to a certain degree of collective forgetting.

What Future for Intersections of Law and Memory?

Looking back at this brief overview of the main points I made throughout this book, one might be tempted to ask why I did not choose to entitle it "Legal Institutions of Memory." Tempting as though such a straightforward title might have been, I chose the much broader and more universal notion of intersections for reasons explained in the Introduction. Having completed my study, I stand by my choice. While one of the goals of this book was the conceptualisation of a new law and memory framework, I hope that my deliberations will shed light not only on the six distinguished legal institutions of memory but also on other instances of law and memory's intersections.

As the present-day geopolitical situation shows, the issues relating to questions of law and memory continue to be of major importance to not only the societies in question but also international relations. While not the main reason behind the current Russo-Ukrainian war, Russia's politicisation of collective memory over the years, from particularly chosen commemoration days to its plethora of memory legislation, provided an ample basis for its 2022 invasion of the neighbouring country. A detailed study of these law and memory intersections and the Ukrainian responses to counteract them following the 2014 power shift in the country would be the next large test for my framework proposed in this book. Additionally, a deeper analysis of certain case studies, one also including the post-colonial dimension as remarked upon already in the Introduction, could present another challenge for the law and memory framework introduced here.

Turning once again to the big picture, conflict is an inherent element of all law and memory intersections, as they are also a vital part of more general conflicts between the past and the present, of which narratives get to control the present for the future:

> Contests over the meaning of the past are also contests over the meaning of the present and over ways of taking the past forward. Ideas of restitution and reparation, evoking both financial or political justice and more abstruse compensations such as recognition of wrongs done, or readiness to hear and acknowledge hidden stories, all draw on a sense that the present is obliged to accommodate the past in order to move on from it.[8]

8 Katharine Hodgkin and Susannah Radstone, "Introduction: Contested Pasts" in Katharine Hodgkin and Susannah Radstone (eds), *Memory History Nation: Contested Pasts* (Oxon/New York, NY: Routledge, 2003) 1 at 1.

Thus, law, as this book shows, is an indispensable element of the process of coming to terms with the past. While also not free from contestation, if legal institutions of memory are chosen to fit the circumstances well and applied properly, with low levels of politicisation, they may provide societies with the necessary instruments to work through their traumas, achieving what would not have been possible without law, which continues to stand, to paraphrase Proust, like a giant immersed in Time – and Memory.

Index

Note: Page numbers followed by "n" with numbers refer to notes.

accountability 103, 118, 138, 140; collective 109
agents of memory 44–46, 153; governments as 45; instantaneous 46; media as 46; mnemonic abnegators 45; mnemonic activists 45; mnemonic pluralists 45; mnemonic prospectives 45; mnemonic warriors 45; unintentional 46; use of law 154; *vs.* carriers of memory 47
amnesty/amnesties 5, 80, 129, 131, 134, 148, 151, 171–173, 184, 186, 256, 267, 286, 295–296; classification of 137–138; *de facto* 136; goals of 137; law 171, 186, 246, 248, 252, 289; legal amnesia in 134; legitimacy of 138; mistrust of 139; as official forgetting 136; role of 133, 135–140, 173, 186; truth commissions and 133
"anti-communist" institutions 160–161
Argentina's collective memories of foreign interventions 75–78
Armenian massacre of 1915 xvii, xviii–xx, 144, 217–218
Assmann, Aleida 24–25
Assmann, Jan 24–25
Australia 184, 190

Beim, Aaron 25
Bergson, Henri 10, 50, 55–59, 75, 147, 291; division between individual and collective memory 57–58; *Matter and Memory* 55; present and past experiences 57; relationship between law and memory 58; "third way" of looking at memory 55
Bergson's theory of memory 20, 57–58, 75
Bohley, Bärbel 82
Brazil *see* Brazilian National Truth Commission
Brazilian memorialisation initiatives 246–248
Brazilian National Truth Commission 11, 166, 185, 227, 245–254, 295; agreement with Brazilian National History Association (ANPUH) 249; criticisms against 248–249; goals of 250; impact on collective memory 252–253; influence of internal issues 248; at intersections of law and memory 252–254; investigation of Brazilian dictatorship (1964–1985) 245–246; members 249; "myths" regarding junta period 253; official narratives 254; perspective of legal institutions of memory 254; problems regard to obtaining confessions from perpetrators 250; proceedings 250–251; reports and propositions 251–252; transition to democracy 246–247
Bulgarian Committee on Disclosing of Documents and Announcing Affiliation of Bulgarian Citizens to the State Security and the Intelligence Services of the Bulgarian National Army (CRDOPBGDSRSBNA) 159

Canada 8–9, 184, 190
Carnation Revolution 1974 256–259
carriers of memory 46–48; intentional 47; unintentional 47

Chainoglou, Kalliopi 71n7, 170n148, 177
Charter of the International Military Tribunal xvi–xvii
Chirac, Jacques xix
civil amnesia 133–134
collective consciousness 52
collective forgetting 10, 31–36, 110, 112, 131–132, 134, 139–140, 172, 178, 202, 295; as annulment 34; as humiliated silence 34–35; individual processes of 32; mechanisms of 32; as planned obsolesce 34; through distorted connotation 35
collective identity 39, 43–44, 153
collective memory 179, 291–292; actual 30; agents of 44–46; carriers of 46–48; critical views 31; definition 15, 52, 91; Eurocentrism of 31; European memory 156; fallible nature 32; familial 153; formal- and global-oriented 25–27; Halbwachs's theory 16–21; innovative or critical concepts 28–31; Lavabre's dynamic concept of 30; as *lieux de mémoire* 48; meta-narratives 44; past-oriented and present-oriented 22–23; persistence of memory 20; places of 47–48; private and public 47; social- and cultural-oriented 23–25; of social group 19; of trauma 36–44; of various religions 19–20
collective mourning 107, 129
collective remembering 28, 126, 141, 151, 169; history and 28, 30
collective trauma 36–44, 177; case of Israel 42–43; cultural perspective 39–40; relationship between collective memory and 43; social concept 41–42; transgenerational transmission of 41
communicative/everyday memory 24–25
competitive victimhood 146, 169
Connerton, Paul 33–35
Convention on the Prevention and Punishment of Genocide 1948 166, 211
Conway, Brian 21
counter-memory /history 64, 66, 84
Craps, Stef 5
cultural memory of trauma 39–40
cultural theories of memory 23–25; influence of cultural differences 25
cultural trauma 10, 37
Czech Institute for the Study of Totalitarian Regimes (USTR) 159

de-Ba'athification process 228–236
decommunisation 117–118
Delgado, Richard 68
Durkheim, Émile 10, 50–55, 69, 96, 291; collective consciousness 52; institutions of law 52–53; observations on religion and religious ceremonies 53–54, 75, 116; rituals 152, 164, 226, 236, 244, 255, 288; role of collective memories in society 51–52; symbolic objects 54

elusiveness 28, 31
ethno-national-political genocide 218
European Court of Human Rights (ECtHR) 11, 107, 111, 163, 171, 185–186; abuse clause (guillotine effect) 210–211; criteria to examine interplay between articles 8 and 10, 214; decisions 212–213; intersections of law and memory 217–220; *Janowiec* (and Others) *v.* Russia case 222–224, 287; Katyń massacre 186, 220–222, 224–226; as legal institution of memory 220; *nulla poena sine lege* rule, establishment of 212; *Perinçek* case 213–214, 287; protection of human rights 211; right to freedom of expression 209; right to freedom of speech 210; validity of genocide laws 212–213; *Vasiliauskas* and *Drėlingas* cases 215–217, 287
European Network of Official Authorities in Charge of the Secret-Police Files (ENOA) 160
European Network Remembrance and Solidarity (ENRS) 160
European Union (EU) xx–xxi, 75, 146, 163, 173, 176, 284

Far Eastern Commission (FEC) 190–191
forgiveness 103–104
formal collective memory 25–27; hermetic concept of 27
Foucault, Michel 10, 51, 63–68, 84, 115, 292; counter-memories/histories 67; Gaullist France 152–153; genealogy 66; heterotopias 64–66, 121–122, 158, 164; history's place 67; perceptions of collective memory 63–64; places of

memory 66; power-memory relations 152; power relations 67; racial relations in the United States 68
France 96, 141, 184; Charter of 1814 135; memory law 148
French colonial past xviii–xix
French memory laws: protection of genocide from denial xvii; war criminals, prosecution and punishment of xvi

General Assembly of American States 170–171
General Data Protection Regulation (GDPR) 2018 174–175
Germany 142, 184; fiscal policy 75; Gauck-Birthler Institute (BStU) 158–160, 158n57; international tribunals in 109; lustration and truth commissions, use of 124; relations with Poland 199–206
global collective memories 25–27
Greece 33, 133, 135
Greenawalt, Kent 136

habit memory 56–57
Halbwachs, Maurice 16–21, 49, 52; collective memory concept 16–21; theory of remembering 16
hard legal institutions of memory 151, 183, 293; legal amnesia 132–141, 151; memory legislation 141–149, 151
Hespanha, Antonio Manuel 6
Hiroshima and Nagasaki bombing 27, 71
Hirsch, Moshe 107
Historical Archives of State Security (ABTL) 159
historical trauma 40–41
Holocaust (Shoah) 9, 59, 142, 210, 218, 293; denial xvi, xxi–xxii, 142, 144–145, 211, 214, 218
Holocaust Remembrance Day 74, 284
human rights–collective memory intersections 69–73; abuses of human rights violations 70–71, 73; access to legal protection 73; contemporary human rights movement 70; cultural rights 70; domestic 75–76; function of trials 71–72; global trauma-memories 72; indirect intersections 71; retroactive and perpetual 102; sites of memory production 71
Hungary 33, 119, 159
Huyssen, Andreas 165, 171

individual memory 15, 18, 20, 55, 60, 112, 131
innovative theory of collective memory 28–31
Institute of National Memory (IPN), Poland 158–160
institutional memory 26–27
Inter-American Court of Human Rights (IACtHR) 112, 114, 166, 170, 248
International Court of Justice (ICJ) 171
International Criminal Court (ICC) 80, 114, 138–139
International Criminal Tribunal for Rwanda (ICTR) 77, 112
International Criminal Tribunal for the former Yugoslavia (ICTY) 78, 112–113, 115, 184
international law–collective memory intersections 73–78; everyday relations 74; implementation of international legal rules 75; international institutions' resolutions 74, 77–78; judicial recognition of crime 76–77; jurisdiction 77; principles of international customary law 74; trials 75–76
International Military Tribunal for the Far East in Tokyo (IMTFE Tokyo) 110
International Military Tribunal in Nuremberg (IMT Nuremberg) 109
international tribunals 106–116, 150; application of legalistic principles 108; decisions 108; decisions, effect of 109, 111; ICTR's recognition of rape as an element of genocide 112; ICTY's recognition of the war crime of sexual assault 112; issues of power 115; judgement on collective memory 108; as legal institutions of memory 107–108; power of 107; reconciliation work of 113–114; relationship with collective memory 106–107; reworking of collective trauma-memories 113; role in official narratives 111–113; as soft legal institutions of memory 106, 115–116
intersections of law and memory 1–2, 291–297; Bergson's view 55–59; de-Ba'athification process 232–236; demarcations 13; Durkheim's

view 51–55; Foucault's view 63–68; framework 5–8, 93–94; future for 297–298; impact on society 5; international law 73–78; international tribunals 106–116; law and humanities approach 7; Levinas's view 59–63; between official narrative and counter-memory 6; paradoxical nature 297; perspective of memory studies 8; post-colonial perspective 9; spatial situatedness of law 7; in terms of human rights 69–73; theoretical aspects of 3–5; transitional justice 5
Iraq 287–288, 295; collective memories 236; Democratic Principles Working Group of the Iraqi Opposition 229; Future of Iraq Study project 229; Higher National de-Ba'athification Commission (HNDBC) 231; Iraqi de-Ba'athification Council (IDC) 230; Iraqi National Accord (INA) 228; Iraqi National Congress (INC) 228; Liberation Act in 1998 228; lustration in 11, 116, 185, 227–232, 234–235; memory policies 9; 2003 military intervention 116, 227; process of de-Ba'athification 228–229, 232–236; US Iraq policy 229

Janowiec (and Others) *v.* Russia case 222–224
Japan: apology diplomacy 195–197; international tribunals in 109–110; issues with reparations 199; material reparations in 185, 190–194, 197–198; Nanking Massacre of 1937–1938 debate 194; "obvious excess" programme 190; post-war identity 197; question of military comfort women 194–195; symbolic reparations in 185, 194–198; Yasukuni Shrine visits 196, 198
Joinet, Louis 168

Karstedt, Susanne 290
Katyń massacre 186, 220–222, 224–226
Knutsen, Ketil 178
Kominek, Bolesław 201, 203, 206
Kossak- Szczucka, Zofia 204
Kwaśniewski, Aleksander 186

Lavabre, Marie-Claire 30, 91
law–collective memory relationship 1–4, 177, *180*, 183, 289
Lawlor, Leonard 55–56
Law on the freedom of press 1881 xvi, xvii
Lefebvre, Alexandre 58
legal amnesia 132–141, 148, 151, 173, 184; as an institution of law 133; Athenian 133–134; classification of amnesties 137–138; collective forgetting by 132, 134, 139–140; desired 133; goals of amnesty 137; ideal 134; impact on society's collective memory 132, 134; legal constructs 132; manifestations of 132; of Portugal 256–268; role of amnesties 133, 135–140, 173, 186
legal institutions of memory 10, 93, 152, 156, 164, 171, 176, 178, 181, 293–294; general observations 297; goals of 149; *see also* hard legal institutions of memory; medium legal institutions of memory; soft legal institution of memory
Letter of Polish to German Bishops 1965 199–206; adoption and contents 200–202; aftermath of 202–206; bilateral experiences 202; religious arguments 202
Levinas, Emmanuel 10, 51, 59–63, 86, 292; dedications 59–61; diachronic theory of ethics 61; difference between individual and collective memory 59–60; ethical responsibilities 61–63; *Otherwise than Being* 59; social encounters 62
Lithuania 215, 220, 287; *Drélingas* case 218–219; genocide 215–216; *Vasiliauskas* case 216
loi Gayssot xix, xvi
loi Taubira xviii, xx, xxi
lustration 116–124, 151, 162; accountability and 118; decommunisation and 117–118; delivery of 117; goals 119; in Iraq 11, 116, 185, 227–232, 234–235; as legal institution of memory 116–118, 122–123; link with collective memory 122; in Poland 236–245; process of conducting 120–121; regulations 117

medium legal institutions of memory 151, 183, 293; lustration 116–124, 151; truth commissions 123–131, 151
memory-images 56–57

memory institutes 158–164; agents of memory, influence of 163; organisations 160–162; range of activities 161–162; transitional justice in 164; in Western Europe 158–159
memory inversion 67, 290, 292
memory legislation/laws 141–149, 151; dangers of 147; groups 144; impact on collective memory 147; international level 146; non-punitive and punitive 143, 145; positive and negative 143; punitive 141–142; regarding genocides and mass atrocities 144; uses 143
memory politics 11, 152, 178, 181, 254; characteristics of stasis 154; expressions of power 153; institutionalisation of 158–164; internal and external 155–157; in non-democratic regimes 155; success of 157; transitional 155–156
Mills, Charles W., 68

Nazi crimes 34, 186
Nora, Pierre 48
Nuremberg trials 80, 134
Nuremberg Tribunal xvii, 134, 225

Olick, Jeffrey K., 29
organisational memory 26
Osiel, Mark 106–107
overt silences 35

pardon 136–137
participatory element of public apologies 101–102
Perinçek case 213–214
places of memory 47–48, 172–173
Platform of European Memory and Conscience (Platform) 160
Poland 288, 296; Act on the Institute of National Memory 1998 278; collective memory 183, 185; extermination of concentration and annihilation camps 276–277; law and memory relationship 186; Letter of Polish to German Bishops 1965 199–206; lustration in 236–245; Polish negationism ban 278; public apology for Jedwabne massacre 186–187; reconciliation with Germany and 199–206, 295; symbolic reparations 206–209
Polish memory legislation 276–286, 296; banned denialism 1998 277–278; collective protection of memory 280; criticisms 284–285; educational programmes 285; at intersections of law and memory 283–286; IPN Act Chapter 6c 280–284; legal scrutiny 284–285; perspective of legal institutions of memory 285–286; safeguarding of personal interests 279
Portugal 9, 11, 43, 185, 256, 257, 258–268, 286, 287, 290, 295: Armed Forces Movement (MFA) 260; Carnation Revolution 1974 256–259; education system 262; establishment of military tribunals 261; *Estado Novo* regime 256–260, 263; Operation Command for Continental Portugal (COPCON) 261; purge commissions 262–263; reconciliation period 261
Portuguese legal amnesia 185, 256–268, 295; at intersections of law and memory 263–268
Prager, Jeffrey 41–42, 80
prescriptive forgetting 32–33; legal mechanisms of 33
Proust, Marcel 1, 298
public apologies 100–106; actual act of 102; for atrocities committed in the past 102; attributive element 101; cathartic effect 104; characteristics 103; contemporary and retrospective 103; definition 101; delivery of 102; goals 103–104; interstate 102; Japan's apology diplomacy 195–197; Letter of Polish to German Bishops 1965 199–206; long-term effects 104; participatory element 101–102; reconciliation 104–105, 104*fn*[80]; state-sponsored 105; transactional apology 101; transnational 102; verdictive element 101
public apology 100–106
public memory 19, 23
pure memory 56–57

reconciliation 50, 133, 186, 202; between Poland and Germany 199–206, 295; Portuguese 261

religion and religious ceremonies 53–54
remembering 55; collective 28, 30, 126, 141, 151, 169
reparations 96–100, 150; atrocity memories 99–100; functions of 98; human rights law and 97; in law and memory sense 98; material 97–98, 100; relations between victims and perpetrators 99; successful 99; symbolic 97–98, 100–106, 130 *see also* Japan
representational memory 56–57
repressive erasure 32–33
Ricoeur, Paul 8–9, 50
right to be forgotten (RtbF) 173–176
right to be remembered 170–172; in cases of forced disappearances 170; IACtHR's jurisprudence 170–171; limitations 171
right to forget 172–173; for cleansing images 176; renouncing collective memories 173; social rituals 172–173
right to memory 164–167, 172, 177–178; challenges 176–177; enforceability 176; legally enforceable 165, 176; in legal texts 166; schema *175*
right to remember 166–170; challenges 169; with reparations and memory laws 176; State's duty to remember 168
right to truth 170–172
Romania 186; memory institutes 159, 162
Russia 145, 160, 163, 200, 219–225
Rwanda 77, 288; genocide 144; memory legislation 185, 268–276, 296

San Francisco Peace Treaty 1951 191, 193, 197
shared memories 30, 71
shared memory 30, 70
silence: covert 35; humiliated 34–35; overt 35
Slovakian Nation's Memory Institute (UPN) 158–159
social memory 15, 92
social theories of memory 23–25
soft legal institution of memory 150, 183, 293; international tribunals 106–116; public apology 100–106; reparations 96–100; *see also* European Court of Human Rights (ECtHR)
Sontag, Susan 31
Statute of the International Criminal Court xviii, xxii

Taubira, Christiane xviii, xx, xxi, 164–165
Teitel, Ruti G., 179, 181
Tendera, Karol 279
transitional justice 10, 23, 40, 58, 69, 78–89, 179, 290; counter-memories 84; ethnic identity conflicts phase 80; goals of 79, 81, 84–85; influence of human rights and international law 78; institutionalisation of 80; intersections with collective memory 81, 83–89; processes of 80–83, 87–88; reconciliation 81–82; reconciliatory phase 80, 88–89; time of 86–87; waning dictatorships phase 80; as Western concept 83
truth and reconciliation commission123–131, 135, 151, 186; approach towards reconciliation 129; amnesty and 133; archives of 130; goal of 126, 128; impact on collective memory 131; investigation of atrocities 125–126; as medium legal institution of memory 124; in non-transitional contexts 124; potential benefits of 127; proceedings 125–126; publication of report 130; role as an agent of nationalism 128; in transitional contexts 124; truth categorisation 128; *see also* Brazilian National Truth Commission

Universal Declaration of Human Rights (UDHR) 70–71, 166

Vasiliauskas and *Drėlingas* cases 215–217

Wang, Qi 25
war criminals, prosecution and punishment of xvi, 282
Wojtyła, Karol 205
Wyszyński, Stefan 200–201, 203, 205–206

FSC
www.fsc.org
MIX
Papier | Fördert gute Waldnutzung
FSC® C083411

Kolibri 360 GmbH
Ferdinand-Jühlke-Straße 7
99095 Erfurt, Deutschland
produktsicherheit@kolibri360.de